The 70-620 Cram Sheet

This Cram Sheet contains the distilled, key facts about the MCTS: Microsoft Windows Vista, Configuring exam. Review this information as the last thing you do before you enter the testing center, paying special attention to those areas in which you think you need the most review.

INSTALLING AND UPGRADING WINDOWS VISTA

1. Microsoft defines three hardware levels for Windows Vista: Minimum, Windows Vista Capable, and Windows Vista Premium Ready.
2. For a system to be Windows Vista Capable (capable to run Windows Vista Business and Windows Vista Enterprise editions), it must have an 800-MHz processor, 512MB of RAM, and 15GB of free disk space.
3. For a system to be Windows Vista Premium Ready (runs all versions of Windows Vista and supports the new Windows Aero interface), it must have a 1-GHz processor, 1GB of RAM, and 15GB of free disk space.
4. Windows System Image Manager (Windows SIM) is a tool that enables you to create answer files and network shares or to modify the files contained in a configuration set. The Windows SIM is part of the Windows Automated Installation Kit (WAIK), which is included with Business Desktop Deployment (BDD) 2007.
5. The answer file is an Extensible Markup Language (XML) file that scripts the answers for a series of graphical user interface (GUI) dialog boxes and other configuration settings to be used to install Windows Vista.
6. A Windows image is a single compressed file that contains a collection of files and folders that duplicate a Windows installation on a disk volume. Windows Vista is built and distributed as a single image using the new Windows Imaging (WIM) file format.
7. A catalog is a binary file (CLG) that contains the state of the settings and packages in a Windows image.
8. Windows Preinstallation Environment (PE) is a bootable tool that replaces MS-DOS as the preinstallation environment to install, troubleshoot, and recover Windows Vista.
9. ImageX is a command-line tool that captures, modifies, and applies installation images for deployment in a manufacturing or corporate environment.
10. Windows Setup (Setup.exe) is the program that installs the Windows Vista operating system.
11. Diskpart is a command-line hard disk configuration utility.
12. Sysprep is a utility that facilitates image creation for deployment to multiple destination computers by removing the original security identifiers (SIDs) from the image and cleaning up various user and machine settings and log files.
13. You can upgrade (in-place) Windows XP Pro to Windows Vista Business and Ultimate editions. You can upgrade Windows XP Home to Windows Vista Home Basic, Home Premium, Business, and Ultimate editions.
14. You can use the Windows Vista Upgrade Advisor to determine which edition of Windows Vista is right for you.
15. To migrate user settings from one computer to a Windows Vista computer, use Windows Easy Transfer (WET) and User State Migration Tool (USMT).
16. You can upgrade Windows Vista to higher editions of Windows Vista:
    - Home Basic edition to Home Premium, Business, Enterprise, and Ultimate editions
    - Business edition to Enterprise and Ultimate editions
    - Enterprise edition to Ultimate edition
17. Windows Vista Startup Repair (executed from the Windows installation disc or loaded on your hard drive) is a Windows recovery tool that can fix certain problems, such as missing or damaged system files that might prevent Windows from starting correctly.
18. Device drivers are programs that control a device. They each act like a translator between the device and programs that use the device.

78. Windows ReadyBoost boosts system performance by using USB flash devices as additional sources for caching.
79. Windows ReadyDrive boosts system performance on mobile computers equipped with hybrid drives.
80. System Configuration (**msconfig**) is an advanced tool that can help identify problems that might prevent Windows from starting correctly. You can start Windows with common services and startup programs turned off and then turn them back on, one at a time.
81. The Advanced Boot Options menu lets you start Windows in advanced troubleshooting modes.
82. Safe mode, found in the Advanced Boot Options, starts Windows with a minimal set of drivers and services.
83. Safe mode boots to the Windows GUI in minimal VGA mode using the standard VGA drivers (640x480 resolution and 16 colors), which comes in handy when you load an incompatible video driver.
84. The Last Known Good Configuration (advanced) option starts Windows with the last registry and driver configuration that worked for the most recently successful logon.

CONFIGURING AND TROUBLESHOOTING MOBILE COMPUTING

85. To make finding these settings quick and easy, Windows Vista includes the Windows Mobility Center, which provides a single location that enables you to quickly adjust mobile PC settings.
86. Presentation settings, found with the Windows Mobility Center, enable you to adjust settings such as the speaker volume and the desktop background image, to enhance presentations.
87. A power plan is a collection of hardware and system settings that manages how your computer uses and conserves power.
88. Windows Vista offers two other modes besides Shutdown: Hibernate, which saves the system state and the system memory saved to a file (Hiberfil.sys) on the hard disk; and Sleep, a power-saving state that saves work and opens programs to memory, maintained by a small amount of power.
89. Hybrid Sleep mode, a combination of Sleep and Hibernate, saves your work to your hard disk and puts your mobile PC into a power-saving state.
90. Displayed in the notification area of the Windows taskbar, the battery meter helps you manage your computer's power consumption by indicating how much charge is remaining on your battery and which power plan your computer is using.
91. The new Windows Vista Sync Center provides a single easy-to-use interface to manage data synchronization between multiple computers, including network servers, and mobile devices you connect to your computer.
92. When an offline folder is created, Windows automatically creates a copy of that file or folder on your computer. Anytime you reconnect to that network folder, Windows syncs the files between your computer and the network folder. You can also sync them manually at any time.
93. To configure a Tablet PC, you use the Tablet PC Settings tool, which is found under Mobile PC in the Control Panel.
94. All tablet PCs have several hardware buttons for common tasks, which can be programmed as needed. In addition, you can program the digital pen by assigning key commands or actions to simple pen gestures called flicks.
95. The Handwriting Recognition Personalization Tool enables you to tailor recognition results to your own personal handwriting style.
96. Windows Touch Technology provides support for touchscreens, including accessing context menus and accessing small components with your finger.

CONFIGURING NETWORK CONNECTIVITY

49. The Network and Sharing Center enables you to check your connection status, view your network visually, and troubleshoot connection problems.
50. Windows Network Diagnostics analyzes the problem and, if possible, presents a solution or a list of possible causes.
51. The **ipconfig** command displays current TCP/IP configuration. It can also be used to release (**/release** option) and renew (**/renew** option) TCP/IP configuration and for flushing the Domain Name System (DNS) cache (**/flushdns** option).
52. The **ping** command verifies connections to a remote computer by verifying configurations and testing IP connectivity.
53. The **tracert** command traces the route that a packet takes to a destination and displays the series of IP routers that are used in delivering packets to the destination.
54. The **nslookup** command displays information that you can use to diagnose your DNS infrastructure.
55. You use Remote Desktop to access one computer from another remotely.
56. You use Remote Desktop Connection (RDC) to connect to computers running Windows Vista Starter, Windows Vista Home Basic, Windows Vista Home Basic N, or Windows Vista Home Premium.
57. To connect to a remote computer using Remote Desktop, the computer must be turned on, it must have a network connection and network access, Remote Desktop must be enabled, and you must have permission to connect (a member of the Administrators group or the Remote Desktop Users group).
58. To use Remote Assistance, first invite a person to help you, using e-mail or an instant message. You can also reuse an invitation that you have sent before.

CONFIGURING APPLICATIONS INCLUDED WITH WINDOWS VISTA

59. Windows Media Player 11 is an all-in-one media player that enables you to play most media files with an easy-to-use, intuitive interface.
60. Codecs, an abbreviation for compressor/decompressor, are software or hardware used to compress and decompress digital media, such as a song or video.
61. If you want to play a DVD, you need a DVD decoder, also known as an MPEG-2 decoder. Only Windows Vista Home Premium and Windows Vista Ultimate ship with an MPEG-2 decoder.
62. The commercial DVD video player specification dictates that DVD players must be coded to play discs that contain the region code for the country in which they were sold.
63. The Windows Media Center enables you to manage and play back all of your digital media through one interface, including live and recorded TV, movies, music, and pictures.
64. If your computer has no TV tuner, an optional analog or digital TV tuner is required to play and record TV in Windows Media Center.
65. Windows Mail is used to send, receive, and organize e-mail. It also includes improved stability over Outlook Express, enables real-time search, and provides enhanced security via the Phishing Filter and Junk Mail Filter.
66. Windows Calendar is a new calendar and task application.
67. To view several calendars together, you can create a calendar group, which then enables you to view the appointments in each calendar individually, or together.
68. The Windows Fax and Scan program enables users to scan a document or picture into the system with a scanner, e-mail those documents, and fax documents using a fax modem or fax server and receive faxes from other fax machines.
69. Windows Meeting Space, which is a replacement for NetMeeting, enables you to share documents, programs, or your entire desktop with other people.
70. One of the advantages of using Windows Meeting Space is that it uses peer-to-peer technology that automatically sets up an ad hoc network if it cannot find an existing network.
71. People Near Me, used in Windows Meeting Space, identifies people using computers near you so that you can use Windows Meeting Space and other programs.
72. The Windows Sidebar is a pane that keeps your gadgets organized and always available.
73. Gadgets are easy-to-use mini programs (tools) that give you information at a glance for frequently performed tasks such as checking the weather, checking the time (via a digital clock), and checking e-mail (without opening other programs).

MAINTAINING AND OPTIMIZING SYSTEMS THAT RUN WINDOWS VISTA

74. Windows Reliability and Performance Monitor is a Microsoft Management Console (MMC) snap-in that provides tools for analyzing system performance. From a single console, you can monitor application and hardware performance in real time, customize what data you want to collect in logs, define thresholds for alerts and automatic actions, generate reports, and view past performance data in a variety of ways.
75. Another tool that you can use to view system performance is the Windows Task Manager.
76. You should periodically use the Check Disk tool (**chkdsk**) to check the integrity of disks, which will examine and correct many types of common errors.
77. To reduce fragmentation, Windows Vista automatically defragments your hard disk using Disk Defragmenter.

19. To ensure reliable drivers, a signed driver is a device driver that includes a digital signature, which is an electronic security mark that can indicate the publisher of the software and information that can show whether a driver has been altered.
20. By default, if a driver is not signed, signed by a publisher that could not be properly identified, or has been altered since its release, Windows Vista will notify you.
21. The Device Manager lists all hardware devices on your computer and enables you to change the properties for any device and update drivers.
22. You can use the Add Hardware component in the Control Panel to add device drivers.

CONFIGURING AND TROUBLESHOOTING POST-INSTALLATION SYSTEM SETTINGS

23. Windows Aero is the premium visual experience of Windows Vista that features a transparent glass design with subtle window animations and new window colors.
24. Part of the Windows Aero experience is Windows Flip 3D, which is a way to arrange your open windows in a three-dimensional stack that you can quickly flip through without having to click the taskbar.
25. To enable Windows Aero, you need to set the color depth of 32 bits per pixel (bpp), a refresh rate that is higher than 10 hertz, the theme to Windows Vista, the color scheme to Windows Aero, and confirm that the window frame transparency is on.
26. Parental controls enable administrators to control which websites, programs, and games each standard user can use and install and what time those users can use the computer.
27. The Ease of Access Center is a central location that you can use to set up the accessibility settings and programs available in Windows.
28. Internet Explorer Zoom (from 10% to 1000%) lets you enlarge or reduce the view of a web page.
29. The Internet Explorer has a Security status bar that keeps you notified of the website security and privacy settings by using color-coded notifications next to the address bar.
30. Internet Explorer 7.0 offers a Phishing Filter that helps protect you from online phishing attacks, fraud, and spoofed websites.
31. Internet Explorer 7.0 offers Protected mode, which helps protect you from websites that try to save files or install programs on your computer.
32. Dynamic Security options for Internet Explorer 7.0 offers multiple security features to defend your computer against malware and data theft.
33. To reset Windows Explorer, click the Reset button within the Advanced tab. If you want to reset only the Advanced options, click the Restore Advanced Settings button.
34. A website that wants to allow other sites to publish some of its content creates an RDF Site Summary (RSS) document and registers the document with an RSS publisher. Users who can read RSS-distributed content or feed can get data such as news feeds, events listings, news stories, headlines, project updates, excerpts from discussion forums, and even corporate information.
35. When you subscribe to an RSS feed, Internet Explorer automatically checks the website and downloads new content so that you can see what is new since you last visited the feed.

CONFIGURING WINDOWS SECURITY FEATURES

36. User Account Control (UAC) is a feature in Windows that can help prevent unauthorized changes to your computer. If you are logged in as an administrator, UAC asks you for permission to perform a task; and if you are logged in as a standard user, UAC asks you for an administrator username and password that can perform the task.
37. UAC can be enabled or disabled for any individual user account by using the Control Panel. You can also control the behavior of the UAC by using local or group policies.
38. If you have an older application that requires administrative permissions to run, you can use the Application Compatibility tab to select this Run This Program as an Administrator option, which will allow the application to use the UAC system to request privilege escalation.
39. Windows Defender helps users detect and remove known spyware and other potential unwanted software.
40. A quick scan using Windows Defender checks areas on a hard disk that spyware is most likely to infect.
41. When you perform a scan, you can configure what Windows Defender will do when it identifies unwanted software.
42. If you want to prevent a program from being flagged as possible spyware, you should select Always Allow.
43. Software Explorer can remove any program that executes during startup.
44. Windows Defender automatically blocks all startup items in Windows Vista that require administrator privileges to run.
45. Windows Firewall is a packet filter and stateful host-based firewall that allows or blocks network traffic according to the configuration.
46. By default, Windows Firewall is on.
47. By default, Windows Firewall blocks most programs from communicating through the firewall. Therefore, you will need to add an exception for a port or program.
48. The new Windows Firewall with Advanced Security is a Microsoft Management Console (MMC) snap-in that provides more advanced options for IT professionals that enable you to set up and view detailed inbound and outbound rules and integrate with Internet Protocol Security (IPSec).

MCTS 70-620:

Microsoft® Windows™ Vista, Configuring

Patrick Regan

MCTS 70-620 Exam Cram: Microsoft® Windows™ Vista, Configuring

ISBN-13: 978-0-7897-3688-8
ISBN-10: 0-7897-3688-8

Library of Congress Cataloging-in-Publication Data

Regan, Patrick E.

MCTS 70-620 exam cram : Microsoft Windows Vista client, configuring / Patrick Regan.

p. cm.

Includes index.

ISBN 978-0-7897-3688-8 (pbk. w/cd)

1. Electronic data processing personnel--Certification. 2. Microsoft software--Examinations--Study guides. 3. Microsoft Windows (Computer file) I. Title.

QA76.3.R4554 2007
005.4'46--dc22

2007033809

Printed in the United States of America

First Printing: October 2007

Trademarks

Warning and Disclaimer

Bulk Sales

Que Publishing offers excellent discounts on this book when ordered in quantity for bulk purchases or special sales. For more information, please contact

U.S. Corporate and Government Sales
1-800-382-3419
corpsales@pearsontechgroup.com

For sales outside of the U.S., please contact

International Sales
international@pearsoned.com

Publisher
Paul Boger

Associate Publisher
David Dusthimer

Acquisitions Editor
Betsy Brown

Development Editor
Ginny Bess Munroe

Managing Editor
Patrick Kanouse

Technical Editor
Chris Crayton

Project Editor
Meg Shaw

Copy Editor
Keith Cline

Indexer
Wordwise Publishing Services,LLC

Proofreader
Katherin Bidwell

Publishing Coordinator
Vanessa Evans

Multimedia Developer
Dan Scherf

Designer
Gary Adair

Contents at a Glance

	Introduction	1
	Self-Assessment	15
	Exam Layout and Design	29

Part I: Exam Preparation

CHAPTER 1	Introduction to Windows Vista	47
CHAPTER 2	Installing Windows Vista	63
CHAPTER 3	Using Windows Vista	87
CHAPTER 4	Configuring Advanced Networking	123
CHAPTER 5	NTFS Security Features and File Sharing	151
CHAPTER 6	Configuring User Account Security	183
CHAPTER 7	Configuring Network Security	207
CHAPTER 8	Configuring Internet Explorer 7.0	231
CHAPTER 9	Maintaining and Optimizing Windows Vista Systems	253
CHAPTER 10	Configuring Windows Vista Media Applications	281
CHAPTER 11	Configuring Windows Vista Productivity Applications	293
CHAPTER 12	Configuring Mobile Computers	317

Part II: Practice Exams

CHAPTER 13	Practice Exam 1	339
CHAPTER 14	Answers to Practice Exam 1	353
CHAPTER 15	Practice Exam 2	365
CHAPTER 16	Answers to Practice Exam 2	379
APPENDIX	What's on the CD-ROM?	391
	Glossary	395
	Index	411

Table of Contents

Introduction 1

The Value of Certification 2

The Microsoft Certification Program 4

Microsoft Certified Technology Specialist 6

Microsoft Certified IT Professional 7

Microsoft Certified Technology Specialist: Windows Vista, Configuration 8

Taking a Certification Exam 9

Tracking Certification Status 10

About This Book 11

Self-Assessment 15

Microsoft Certification in the Real World 15

The Ideal Microsoft Certification Candidate 16

Put Yourself to the Test 17

Educational Background 17

Hands-On Experience 18

How to Prepare for an Exam 21

Studying for the Exam 22

Testing Your Exam Readiness 24

Assessing Readiness for Exam 70-620 25

Day of the Exam 25

Dealing with Test Anxiety 27

Exam Layout and Design 29

Common Question Formats 29

Special Exam Question Formats 37

Microsoft's Testing Formats 40

The Fixed-Length and Short-Form Exam Strategy 42

Question-Handling Strategies 44

Mastering the Test-Taking Mindset 44

Additional Resources 45

CHAPTER 1:
Introduction to Windows Vista 47

Features of the Windows Vista Operating System. 48
End-User Features 48
Application Enhancements 51
Core Technologies 53
Security Enhancements 55
Windows Vista Versions. 57
Exam Prep Questions. 59
Answers to Exam Prep Questions 61
Recommended Readings and Resources 62

CHAPTER 2:
Installing Windows Vista 63

System Requirements. 64
Windows Vista Installation Methods. 65
Business Desktop Deployment Solution Accelerator 2007. 65
Performing a Clean Installation of Windows Vista 68
Methods to Perform a Clean Installation 68
Troubleshooting Problems with Clean Installation 70
Windows Updates. 71
Upgrading and Migrating to Windows Vista from a Previous Version of Windows. 72
Windows Vista Upgrade Advisor 73
Upgrading to Windows Vista 75
Migrating User Settings to a Windows Vista Computer 76
Troubleshooting an Upgrade or Migration to Windows Vista . . 77
Upgrading Between Windows Vista Editions. 77
Restoring a Computer to a Previous Windows Installation 78
Dual Booting Windows XP and Windows Vista 79
Repairing a Windows Installation 79
Activating Windows Vista 80
Exam Prep Questions. 81
Answers to Exam Prep Questions 84
Recommended Readings and Resources 86

CHAPTER 3:
Using Windows Vista **87**

Desktop 88
Managing Desktop Icons 89
Taskbar and Sidebar 91
Start Menu 91
Search Box 93
Right Pane 94
Taskbar 95
Quick Launch Toolbar 96
Notification Area 96
Control Panel 97
Welcome Center 98
Managing Device Drivers 99
Plug-and-Play Devices 100
Signed Drivers 100
Device Manager 100
Display Settings 102
Adjusting the Screen Settings 103
Windows Aero 106
Configuring Accessibility 110
Parental Control 112
Administrative Tools 114
Exam Prep Questions 116
Answers to Exam Prep Questions 120
Recommended Readings and Resources 121

CHAPTER 4:
Configuring Advanced Networking **123**

Introduction to TCP/IP 124
IPv4 TCP/IP Addressing 124
IPv6 TCP/IP Addressing 126
Name Resolution 127
IP Configuration on Windows Vista Machines 128
Tools to Help Diagnose Network Problems 131

Wireless Connections 133
Wireless Technology 133
Wireless Security 134
Configuring a Wireless Connection 135
Remote Access 139
Dial-Up Connections 139
Broadband Connections 141
Virtual Private Networking 141
Exam Prep Questions 143
Answers to Exam Prep Questions 147
Recommended Readings and Resources 149

CHAPTER 5:
NTFS Security Features and File Sharing 151

File Systems 152
NTFS File Permissions 153
Sharing Files and Folders 156
Network Discovery and Browsing 157
Public Folder 160
Standard Sharing 161
Accessing a Shared Folder 165
File Encryption 166
Encryption File System 167
BitLocker Drive Encryption 170
Workings of BitLocker Drive Encryption 170
System Requirements of BitLocker 172
Enabling and Disabling BitLocker 173
Compression 174
Exam Prep Questions 176
Answers to Exam Prep Questions 180
Recommended Readings and Resources 181

CHAPTER 6:
Configuring User Account Security 183

User Accounts and Groups 184
Default User Accounts 185
Windows Vista Local Accounts 186

Managing Local Logon Accounts 188
Creating a New Local Account 188
Giving Domain Accounts Local Access 189
Changing Accounts 190
Creating and Changing Passwords 191
Removing Local User Accounts 191
Local User Accounts and Groups in the Computer Management Console 192
User Account Control 193
Program Compatibility 197
Controlling UAC 197
Exam Prep Questions 201
Answers to Exam Prep Questions 204
Recommended Readings and Resources 205

CHAPTER 7:
Configuring Network Security 207

Spyware 208
Windows Defender 209
Windows Firewall Settings 215
Basic Configuration 216
Advanced Configuration 219
Computer Connection Security Rules 221
Exam Prep Questions 224
Answers to Exam Prep Questions 228
Recommended Readings and Resources 230

CHAPTER 8:
Configuring Internet Explorer 7.0 231

New Features of IE 7.0 232
Common IE Settings 233
Plug-Ins, Add-Ons, and Scripting Languages 236
IE Security Features 238
Cookies and Privacy Settings 239
Content Zones 240
Dynamic Security and Protected Mode 242

RSS Feeds . . . 246
Reset IE to Default Settings . . . 247
Exam Prep Questions . . . 248
Answers to Exam Prep Questions . . . 250
Recommended Readings and Resources . . . 251

CHAPTER 9:
Maintaining and Optimizing Windows Vista Systems . . . 253

Windows Reliability and Performance Monitor and Task Manager . . 254
Optimizing the Disk . . . 258
Monitoring Disk Space . . . 258
Running Check Disk . . . 258
Defragging the Hard Drive . . . 259
Memory Usage and the Paging File . . . 260
ReadyBoost and ReadyDrive . . . 262
Diagnostic Tools . . . 264
Memory Diagnostic Tool . . . 264
Network Diagnostic Tool . . . 265
System Configuration . . . 266
Advanced Startup Options . . . 267
Startup Repair Tool . . . 269
Event Viewer . . . 269
Problem Reports and Solutions Tool . . . 270
Restore a Driver to Its Previous Version . . . 270
System Restore . . . 271
Remote Desktop and Remote Assistance . . . 271
Exam Prep Questions . . . 275
Answers to Exam Prep Questions . . . 278
Recommended Readings and Resources . . . 280

CHAPTER 10:
Configuring Windows Vista Media Applications . . . 281

Windows Media Player . . . 282
Security Options . . . 282
Codecs . . . 284
Regions . . . 285
Windows Media Center . . . 286

Practice Exam Questions . . . 289
Answers to Exam Prep Questions . . . 290
Recommended Readings and Resources . . . 291

CHAPTER 11:
Configuring Windows Vista Productivity Applications . . . 293

Windows WordPad and Notepad . . . 294
Windows Mail . . . 294
Using Windows Mail . . . 295
Configuring Windows Mail . . . 296
Dealing with Junk E-Mail . . . 297
Phishing Options . . . 299
Securing Windows Mail . . . 300
Windows Calendar . . . 300
Windows Fax and Scan . . . 303
Meeting Space . . . 307
Windows Sidebar . . . 309
Practice Exam Questions . . . 311
Answers to Exam Prep Questions . . . 315
Recommended Readings and Resources . . . 316

CHAPTER 12:
Configuring Mobile Computers . . . 317

Control Panel and Windows Mobility Center . . . 318
Power Management . . . 320
Power Plans . . . 320
Shutdown Options . . . 323
Battery Meter . . . 323
File and Data Synchronization . . . 325
Offline Folders . . . 326
Connecting Mobile Devices . . . 328
Giving Presentations . . . 329
Windows SideShow . . . 331
Configuring Tablet PCs . . . 332
Practice Exam Questions . . . 334
Answers to Exam Prep Questions . . . 336
Recommended Readings and Resources . . . 338

CHAPTER 13:
Practice Exam 1 339

Exam Questions 340

CHAPTER 14:
Answers to Practice Exam 1 353

CHAPTER 15:
Practice Exam 2 365

Exam Questions 366

CHAPTER 16:
Answers to Practice Exam 2 379

APPENDIX:
What's on the CD-ROM? 391

Multiple Test Modes 391
Study Mode 391
Certification Mode 391
Custom Mode 392
Attention to Exam Objectives 392
Installing the CD 392
Creating a Shortcut to the MeasureUp Practice Tests 394
Technical Support 394

Glossary 395

Index 411

About the Author

Patrick Regan has been a PC technician, network administrator/engineer, design architect, and security analyst for the past 16 years after graduating with a bachelor's degree in physics from the University of Akron. He has taught many computer and network classes at Sacramento local colleges (Heald College and MTI College), and participated in and led many projects (Heald College, Intel Corporation, Miles Consulting Corporation, and Pacific Coast Companies). For his teaching accomplishments, he received the Teacher of the Year award from Heald College and he has received several recognition awards from Intel. Previously, he worked as a product support engineer for the Intel Corporation Customer Service, a senior network engineer for Virtual Alert supporting the BioTerrorism Readiness suite and as a senior design architect/engineer and training coordinator for Miles Consulting Corp (MCC), a premiere Microsoft Gold Certified Partner and consulting firm. He is currently a senior network engineer at Pacific Coast Companies supporting a large enterprise network.

He holds many certifications including the Microsoft MCSE, MCSA, MCT; CompTIA's A+, Network+, Server+, Linux+, Security+, and CTT+; Cisco CCNA; and Novell's CNE and CWNP Certified Wireless Network Administrator (CWNA).

Over the past several years, he has written several textbooks for Prentice Hall Publisher, including *Troubleshooting the PC*, *Networking with Windows 2000 and 2003*, *Linux*, *Local Area Networks*, *Wide Area Networks* and the Acing Series (*Acing the A+*, *Acing the Network+*, *Acing the Security+* and *Acing the Linux+*). He has also co-authored the *ExamCram 70-290 MCSA/MCSE Managing and Maintaining a Microsoft Windows Server 2003 Environment, 2nd Edition*.

You can write with questions and comments to the author at Patrick_Regan@hotmail.com. (Because of the high volume of mail, every message might not receive a reply.)

About the Reviewer

Chris Crayton is a technical consultant, security consultant, and trainer. Formerly, he worked as a networking instructor at Keiser College and as a network administrator for Protocol, an electronic customer relationship management (eCRM) company. Chris has authored several print and online books including *Microsoft Windows Vista 70-620 Exam Guide Short Cut* (O'Reilly, 2007), *CompTIA A+ Essentials 220-601 Exam Guide Short Cut* (O'Reilly, 2007), *A+ Adaptive Exams* (Charles River Media, 2002), and *The Security+ Exam Guide* (Charles River Media, 2003). He holds MCSE, MCP+I, A+, and Network+ certifications.

Dedication

I dedicate this book to the most beautiful woman, most wonderful person, and the greatest Mom, Lidia. She is the best there is.

We Want to Hear from You!

As the reader of this book, *you* are our most important critic and commentator. We value your opinion and want to know what we're doing right, what we could do better, what areas you'd like to see us publish in, and any other words of wisdom you're willing to pass our way.

As an acquisitions editor for Que Publishing, I welcome your comments. You can email or write me directly to let me know what you did or didn't like about this book—as well as what we can do to make our books better.

Please note that I cannot help you with technical problems related to the topic of this book. We do have a User Services group, however, where I will forward specific technical questions related to the book.

When you write, please be sure to include this book's title and author as well as your name, email address, and phone number. I will carefully review your comments and share them with the author and editors who worked on the book.

Email: scorehigher@pearsoned.com

Mail: Betsy Brown
Acquisitions Editor
Que Publishing
800 East 96th Street
Indianapolis, IN 46240 USA

Reader Services

Visit our website and register this book at www.quepublishing.com/register for convenient access to any updates, downloads, or errata that might be available for this book.

Introduction

Welcome to *MCTS 70-620 Exam Cram: Microsoft Windows Vista Client Configuration*! Whether this book is your first or your fifteenth *Exam Cram* series book, you'll find information here that will help ensure your success as you pursue knowledge, experience, and certification. This book aims to help you get ready to take and pass the Microsoft certification exam "TS: Microsoft Windows Vista, Configuring" (Exam 70-620). When you pass this exam, you will earn the Microsoft Certified Technology Specialist: Windows Vista, Configuration certification.

This introduction explains the Microsoft certification programs in general and talks about how the *Exam Cram* series can help you prepare for the latest certification exams from Microsoft. Chapters 1 through 12 are designed to remind you of everything you need to know to pass the 70-620 certification exam. The two sample tests at the end of the book should give you a reasonably accurate assessment of your knowledge and, yes, we've provided the answers and their explanations for these sample tests. Read the book, understand the material, and you'll stand a very good chance of passing the real test.

Exam Cram books help you understand and appreciate the subjects and materials you need to know to pass Microsoft certification exams. *Exam Cram* books are aimed strictly at test preparation and review. They do not teach you everything you need to know about a subject. Instead, the author streamlines and highlights the pertinent information by presenting and dissecting the questions and problems he has discovered that you're likely to encounter on a Microsoft test.

Nevertheless, to completely prepare yourself for any Microsoft test, we recommend that you begin by taking the "Self Assessment" that is included in this book, immediately following this introduction. The self-assessment tool will help you evaluate your knowledge base against the requirements for becoming a Microsoft Certified Technology Specialist (MCTS) and will be the first step in earning more advanced certifications including Microsoft's IT Professional and Professional Developer (MCITP and MCPD) and Architect (MCA).

Based on what you learn from the Self-Assessment, you might decide to begin your studies with classroom training or some background reading. On the other hand, you might decide to pick up and read one of the many study guides available from Microsoft or third-party vendors. We also recommend that you supplement your study program with visits to http://examcram.com for additional practice questions and to get advice and track the Windows certification programs.

This book also offers you an added bonus of access to Exam Cram practice tests online. All you need is a connection to the Internet and you can take advantage of these practice exam questions right from your very own web browser! This software simulates the Microsoft testing environment with similar types of questions that you're likely to see on the actual Microsoft exam. We also strongly recommend that you install, configure and play around with the Microsoft Windows Vista operating system. Nothing beats hands-on experience and familiarity when it comes to understanding the questions you're likely to encounter on a certification test. Book learning is essential, but without a doubt, hands-on experience is the best teacher of all!

The Value of Certification

It is an established fact that computers and networking is a fast-paced environment. Therefore, employees who work in information technology (IT) must learn to keep up with the ever-changing technology and have the ability to learn new technology. It is said that those in IT must be able to learn or retrain themselves every 1 to 1.5 years.

According to *Certification* magazine (http://www.certmag.com), the successful IT worker must

- Be proficient in two or more technical specialties
- Be able to wear multiple hats
- Be more business-oriented because hiring managers will be looking for employees who see the big picture of profit, loss, competitive advantage and customer retention and understand how IT fits into this picture
- Be able to work easily with nontechnical personnel
- Have soft skills of good listening, problem-solving, and effective written and verbal communication

In addition, there is a demand for those who can demonstrate expertise in IT project management. Those moving to a mid- to high-level position will have a mix of academic credentials and industry certifications, and increasing levels of responsibility.

Today, technical certifications are highly valuable. Depending on which certification or certifications you have, they can allow you to begin as an entry-level technician or administrator or demonstrate the knowledge and capabilities of a current technician or administrator. Technical companies consider some technical certifications as valuable as a college degree and nontechnical companies consider them just a little less than a college degree.

In 2001 researchers from Gartner Consulting surveyed nearly 18,000 IT managers, certified professionals, and certification candidates. They reported the following:

- IT professionals seek certification to increase compensation, find employment, or boost productivity.
- Of those certified, 66 percent of certified professionals received an increase in salary after becoming certified, and 83 percent reported that certification helped them gain a new position.
- Although most certification candidates combine several study methods, printed materials designed for self-study and instructor-led training were reported as the most useful preparation methods.

From the employer's perspective, although many managers (42 percent) feared that certified employees would move on to another organization, 71 percent of IT professionals gaining certification stay put. IT managers cited a higher level of service, competitive advantage, and increased productivity as key benefits of having certified staff. Of course, the drawbacks include cost of training and testing.

As you can see, many people in IT see certification as a valuable tool. You can see that certification is

- A demonstration of specific areas of competence with particular technologies
- A credential desired or required by an increasing number of employers
- A tool people use successfully to challenge themselves
- A road map for continuing education
- A potential bridge to a new specialty
- Evidence that you are self-motivated and actively working to stay current

On the other hand, certification is not a substitute for extensive hands-on experience and it is not a career cure-all. Finally, passing these exams requires a little bit of work and discipline.

The Microsoft Certification Program

Microsoft currently offers multiple certification titles, each of which boasts its own special abbreviation. (As a certification candidate and computer professional, you need to have a high tolerance for acronyms.)

The certification for end users is this:

- **Microsoft Office Specialist.** Recognized for demonstrating advanced skills with Microsoft desktop software (including Microsoft Office).

The older certifications associated with the Windows Server 2003 operating system and related network infrastructure are as follows:

- **Microsoft Certified Professional (MCP).** For professionals who have the skills to successfully implement a Microsoft product (such as Windows XP or Windows Server 2003) or technology as part of a business solution in an organization.
- **Microsoft Certified Desktop Support Technician (MCDST).** For professionals who have the technical and customer service skills to troubleshoot hardware and software operation issues in Microsoft Windows environments.
- **Microsoft Certified Systems Administrator (MCSA).** For professionals who administer network and systems environments based on the Microsoft Windows operating systems. Specializations include MCSA: Messaging and MCSA: Security.
- **Microsoft Certified Systems Engineer (MCSE).** For professionals who design and implement an infrastructure solution that is based on the Windows operating system and Microsoft Windows Server System software. Specializations include MCSE: Messaging and MCSE: Security.

The newer certification based on Windows Vista and related server products are as follows:

- **Microsoft Certified Technology Specialist (MCTS).** For professionals who target specific technologies and want to distinguish themselves by demonstrating in-depth knowledge and expertise in the various Microsoft specialized technologies. The MCTS is a replacement for the MCP program.

- **Microsoft Certified IT Professional (MCITP).** For professionals who demonstrate comprehensive skills in planning, deploying, supporting, maintaining, and optimizing IT infrastructures. The MCITP is a replacement for the MCSA and MCSE programs.
- **Microsoft Certified Architect (MCA).** For professionals who are identified as top industry experts in IT architecture that use multiple technologies to solve business problems and provide business metrics and measurements. Candidates for the MCA program are required to present to a review board—consisting of previously certified architects—to earn the certification.

For database professionals, the certification is this:

- **Microsoft Certified Database Administrator (MCDBA).** For professionals who design, implement, and administer Microsoft SQL Server databases.

For developers and programmers, certifications are as follows:

- **Microsoft Certified Professional Developer (MCPD).** Professionals who are recognized as expert Windows Application Developer, Web Application Developer, or Enterprise Application Developer. They demonstrate that you can build rich applications that target a variety of platforms such as the Microsoft .NET Framework 2.0.
- **Microsoft Certified Application Developer (MCAD).** For professionals who use Microsoft technologies to develop and maintain department-level applications, components, web or desktop clients, or back-end data services.

For trainers and curriculum developers, certifications are as follows:

- **Microsoft Certified Trainer (MCT).** For qualified instructors who are certified by Microsoft to deliver Microsoft training courses to IT professionals and developers.
- **Microsoft Certified Learning Consultant (MCLC).** Recognizes MCTs whose job roles have grown to include frequent consultative engagements with their customers and who are experts in delivering customized learning solutions that positively affect customer return on investment (ROI).

To best keep tabs on all Microsoft certifications, visit the following website:

www.microsoft.com/learning/default.mspx.

Because Microsoft changes its website often, this URL might not work in the future, so you should use the Search tool on the Microsoft site to find more information about specific certifications.

Microsoft Certified Technology Specialist

Technology Specialist certifications enable professionals to target specific technologies and to distinguish themselves by demonstrating in-depth knowledge and expertise in their specialized technologies. Microsoft Technology Specialists are consistently capable of implementing, building, troubleshooting, and debugging a particular Microsoft technology.

At the time of this writing, there are 17 Microsoft Certified Technology Specialist (MCTS) certifications:

- Technology Specialist: .NET Framework 2.0 Web Applications
- Technology Specialist: .NET Framework 2.0 Windows Applications
- Technology Specialist: .NET Framework 2.0 Distributed Applications
- Technology Specialist: SQL Server 2005
- Technology Specialist: SQL Server 2005 Business Intelligence
- Technology Specialist: BizTalk Server 2006
- Technology Specialist: Microsoft Office Live Communications Server 2005
- Technology Specialist: Microsoft Exchange Server 2007, Configuration
- Technology Specialist: Microsoft Office SharePoint Server 2007, Configuration
- Technology Specialist: Microsoft Office SharePoint Server 2007, Application Development
- Technology Specialist: Windows Mobile 5.0, Applications
- Technology Specialist: Windows Mobile 5.0, Implementing and Managing

- Technology Specialist: Windows Server 2003 Hosted Environments, Configuration, and Management
- Technology Specialist: Windows SharePoint Services 3.0, Application Development
- Technology Specialist: Windows SharePoint Services 3.0, Configuration
- Technology Specialist: Windows Vista and 2007 Microsoft Office System Desktops, Deploying and Maintaining
- Technology Specialist: Windows Vista, Configuration

Microsoft Certified IT Professional

The new Microsoft Certified IT Professional (MCITP) credential lets you highlight your specific area of expertise. Now, you can easily distinguish yourself as an expert in database administration, database development, business intelligence, or support. At the time of this writing, the following Microsoft Certified IT Professional certifications exist:

- IT Professional: Database Developer
- IT Professional: Database Administrator
- IT Professional: Business Intelligence Developer
- IT Professional: Enterprise Support Technician

The MCTS on Windows Server 2008 will help you and your organization to take advantage of advanced server technology with the power to increase the flexibility of your server infrastructure, save time, and reduce costs. In 2008, Microsoft will introduce two MCITP programs aimed at the Windows Server 2008 platform: the MCITP—Server Administrator and MCITP—Enterprise Administrator.

The MCITP—Server Administrator program consists of the following certifications:

- Windows Server 2008 Active Directory (70-640)
- Windows Server 2008 Network Infrastructure (70-642)
- Windows Server 2008 Administrator (70-646)

The MCITP—Enterprise Administrator program consists of the following certifications:

- Windows Vista (70-620 or 70-624)
- Windows Server 2008 Application/Platform Configuration (70-643)
- Windows Server 2008 Network Infrastructure (70-642)
- Windows Server 2008 Active Directory (70-640)
- Enterprise Administrator (70-647)

Transition certifications are available today for Windows Server 2003 certified professionals, and full certification paths will be available soon after the Windows Server 2008 product release. For more details about these certifications, visit the following website:

www.microsoft.com/learning/mcp/windowsserver2008/default.mspx

If the URL is no longer available, don't forget to search for "MCTS" and "Windows Server 2008" using the Microsoft Search tool found on the Microsoft website.

Microsoft Certified Technology Specialist: Windows Vista, Configuration

The Microsoft Certified Technology Specialist certifications enable professionals to target specific technologies and distinguish themselves by demonstrating in-depth knowledge and expertise in their specialized technologies. A Microsoft Certified Technology Specialist in Windows Vista, Configuration possesses the knowledge and skills to configure Windows Vista for optimal performance on the desktop, including installing, managing, and configuring the new security, network, and application features in Windows Vista.

To earn the Microsoft Certified Technology Specialist: Windows Vista, Configuration, you must pass one exam that focuses on supporting end-user issues about network connectivity, security, and application installation and compatibility, and logon problems that include account issues and password resets:

- Exam 70-620: TS: Microsoft Windows Vista Client, Configuring

If you decide to take a Microsoft-recognized course, you need to take two classes:

- Course 5115: Installing and Configuring the Windows Vista Operating System (3 days)
- Course 5116: Configuring Windows Vista Applications and Tools (2 days)

You can find the preparation guide (including exam objectives) for Exam 70-620 TS: Microsoft Windows Vista, Configuring at www.microsoft.com/learning/exams/70-620.mspx

Taking a Certification Exam

After you prepare for your exam, you need to register with a testing center. At the time of this writing, the cost to take Exam 70-620 is (U.S.) $125, and if you don't pass, you can take each again for an additional (U.S.) $125 for each attempt. In the United States and Canada, tests are administered by Prometric. You can sign up for a test through the company's website, www.2test.com or www.prometric.com. Within the United States and Canada, you can register by phone at 800-755-3926. If you live outside this region, check the Prometric website (www.microsoft.com/learning/mcpexams/register/prometric.mspx) for the appropriate phone number.

To sign up for a test, you must have a valid credit card. Alternatively, you can contact Prometric for mailing instructions to send a check (in the United States). Only when payment has been verified, or a check has cleared, can you actually register for a test.

To schedule an exam, you need to call the phone number or visit Prometric websites at least one day in advance. To cancel or reschedule an exam in the United States or Canada, you must call before 3 p.m. Eastern time the day before the scheduled test time (or you might be charged, even if you don't show up to take the test). When you want to schedule a test, you should have the following information ready:

- Your name, organization, and mailing address.
- Your Microsoft test ID. (In the United States, this means your Social Security number; citizens of other countries should call ahead to find out what type of identification number is required to register for a test.)

- The name and number of the exam you want to take.
- A method of payment. (As mentioned previously, a credit card is the most convenient method, but alternative means can be arranged in advance, if necessary.)

After you sign up for a test, you are told when and where the test is scheduled. You should arrive at least 15 minutes early. You must supply two forms of identification, one of which must be a photo ID to be admitted into the testing room.

Tracking Certification Status

As soon as you pass a qualified Microsoft exam and earn a professional certification, Microsoft generates transcripts that indicate the exams you have passed. You can view a copy of your transcript at any time by going to the MCP-secured site (this site might change as the MCP is retired) and selecting the Transcript Tool. This tool enables you to print a copy of your current transcript and confirm your certification status.

After you pass the necessary set of exams, you are certified. Official certification is normally granted after six to eight weeks, so you shouldn't expect to get your credentials overnight. The package for official certification that arrives includes a Welcome Kit that contains a number of elements (see the Microsoft website for other benefits of specific certifications):

- A certificate that is suitable for framing, along with a wallet card and lapel pin.
- A license to use the related certification logo, which means you can use the logo in advertisements, promotions, and documents and on letterhead, business cards, and so on. Along with the license comes a logo sheet, which includes camera-ready artwork. (Note that before you use any of the artwork, you must sign and return a licensing agreement that indicates you'll abide by its terms and conditions.)
- Access to the *Microsoft Certified Professional Magazine Online* website, which provides ongoing data about testing and certification activities, requirements, changes to the MCP program, and security-related information on Microsoft products.

Many people believe that the benefits of MCP certification go well beyond the perks that Microsoft provides to newly anointed members of this elite group.

We're starting to see more job listings that request or require applicants to have Microsoft and other related certifications, and many individuals who complete Microsoft certification programs can qualify for increases in pay and responsibility. As an official recognition of hard work and broad knowledge, a certification credential is a badge of honor in many IT organizations.

About This Book

Each topical *Exam Cram* chapter follows a regular structure and contains graphical cues about important or useful information. Here's the structure of a typical chapter:

- **Opening hotlists.** Each chapter begins with a list of the terms, tools, and techniques that you must learn and understand before you can be fully conversant with that chapter's subject matter. The hotlists are followed with one or two introductory paragraphs to set the stage for the rest of the chapter.
- **Topical coverage.** After the opening hotlists and introductory text, each chapter covers a series of topics related to the chapter's subject. Throughout that part of the chapter, we highlight topics or concepts that are likely to appear on a test, using a special element called an alert:

EXAM ALERT

This is what an alert looks like. Normally, an alert stresses concepts, terms, software, or activities that are likely to relate to one or more certification-test questions. For that reason, we think any information in an alert is worthy of unusual attentiveness on your part.

You should pay close attention to material flagged in Exam Alerts; although all the information in this book pertains to what you need to know to pass the exam, Exam Alerts contain information that is important. You'll find what appears in the meat of each chapter to be worth knowing, too, when preparing for the test. Because this book's material is condensed, we recommend that you use this book along with other resources to achieve the maximum benefit.

In addition to the alerts, we provide tips that will help you build a better foundation for Windows Server 2003 knowledge. Although the tip information might not be on the exam, it is certainly related and it will help you become a better-informed test taker.

TIP

This is how tips look. Keep your eyes open for these and you'll become a Windows Server 2003 guru in no time!

NOTE

This is how notes look. Notes direct your attention to important pieces of information that relate to Windows Server 2003 and Microsoft certification.

- **Exam prep questions.** Although we talk about test questions and topics throughout the book, this section at the end of each chapter presents a series of mock test questions and explanations of both correct and incorrect answers.
- **Details and resources.** Every chapter ends with a section titled "Recommended Readings and Resources." That section provides direct pointers to Microsoft and third-party resources that offer more details about the chapter's subject. In addition, that section tries to rank or at least rate the quality and thoroughness of the topic's coverage by each resource. If you find a resource you like in that collection, you should use it; but don't feel compelled to use all the resources. On the other hand, we recommend only resources that we use on a regular basis, so none of our recommendations will be a waste of your time or money (but purchasing them all at once probably represents an expense that many network administrators and Microsoft certification candidates might find hard to justify).

The bulk of the book follows this chapter structure, but there are a few other elements. Chapters 13 through 16, "Practice Exam 1" and "Practice Exam 2," and their answers chapters, provide good reviews of the material presented throughout this book to ensure that you're ready for the exam.

Finally, the tear-out Cram Sheet attached next to the inside front cover of this *Exam Cram* book represents a condensed and compiled collection of facts and tips that we think are essential for you to memorize before taking the test. Because you can dump this information out of your head onto a sheet of paper before taking the exam, you can master this information by brute force; you need to remember it only long enough to write it down when you walk into the testing room. You might even want to look at it in the car or in the lobby of the testing center just before you walk in to take the exam.

We've structured the topics in this book to build on one another. Therefore, some topics in later chapters make the most sense after you've read earlier chapters. That's why we suggest that you read this book from front to back for your initial test preparation. If you need to brush up on a topic or if you have to bone up for a second try, you can use the index or table of contents to go straight to the topics and questions that you need to study. Beyond helping you prepare for the test, we think you'll find this book useful as a tightly focused reference to some of the most important aspects of Windows Vista.

The book uses the following typographical conventions:

- Command-line strings that are meant to be typed into the computer are displayed in monospace text, such as

  ```
  net use lpt1: \\print_server_name\printer_share_name
  ```

- *New terms* are introduced in italics.

Given all the book's elements and its specialized focus, we've tried to create a tool that will help you prepare for and pass Microsoft Exam 70-620. Please share with us your feedback on the book, especially if you have ideas about how we can improve it for future test takers. Send your questions or comments about this book via email to feedback@quepublishing.com. We'll consider everything you say carefully, and we'll respond to all suggestions. For more information about this book and other Que Certification titles, visit our website at www.quepublishing.com. You should also check out the new *Exam Cram* website at www.examcram.com, where you'll find information updates, commentary, and certification information.

Thanks for making this *Exam Cram* book a pivotal part of your certification study plan. Best of luck on becoming certified!

Self-Assessment

The reason we include a self-assessment in this *Exam Cram* book is to help you evaluate your readiness to tackle Microsoft certifications. It should also help you to understand what you need to know to master the main topic of this book: namely, Exam 70-620 TS: Microsoft Windows Vista, Configuring. You might also want to check out the Microsoft Skills Assessment web page (www.microsoft.com/learning/assessment) on the Microsoft Training and Certification website. But, before you tackle this self-assessment, let's talk about concerns you might face when pursuing a Microsoft certification credential on Windows and what an ideal Microsoft certification candidate might look like.

Microsoft Certification in the Real World

In the next section, we describe the ideal Microsoft certification candidate, knowing full well that only a few real candidates meet that ideal. In fact, our description of those ideal candidates might seem downright unrealistic, especially with the changes that have been made to the Microsoft certifications to support Windows. But don't worry: Although the requirements to obtain the advanced Microsoft certification might seem formidable, they are by no means impossible to meet. However, you need to be keenly aware that getting through the process takes time, involves some expense, and requires real effort.

Increasing numbers of people are attaining Microsoft certifications. You can get all the real-world motivation you need from knowing that many others have gone before, so you will be able to follow in their footsteps. If you're willing to tackle the process seriously and do what it takes to obtain the necessary experience and knowledge, you can take and pass all the certification tests involved in obtaining the credentials. In fact, at Que Publishing, we've designed the *Exam Cram 2* series and the *MCSE Training Guide* series to make it as easy for you as possible to prepare for these exams. We've also greatly expanded our website, www.examcram2.com, to provide a host of resources to help you prepare for the complexities of Windows.

The Ideal Microsoft Certification Candidate

To give you an idea of what an ideal Microsoft certification candidate is like, here are some relevant statistics about the background and experience such an individual might have:

> **NOTE**
>
> Don't worry if you don't meet these qualifications or even come close to meeting them: This world is far from ideal, and where you fall short is simply where you have more work to do.

- Academic or professional training in network theory, concepts, and operations. This area includes everything from networking media and transmission techniques through network operating systems, services, and applications.
- Two or more years of professional networking experience, including experience with Ethernet, Token Ring, modems, and other networking media. This experience must include installation, configuration, upgrading, and troubleshooting experience.

> **NOTE**
>
> Some of the more advanced exams require you to solve real-world case studies and network-design issues, so the more hands-on experience you have, the better.

- Two or more years in a networked environment that includes hands-on experience with Windows Server 2003, Windows 2000 Server, Windows 2000/XP Professional, Windows NT 4.0 Server, Windows NT 4.0 Workstation, and Windows 98 or Windows 95. A solid understanding of each system's architecture, installation, configuration, maintenance, and troubleshooting is also essential.
- Knowledge of the various methods for installing Windows Server 2003 and Windows XP, including manual and unattended installations.
- A thorough understanding of key networking protocols, addressing, and name resolution, including Transmission Control Protocol/Internet Protocol (TCP/IP).

- Familiarity with key Windows Server 2003–based TCP/IP utilities and services, including Hypertext Transport Protocol (HTTP—used for web servers), Dynamic Host Configuration Protocol (DHCP), Windows Internet Naming Service (WINS), and Domain Name System (DNS), plus familiarity with one or more of the following: Internet Information Services (IIS), Internet Protocol Security (IPSec), Internet Connection Sharing (ICS), Internet Connection Firewall (ICF), and Terminal Services.
- An understanding of how to implement security for key network data in a Windows Server 2003 environment.
- A good understanding of Active Directory.

To meet all of these qualifications, you need a Bachelor's degree in computer science plus three years' work experience in PC networking design, installation, administration, and troubleshooting. Don't be concerned if you don't have all of these qualifications. Fewer than half of all Microsoft certification candidates meet these requirements. This self-assessment chapter is designed to show you what you already know and to prepare you for the topics that you need to learn.

Put Yourself to the Test

The following series of questions and observations is designed to help you figure out how much work you must do to pursue Microsoft certification and what kinds of resources you can consult on your quest. Be absolutely honest in your answers; otherwise, you'll end up wasting money on exams that you're not yet ready to take. There are no right or wrong answers—only steps along the path to certification. Only you can decide where you really belong in the broad spectrum of aspiring candidates. Two things should be clear from the outset, however:

- Even a modest background in computer science is helpful.
- Hands-on experience with Microsoft products and technologies is an essential ingredient in certification success.

Educational Background

The following questions concern your level of technical computer experience and training. Depending on your answers to these questions, you might need to review some additional resources to get your knowledge up to speed for the types of questions that you will encounter on Microsoft certification exams:

1. Have you ever taken any computer-related classes? [Yes or No]

   If Yes, proceed to Question 2; if No, proceed to Question 3.

2. Have you taken any classes on computer operating systems? [Yes or No]

   If Yes, you will probably be able to handle the Microsoft architecture and system component discussions. If you're rusty, you should brush up on basic operating system concepts, especially virtual memory, multitasking regimes, User mode versus Kernel mode operation, and general computer security topics.

   If No, you should consider doing some basic reading in this area. We strongly recommend a good general operating systems book, such as *Operating System Concepts*, by Abraham Silberschatz and Peter Baer Galvin (John Wiley & Sons). If this book doesn't appeal to you, check out reviews for other similar books at your favorite online bookstore.

3. Have you taken any networking concepts or technologies classes? [Yes or No]

   If Yes, you will probably be able to handle the Microsoft networking terminology, concepts, and technologies. (Brace yourself for frequent departures from normal usage.) If you're rusty, you should brush up on basic networking concepts and terminology, especially networking media, transmission types, the Open System Interconnection (OSI) reference model, and networking technologies, such as Ethernet, Token Ring, Fiber Distributed Data Interface (FDDI), and wide area network (WAN) links.

   If No, you might want to read one or two books in this topic area. The two best books that we know are *Computer Networks*, by Andrew S. Tanenbaum (Prentice Hall), and *Computer Networks and Internets*, by Douglas E. Comer and Ralph E. Droms (Prentice Hall).

Hands-On Experience

The most important key to success on all the Microsoft tests is hands-on experience, especially when it comes to Windows Server 2003 and Windows XP and the many add-on services and components around which so many of the Microsoft certification exams revolve. If we leave you with only one realization after you take this self-assessment, it should be that there's no substitute for time spent installing, configuring, and using the various Microsoft products on which you'll be tested. The more in-depth understanding you have of how these software products work, the better your chance of selecting the right answers on the exam:

1. Have you installed, configured, and worked with the following:

    - Windows Server 2003? [Yes or No]

      If No, you must obtain one or two machines and a copy of Windows Server 2003. (A trial version is available on the Microsoft website.) Then, you should learn about the operating system and any other software components on which you'll also be tested. In fact, we recommend that you obtain two computers, each with a network interface, and set up a two-node network on which to practice. With decent Windows Server 2003–capable computers selling for about $500 to $600 apiece these days, this setup shouldn't be too much of a financial hardship. You might have to scrounge to come up with the necessary software, but if you scour the Microsoft website, you can usually find low-cost options to obtain evaluation copies of most of the software that you'll need.

NOTE

You can download objectives, practice exams, and other data about Microsoft exams from the Training and Certification page at www.microsoft.com/traincert. You can use the Exams link to obtain specific exam information.

    - Windows XP Professional? [Yes or No]

      If No, you should obtain a copy of Windows XP Professional and learn how to install, configure, and maintain it. Pick up a well-written book to guide your activities and studies (such as *MCSE Windows XP Professional Exam Cram 2*), or you can work straight from the Microsoft exam objectives, if you prefer.

    - Windows Vista? [Yes or No]

      If No, you should obtain a copy of Windows Vista and learn how to install, configure, and maintain it. Pick up a well-written book to guide your activities and studies, or you can work straight from the Microsoft exam objectives, if you prefer.

Use One Computer to Simulate Multiple Machines

If you own a powerful enough computer—one that has plenty of available disk space, a lot of RAM (at least 512 MB), and a Pentium 4-compatible processor or better—you should check out the VMware and Virtual PC virtual-machine software products that are on the market. These software programs create an emulated computer environment within separate windows that are hosted by your computer's main operating system—Windows Server 2003, Windows XP, Windows 2000, and so on. So, on a single computer, you can have several different operating systems running simultaneously in different windows! You can run everything from DOS to Linux, from Windows 95 to Windows Server 2003. Within a virtual-machine environment, you can "play" with the latest operating systems, including beta versions, without worrying about "blowing up" your main production computer and without having to buy an additional PC. VMware is published by VMware, Inc.; you can get more information from its website at www.vmware.com. Virtual PC is published by Connectix Corporation; you can find out more information from its website at www.connectix.com. Microsoft recently acquired the Virtual PC technology from Connectix Corporation. For more information about this acquisition, visit www.microsoft.com/windowsxp/pro/evaluation/news/windowsvpc.asp.

TIP

For any and all of these Microsoft operating systems exams, the Resource Kits for the topics involved always make good study resources. You can purchase the Resource Kits from Microsoft Press (you can search for them at http://microsoft.com/mspress), but they also appear on the TechNet CDs, DVDs, and website (www.microsoft.com/technet). Along with the *Exam Cram 2* books, we believe that the Resource Kits are among the best tools you can use to prepare for Microsoft exams. Take a look at the Windows Deployment and Resource Kits web page for more information: www.microsoft.com/windows/reskits/default.asp.

If you have the funds, or if your employer will pay your way, consider taking a class at a Microsoft Certified Training and Education Center (CTEC). In addition to classroom exposure to the topic of your choice, you get a copy of the software that is the focus of your course, along with a trial version of whatever operating system it needs, as part of the training materials for that class.

Before you even think about taking any Microsoft exam, make sure you've spent enough time with the related software to understand how to install and configure it, how to maintain such an installation, and how to troubleshoot the software when things go wrong. This time will help you in the exam—and in real life!

How to Prepare for an Exam

Preparing for any Microsoft certification test (including Exam 70-620) requires that you obtain and study materials designed to provide comprehensive information about the product and its capabilities that will appear on the specific exam for which you are preparing. The following list of materials can help you study and prepare:

- The Windows Vista product DVD-ROM. This disc includes comprehensive online documentation and related materials; it should be one of your primary resources when you are preparing for the test.
- The exam preparation materials, practice tests, and self-assessment exams on the Microsoft Training and Certification site, at www.microsoft.com/learning/default.mspx. The Exam Resources link offers samples of the new question types on the Windows Server 2003 Microsoft Certification track series of exams. You should find the materials, download them, and use them!
- The exam preparation advice, practice tests, questions of the day, and discussion groups at www.examcram2.com.

In addition, you might find any or all of the following materials useful in your quest for Windows Vista expertise:

- **Microsoft training kits.** Microsoft Learning offers a training kit that specifically targets Exam 70-620. For more information, visit www.microsoft.com/learning/books/. This training kit contains information that you will find useful in preparing for the test.
- **Microsoft TechNet CD or DVD and website.** This monthly CD- or DVD-based publication delivers numerous electronic titles that include coverage of Windows Server 2003 and related topics on the Technical Information (TechNet) series on CD or DVD. Its offerings include product facts, technical notes, tools and utilities, and information about how to access the Seminars Online training materials for Windows Server 2003 and the Windows Server System line of products. Visit http://technet.microsoft.com and check out the information for TechNet subscriptions. You can use a large portion of the TechNet website at no charge.

- **Study guides.** Several publishers, including Que Publishing, offer Windows Server 2003, Windows Vista, Windows XP, and Windows 2000 titles. Que Publishing offers the following:
  - **The *Exam Cram 2* series.** These books give you the insights about the material that you need to know to successfully pass the certification tests.
  - **The *MCSE Training Guide* series.** These books provide a greater level of detail than the *Exam Cram 2* books and are designed to teach you everything you need to know about the subject covered by an exam. Each book comes with a CD-ROM that contains interactive practice exams in a variety of testing formats.

  Together, these two series make a perfect pair.
- **Classroom training.** CTECs, online partners, and third-party training companies (such as Wave Technologies, New Horizons, and Global Knowledge) all offer classroom training on Windows Server 2003, Windows Vista, Windows XP, and Windows 2000. These companies aim to help you prepare to pass Exam 70-620 and several others. Although this type of training tends to be pricey, most of the individuals lucky enough to attend find this training to be quite worthwhile.
- **Other publications.** There's no shortage of materials available about Windows Vista. The "Recommended Readings and Resources" sections at the end of each chapter in this book give you an idea about where we think you should look for further discussion.

This set of required and recommended materials represents an unparalleled collection of sources and resources for Windows Vista and related topics. We anticipate that you'll find this book belongs in this company.

Studying for the Exam

Although many websites offer information about what to study for a particular exam, few sites explain how you should study for an exam. The study process can be broken down into various stages. However, key to all of these stages is the ability to concentrate. Concentration, or the lack of, plays a big part in the study process.

To be able to concentrate, you must remove all distractions. Although you should plan for study breaks, it is the unplanned breaks caused by distractions that do not allow you to concentrate on what you need to learn. Therefore, first, you need to create an environment that's conducive to studying or seek out an existing environment that meets these criteria, such as a library.

Do *not* study with the TV on, and do not have other people in the room. It is too easy for something on TV to grab your attention and break your concentration And, do not study with others in the room who might not share your dedication to passing this exam. Opinions differ on whether it is better to study with or without music playing. Some people need to have a little white noise in the background to study; if you choose to have music, keep the volume on a low level and listen to music without vocals.

After you find a place to study, you must schedule the time to study. And, don't study on an empty stomach. You should also not study on a full stomach; a full stomach tends to make people drowsy. You may also consider having a glass of water near to sip on.

In addition, make sure that you are well rested so that you don't start dozing off. Make sure that you find a position that is comfortable and use furniture that is also comfortable. And finally, make sure that your study area is well lit. Natural light is best for fighting fatigue.

The first thing that you should do when you begin to study is to clear your mind of distractions. So, take a minute or two, close your eyes, and empty your mind.

When you prepare for an exam, the best place to start is to take the list of exam objectives and study the list carefully for its scope. You can then organize your study with these objectives in mind, narrowing down your focus area to specific topics/subtopics. In addition, you need to understand and visualize the process as a whole, to help prepare you to address practical problems in a real environment and to deal with unexpected questions.

In a multiple-choice exam, you do have one advantage: The answer or answers are already there, and you just have to choose the correct one(s). Because the answers are already there, you can start eliminating the incorrect answers by using your knowledge and some logical thinking. One common mistake is to select the first obvious-looking answers without checking the other options. Don't fall into this trap: *Always* review all the options, think about them, and then choose the right answer. Of course, with multiple-choice questions, you have to be exact and should be able to differentiate between similar answers. This is one reason you need a peaceful place of study without distractions, so that you can read between the lines and don't miss key points.

Testing Your Exam Readiness

Whether you attend a formal class on a specific topic to get ready for an exam or use written materials to study on your own, some preparation for the Microsoft certification exams is essential. At $125 each—whether you pass or fail—you'll want to do everything you can to pass on your first try. That's where studying comes in.

We include two practice tests in this book (Chapters 13 through 16, "Practice Exam 1," "Practice Exam 2" and answers to Practice Exam 1 and 2, respectively), so if you don't score very well on these tests, you can study the practice exams more and then tackle the test again. We also have practice questions that you can sign up for online through www.examcram2.com. The PrepLogic CD-ROM in the back of this book has sample questions to quiz you on; however, you can also purchase additional practice questions from www.PrepLogic.com. If you still don't hit a score of at least 70 percent after practicing with these tests, investigate the other practice test resources mentioned in this section.

For any given subject, consider taking a class if you've tackled self-study materials, taken the test, and failed anyway. The opportunity to interact with an instructor and fellow students can make all the difference in the world, if you can afford that luxury. For information about Microsoft classes, visit the Training and Certification page at www.microsoft.com/traincert/training/find/findcourse.asp to find training courses offered at Microsoft CTECs.

If you can't afford to take a class, visit the Training and Certification pages anyway; they include pointers to free practice exams and to Microsoft-approved study guides and other self-study tools. And, even if you can't afford to spend much money at all, you should still invest in some low-cost practice exams from commercial vendors. The Microsoft Training and Certification "Assess Your Readiness" page, at www.microsoft.com/traincert/assessment, offers several skills-assessment evaluations that you can take online to show you how far along you are in your certification preparation.

The next question deals with your personal testing experience. Microsoft certification exams have their own style and idiosyncrasies. The more acclimated that you become to the Microsoft testing environment, the better your chances are to score well on the exams:

1. Have you taken a practice exam on your chosen test subject? [Yes or No]

   If Yes, and if you scored 70 percent or better, you're probably ready to tackle the real thing. If your score isn't above that threshold, you should keep at it until you break that barrier.

If No, you should obtain all the free and low-budget practice tests you can find and get to work. Keep at it until you can break the passing threshold comfortably.

TIP

When it comes to assessing your test readiness, there is no better way than to take a good-quality practice exam and pass with a score of 70 percent or better. When preparing, aim for 80 percent or higher, just to leave room for the unexpected or confusing question that sometimes shows up on Microsoft exams.

Assessing Readiness for Exam 70-620

In addition to the general exam-readiness information in the preceding section, you can do several things to prepare for Exam 70-620. As you're getting ready for the exam, visit the *Exam Cram 2* website at www.examcram2.com. We also suggest that you join an active MCSE/MCSA e-mail list and e-mail newsletter. Some of the best list servers and e-mail newsletters are managed by Sunbelt Software. You can sign up at www.sunbelt-software.com.

Microsoft exam mavens also recommend that you check the Microsoft Knowledge Base (available on its own CD as part of the TechNet collection, and on the Microsoft website at http://support.microsoft.com) for "meaningful technical support issues" that relate to your exam's topics. Although we're not sure exactly what the quoted phrase means, we have also noticed some overlap between technical-support questions on particular products and troubleshooting questions on the exams for those products.

Day of the Exam

Before you take an exam, eat something light, even if you have no appetite. If your stomach is actively upset, try mild foods such as toast or crackers. Plain saltine crackers are great for settling a cranky stomach. Keep your caffeine and nicotine consumption to a minimum; excessive stimulants aren't exactly conducive to reducing stress. Plan to take a bottle of water or some hard candies, such as lozenges or mints, with you to combat dry mouth.

When you take the exam, dress comfortably. And, arrive at the testing center early. If you have never been to the testing center before, make sure that you know where it is. You might even consider taking a test drive. If you arrive between 15 and 30 minutes early for any certification exam, it gives you

- Ample time for whatever relaxes you: prayer, meditation, or deep breathing
- Time to scan glossary terms and quick access tables before taking the exam so that you can get the intellectual juices flowing and to build a little confidence
- Time to visit the washroom before you begin the exam.

But, don't arrive too early.

When you are escorted into the testing chamber, you will be usually given two sheets of paper (or laminated paper) with pen (or wet erase pen). As soon as you hear the door close behind you, immediately jot down onto the paper information that you might need to quickly recall. Then, throughout the exam, you can refer to this information and not have to "think" about it. Instead, you can use this information as a reference and focus on answering the questions. Before you actually start the exam, close your eyes and take deep breath to clear your mind of distractions.

Typically, the testing room is furnished with anywhere from one to six computers, and each workstation is separated from the others by dividers designed to keep anyone from seeing what's happening on someone else's computer screen. Most testing rooms feature a wall with a large picture window. This layout permits the exam coordinator to monitor the room, to prevent exam takers from talking to one another, and to observe anything out of the ordinary that might go on. The exam coordinator will have preloaded the appropriate Microsoft certification exam—for this book, that's Exam 70-620: TS: Microsoft Windows Vista Client, Configuring—and you are permitted to start as soon as you're seated in front of the computer.

EXAM ALERT

Always remember that the testing center's test coordinator is there to assist you in case you encounter some unusual problems, such as a malfunctioning test computer. If you need some assistance, feel free to notify one of the test coordinators—after all, they are there to make your exam-taking experience as pleasant as possible.

All exams are completely closed book. In fact, you are not permitted to take anything with you into the testing area, but you receive a blank sheet of paper and a pen or, in some cases, an erasable plastic sheet and an erasable pen. We suggest that you immediately write down on that sheet of paper all the information you've memorized for the test. In *Exam Cram 2* books, this information appears on the tear-out sheet (Cram Sheet) inside the front cover of each book. You are given some time to compose yourself, record this information, and take a sample orientation exam before you begin the real thing. We suggest that you take the orientation test before taking your first exam; but because all the certification exams are more or less identical in layout, behavior, and controls, you probably don't need to do so more than once.

All Microsoft certification exams allow a certain maximum amount of testing time. (This time is indicated on the exam by an onscreen timer clock, so you can check the time remaining whenever you like.) All Microsoft certification exams are computer generated. In addition to multiple-choice questions, most exams contain select–and-place (drag-and-drop), create-a-tree (categorization and prioritization), drag-and-connect, and build-list-and-reorder (list prioritization) types of questions. Although this format might sound quite simple, the questions are constructed not only to check your mastery of basic facts and figures about Windows Vista, but also to require you to evaluate one or more sets of circumstances or requirements. Often, you are asked to give more than one answer to a question. Likewise, you might be asked to select the best or most effective solution to a problem from a range of choices—all of which are technically correct. Taking the exam is quite an adventure, and it involves real thinking and concentration. This book shows you what to expect and how to deal with the potential problems, puzzles, and predicaments.

Dealing with Test Anxiety

Because a certification exam costs money to take and time to prepare for, and because failing an exam can be a blow to your self-confidence, most people feel a certain amount of anxiety when they are about to take a certification exam. It is no wonder that most of us are a little sweaty in the palms when taking the exam. However, certain levels of stress can actually help you to raise your level of performance when taking an exam. This anxiety usually serves to help you focus your concentration and think clearly through a problem.

For some people, exam anxiety is more than just a nuisance. For these people, exam anxiety is a debilitating condition that negatively affects their performance (and therefore their exam results).

Exam anxiety reduction begins with the preparation process. Remember, if you know the material, you really don't have anything to be nervous about. The better prepared you are for an exam, the less stress you will experience when taking it. Always give yourself plenty of time to prepare for an exam; don't place yourself under unreasonable deadlines. But again, make goals and make every effort to meet those goals. Procrastination and making excuses will just lead to more anxiety.

No hard-and-fast rule applies to how long it takes to prepare for an exam. The time required will vary from student to student and depends on a number of different factors, including reading speed, access to study materials, personal commitments, and so on. In addition, don't compare yourself to peers, especially if doing so has a negative effect on your confidence.

For many students, practice exams are a great way to shed some of the fears that arise in the test center. Practice exams are best used near the end of the exam preparation, and be sure to use them as an assessment of your current knowledge, not as a method to try to memorize key concepts. When reviewing these questions, be sure you understand the questions and all the answers (right and wrong). And finally, set time limits on the practice exams.

If you know the material, don't plan to study the day of your exam. You should end your studying the evening before the exam. In addition, don't make it a late night; get a full night's rest. Of course, because you'll be studying regularly for at least a few weeks before the evening before the exam, you won't need any last-minute cramming.

Exam Layout and Design

This section explains different types of questions you might see on the exam. You learn strategies for handling questions and techniques for preparing for the exam.

Common Question Formats

Historically, there have been six types of question formats on Microsoft certification exams. These types of questions continue to appear on current Microsoft tests, and they are discussed in the following sections:

- Multiple-choice, single answer
- Multiple-choice, multiple answers
- Build-list-and-reorder (list prioritization)
- Create-a-tree
- Drag-and-connect
- Select-and-place (drag-and-drop)

The Single-Answer and Multiple-Answers Multiple-Choice Question Formats

Some exam questions require you to select a single answer, whereas others ask you to select multiple correct answers. The following multiple-choice question requires you to select a single correct answer. Following the question is a brief summary of each potential answer and why it is either right or wrong.

Question 1

You have three domains connected to an empty root domain under one contiguous domain name: `tutu.com`. This organization is formed into a forest arrangement, with a secondary domain called `frog.com`. How many schema masters exist for this arrangement?

A. 1

B. 2

C. 3

D. 4

The correct answer is A because only one schema master is necessary for a forest arrangement. The other answers (B, C, and D) are misleading because they try to make you believe that schema masters might be in each domain or perhaps that you should have one for each contiguous namespace domain.

This sample question format corresponds closely to the Microsoft certification exam format. The only difference is that on the exam, the questions are not followed by answers and their explanations. To select an answer, you position the cursor over the option button next to the answer you want to select. Then, you click the mouse button to select the answer.

Let's examine a question for which one or more answers are possible. This type of question provides check boxes rather than option buttons for marking all appropriate selections.

Question 2

What can you use to seize FSMO roles? (Choose two.)

A. The `ntdsutil.exe` utility

B. The Active Directory Users and Computers console

C. The `secedit.exe` utility

D. The `utilman.exe` utility

Answers A and B are correct. You can seize roles from a server that is still running through the Active Directory Users and Computers console, or in the case of a server failure, you can seize roles with the `ntdsutil.exe` utility. You use the `secedit.exe` utility to force group policies into play; therefore, answer C is incorrect. The `utilman.exe` tool manages accessibility settings in Windows Server 2003; therefore, Answer D is incorrect.

This particular question requires two answers. Microsoft sometimes gives partial credit for partially correct answers. For Question 2, you have to mark the check boxes next to answers A and B to obtain credit for a correct answer. Notice that choosing the right answers also means knowing why the other answers are wrong.

Build-List-and-Reorder Question Format

Questions in the build-list-and-reorder format present two lists of items—one on the left and one on the right. To answer the question, you must move items from the list on the right to the list on the left. The final list must then be reordered into a specific sequence.

These questions generally sound like this: “From the following list of choices, pick the choices that answer the question. Arrange the list in a certain order.” Question 3 shows an example of how they appear in this book; for an example of how they appear on the test, see Figure I.1.

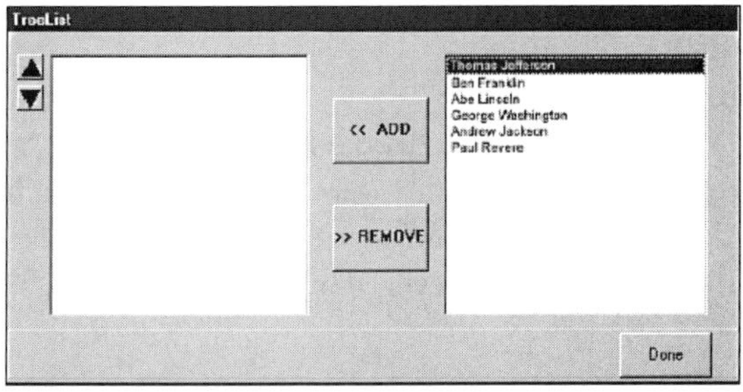

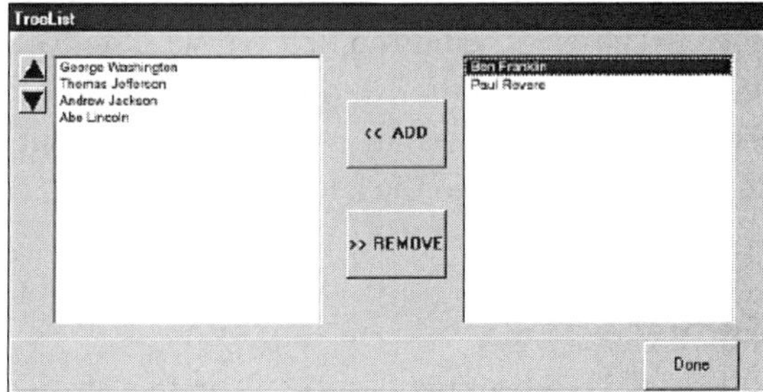

FIGURE I.1 The format for build-list-and-reorder questions.

Question 3

From the following list of famous people, choose those who have been elected president of the United States. Arrange the list in the order in which the presidents served.

- Thomas Jefferson
- Ben Franklin
- Abe Lincoln
- George Washington
- Andrew Jackson
- Paul Revere

The correct answer is

1. George Washington
2. Thomas Jefferson
3. Andrew Jackson
4. Abe Lincoln

On an actual exam, the entire list of famous people would initially appear in the list on the right. You would move the four correct answers to the list on the left and then reorder the list on the left. Notice that the answer to Question 3 does not include all the items from the initial list. However, that might not always be the case.

To move an item from the right list to the left list on the exam, you first select the item by clicking it, and then you click the Add button (left arrow). After you move an item from one list to the other, you can move the item back by first selecting the item and then clicking the appropriate button (either the Add button or the Remove button). After you move items to the left list, you can reorder an item by selecting the item and clicking the up or down arrow buttons.

Create-a-Tree Question Format

Questions in the create-a-tree format also present two lists—one on the left side of the screen and one on the right side of the screen. The list on the right consists of individual items, and the list on the left consists of nodes in a tree. To answer the question, you must move items from the list on the right to the appropriate node in the tree.

These questions can best be characterized as simply a matching exercise. Items from the list on the right are placed under the appropriate category in the list on the left. Question 4 shows an example of how they appear in this book; for an example of how they appear on the test, see Figure I.2.

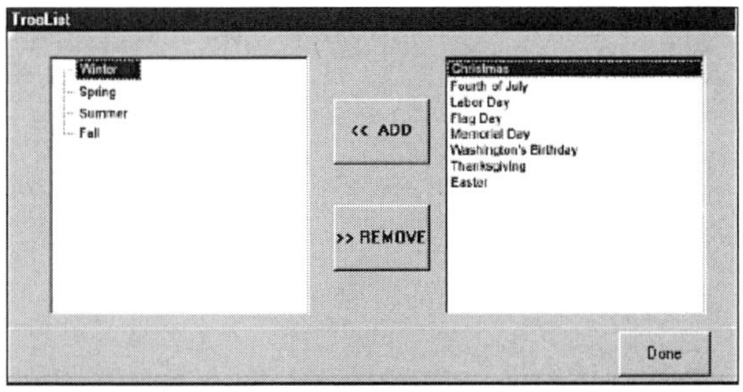

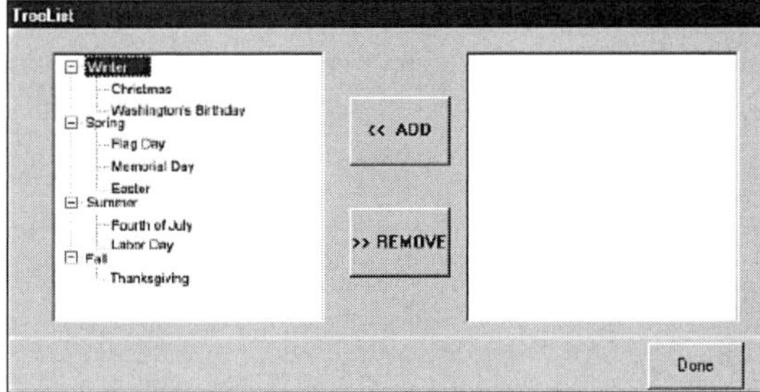

FIGURE I.2 The create-a-tree question format.

Question 4

The calendar year is divided into four seasons:

1. Winter
2. Spring
3. Summer
4. Fall

Identify the season during which each of the following holidays occurs:

- Christmas
- Fourth of July
- Labor Day
- Flag Day
- Memorial Day
- Washington's Birthday
- Thanksgiving
- Easter

The correct answers are

1. Winter
    - Christmas
    - Washington's Birthday
2. Spring
    - Flag Day
    - Memorial Day
    - Easter
3. Summer
    - Fourth of July
    - Labor Day
4. Fall
    - Thanksgiving

In this case, you use all the items in the list. However, that might not always be the case.

To move an item from the right list to its appropriate location in the tree, you must first select the appropriate tree node by clicking it. Then, you select the item to be moved and click the Add button. Once you add one or more items to a tree node, the node appears with a **+** icon to the left of the node name. You can click this icon to expand the node and view the items you have added. If you have added any item to the wrong tree node, you can remove it by selecting it and clicking the Remove button.

Drag-and-Connect Question Format

Questions in the drag-and-connect format present a group of objects and a list of "connections." To answer the question, you must move the appropriate connections between the objects.

This type of question is best described using graphics. Question 5 shows an example.

Question 5

The following objects represent the different states of water:

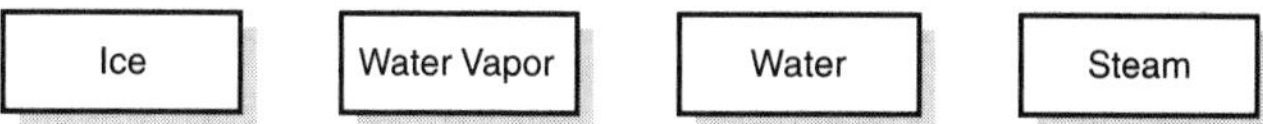

Use items from the following list to connect the objects so that they are scientifically correct:

Sublimates to form

Freezes to form

Evaporates to form

Boils to form

Condenses to form

Melts to form

FIGURE I.3 The drag-and-connect question format.

The correct answer is

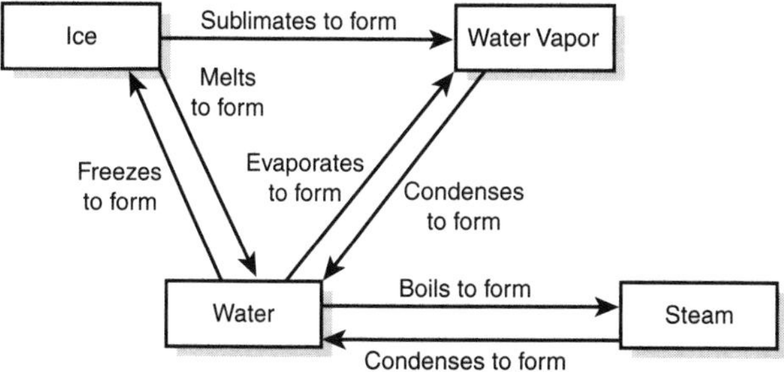

FIGURE I.4 The answer to a drag-and-connect question format.

For this type of question, it isn't necessary to use every object, and you can use each connection multiple times.

The Select-and-Place Question Format

Questions in the select-and-place (drag-and-drop) format display a diagram with blank boxes and a list of labels that you need to drag to correctly fill in the blank boxes. To answer such a question, you must move the labels to their appropriate positions on the diagram.

This type of question is best described using graphics. Question 6 shows an example.

Question 6

Place the items in their proper order, by number, on the following flowchart. Some items may be used more than once, and some items may not be used at all.

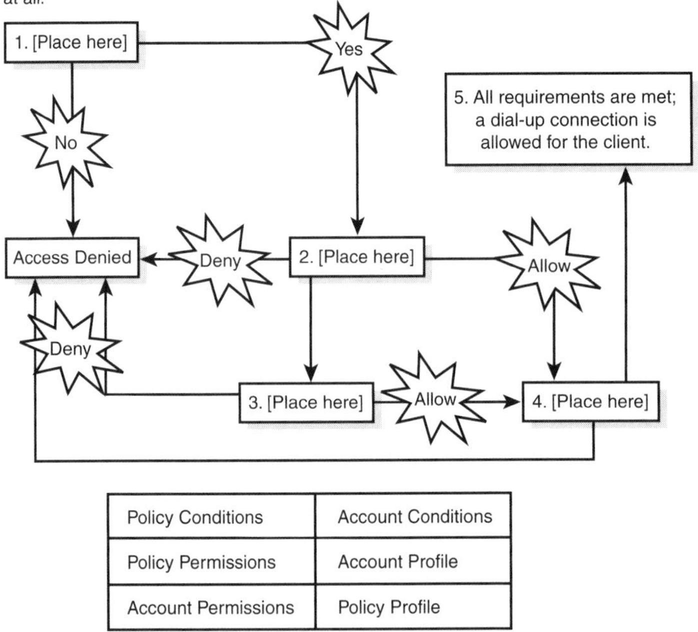

Policy Conditions	Account Conditions
Policy Permissions	Account Profile
Account Permissions	Policy Profile

FIGURE I.5 The select-and-place question format.

The correct answer is

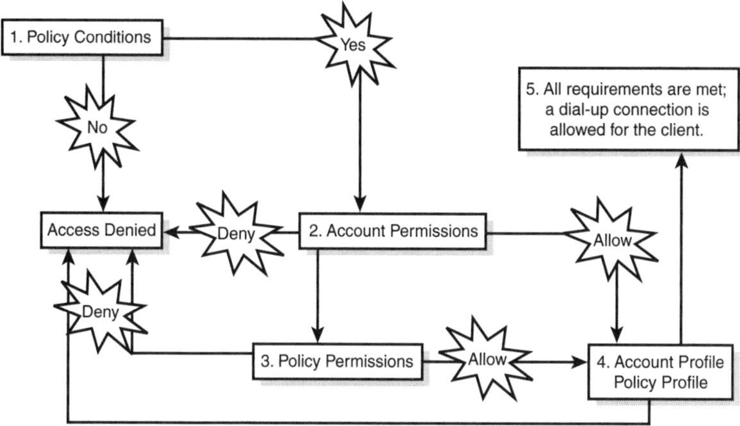

FIGURE I.6 The answer to a select-and-place question format.

Special Exam Question Formats

Starting with the exams released for the Windows Server 2003 MCSE track, Microsoft introduced several new question types in addition to the more traditional types of questions that are still widely used on all Microsoft exams. These innovative question types have been highly researched and tested by Microsoft before they were chosen to be included in many of the "refreshed" exams for the MCSA/MCSE on the Windows 2000 track and for the new MCSA/MCSE exams on the Windows Server 2003 track. These special question types are as follows:

- Hot area questions
- Active screen questions
- Drag-and-drop–type questions
- Simulation questions

Hot Area Question Types

Hot area questions ask you to indicate the correct answer by selecting one or more elements within a graphic. For example, you might be asked to select multiple objects within a list, as shown in Figure I.7.

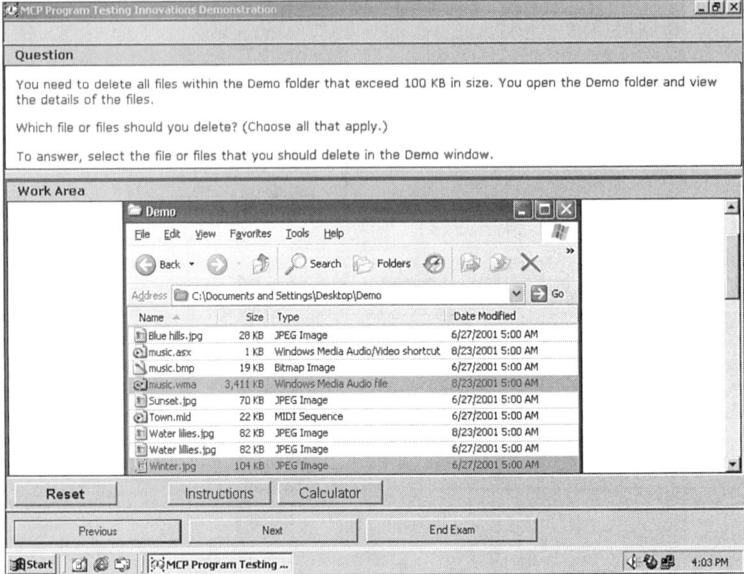

FIGURE I.7 Selecting objects within a list box to answer a hot area question.

Active Screen Question Types

Active screen questions ask you to configure a dialog box by modifying one or more elements. These types of questions offer a realistic interface in which you must properly configure various settings, just as you would within the actual software product. For example, you might be asked to select the proper option within a drop-down list box, as shown in Figure I.8.

Drag-and-Drop Question Types

New drag-and-drop questions ask you to drag source elements to their appropriate corresponding targets within a work area. These types of questions test your knowledge of specific concepts and their definitions or descriptions. For example, you might be asked to match a description of a computer program to the actual software application, as shown in Figure I.9

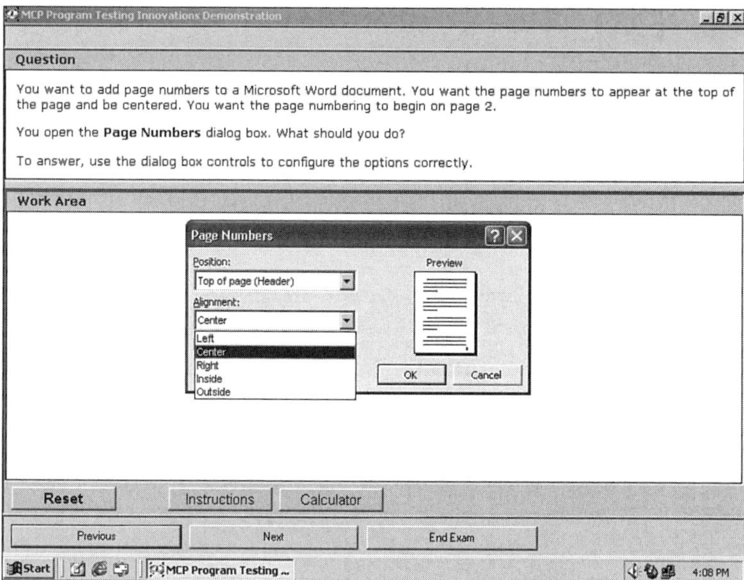

FIGURE I.8 Configuring an option from a dialog box's drop-down list box to answer an active screen question.

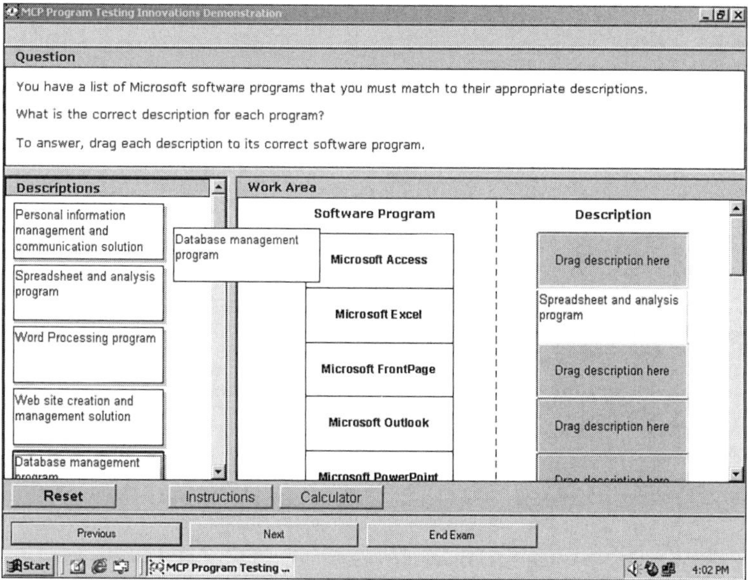

FIGURE I.9 Using drag and drop to match the correct application description to each software program.

Simulation Question Types

Simulation questions ask you to indicate the correct answer by performing specific tasks, such as configuring and installing network adapters or drivers, configuring and controlling access to files, or troubleshooting hardware devices. Many of the tasks that systems administrators and systems engineers perform can be presented more accurately in simulations than in most traditional exam question types (see Figure I.10).

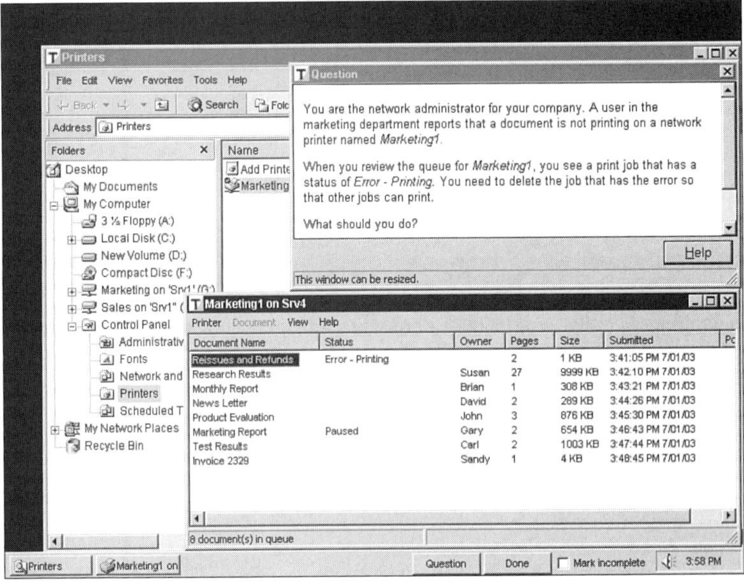

FIGURE I.10 Answering a simulation question about how to troubleshoot a network printing problem.

Microsoft Testing Formats

Currently, Microsoft uses three different testing formats:

- Fixed length
- Short form
- Case study

Other Microsoft exams employ advanced testing capabilities that might not be immediately apparent. Although the questions that appear are primarily multiple-choice, the logic that drives them is more complex than that in older Microsoft tests, which use a fixed sequence of questions, called a *fixed-length test*. Some questions employ a sophisticated user interface, which Microsoft calls a *simulation*, to test your knowledge of the software and systems under consideration in a more-or-less "live" environment that behaves just like the real thing. You should review the Microsoft Learning, Reference, and Certification Web pages at http://www.microsoft.com/learning/default.mspx for more detailed information.

In the future, Microsoft might choose to create exams using a well-known technique called *adaptive testing* to establish a test taker's level of knowledge and product competence. In general, adaptive exams might look the same as fixed-length exams, but they discover the level of difficulty at which an individual test taker can correctly answer questions. Test takers with differing levels of knowledge or ability therefore see different sets of questions; individuals with high levels of knowledge or ability are presented with a smaller set of more difficult questions, whereas individuals with lower levels of knowledge are presented with a larger set of easier questions. Two individuals might answer the same percentage of questions correctly, but the test taker with a higher knowledge or ability level will score higher because his or her questions are worth more. Also, the lower-level test taker will probably answer more questions than his or her more-knowledgeable colleague. This explains why adaptive tests use ranges of values to define the number of questions and the amount of time it takes to complete the test.

NOTE

Microsoft does ***not*** offer adaptive exams at the time that this book was published.

Most adaptive tests work by evaluating the test taker's most recent answer. A correct answer leads to a more difficult question, and the test software's estimate of the test taker's knowledge and ability level is raised. An incorrect answer leads to a less difficult question, and the test software's estimate of the test taker's knowledge and ability level is lowered. This process continues until the test targets the test taker's true ability level. The exam ends when the test taker's level of accuracy meets a statistically acceptable value (in other words, when his or her performance demonstrates an acceptable level of knowledge and ability) or when the maximum number of items has been presented (in which case, the test taker is almost certain to fail).

Microsoft has also introduced a short-form test for its most popular tests. This test delivers 25 to 30 questions to its takers, giving them exactly 60 minutes to complete the exam. This type of exam is similar to a fixed-length test in that it allows readers to jump ahead or return to earlier questions and to cycle through the questions until the test is done. Microsoft does not use adaptive logic in short-form tests, but it claims that statistical analysis of the question pool is such that the 25 to 30 questions delivered during a short-form exam conclusively measure a test taker's knowledge of the subject matter in much the same way as an adaptive test. You can think of the short-form test as a kind of "greatest hits exam" (that is, it covers the most important questions) version of an adaptive exam on the same topic.

Because you won't know which form the Microsoft exam might take, you should be prepared for either a fixed-length or short-form exam. The layout is the same for both fixed-length and short-form tests—you are not penalized for guessing the correct answer(s) to questions, no matter how many questions you answer incorrectly.

The Fixed-Length and Short-Form Exam Strategy

One tactic that has worked well for many test takers is to answer each question as well as you can before time expires on the exam. Some questions you will undoubtedly feel better equipped to answer correctly than others; however, you should still select an answer to each question as you proceed through the exam. You should click the Mark for Review check box for any question that you are unsure of. In this way, at least you have answered all the questions in case you run out of time. Unanswered questions are automatically scored as incorrect; answers that are guessed at have at least some chance of being scored as correct. If time permits, once you answer all questions, you can revisit each question that you have marked for review. This strategy also allows you to possibly gain some insight to questions that you are unsure of by picking up some clues from the other questions on the exam.

TIP

Some people prefer to read over the exam completely before answering the trickier questions; sometimes, information supplied in later questions sheds more light on earlier questions. At other times, information you read in later questions might jog your memory about facts, figures, or behavior that help you answer earlier questions. Either way, you could come out ahead if you answer only those questions on the first pass that you're absolutely confident about. However, be careful not to run out of time if you choose this strategy!

Fortunately, the Microsoft exam software for fixed-length and short-form tests makes the multiple-visit approach easy to implement. At the top-left corner of each question is a check box that permits you to mark that question for a later visit.

Here are some question-handling strategies that apply to fixed-length and short-form tests. Use them if you have the chance:

- When returning to a question after your initial read-through, read every word again; otherwise, your mind can miss important details. Sometimes, revisiting a question after turning your attention elsewhere lets you see something you missed, but the strong tendency is to see what you've seen before. Avoid that tendency at all costs.
- If you return to a question more than twice, articulate to yourself what you don't understand about the question, why answers don't appear to make sense, or what appears to be missing. If you chew on the subject awhile, your subconscious might provide the missing details, or you might notice a "trick" that points to the right answer.

As you work your way through the exam, another counter that Microsoft provides will come in handy—the number of questions completed and questions outstanding. For fixed-length and short-form tests, it's wise to budget your time by making sure that you've completed one-quarter of the questions one-quarter of the way through the exam period and three-quarters of the questions three-quarters of the way through.

If you're not finished when only five minutes remain, use that time to guess your way through any remaining questions. Remember, guessing is potentially more valuable than not answering. Blank answers are always wrong, but a guess might turn out to be right. If you don't have a clue about any of the remaining questions, pick answers at random or choose all As, Bs, and so on. (Choosing the same answer for a series of question all but guarantees you'll get most of them wrong, but it also means you're more likely to get a small percentage of them correct.)

EXAM ALERT

At the very end of your exam period, you're better off guessing than leaving questions unanswered.

Question-Handling Strategies

For those questions that have only one right answer, usually two or three of the answers will be obviously incorrect and two of the answers will be plausible. Unless the answer leaps out at you (if it does, reread the question to look for a trick; sometimes those are the ones you're most likely to get wrong), begin the process of answering by eliminating those answers that are most obviously wrong.

You can usually immediately eliminate at least one answer out of the possible choices for a question because it matches one of these conditions:

- The answer does not apply to the situation.
- The answer describes a nonexistent issue, an invalid option, or an imaginary state.

After you eliminate all answers that are obviously wrong, you can apply your retained knowledge to eliminate further answers. You should look for items that sound correct but refer to actions, commands, or features that are not present or not available in the situation that the question describes.

If you're still faced with a blind guess among two or more potentially correct answers, reread the question. Picture how each of the possible remaining answers would alter the situation. Be especially sensitive to terminology; sometimes the choice of words ("remove" instead of "disable") can make the difference between a right answer and a wrong one.

You should guess at an answer only after you've exhausted your ability to eliminate answers and you are still unclear about which of the remaining possibilities is correct. An unanswered question offers you no points, but guessing gives you at least some chance of getting a question right; just don't be too hasty when making a blind guess.

Numerous questions assume that the default behavior of a particular utility is in effect. If you know the defaults and understand what they mean, this knowledge will help you cut through many of the trickier questions. Simple "final" actions might be critical as well. If you must restart a utility before proposed changes take effect, a correct answer might require this step as well.

Mastering the Test-Taking Mindset

In the final analysis, knowledge breeds confidence, and confidence breeds success. If you study the materials in this book carefully and review all the practice questions at the end of each chapter, you should become aware of the areas where you need additional learning and study.

After you've worked your way through the book, take the practice exams in the back of the book. Taking these tests provides a reality check and helps you identify areas to study further. Make sure you follow up and review materials related to the questions you miss on the practice exams before scheduling a real exam. Don't schedule your exam appointment until after you've thoroughly studied the material and you feel comfortable with the whole scope of the practice exams. You should score 80% or better on the practice exams before proceeding to the real thing. (Otherwise, obtain some additional practice tests so that you can keep trying until you hit this magic number.)

TIP

If you take a practice exam and don't get at least 70% to 80% of the questions correct, keep practicing. Microsoft provides links to practice-exam providers and also self-assessment exams at http://www.microsoft.com/learning/mcpexams/prepare/default.asp.

Armed with the information in this book and with the determination to augment your knowledge, you should be able to pass the certification exam. However, you need to work at it, or you'll spend the exam fee more than once before you finally pass. If you prepare seriously, you should do well.

The next section covers other sources that you can use to prepare for Microsoft certification exams.

Additional Resources

A good source of information about Microsoft certification exams comes from Microsoft itself. Because its products and technologies—and the exams that go with them—change frequently, the best place to go for exam-related information is online.

Microsoft offers training, certification, and other learning-related information and links at the http://www.microsoft.com/learning web address. If you haven't already visited the Microsoft Training and Certification website, you should do so right now. The Microsoft Training and Certification home page resides at http://www.microsoft.com/learning/default.mspx.

Coping with Change on the Web

Sooner or later, all the information we've shared with you about the Microsoft Certified Professional pages and the other Web-based resources mentioned throughout the rest of this book will go stale or be replaced by newer information. In some cases, the URLs you find here might lead you to their replacements; in other cases, the URLs will go nowhere, leaving you with the dreaded "404 File not found" error message. When that happens, don't give up.

There's always a way to find what you want on the Web if you're willing to invest some time and energy. Most large or complex websites—and the Microsoft website qualifies on both counts—offer search engines. All of the Microsoft web pages have a Search button at the top edge of the page. As long as you can get to the Microsoft site (it should stay at http://www.microsoft.com for a long time), you can use the Search button to find what you need.

The more focused (or specific) that you can make a search request, the more likely the results will include information you can use. For example, you can search for the string

```
"training and certification"
```

to produce a lot of data about the subject in general, but if you're looking for the preparation guide for Exam 70-620, TS: Microsoft Windows Vista, Configuring, you'll be more likely to get there quickly if you use a search string similar to the following:

```
"Exam 70-620" AND "preparation guide"
```

Likewise, if you want to find the Training and Certification downloads, you should try a search string such as this:

```
"training and certification" AND "download page"
```

Finally, you should feel free to use general search tools—such as http://www.google.com, http://www.yahoo.com, http://www.excite.com, and http://www.ask.com—to look for related information. Although Microsoft offers great information about its certification exams online, there are plenty of third-party sources of information and assistance that need not follow the Microsoft party line. Therefore, if you can't find something where the book says it lives, you should intensify your search.

CHAPTER ONE

Introduction to Windows Vista

Terms you'll need to understand:

- ✓ Windows Vista
- ✓ Windows Aero
- ✓ Windows Sidebar
- ✓ Gadgets
- ✓ Internet Explorer
- ✓ Atomic Transaction Operations

Techniques/concepts you'll need to master:

- ✓ Describe the functions of Windows Vista.
- ✓ List the differences between Windows XP and Windows Vista.
- ✓ List and describe the various versions of Windows Vista.

Windows Vista (formerly known as Longhorn, Microsoft's internal codename) is the latest workstation release of Microsoft Windows operating system that is designed for both home and business users. It was released to manufacturers on November 8, 2006, and released to the general public on January 30, 2007. Its predecessor, Windows XP, was released more than five years before Windows Vista. As any modern operating system, Windows Vista coordinates the actions of the hardware, software, and the user so that they can work as one. Although Windows Vista is built on top of the Windows XP architecture, Windows Vista contains hundreds of new features, including an updated graphical user interface dubbed Windows Aero; improved searching features; new multimedia-creation tools such as Windows DVD Maker; and completely redesigned networking, audio, print, and display subsystems. In addition, it has increased its peer-to-peer technology to make it easier to share files and digital media between computers and devices. And, the security of Vista has been enhanced to minimize security vulnerabilities and overall susceptibility to malware, viruses, and buffer overflows. This chapter introduces many of the features of Windows Vista and describes the different versions of Windows Vista.

Features of the Windows Vista Operating System

Windows Vista introduces many new features that enable users to be more productive, make it easier to carry out common tasks, and provide a more secure desktop environment and a higher level of reliability. Although its interface and tools make it easier for users to organize, search for, and view information, it is designed to enable users to focus on the most important aspects of their jobs.

One of the most important improvements over previous Windows versions is that Windows Vista includes many security features and improvements that protect client computers from the latest generation of threats, including worms, viruses, and malicious software (malware) that often attempt to install silently without a user's knowledge. This is accomplished by having all users in Windows Vista, including administrators, work at the user level, unless they need a higher level to perform a particular task.

End-User Features

The graphical interface that a user uses to run Windows and the applications running on Windows is a built on the shell to provide the entire user interface, including the taskbar, the desktop, Windows Explorer, the dialog boxes, and the interface controls. It is also used to manage your folders and files. Different from previous versions of Windows, the Windows shell used in Windows Vista offers a new range of organization, navigation, and search capabilities.

Depending on the system hardware and the desires of the user, Windows Vista offers four user interfaces, including Basic, Windows Classic, Standard, and Windows Aero. *Windows Aero* is the new hardware-based graphical user interface intended to be cleaner and more aesthetically pleasing than those of previous Windows versions.

Different from Windows XP, the Windows Vista task pane has been removed and integrated into the task options of the toolbar. The Favorite Links pane has been added, enabling one-click access to common directories. The address bar has been replaced with a breadcrumb navigation system for easier navigation. In addition, the Start menu has changed; it does not use ever-expanding boxes when navigating through programs.

NOTE

As with many other Microsoft-made Windows Vista applications, the menu bar is hidden by default. Press the Alt key to make the menu bar display.

One of the biggest complaints about previous versions of Windows is the difficulty with quickly finding information such as documents and e-mail. Therefore, Vista includes Windows Search (also known as Instant Search or "search as you type"), which is significantly faster and more thorough than before. In addition, search boxes have been added to the Start menu, Windows Explorer, and several of the applications included with Vista.

NOTE

By default, Instant Search indexes only a small number of folders such as the Start menu, the names of files opened, the Documents folder, and the user's e-mail. Advanced options enable you to search for a specific file type, the properties of the file, and the content of the file. In addition, it enables you to exclude the same search criteria and to specify how the searches should be indexed.

New to Windows, Windows Vista includes *Windows Sidebar*, a transparent panel anchored to the side of the screen where a user can place desktop *gadgets* (small applets designed for a specialized purpose such as displaying the date, time, weather, or sports scores). Gadgets can also be placed on other parts of the desktop, if desired.

Other end-user enhancements to Windows Vista include the following:

- **Windows Mobility Center.** A new control panel that enables users to view and control the settings for mobile computers, including brightness, sound, battery level, power-scheme selection, wireless network, and presentation settings.
- **Backup and Restore Center.** A backup/restore application that can be easily configured to periodically back up files on users' computers. To minimize the disk usage, backups are stored incrementally, which means it stores only the changes each time. In addition, if you have the Business, Enterprise, or Ultimate version, you can back up the entire computer disk onto a hard disk or DVD as an image file. And, you can then use CompletePC Backup to automatically re-create a machine setup onto new hardware or hard disk in case of any hardware failures.
- **Previous Versions.** If you have the Business, Enterprise, or Ultimate edition, Windows Vista includes Previous Version, which is technology that automatically creates daily backup copies of files and folders. If you enable this feature by creating a System Protection Point, you can restore previous versions of the document.
- **Windows Update.** Different from previous Windows versions, Windows Update has been simplified and is controlled through a control panel rather than a web application.
- **Parental controls.** Parental controls enable administrators to control which websites, programs, and games each standard user can use and install.
- **Problem Reports and Solutions.** A new control panel that enables users to see previously sent problems and any solutions or additional information that is available.
- **Fonts.** Windows Vista includes several designed fonts for screen reading, and new high-quality Chinese (Yahei, JhengHei), Japanese (Meiryo), and Korean (Malgun) fonts. In addition, ClearType (a technology used by fonts for better viewing on computer displays) has been enhanced and enabled by default.
- **Improved audio controls.** New controls enable the control of systemwide volume, volume of individual audio devices, and volume of individual applications. It also includes new functionality such as Room Correction, Bass Management, and Speaker Fill.

- **System Performance Assessment.** System Performance Assessment is a benchmark used by Windows Vista (and certain applications) so that it can determine whether the application needs to slow down or speed up so that it can run at the optimum effect. The benchmark includes benchmarks for the processor, RAM, graphics acceleration (2D and 3D), and disk access.

Application Enhancements

Although *Internet Explorer (IE)* 7 has been available as a download for Windows XP, IE 7 is included with Windows Vista. IE 7 includes a new user interface that includes tabbed browsing, RDF Site Summary (RSS) support, a search box, improved printing, Page Zoom, and Quick Tabs (thumbnails of all open tabs). It also includes a number of new security-protection features that run in isolation from other applications in the operating system (Protected mode), restricting exploits and malicious software from writing to any location beyond Temporary Internet Files without explicit user consent.

NOTE

RSS is an Extensible Markup Language (XML) format for syndicating web content. A website that wants to allow another site to publish some of its content creates an RSS document and registers the document with an RSS publisher. A user that can read RSS-distributed content can use the content on a different site. Syndicated content includes such data as news feeds, events listings, news stories, headlines, project updates, and excerpts from discussion forums or even corporate information.

CAUTION

Make sure that you don't confuse Windows Explorer and Internet Explorer (IE). Windows Explorer is an application that is part of Microsoft Windows operating system and provides a graphical user interface for accessing the file systems. It is the component of the operating system that presents the user interface on the monitor and enables the user to control the computer. It is sometimes referred to as the Windows GUI shell, or simply Explorer. IE is a series of proprietary graphical web browsers developed by Microsoft and included as part of the Microsoft Windows line of operating systems starting in 1995.

Another popular application that has been revamped is Windows Media Player 11, which enables users to play and organize their music and video. New features include a new graphical interface, word wheeling (or "search as you type"), and the ability to share music libraries over a network with other Vista and Xbox 360 machines. Similar to IE 7, Windows Media Player 11 is available for Windows XP as a download.

Other application enhancements include the following:

- **Windows Mail.** A replacement for Outlook Express used to send, receive, and organize e-mail. Different from Outlook Express, Windows Mail includes a completely replaced mail store (database/file that stores all the individual e-mail messages) that improves stability and enables real-time search. It also provides enhanced security through a Phishing filter and a Junk Mail filter, both of which are regularly updated through Windows Update.
- **Windows Calendar.** A new calendar and task application.
- **Windows Photo Gallery.** A photo and movie library management application that enables the user to import JPG files from digital cameras, tag and rate individual items, adjust colors and exposure, create and display slideshows (with pan and fade effects), and burn slideshows to DVD.
- **Windows DVD Maker.** A program that enables users to create video DVDs based on a user's content.
- **Windows Meeting Space.** A program that replaces NetMeeting that enables you to share applications (or their entire desktop) with other users on the local network or over the Internet using peer-to-peer technology.
- **Windows Media Center.** Included with the Home Premium or Ultimate editions, the Windows Media Center provides an application to view TV programs; record and play back TV programs; DVD, video, and music playback; and photo viewing. As part of the Media Center controls, it includes a large-font interface that can be seen up to 10 feet away.
- **Games.** As with previous versions of Windows, Windows Vista includes games. Different from previous versions of Windows, the games have been rewritten to take advantage of Vista's new graphics capabilities. In addition, Windows Vista includes Chess Titans, Mahjong Titans, and Purple Place.
- **Speech recognition.** Windows Vista includes an improved version of Microsoft Speech Recognition that enables the user to activate the computer by voice.

- **Windows Ultimate Extras.** The Ultimate edition of Windows Vista provides access to extra games and tools, available through Windows Update.

Core Technologies

To make Windows Vista more powerful and more flexible than previous versions of Windows, Vista includes an improved memory manager, process scheduler, heap manager, and I/O schedule, all of which manage the memory and processing resources on the computer. In addition, a Kernel Transaction Manager has been implemented that gives applications the capability to work with the file system and registry using *atomic transaction operations*. An atomic transaction takes an all-or-nothing approach with a related set of changes when saving those changes, making sure that the updates are processed and fully completed. As a result, the atomic transactions will help prevent database inconsistencies and corruption.

In addition to the obvious enhancements to the graphical user interface, the audio, print, display, and networking subsystems have been redesigned. What most users don't realize is that although these redesigns make Windows Vista more powerful and more reliable, they also provide an enhanced development environment for software developers.

To support the new graphics interface and to extend the capability of the video system, Vista introduced the new Windows Vista Display Driver Model (WDDM) and a major revision to Direct3D, both of which can be used to access the Windows interface and to provide its special effects. Direct3D 10, which was developed in conjunction with major display driver manufacturers, is a new architecture that has more advanced shader support and enables the graphics processing unit to render more complex scenes without assistance from the processor. It also features improved load balancing between the processor and the graphics processing unit and optimizes the data transfer between the two.

As part of the networking subsystem redesign, Windows Vista now fully supports IPv6, an enhanced TCP/IP protocol suite that supports many more addresses and has its own performance and security enhancements. Windows Vista also supports TCP windows scaling, which is an option that can adjust the size of the window or amount of data that can be sent and received at once depending on congestion and reliability of the network signals. In addition, Windows Vista includes built-in, comprehensive wireless-networking software.

Vista includes ReadyBoost and ReadyDrive, which employ fast flash memory (located on USB drives and hybrid hard disk drives, respectively) to improve system performance by caching commonly used programs and data. In addition, it is used to improve battery life on notebook computers so that it can intelligently spin down a hybrid drive when not in use. Next, SuperFetch uses machine-learning techniques to analyze usage patterns to allow Windows Vista to make intelligent decisions about what content should be present in system memory at any given time.

Other core technologies that have been added or enhanced include the following:

- The WIM image format (Windows IMage) is Microsoft's new deployment and packaging system. WIM files, which contain an image of Windows Vista, can be maintained and patched without having to rebuild new images. ImageX is the Microsoft tool used to create and customize images.
- Windows Deployment Services replaces Remote Installation Services for deploying Vista and earlier versions of Windows.
- Approximately 700 new Group Policy settings have been added, covering most aspects of the new features in the operating system, and significantly expanding the configurability of wireless networks, removable storage devices, and user desktop experience.
- Windows Vista includes the Multilingual User Interface (MUI). Unlike earlier version of Windows, which required language packs to be loaded to provide local language support, Windows Vista Enterprise edition supports the ability to dynamically change languages based on the logged-on user's preference.
- Windows Vista includes network projector support for a projector that is connected to a network through a wired or wireless connection, rather than one that is connected directly to a computer.
- Applications are more reliable because they can recover from deadlocked situations, and improved error-reporting enables developers to fix common problems.
- Windows Vista includes the Startup Repair Tool (SRT). This tool automatically fixes many common problems, and can be used manually to diagnose and repair more complex startup failures.
- Windows Vista can help detect and recover failing hard disks and memory.

- The auto-tuning network stack of Windows Vista provides improved performance, by analyzing the available bandwidth and using it more efficiently.
- Windows Vista includes .NET Framework 3.0. .NET Framework provides a large collection of precoded solutions to common program requirements, and manages the execution of programs written specifically for the framework. The .NET Framework is intended to be used by most new applications created for the Windows platform. Although .NET Framework 3.0 can be downloaded for Windows XP and Windows Server 2003, it is included with Windows Vista and it includes a new set of managed code application programming interfaces (APIs) that are an integral part of Windows Vista and new upcoming Windows Server operating systems.

Security Enhancements

During 2005 and 2006, Microsoft made a security push to make all their operating system and applications more secure. One of the primary design goals of Windows Vista is to improve security, and as a result, Windows Vista offers a number of new security and safety features.

User Account Control

One of the most significant changes to security, which is visible to users, is the User Account Control (UAC). UAC is a security technology that makes it possible for users to use their computers with fewer privileges by default. When an action requires administrative rights, the user is prompted for an administrator name and password. If the person is an administrator, the user is prompted to confirm the action he is about to take. UAC asks for credentials in a Secure Desktop mode, where the entire screen is blacked out and temporarily disabled and only the authorization window is enlightened. This is to stop a malicious program "spoofing" it and attempting to capture admin credentials. In addition, changes to various system configuration settings (such as new auto-starting applications) are blocked unless the user consents.

In addition to the UAC, Windows Vista has taken extra steps to make sure rogue processes do not access other processes that they should not be accessing. For example, Microsoft followed closely the concept of "integrity levels"; that is, user processes (which have a lower security level) cannot interact with processes with a higher security level. This prevents certain system services, such as those that listen on the network, from interacting with other parts of the operating system that they do not need to interact with. In addition, Microsoft used obfuscation techniques such as address space layout randomization and kernel patch protection to obscure key parts of the operating system as it runs in memory. All of these security enhancements increase the amount of effort required by malware to infiltrate a system.

BitLocker Drive Encryption

Another significant new feature is BitLocker Drive Encryption, a data-protection feature included in the Enterprise and Ultimate editions of Vista that provides encryption for the entire operating system volume. BitLocker can work in conjunction with a Trusted Platform Module chip (version 1.2) that is on a computer's motherboard or with a USB key.

Windows Defender

To help protect the system, Microsoft now includes Microsoft's antispyware product called Windows Defender to help protect from malware and other threats.

ASCII Characters

IE7 imposes restrictions on displaying non-ASCII domain names (non-ASCII character can look like other ASCII characters, tricking users thinking they are at a different site, but instead they are on a spoof site designed to steal users' private information) based on a user-defined list of allowed languages and provides an antiphishing filter that checks suspicious websites against a remote database of known phishing sites. ActiveX controls are disabled by default. ActiveX controls can be used to access or remotely control a computer without the user's knowledge. Following the concept of integrity levels, IE operates in a Protected mode, which operates with lower permissions than the user, and it runs in isolation from other applications in the operating system, preventing it from accessing or modifying anything besides the Temporary Internet Files directory. In addition, IE is no longer integrated with the Explorer shell; local files typed in IE are opened using the Explorer shell, and websites typed in Explorer are opened using the default web browser.

Windows Firewall

Windows Vista includes a newly redesigned Windows Firewall that filters both incoming and outgoing traffic. Advanced packet-filter rules can be created that can grant or deny communications to specific services. Vista also adds new Secure Sockets Layer (SSL) and Transport Layer Security (TLS) cryptographic extensions, which enable the support of both Advanced Encryption Standard (AES) and new Elliptic Curve Cryptography (ECC) cipher suites.

Windows Vista Versions

Different from earlier versions of Windows, Windows Vista comes in five different versions, which vary in price and features, as follows:

- **Windows Vista Home Basic.** Similar to Windows XP Home edition, Home Basic is intended for users who do not require advanced media support for home use or the need to be added to a domain. It does not support Windows Aero.
- **Windows Vista Home Premium.** Similar to Windows XP Media Center. It contains all the features from Home Basic, and it also supports more advanced features aimed for the home market segment, such as HDTV support and DVD authoring. Also included are extra premium games and support for mobile and tablet PC, network projector, touch screen, and auxiliary display (via Windows SideShow). It also includes a utility to schedule backups. Home Premium supports 10 simultaneous peer network connections and includes Windows Meeting Space. The 64-bit Home Premium will support up to 16 GB of physical memory, and will be supported until 2012.
- **Windows Vista Business.** Comparable to Windows XP Professional, Windows Vista Business edition is aimed at the business market. It includes most of the features of Home Premium (it does not include Windows Media Center and related technologies, parental controls, and Windows DVD and Movie Maker HD), and it includes the Internet Information Server (IIS) web server, fax support, Rights Management Services (RMS) client, file system encryption, dual processor (two sockets) support, system image backup and recovery, offline file support, a full version of Remote Desktop that supports incoming connections, ad-hoc peer-to-peer (P2P) collaboration capabilities, Previous Versions (Windows ShadowCopy), and several other business features not in Home Premium.
- **Windows Vista Enterprise.** This edition is aimed at the enterprise segment of the market, and is a superset of the Business edition. Windows Vista Enterprise is available as part of the Software Assurance Enterprise licensing, and it will not be available through retail or original equipment manufacturer (OEM) channels. It includes Multilingual User Interface support, BitLocker Drive Encryption, and UNIX application support. It also includes a license allowing for multiple virtual machines to be run, access to Virtual PC Express, and activation via Volume License Key (VLK).

- **Windows Vista Ultimate.** This edition combines all the features of the Home Premium and Enterprise editions, a game performance tweaker (WinSAT), and Ultimate Extras.

NOTE

There is also a sixth version, Windows Vista Starter, that is limited to emerging markets such as Colombia, India, Thailand, Indonesia, and the Philippines and will not be available in the United States, Canada, Europe, or Australia. It will have many significant limitations, such as allowing a user to launch only three applications with a user interface at one time, not accepting incoming network connections, a physical memory limit of 256 MB, and it will run only in 32-bit mode.

All the previously mentioned versions come in 32-bit and 64-bit variants, except the Windows Vista Starter, which comes only in a 32-bit edition. The 64-bit editions of Windows Vista are for the serious computer users who have advanced high-performance needs and are running a computer system with a 64-bit processor. The 64-bit editions require a system with a 64-bit processor and 64-bit system drivers. In addition, you need to confirm that your system, applications, and devices are compatible with a 64-bit edition of Windows Vista before installing and that the appropriate drivers are available.

All Windows Vista 64-bit editions provide increased memory support beyond the standard 4 GB available with 32-bit editions. Refer to the specific Windows Vista 64-bit edition to determine maximum memory capacity.

TABLE 1.1 Maximum Amount of Memory Support by the Various Editions of Windows Vista

Windows Vista Edition	64-Bit Memory Support
Home Basic	8 GB
Home Premium	16 GB
Business	128+ GB
Enterprise	128+ GB
Ultimate	128+ GB

Exam Prep Questions

1. Which of the following is not a user interface for Windows Vista? (Choose the best answer.)

   ❍ **A.** Basic

   ❍ **B.** Classic

   ❍ **C.** Standard

   ❍ **D.** X

   ❍ **E.** Aero

2. Which of the following are new features or updates that have been added to Windows Vista? (Choose all that apply.)

   ❍ **A.** Sidebar with gadgets

   ❍ **B.** Internet Explorer 7

   ❍ **C.** Media Player 11

   ❍ **D.** Full support for IPv6

3. Which of the following are new features of Windows Vista? (Choose all that apply.)

   ❍ **A.** Enables users to be more productive

   ❍ **B.** Makes it easier to carry out common tasks

   ❍ **C.** Provides a more secure desktop environment

   ❍ **D.** Provides a higher level of reliability

4. Which of the following does Windows Vista include to make it easier for users to quickly find information such as documents and e-mail? (Choose the best answer.)

   ❍ **A.** Windows Search (also known as Instant Search), which searches as you type

   ❍ **B.** A new index service that indexes 25 percent faster than previous versions

   ❍ **C.** A new folder structure to help better organize documents and e-mails

   ❍ **D.** All of the above

5. Which of the following is not a new security feature of Windows Vista? (Choose the best answer.)

   ❍ **A.** User Account Control, which makes it possible for users to use their computers with fewer privileges by default

   ❍ **B.** BitLocker Drive Encryption, which provides encryption for the entire operating system volume

   ❍ **C.** Enhanced file system to prevent viruses from spreading from file to file

   ❍ **D.** Windows Defender

   ❍ **E.** Enhanced Internet Explorer to prevent being tricked into using a spoofed site and to prevent phishing

   ❍ **F.** Redesigned Windows Firewall, which filters both incoming and outgoing traffic

6. Which of the following describes Windows Aero?

   ❍ **A.** A new hardware-based graphical user interface intended to be cleaner and more aesthetically pleasing than those of previous Windows operating systems

   ❍ **B.** A special theme based on the aerospace industry

   ❍ **C.** A background theme that shows the blue skyline

   ❍ **D.** A search-oriented desktop interface

7. Which of the following does not support adding Windows Vista to a Windows domain? (Choose all that apply.)

   ❍ **A.** Windows Vista Starter

   ❍ **B.** Windows Vista Home Basic

   ❍ **C.** Windows Vista Home Premium

   ❍ **D.** Windows Vista Business

   ❍ **E.** Windows Vista Enterprise

   ❍ **F.** Windows Vista Ultimate

8. Which of the following describes the Windows Sidebar?

   ❍ **A.** An abbreviated Start menu of commonly used programs

   ❍ **B.** A mini browser used to open favorite websites quickly

   ❍ **C.** A virtual PC environment that allows you to run older software packages

   ❍ **D.** A transparent panel where a user can place desktop gadgets

Answers to Exam Prep Questions

1. **Answer D is correct.** X is a reference to the operating system used by some Apple Macintosh computers. Depending on the system hardware and the desires of the user, Windows Vista offers four user interfaces: Basic, Windows Classic, Standard, and Windows Aero. Therefore, answers A, B, C, and E are incorrect.

2. **Answers A, B, C, and D are correct.** Sidebar with gadgets, Internet Explorer 7, Media Player 11, and full support for IPv6 have been added to Windows Vista. Internet Explorer 7 is available as download for Windows XP. Media Player 11 is available as a download for Windows XP. Windows XP had a test environment only for IPv6. The Sidebar with gadgets is introduced in Windows Vista.

3. **Answers A, B, C, and D are correct.** Windows Vista introduces many new features that enable users to be more productive, make it easier to carry out common tasks, and provide a more secure desktop environment and a higher level of reliability. Although its interface and tools make it easier for users to organize, search for, and view information, it is designed to allow users to focus on the most important aspects of their job.

4. **Answer A is correct.** Vista includes Windows Search (also known as Instant Search or "search as you type"), which is significantly faster and more thorough than before. In addition, search boxes have been added to the Start menu, Windows Explorer, and several of the applications included with Vista. Although the Windows folders structure is slightly different from Windows XP, these changes will not necessarily help find files faster and will not help search through e-mail. Therefore, answer C is incorrect. In addition, answer B is incorrect because the indexing service has not been significantly changed. Because B and C are incorrect, answer D is incorrect.

5. **Answer C is correct.** Windows XP and Windows Vista use the same file systems, which include FAT and NTFS. Therefore, at its initial release, Windows Vista does not include a new or different file system. Windows Vista includes User Account Control (answer A), BitLocker Drive Encryption (answer B), Windows Defender (answer D), Internet Explorer 7 (answer E), and a newly redesigned Windows Firewall (answer F).

6. **Answer A is correct.** Windows Aero is a new hardware-based graphical user interface intended to be cleaner and more aesthetically pleasing than those of previous Windows operating systems. Answers B, C, and D have nothing or little to do with the Windows theme, or desktop background. Answers B and C are incorrect because Aero is not a theme, and answer D is incorrect because it is not a search-oriented desktop interface.

7. **Answers A, B, and C are correct.** Windows Vista Starter, Windows Vista Home Basic, and Windows Vista Home Premium are designed as operating systems for the home (and so do not require connecting to a company's Windows domain). Answers D, E, and F are incorrect because Windows Vista Business, Windows Vista Enterprise, and Windows Vista Ultimate support adding to a domain.

8. **Answer D is correct.** The Sidebar is a transparent panel where a user can place desktop gadgets. Answer A deals with the Quick Launch program. Answers B and C do not exist with the Windows Vista operating system.

Recommended Readings and Resources

Visit the Microsoft website to see highlights, feature lists, and an overview of Windows Vista at http://www.microsoft.com/windows/products/windowsvista/default.mspx.

Download the Windows Vista Product Guide from http://www.microsoft.com.

Mitch Tulloch, Tony Northrup, Jerry Honeycutt, Ed Wilson, Ralph Ramos, and the Windows Vista Team, *Windows Vista Resource Kit (Pro - Resource Kit)* (Redmond, Washington: Microsoft Press, 2007).

William R. Stanek, *Introducing Microsoft Windows Vista* (Redmond, Washington: Microsoft Press, 2006).

CHAPTER TWO

Installing Windows Vista

Terms you'll need to understand:

- ✓ Windows Deployment Services (WDS)
- ✓ Business Desktop Deployment Solution Accelerator 2007 (BDD 2007)
- ✓ Windows System Image Manager (Windows SIM)
- ✓ Answer file
- ✓ Windows image
- ✓ Catalog
- ✓ Windows PE
- ✓ Windows PXE
- ✓ ImageX
- ✓ Diskpart
- ✓ Sysprep
- ✓ Service pack
- ✓ Windows Vista Upgrade Advisor
- ✓ System Recovery Option
- ✓ Windows activation

Techniques/concepts you'll need to master:

- ✓ List the system requirements for Windows Vista.
- ✓ Given a scenario, recommend to do a clean installation, an upgrade, or a migration.
- ✓ Perform a clean installation of Windows Vista.
- ✓ Perform an upgrade installation of Windows Vista.
- ✓ Install Windows Vista using an answer file and ImageX.
- ✓ Check for and install Windows Vista fixes, patches, and service packs.
- ✓ Upgrade Windows Vista to another version of Windows Vista.
- ✓ Determine whether a machine meets system requirements by running the Windows Upgrade Advisor.
- ✓ Repair a Windows Vista installation using the installation DVD.
- ✓ When necessary, activate Windows Vista.

The first step to becoming a desktop technician is to know how to install Windows Vista onto a computer. Although you might think that this is a simple operation in which you insert the DVD into the drive and install it, you will quickly learn that you must first verify whether your system meets system requirements. You must then determine whether it is best to perform a clean install, upgrade a current system, or perform a clean install and migrate system settings from another system. Of course, if problems occur during the installation, you must determine the best way to overcome those problems.

System Requirements

Before installing Windows Vista, you need to look at the system and verify whether it has the necessary hardware to effectively run Windows Vista. If the system that you choose does not meet the system requirements, Windows Vista might not install completely, some Windows Vista features might not function properly, or system performance will be poor and unacceptable.

In contrast to previous versions of Windows, Microsoft defines three hardware levels for Windows Vista:

- **Minimum.** The minimum hardware requirements are the minimum hardware to install Windows Vista.
- **Windows Vista Capable.** Vista Capable PCs will meet or exceed the core Windows Vista experience and features found on Windows Vista Business and Windows Vista Enterprise versions.
- **Windows Vista Premium Ready.** If a PC is Windows Vista Premium Ready, it delivers or exceeds the Windows Vista Capable PC, and it supports the new Windows Aero interface.

See Table 2.1 for the system requirements for Windows Vista as defined by Microsoft. Of course, if a system has a faster processor or additional RAM, your system will run faster.

TABLE 2.1 System Requirements for Windows Vista

	Minimum	Vista Capable	Premium Ready*
CPU	800 MHz	800 MHz	1 GHz
RAM	512 MB	512 MB	1 GB
GPU	SVGA	Direct 9 Capable	Aero Capable
Video RAM			128 MB

TABLE 2.1 *Continued*

	Minimum	Vista Capable	Premium Ready*
HDD	20 GB	20 GB	40 GB
HDD Free	15 GB	15 GB	15 GB
Optical Drive	CD	CD	DVD

*Requires an aero Capable GPU supports Direct 9 with a WDDM driver, Pixel Shader 2.0, and 32 bits per pixel.

Windows Vista Installation Methods

There several ways to install Windows Vista. The method you use will depend on whether you are installing on a new computer or on a computer that is currently running another version of Windows. The three types of installations are as follows:

- **Clean.** Performed on a new partition or when you want to completely replace the operating system on a partition. On a computer without an operating system, you boot directly from the CD or DVD. If an operating system is already on the system, you can also run Setup.exe to start the installation. You can also use an image to create a clean installation.
- **Upgrade.** Also known as an in-place upgrade, it is used to replace or upgrade an existing version of Windows (Windows 2000, Windows XP, or Windows Vista).
- **Migration.** Provides a clean installation of Windows Vista while migrating all current Windows settings to the new Windows Vista installation (backing up the user's files and settings, performing a clean installation or upgrade, restoring the user's files and settings, and reinstalling the applications).

Business Desktop Deployment Solution Accelerator 2007

If you work for an organization that has hundreds of computers, it is a huge task to install or upgrade Windows Vista on each computer. To assist with the deployment of Windows Vista, Microsoft offers *Windows Deployment Services (WDS)*.

Microsoft WDS is the updated and redesigned version of Remote Installation Services (RIS), which can be installed on Windows Server 2003 and will be included with future versions of Windows servers. WDS helps organizations rapidly and remotely deploy Windows operating systems, particularly Windows Vista. Using WDS, you can deploy Windows operating systems over a network without having to be physically present at the destination computer and without using installation media.

Part of the WDS is the *Business Desktop Deployment Solution Accelerator 2007 (BDD 2007)*, which provides end-to-end guidance for planning, building, testing, and deploying Windows Vista. BDD 2007 enables you to do the following:

- Create a software and hardware inventory to assist in deployment planning.
- Test applications for compatibility with Windows Vista, and mitigate any compatibility issues discovered during the process.
- Set up an initial lab environment with deployment and imaging servers.
- Customize and package core and supplemental applications.
- Automate creating and deploying desktop images.
- Ensure that the desktop is hardened to improve security within the environment.
- Manage processes and technologies to produce a comprehensive and integrated deployment.

BDD 2007 includes the following tools:

- **Windows System Image Manager (Windows SIM).** A tool that enables you to create answer files and network shares or to modify the files contained in a configuration set. The Windows SIM is part of the Windows Automated Installation Kit (WAIK), which is included with BDD 2007.
- **Answer file.** An Extended Markup Language (XML) file that scripts the answers for a series of graphical user interface (GUI) dialog boxes and other configuration settings. The answer file for Windows Setup is commonly called autounattend.xml. You can create and modify this answer file by using Windows SIM from the WAIK.
- **Windows image.** A single compressed file that contains a collection of files and folders that duplicate a Windows installation on a disk volume.

Windows Vista is built and distributed as a single image using the new Windows Imaging (WIM) file format. The WIM file format can contain multiple images; this enables you to package several custom installations into one file.

- **Catalog.** A binary file (CLG) that contains the state of the settings and packages in a Windows image. There must be a catalog for each version of Windows Vista contained within the image.
- **Windows PE.** Microsoft Windows Preinstallation Environment (Windows PE) is a bootable tool that replaces MS-DOS as the preinstallation environment. Windows PE is not a general-purpose operating system. Instead, it is used to provide operating system features for installation, troubleshooting, and recovery. Windows PE can be run from CD/DVD, USB pen drive, or a network using *Pre-boot Execution Environment (PXE)*. Windows PE 2.0, built for Windows Vista, is available for download as part of the BDD 2007 solution.

NOTE

PXE (pronounced pixie) is short for Pre-boot Execution Environment. PXE allows a computer to boot from a server on a network instead of booting the operating system on the local hard drive. For a system to support PXE, the PXE must be supported by the computer's BIOS and its network interface card (NIC).

- **ImageX.** A command-line tool that captures, modifies, and applies installation images for deployment in a manufacturing or corporate environment.
- **Windows Setup (Setup.exe).** The program that installs the Windows Vista operating system.
- **Diskpart.** A command-line hard disk configuration utility.
- **Sysprep.** The utility that facilitates image creation for deployment to multiple-destination computers. Sysprep prepares an installed system ready to be duplicated as an image. It does this by removing the original security identifiers (SIDs) from the image and cleaning up various user and machine settings and log files.

The BDD 2007 can be downloaded from http://www.microsoft.com/downloads/details.aspx?FamilyId=13F05BE2-FD0E-4620-8CA6-1AAD6FC54741&displaylang=en.

Performing a Clean Installation of Windows Vista

When you perform a clean installation of Windows Vista, any existing data is removed, including personal data and settings. You must also reinstall all programs. Of course, before you do any installation of any machine that has any kind of data, it is recommended that you back up all personal data before you perform a clean installation.

Methods to Perform a Clean Installation

You can perform a clean installation of Windows using the following methods:

- Install from DVD.
- Install from a network share.
- Install using an image.

To perform a clean installation of Windows Vista, the most common method is to install it from the installation DVD. To install it by starting the computer using the Windows DVD, follow these steps:

1. Insert the Windows Vista DVD into the computer's DVD drive.
2. Restart the computer.
3. When the "Press any key to boot from CD" message shows on the screen, press a key.
4. Follow the instructions that are displayed on the screen to install Windows Vista.

To start the computer from the Windows Vista DVD, the computer must be configured to start from the DVD drive, usually in the BIOS settings. For more information about how to configure the computer to start from the DVD drive, refer to the documentation that is included with the computer or contact the computer manufacturer.

To start the installation process from a current operating system, follow these steps:

1. Start the computer by using the current operating system.
2. Insert the Windows Vista DVD into the computer's DVD drive.

3. If Windows automatically detects the DVD, the Install Now screen appears. Click Install Now. If Windows does not automatically detect the DVD, click Start, click Run, enter ***Drive*:\setup.exe** (where the *Drive* is the drive letter of the computer's DVD drive), and then click OK.
4. Click the Install Now button option.
5. When you reach the "Which type of installation do you want?" screen, click Custom (advanced), and then follow the instructions that are displayed on the screen to install Windows Vista.

To install Windows Vista from a network share, follow these steps:

1. Boot a computer that has network connectivity by using a network boot disk such as PXE boot or Windows PE.
2. To start the installation, either connect to a network share containing the Windows Vista files or connect to a WDS server using PXE. The network source could be a share on a file server (such as *servername**sharename*) or a WDS server. If you connect to a network share on a file server, run Setup.exe. If you connect to a WDS server using PXE, installation will start automatically.
3. Complete the wizard.

To install Windows Vista by using an Image, you use an answer file or the command-line utility ImageX. When installing using the answer file, it will install Windows with the same parameters that are specified in the answer file. To install Windows Vista by using an answer file, follow these steps:

1. Build a source computer.
2. Use Windows SIM to create an answer file (autounattend.xml) on removable media using the source computer. Save the autounattend.xml file to removable media, such as a USB flash device or floppy disk.
3. Insert the removable media into the destination computer.
4. Boot the destination computer from DVD; Setup automatically searches for autounattend.xml.

To deploy Windows Vista by using ImageX, follow these steps:

1. Install and configure Windows Vista on a source PC.
2. Use Sysprep on the PC so that the operating system can be deployed by removing some computer-specific information such as the workstation's SID, which must be unique.

3. Boot the master with the Windows PE CD.
4. Use ImageX on the master to create the image file.
5. Boot the target with the Windows PE CD.
6. Use Diskpart to format the drive. Diskpart is a PE tool that is used to configure the hard drive on a PC.
7. Use ImageX to apply the image to the target.

EXAM ALERT

During the exam, you will need to know the steps for setting up a Windows Vista computer using the answer file and using images.

For more information, refer to the Windows Vista Deployment Step-by-Step Guide at http://technet2.microsoft.com/WindowsVista/en/library/88f80cb7-d44f-47f7-a10d-e23dd53bc3fa1033.mspx.

For more information about Windows PE 2.0 for Windows Vista, visit http://technet.microsoft.com/en-us/windowsvista/aa905120.aspx.

Troubleshooting Problems with Clean Installation

If your machine meets the minimum requirements, the installation should complete without problems. If a problem does occur, follow a standard troubleshooting approach to isolate and fix the problem:

1. Determine what has changed.
2. Eliminate possible causes to determine probable cause.
3. Identify a solution.
4. Test the solution.

If your solution does not fix the problem, start at step 3 again.

To help identify specific problems, do the following:

- Review and research error messages.
- Verify the system meets minimum requirements. A common reason for an upgrade to fail is that the computer does not meet the minimum

hardware requirements to support the edition of Windows Vista that you are installing.

- Verify that the hardware has been installed properly.
- Check to see whether there are compatibility problems with the installed devices.
- Check whether a BIOS upgrade is needed. Check your computer supplier's website to see whether a BIOS upgrade is available for Windows Vista.
- Verify the installation media. Make sure that the installation media is not damaged or corrupt.

Windows Updates

After installing Windows, check whether Microsoft has any fixes, patches, service packs, or device drivers, and apply them to the Windows system. By adding fixes and patches, you will keep Windows stable and secure. If there are many fixes or patches, Microsoft releases them together as a *service pack*. To update Windows Vista, Internet Explorer, and other programs that ship with Windows, go to Windows Update in the Control Panel (see Figure 2.1). Windows will then scan your system to see what you have installed and then list suggested components. This system check ensures that you will get the most current and accurate versions of anything you choose to download from the site.

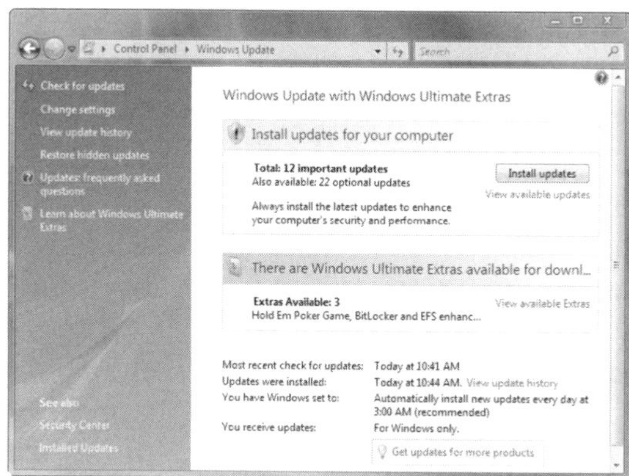

FIGURE 2.1 Windows Update is accessed through the Control Panel.

To help users with the Windows updates, Windows Vista also offers Dynamic Update and Auto Update. Dynamic Update is a feature built in to Windows Setup that automatically checks for new drivers, compatibility updates, and security fixes while Windows is beings installed. All that is required is that you have a working connection to the Internet. During installation, you can choose to have Dynamic Update check for updates. It automatically downloads any device or application updates and uses these replacement files rather than the installation files, thereby ensuring you have the latest updates available. By updating your installation files as needed, Windows can quickly integrate new, certified device drivers, critical security fixes, and compatibility updates.

After you install Windows, you can use Auto Update to ensure that critical security and compatibility updates are made available for installation automatically, without significantly affecting your regular use of the Internet. Auto Update works in the background when you are connected to the Internet to identify when new updates are available and to download them to your computer. The download is managed so that it does not affect your surfing the web, and it picks up where it left off if the download is interrupted.

When the download has completed, you are notified and prompted to install the update. You can install it then, get more details about what is included in the update, or let Windows remind you about it later. Some installations may require you to reboot, but some do not.

Upgrading and Migrating to Windows Vista from a Previous Version of Windows

When you perform a clean installation of Windows Vista, you do not transfer user settings from the previous operating system on the system. To reconfigure the user settings on a new machine is time-consuming for IT administrators and users who use the computers. Because Windows 2000 Professional, Windows XP, and Windows Vista use similar file systems, device drivers, and registry structures, it is possible to upgrade or migrate user settings from one Windows version to a later Windows version under certain conditions. Table 2.2 lists upgrade capabilities of different Windows versions.

TABLE 2.2 Upgrade Options for Windows Vista

	Home Basic	Home Premium	Business	Ultimate
Windows XP Pro*	Requires clean install	Requires clean install	In-place installation option available	In-place installation option available
Windows XP Home	In-place installation option available	In-place installation option available	In-place installation option available	In-place installation option available
Windows XP Media Center	Requires clean install	In-place installation option available	In-place installation option available	In-place installation option available
Windows XP Tablet PC	Requires clean install	Requires clean install	In-place installation option available	In-place installation option available
Windows XP Professional x64	Requires clean install	Requires clean install	Requires clean install	Requires clean install
Windows 2000	Requires clean install	Requires clean install	Requires clean install	Requires clean install

*Requires Windows XP Service Pack 2 (SP2)

Windows Vista Upgrade Advisor

For computers that have not been tested by the manufacturer and do not have the Vista Capable or Premium Ready logos (especially for older computers that were produced before Windows Vista's release), you can also run the *Windows Vista Upgrade Advisor* on individual machines to learn which version of Windows Vista can be successfully installed on the computer.

NOTE

The Windows Vista Upgrade Advisor runs only on computers that are running 32-bit versions of either Windows Vista or Microsoft Windows XP SP2. In addition, it requires both Microsoft Core Extensible Markup Language Services (MSXML) 6.0 and Microsoft .NET Framework 2.0 are installed before it can run, both of which you can download from the Microsoft website.

After you install Windows Vista Upgrade Advisor and perform the scan, it will recommend a suitable edition of Windows Vista to which you can upgrade. You can also use the Windows Vista Upgrade Advisor to select alternative Windows Vista editions, and then view a report of potential problems related to that edition and recommendations on changes that you might need to make (see Figure 2.2). Of course, you can install any edition of Windows Vista as long as the computer meets the minimum hardware requirements for that edition. Of course, you might encounter some problems with Windows Vista and its functionality.

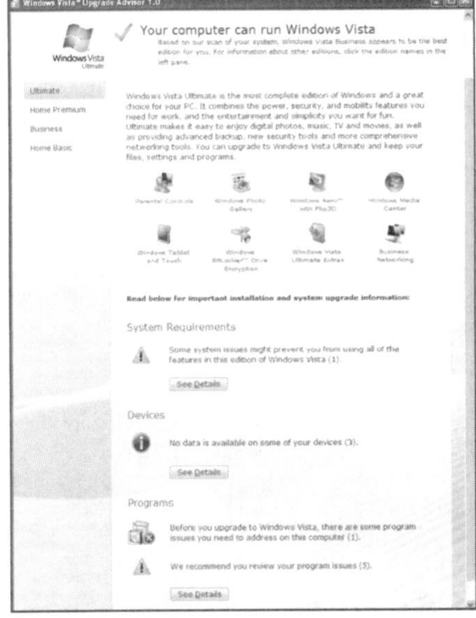

FIGURE 2.2 Windows Vista Upgrade Advisor.

EXAM ALERT

Anytime you need to check a system to see whether it is compatible with Windows Vista, use the Windows Vista Upgrade Advisor.

Another program worth mentioning is the Windows Vista Hardware Assessment tool. The Windows Vista Hardware Assessment solution accelerator is an inventory, assessment, and reporting tool that will find computers on a network and determine whether they are ready to run the Windows Vista operating system. The solution accelerator performs three key functions: hardware inventory, compatibility analysis, and readiness reporting. The Windows Vista Hardware Assessment Wizard can inventory and scan computers on a network that runs an operating system that supports Windows Management Instrumentation (WMI). The supported operating systems are as follows:

- Windows Vista (already migrated)
- Windows XP Professional (SP2)
- Windows Server 2003 or Windows Server 2003 R2
- Windows 2000 Professional or Windows 2000 Server

Upgrading to Windows Vista

If you have Windows XP running SP2, you might be able to perform an in-place upgrade. During an in-place upgrade, the operating system is replaced while retaining all programs, program settings, user-related settings, and user data.

To perform an upgrade, follow these steps:

1. Verify that your system is capable of running Windows Vista by using the Windows Vista Upgrade Advisor. You also need to determine which applications have compatibility problems with Windows Vista and resolve those issues.
2. To protect against data loss, back up any data and personal settings before you start the upgrade.
3. Microsoft recommends that you turn off antivirus software during the install to ensure that it does not interfere with the installation process.
4. Insert the Windows Vista product DVD, and run the installation program. If your computer will support an in-place upgrade to Windows Vista, you will be able to select Upgrade during the installation process. If the Upgrade option is not available, verify the minimum system requirements, including memory and disk space.
5. After the upgrade has completed, log on to your computer and verify that all the applications and hardware devices function correctly. If the Windows Vista Upgrade Advisor made any recommendations relating to program compatibility or devices, follow those recommendations to complete the upgrade process.
6. Using the Microsoft update site, update Windows with the newest patches, fixes, and security packs.

Migrating User Settings to a Windows Vista Computer

When you migrate user settings, you are essentially installing fresh copies of Windows Vista and the applications, and then migrating the user settings from a previously used Windows computer. Two tools are used to migrate user settings:

- **Windows Easy Transfer (WET).** Using removable media or over the network, use WET to perform a side by side migration to migrate the settings to a new computer that is already running Windows Vista.
- **User State Migration Tool V3.0 (USMT).** Use USMT to migrate the files and settings to a removable media or to a network share, and later restore the files and settings to the target computer.

To migrate user settings, follow these steps:

1. Verify that your system is capable of running of Windows Vista by using the Windows Vista Upgrade Advisor. You also need to determine which applications have compatibility problems with Windows Vista and resolve those issues.
2. To protect from data loss, back up any data and personal settings before you start the upgrade.
3. When you have successfully transferred the necessary files from your computer, insert the Windows Vista product DVD and perform a clean installation. To perform a clean installation, select Custom (advanced) during the installation process, and then follow the onscreen instructions to complete the installation.
4. Using the Microsoft update site, update Windows with the newest patches, fixes, and security packs.
5. Reinstall all programs.
6. Use WET or USMT to migrate both your program settings and your user-related settings to complete the migration process.

Troubleshooting an Upgrade or Migration to Windows Vista

If you experience problems during an upgrade or migration to Windows Vista, you would use standard troubleshooting methodology to isolate the problem. Of course, to gather information, you do the following:

- Review and research error messages.
- Check logs. During setup, Windows Vista produces log files (located in Windows\panther) into which it records setup progress and information relating to problems encountered during setup.
- Verify the system meets minimum requirements. A common reason for an upgrade to fail is that the computer does not meet the minimum hardware requirements to support the edition of Windows Vista that you are installing.
- Check the devices and BIOS. If Windows Setup encounters a compatibility problem with a device or with the computer's BIOS, the upgrade might fail.
- Verify the installation media. Make sure that the installation media is not damaged or corrupt.

Upgrading Between Windows Vista Editions

If you install one version of Windows Vista and you want to upgrade to a more enhanced version of Windows Vista, you might be able to perform an in-place upgrade to the new version of Windows Vista. You can perform an in-place upgrade between certain editions of Windows Vista, whereas you must use a clean installation and migration process for other Windows Vista upgrades. Table 2.3 shows which versions can be upgraded.

TABLE 2.3 The Upgradeability of Windows Vista to Other Versions of Windows Vista

	Starter	Home Basic	Home Premium	Business	Enterprise	Ultimate
Starter	Repair	Upgrade	Upgrade	Upgrade	Upgrade	Upgrade
Home Basic	Clean Install	Repair	Upgrade	Upgrade	Upgrade	Upgrade
Home Premium	Clean Install	Clean Install	Repair	Clean Install	Clean Install	Upgrade
Business	Clean Install	Clean Install	Clean Install	Repair	Upgrade	Upgrade
Enterprise	Clean Install	Clean Install	Clean Install	Clean Install	Repair	Upgrade
Ultimate	Clean Install	Clean Install	Clean Install	Clean Install	Clean Install	Repair

The process for upgrading between editions of Windows Vista is broadly similar to the process of upgrading earlier versions of Windows to Windows Vista:

1. Back up your data, program settings, and all user-related settings.
2. Install or upgrade using the Windows Vista DVD. If a direct in-place upgrade is possible, that option will be available to select during installation. Otherwise, select Custom (advanced) and perform a clean installation of the new edition of Windows Vista.
3. When installation has completed, ensure that you apply any updates to the new edition of Windows Vista if you did not do so during the installation process.
4. Install programs if you are performing a clean installation migration.
5. To complete the migration process, you must use WET or USMT to restore application program and user-related settings. You do not need to restore settings if you perform an in-place upgrade between Windows Vista editions.

Restoring a Computer to a Previous Windows Installation

When you perform a clean installation of Windows Vista on a hard disk partition that contains an existing Windows installation (assuming you did not reformat the hard disk), the previous operating system, user data, and program files are saved to a Windows.OLD folder. If the Windows.OLD folder exists on this drive, files from the previous Windows installation are saved during the Windows Vista installation process. Therefore, you can restore the computer to the previous Windows installation by accessing the following Microsoft website:

http://support.microsoft.com/kb/933168

EXAM ALERT

If you upgrade from an older version of Windows, the old Windows is placed in the Windows.OLD folder so that you can retrieve old data and restore a computer to the previous Windows version.

Dual Booting Windows XP and Windows Vista

Often when a new operating system is released, there are software or device compatibility issues with which you have to contend. Some people may find it beneficial to have two partitions on their system, one with Windows XP and one with Windows Vista. In such a scenario, when you boot your system, you can select which operating system you want to boot. This also gives you an opportunity to test Windows Vista while having Windows XP still available.

Repairing a Windows Installation

Windows Vista Startup Repair is a Windows recovery tool that can fix certain problems, such as missing or damaged system files that might prevent Windows from starting correctly. When you run Startup Repair, it scans your computer for problems, and then tries to fix them so that your computer can start correctly.

Startup Repair is located on the *System Recovery Options* menu, which is on the Windows installation disc. Startup Repair might also be installed on your hard disk if your computer has preinstalled recovery options. Startup Repair might prompt you to make choices as it tries to fix problems; if necessary, it might also restart your computer as it makes repairs.

To run System Recovery from the installation DVD, follow these steps:

1. Insert the installation disc.
2. Restart your computer.

3. If prompted, press any key to start Windows from the installation disc.
4. Choose your language settings, and then click Next.
5. Click Repair Your Computer.
6. Select the operating system you want to repair, and then click Next.
7. On the System Recovery Options menu, click Startup Repair.

Activating Windows Vista

Although volume license might not require activation, retail versions of Windows Vista will need to be activated after installation. In the Welcome Center, the Activation Status entry specifies whether you have activated the operating system. If Windows Vista has not been activated, you can activate the operating system by clicking More Details to access the System console and then selecting Click Here to Activate Windows Now under Windows Activation.

Unlike in Windows XP, you can easily change the product key used by the operating system. In the System console, click Change Product Key under Windows Activation. In the Windows Activation window, type the product key, and then click Next. As in Setup, you do not need to type the dashes in the product key.

Exam Prep Questions

1. You work as a desktop support technician at Acme.com. Because you need to connect to the domain, you need to install Windows Vista Business edition on a new computer for the graphics department. The new computer has the following specifications:

   - 1.4-GHz Intel processor
   - 384 MB RAM
   - 15 GB disk space
   - Super VGA video card
   - Integrated sound card
   - Intel 10/100 network adapter

   Which hardware does not meet the minimum requirements to install Windows Vista?

   ❍ **A.** The processor

   ❍ **B.** The amount of RAM

   ❍ **C.** The hard drive

   ❍ **D.** The video card

   ❍ **E.** The network adapter

2. You work as a desktop support technician at Acme.com. Because you need to connect to the domain, you need to install Windows Vista Business Edition on a computer for the graphics department. The computer has the following specifications:

   - 1.5 GHz AMD processor.
   - 512 MB of RAM.
   - Drive C (system drive) has 8 GB of free disk space.
   - Drive D (program drive) has 25 GB of free disk space.
   - Integrated sound card.
   - Intel 10/100 network adapter.

   Which hardware does not meet the minimum requirements to install Windows Vista?

   ❍ **A.** You should add a faster processor to the computer.

   ❍ **B.** You should add more memory to the computer.

   ❍ **C.** You need to free up space on Drive C.

   ❍ **D.** You should install Windows Vista on Drive D.

3. You work as the desktop support technician at Acme.com. You have a computer that has a 120-GB hard drive divided into two partitions. Each partition is 60 GB. Windows XP Professional has been installed on the first partition. The second partition has not been defined. You want to set up the computer to dual boot between Windows XP Professional and Windows Vista Business edition. What do you need to do to set this up?

   ❍ **A.** Format the second partition with the NTFS file system, boot from the Windows Vista DVD, and install Windows Vista on the second partition.

   ❍ **B.** Format the first partition with the NTFS file system, boot from the Windows Vista DVD, and install Windows Vista on the first partition.

   ❍ **C.** Boot from the Windows Vista DVD and upgrade the Windows XP partition to Windows Vista.

   ❍ **D.** Install Windows XP on the first partition, boot from the Windows Vista DVD, and install Windows Vista on the second partition.

4. You work as the desktop support technician at Acme.com. Within your corporation, you have a new computer with Windows Vista Business edition. You need to install the same build and configuration of Windows Vista on 10 other computers. To accomplish this, you burn a bootable Windows PE CD that includes all the required deployment tools. What should you do next with the least amount of administrative effort?

   ❍ **A.** Boot the master with the Windows PE CD. Use ImageX on the master to create the image file. Boot each target with the Windows PE CD. Use Diskpart to format the drive. Use ImageX to apply the image to the target.

   ❍ **B.** Use Sysprep to seal the master. Boot the master with the Windows PE CD. Use ImageX on the master to create the image file. Boot each target with the Windows PE CD. Use ImageX to apply the image to the target.

   ❍ **C.** Boot the master with the Windows PE CD. Use ImageX on the master to create the image file. Boot each target with the Windows PE CD. Use Diskpart to format the drive. Use ImageX to apply the image to the target. Use Sysprep to seal the master.

   ❍ **D.** Use Sysprep to seal the master. Boot the master with the Windows PE CD. Use ImageX on the master to create the image file. Boot each target with the Windows PE CD. Use Diskpart to format the drive. Use ImageX to apply the image to the target.

5. You work as the desktop support technician at Acme.com. You have a new computer that has Windows XP in which you want to install Windows Vista on. You place the DVD into the drive and start the workstation. Unfortunately, it boots to Windows XP without starting the install program. You enter the BIOS program and determine that you are not allowed to boot from the DVD. What do you do next?

   ❍ **A.** Install new drivers for the DVD drive.

   ❍ **B.** Retrieve updates from Microsoft.

   ❍ **C.** Update the PC's BIOS.

   ❍ **D.** Boot from a Windows PE disc.

6. Which versions of Windows can be upgraded to Windows Vista Home edition?

   ❍ **A.** Microsoft Windows XP Professional

   ❍ **B.** Microsoft Windows XP Home

   ❍ **C.** Microsoft Windows XP Tablet PC

   ❍ **D.** Microsoft Windows 2000 Professional SP3

7. You are the network administrator for Acme.com. You have ordered some new computers, and the new computers only have one partition with Windows Vista Home Basic. Unfortunately, each computer must run Windows Vista Business edition so that it can connect to the Windows domain. When you upgrade Windows Vista, which directory will hold the old operating system files and directories in case you need to access the Documents and Settings folders and Program Files folder?

   ❍ **A.** Windows\panther folder

   ❍ **B.** Windows folder

   ❍ **C.** Windows.OLD folder

   ❍ **D.** Files and Settings folder

   ❍ **E.** Explorer Folder

8. You work as a help desk technician for Acme.com. You have a Windows XP computer that you need to upgrade but are unsure whether the older sound card and video card are compatible? What should you do?

   ❍ **A.** Run the Windows Vista Program Compatibility Assistant tool.

   ❍ **B.** Run the Windows Vista Upgrade Advisor.

   ❍ **C.** Run the Windows Update tool.

   ❍ **D.** Open the Device Manager and update its drivers.

9. You work as a help desk technician for Acme.com. You have a new computer that has Windows Vista Home edition. Yet you need to be able to watch and record live television feeds and be able to rip DVDs. What do you need to do that is the most cost-effective?

❍ **A.** Upgrade the system to Windows Vista Home Premium.

❍ **B.** Upgrade the system to Windows Vista Business edition.

❍ **C.** Upgrade the system to Windows Vista Ultimate.

❍ **D.** You don't have to do anything. Windows Home edition already has this functionality.

10. You work as a help desk technician for Acme.com. You have a PC with Windows Vista Business edition. Unfortunately, there are some power glitches, and the system now generates Stop errors during boot. What should you do?

❍ **A.** Run the Update program to make sure all drivers are updated.

❍ **B.** Boot with the Windows Vista DVD and run the Startup Repair utility.

❍ **C.** Run the MSCONFIG program and disable startup items.

❍ **D.** Perform a clean install of the Windows Vista Business edition.

Answers to Exam Prep Questions

1. **Answers B and C are correct.** The system requirements specify a minimum of 512 MB of RAM and a 20-GB hard drive. The system in the question only has 384 MB of RAM and a 15-GB hard drive. The other system requirements include a 1-GHz processor and a Super VGA monitor, which the system already has. Therefore, answers A and D are incorrect. The system requirements do not specify a network card, so answer E is not correct. Of course, you will need a network card to communicate with a network.

2. **Answer C is correct.** The system requirements specify 15 GB of free hard disk space. The system in question only has 8 GB of free disk space. Because the system requirements specify a 1-GHz processor and 512 MB RAM, answers A and B are incorrect. Because it has been specified that Windows will go on drive C: and programs will go on drive D:, answer E is incorrect.

3. **Answer A is correct.** To have a system dual boot between Windows XP and Windows Vista, you have to install each operating system onto two different partitions. Because Windows XP is already on the first partition, you need to install Windows Vista on the other partition. You do not want to format the first partition because it would erase everything on that partition. So, answer B is incorrect. You don't want to upgrade Windows, because Windows XP will not be available. So, answer C is incorrect. Answer D is incorrect because you don't need to install Windows XP; it already exists.

4. **Answer D is correct.** To install the same configuration on 10 different computers, you have to use images. You already have the source system. Answer D then specifies the rest of the steps to install Vista with images. After you have the source computer, the next step is to Sysprep the system. Therefore, answers A and C are incorrect. Because you need to create a new partition before installing the image, answer B is incorrect.

5. **Answer C is correct.** Because the system did not find the DVD disc, you will need to fix that problem. The BIOS not allowing you to specify a DVD to boot from indicates that the BIOS is too old to support bootable DVD drives. Therefore, you need to update the system BIOS. Answers A and B are incorrect because drivers and updates will not help boot from the DVD (because these load when Windows Vista loads, and to boot from a DVD does not require Windows Vista to load). Answer D is incorrect because you don't need the Windows PE disc to load DVD drivers.

6. **Answer B is correct.** The only version that can be upgraded to Windows Vista Home edition is Windows XP Home edition. Because Windows XP Home edition is the only one that can be upgraded to Windows Vista Home edition, answers A, C and D are incorrect.

7. **Answer C is correct.** When you perform a clean installation of Windows Vista on a hard disk partition that contains an existing Windows installation (assuming you did not reformat the hard disk), the previous operating system, user data, and program files are saved to a Windows.OLD folder. Answer A is incorrect because the Windows\panther folder is used for installation logs. Answer B is incorrect because the Windows folder is where the Windows files reside. Answer D and E do not exist in a normal Windows Vista installation.

8. **Answer B is correct.** When you want to see whether a system is compatible with Windows Vista, you should run the Windows Vista Upgrade Advisor. Answer A is incorrect because it will not check hardware compatibility. Answer C is incorrect because Windows Update will not specify whether a device is compatible with Windows Vista. Answer D is incorrect because updating drivers in Windows XP will not specify whether a device is compatible with Windows Vista.

9. **Answer A is correct.** The only two versions of Windows Vista that support DVD ripping and the ability to watch TV are Windows Vista Home Premium and Windows Vista Ultimate. Of course, to be cost-effective, Windows Vista Home Premium is less expensive than Windows Vista Ultimate. Therefore, answer C is incorrect. Answers B and D are incorrect because Windows Vista Home edition and Windows Vista Business edition do not support DVD ripping and the ability to watch TV.

10. **Answer B is correct.** To repair the system startup files, you have to run the Startup Repair utility located on the Windows Vista DVD. Answer A is incorrect because the Update program will replace the corrupt system files. Answer C is incorrect because the MSCONFIG program will replace the corrupt system files. Answer D is incorrect because if you perform a clean install of Windows Vista, it will erase everything on the system including programs.

Recommended Readings and Resources

Mitch Tulloch, Tony Northrup, Jerry Honeycutt, Ed Wilson, Ralph Ramos, and the Windows Vista Team, *Windows Vista Resource Kit (Pro - Resource Kit)* (Redmond, Washington: Microsoft Press, 2007).

William R. Stanek, *Introducing Microsoft Windows Vista* (Redmond, Washington: Microsoft Press, 2006).

For more information about deploying Windows Vista, including a Deployment Step-by-Step Guide and Migration Step-by-Step Guide, go to http://technet2.microsoft.com/WindowsVista/en/library/1d093249-41e9-458a-8297-489935eeabb11033.mspx.

CHAPTER THREE

Using Windows Vista

Terms you'll need to understand:

- ✓ Desktop
- ✓ Sidebar
- ✓ Gadget
- ✓ Start menu
- ✓ Taskbar
- ✓ Quick Launch toolbar
- ✓ Notification area
- ✓ Control Panel
- ✓ Welcome Center
- ✓ Plug-and-play
- ✓ Signed driver
- ✓ Device Manager
- ✓ Windows Aero
- ✓ Color depth
- ✓ Refresh rate
- ✓ Theme
- ✓ Ease of Access Center
- ✓ Parental control
- ✓ Administrative tools

Techniques/concepts you'll need to master

- ✓ Identify parts of the desktop used in Windows Vista.
- ✓ Use the Control Panel to configure certain aspects of Windows Vista.
- ✓ Load and manage device drivers.
- ✓ List the requirements for Windows Aero.
- ✓ Using the Ease of Access Center to enable accessibility technology.
- ✓ Use parental controls to limit access on Windows Vista.

Before learning how to configure and troubleshoot Windows Vista, you need to become familiar with the Windows Vista interface. This includes understanding how to use the desktop, the Start menu, and taskbar. In addition, when you open programs, the programs will appear in windows. You will then need to know how to navigate between the programs and how to manage the windows that the programs are running in. If you are familiar with Windows XP, you will find some similarities between Windows XP and Windows Vista. However, you will find enough differences that will cause you lots of grief if you don't know where to go.

Desktop

Similar to Windows XP, the Windows Vista interface is based on the *desktop*, which is the main screen/graphical space that you see after you turn on your computer and log on to Windows. Like the top of the actual office desk, it serves as a surface for your work (see Figure 3.1).

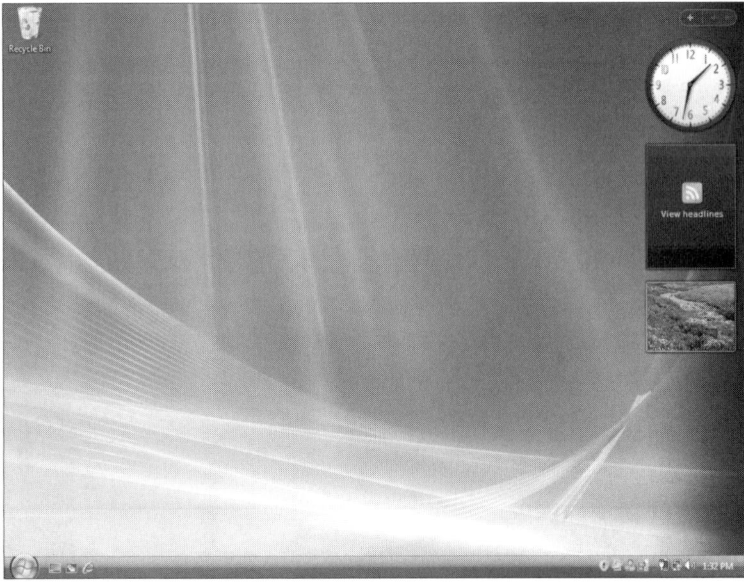

FIGURE 3.1 The Windows Vista desktop.

When you work at your office desk, you will open up folders that contain office documents such as letters and reports. You may spread them on your desk so that you can easily and quickly access them. When working on a Windows Vista machine, you open programs or documents. Sometimes, these programs and documents are located in folders throughout your computer disk drives. Of course, the folders are used to organize your programs and data files so that you can find things in the future. Other times, you place files and folders, shortcuts to files and folders, or shortcuts to programs directly on the desktop, arranging them however you want so that you can easily access them.

To represent the files, folders, and programs, Windows Vista uses icons. A shortcut is an icon that represents a link to an item, rather than the item itself. You can identify shortcuts by the arrow on their icon. Like Windows XP, double-clicking an icon starts or opens the item it represents. If you double-click the Internet Explorer icon Internet Explorer will start. If you double-click a report that was written using Microsoft Word, Microsoft Word will start, and the report will be opened. When you double-click a shortcut, the item opens.

Managing Desktop Icons

By default, when you first start Windows, you'll see at least one icon on your desktop: the Recycle Bin. Depending on how your computer is configured, after its initial installation, you may have additional desktop icons, including the Control Panel, Internet Explorer, or Computer icon. Of course, depending on your preference, you can add or remove icons. Some people like to have a clean, uncluttered desktop with few or no icons, whereas others like to have their frequently used programs, files, and folders.

To add a shortcut to the desktop, follow these steps:

1. Locate the item that you want to create a shortcut for.
2. Right-click the item, click Send To, and then click Desktop (create shortcut). The shortcut icon appears on your desktop.

To add or remove common desktop icons such as Computer, your personal folder (My Documents), Network, the Recycle Bin, Internet Explorer, and Control Panel, follow these steps:

1. Right-click an empty area of the desktop, and then click Personalize.
2. In the left pane, click Change Desktop Icons.
3. Under Desktop icons, select the check box for each icon that you want to add to the desktop, or clear the check box for each icon that you want to remove from the desktop, and then click OK.

To remove an icon from the desktop, right-click the icon, and then click Delete. If the icon is a shortcut, only the shortcut is removed; the original item is not deleted.

To move a file from a folder to the desktop, follow these steps:

1. Open the folder that contains the file.
2. Drag the file to the desktop.

By default, Windows lines up the icons in columns on the left side of the desktop. However, you can move an icon by dragging it to a new place on the desktop.

You can have Windows automatically arrange your icons. Right-click an empty area of the desktop, click View, and then click Auto Arrange. Windows lines up your icons starting in the upper-left corner, locking them into place. To unlock the icons so that you can move them again, click Auto Arrange again, clearing the check mark next to it.

By default, Windows spaces icons evenly on an invisible grid. To place icons closer together or with more precision, turn off the grid. Right-click an empty area of the desktop, click View, and then click Align to Grid to clear the check mark. Repeat these steps to turn the grid back on.

To move or delete a bunch of icons simultaneously, you must first select all of them. Click an empty area of the desktop and drag the mouse to surround the icons with the rectangle that appears. Then release the mouse button. Now you can drag the icons as a group or delete them.

NOTE

In a list of items, you can select multiple items that are sequential (in order) such as files and folders by clicking the first item. You would then click and hold down the Shift key and use the arrows on the keyboard or by the mouse to select the next sequential item or items. To select nonsequential items, click and hold down the Shift key and use the mouse to select each item.

To temporarily hide all of your desktop icons without actually removing them, right-click an empty part of the desktop, click View, and then click Show Desktop Icons to clear the check mark from that option. To get the icons back, click Show Desktop Icons.

Whenever you open a program, file, or folder, it appears on your screen in a box or frame called a window (that's where the Windows operating system gets its name). Of course, these windows will often partially or completely hide the desktop as the windows are placed on top of the desktop. To see the entire desktop without closing the programs or windows, right-click the taskbar and select the Show the Desktop option. You can also click the Show Desktop button on the Quick Launch toolbar. To restore all the windows, click the Show Desktop button again.

Taskbar and Sidebar

Besides icons, the desktop also includes the taskbar and the Windows Sidebar. The taskbar (similar to Windows XP) is located at the bottom of the screen. It shows which programs are running and allows you to switch between the different programs running. The taskbar also contains the Start button, which opens the Start menu so that you can access programs, folders, and computer settings.

The Windows *Sidebar* is a pane on the side of the Microsoft Windows Vista desktop where you can keep your *gadgets* organized and always available. Gadgets are easy-to-use mini programs that give you information at a glance and provide easy access to frequently used tools such as checking the weather, checking the time using a digital clock, or checking e-mail without opening up other programs.

Start Menu

To start programs, access folders, make changes to Windows Vista, access Help, log off the computer, switch to a different user account, or turn off the computer, you should use the *Start menu*. To open the Start menu, click the Start button in the lower-left corner of your screen. You can also press the Windows logo key on your keyboard.

The Start menu is divided into three basic parts:

- The large left pane shows a short list of programs on your computer.
- In the lower-left corner is the Search box, which enables you to look for programs and files on your computer by typing in search terms.
- The right pane provides access to commonly used folders, files, settings, and features. It's also where you go to log off from Windows or turn off your computer.

The Start menu detects which programs you use the most, and it places them in the left pane for quick access (see Figure 3.2).

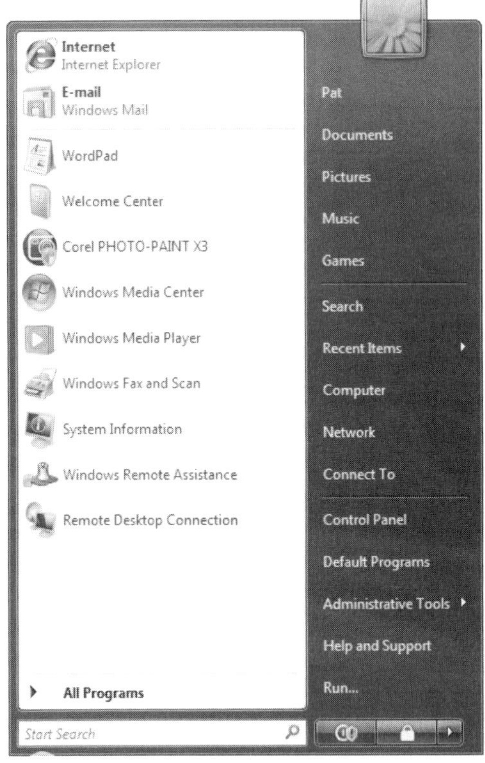

FIGURE 3.2 The Start menu.

One of the most common uses of the Start menu is opening programs installed on your computer. To open a program shown in the left pane of the Start menu, click it. The program opens, and the Start menu closes. If you don't see the program you want to open, click All Programs at the bottom of the left pane, as shown in Figure 3.3. Instantly, the left pane displays a long list of programs in alphabetic order, followed by a list of folders.

NOTE

If you are unsure what a program does, move the cursor over its icon or name, and a box will appear that contains a description of the program.

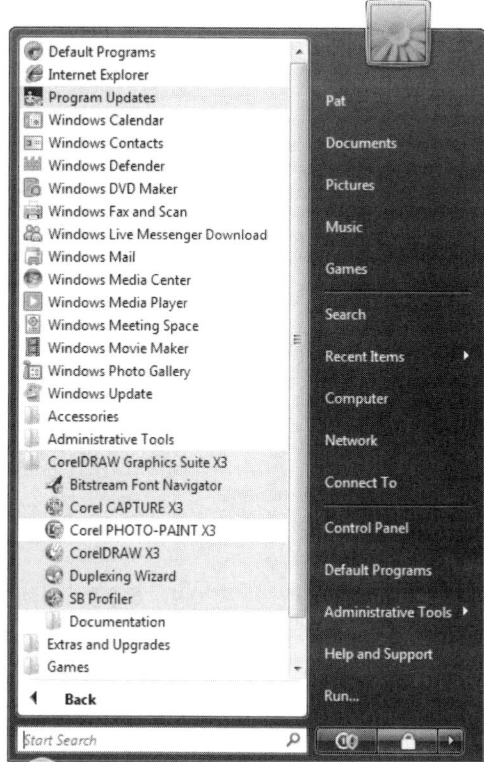

FIGURE 3.3 After you click All Programs, you can then access all programs installed in Window Vista.

Search Box

To find things quickly, use the Windows Vista Search box, which is located in the Start menu. It searches programs, all the folders in your personal folder (which includes Documents, Pictures, Music, Desktop, and other common locations), your e-mail messages, saved instant messages, appointments, contacts, your Internet favorites, and Internet history (see Figure 3.4). A program, file, or folder will appear if the item that you are searching for is in the title, the actual contents of the file, or in the properties of the file (such as the author of the document).

To open a folder or file, click it. You can also click See All Results to display the search results in a folder with more advanced options; or you can click Search the Internet to open your web browser and search the Internet for your term. If your search produces no results, you can click Search Everywhere to search your entire computer. To clear the search results and return to the main programs list, click the Clear button (X).

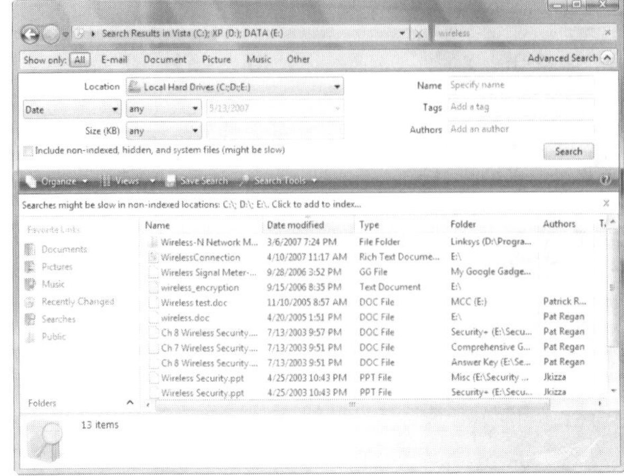

FIGURE 3.4 Using the Search feature in Windows Vista.

Right Pane

The right pane of the Start menu contains links to parts of Windows that you are likely to use frequently, including the following:

- **Personal folder.** Opens for the currently logged-on user and contains user-specific files including the Documents, Music, Pictures, and Videos folders. The folder is named for the name of the user account that is currently logged on.

> **NOTE**
>
> The default location of the personal folder is C:\Users*%UserName%*, where *%UserName%* is the name of the user account.

- **Documents.** Opens the Documents folder, where you can store and open a user's personal documents such as letters, reports, and spreadsheets.
- **Pictures.** Opens the Pictures folder, where you can store and view digital pictures and graphics files.
- **Music.** Opens the Music folder, where you can store and play music and other audio files.
- **Games.** Opens the Games folder, where you can access all the games on your computer.

- **Search.** Opens a window where you can search your computer using advanced options.
- **Recent Items.** Opens a list of files you've opened recently.
- **Computer.** Opens a window where you can access disk drives, cameras, printers, scanners, and other hardware connected to your computer.
- **Network.** Opens a window where you can access the computers and devices on your network.
- **Connect To.** Opens a window where you can connect to a new network.
- **Control Panel.** Opens the Control Panel, where you can customize the appearance and functionality of your computer, add or remove programs, set up network connections, and manage user accounts.
- **Default Programs.** Opens a window where you can choose which program you want Windows to use for activities such as web browsing, editing pictures, sending e-mail, and playing music and videos.
- **Help and Support.** Opens Windows Help and Support, where you can browse and search Help topics about using Windows and your computer.

At the bottom of the right pane, you will find the Power button and the Lock button. The Power button is used to turn off the computer; the Lock button is used to lock your computer without turning it off. After it is locked, you need to use your password to unlock it. Clicking the arrow next to the Lock button displays a menu with additional options for switching users, logging off, restarting, or shutting down.

NOTE

The Switch User option does not appear on the Start menu in Windows Vista Starter.

Taskbar

The *taskbar* is the long horizontal bar at the bottom of your screen. By default, the taskbar is always on top, making it always visible even after you open several windows or programs.

The taskbar has four main sections:

- The Start button, which opens the Start menu
- The Quick Launch toolbar, which enables you to start programs with one click
- The middle section, which shows which programs and documents are open and enables you to quickly switch between them
- The notification area, which includes a clock and small icons that show the status of certain programs and computer settings

Quick Launch Toolbar

To the immediate right of the Start button is the *Quick Launch toolbar*. As mentioned earlier, it enables you to launch or start programs with a single click. By default, the Quick Launch toolbar also contains the Show Desktop button (used to temporarily hide all open windows and show the desktop). You can also click the Switch Between Windows button to switch between open windows using Windows Flip 3D.

To add programs to the Quick Launch toolbar, locate the program in the Start menu, right-click it, and then click Add to Quick Launch. You can also drag the program's icon (and folders) to the Quick Launch toolbar. The program's icon will then appear in the toolbar. To remove an icon from the Quick Launch toolbar, right-click it, click Delete, and then click Yes.

NOTE

If some of the icons are missing on the Quick Launch toolbar, you will see double chevrons, which indicates that the icons won't fit in the toolbar. You can access the double chevrons to access the hidden toolbar programs. To overcome this problem, resize the toolbar so that the entire Quick Launch toolbar will display.

Notification Area

The *notification area*, on the far right side of the taskbar, includes a clock and a group of icons that show the status of a program (or they provide access to certain settings). When you move your cursor to a particular icon, you will see that icon's name or the status of a setting. Double-clicking an icon in the notification area usually opens the program or setting associated with it.

Occasionally, an icon in the notification area will display a small pop-up window (called a notification) to notify you about something. Click the Close button (X) in the upper-right corner of the notification to dismiss it. If you don't do anything, the notification will fade away on its own after a few seconds.

To reduce clutter, Windows hides icons in the notification area when you haven't used them for a while. If icons become hidden, click the Show Hidden Icons button to temporarily display the hidden icons.

Control Panel

The *Control Panel* is a graphical tool used to configure the Windows environment and hardware devices. To access the Control Panel, you can click the Start button on the taskbar and select Control Panel. You can also display the Control Panel in any Windows Explorer view by clicking the leftmost option button in the address bar and then selecting Control Panel (see Figure 3.5).

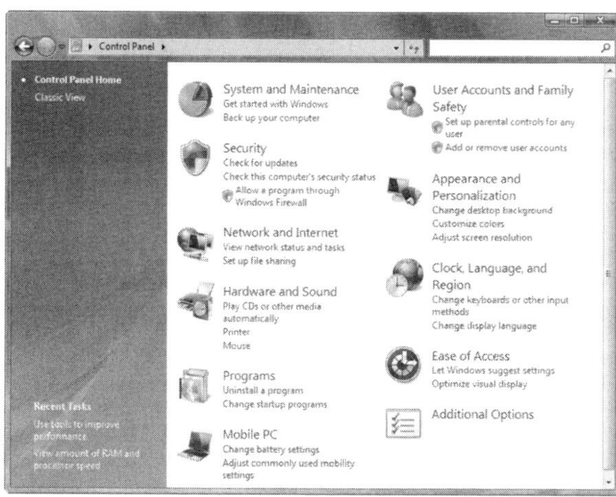

FIGURE 3.5 Window Vista Control Panel in Category view.

Of the 10 categories that are listed, each category includes a top-level link, and under this link are several of the most frequently performed tasks for the category. Clicking a category link provides a list of utilities in that category. Each utility listed within a category includes a link to open the utility, and under this link are several of the most frequently performed tasks for the utility.

As with Windows XP, you can change from the default Category view to Classic view. The Control Panel in Windows Vista has two views: Category view and Classic view. Category view is the default view, which provides access to system utilities by category and task. Classic view is an alternative view that provides the look and functionality of Control Panel in Windows 2000 and earlier versions of Windows (see Figure 3.6).

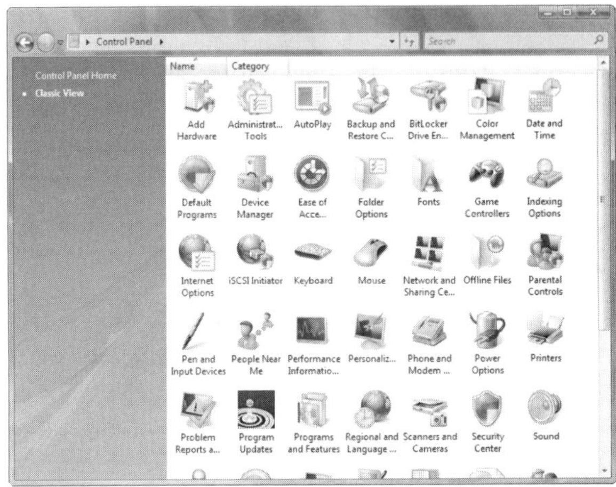

FIGURE 3.6 Window Vista Control Panel in Classic view.

Welcome Center

To simplify the process of setting up a new computer, Windows Vista includes the *Welcome Center*. This screen pulls all the tasks you'll most likely want to complete when you set up your computer into a single location. Such tasks include connecting to the Internet, adding user accounts for different people, and transferring files and settings from another computer using Windows Easy Transfer. You can also identify the edition of Windows Vista by looking at the Welcome Center (see Figure 3.7).

TIP

You can identify the edition of Windows Vista by looking at the Welcome Center.

The Welcome Center automatically displays when you use the computer for the first time. You can choose to have it display every time you start your computer or turn it off. The Welcome Screen displays information about your PC (such as CPU type and amount of RAM) and provides access to both utilities and links to downloads from the Microsoft website (or from the original equipment manufacturer [OEM] where the PC was purchased).

On the lower-left side of the screen, you will find a Run at Startup box. Uncheck this box and close the Welcome Center. When you next reboot, the Welcome

Center will not be displayed. To visit the Welcome Screen in the future, click the Start button, click Control Panel, click System and Maintenance, and then click Welcome Center.

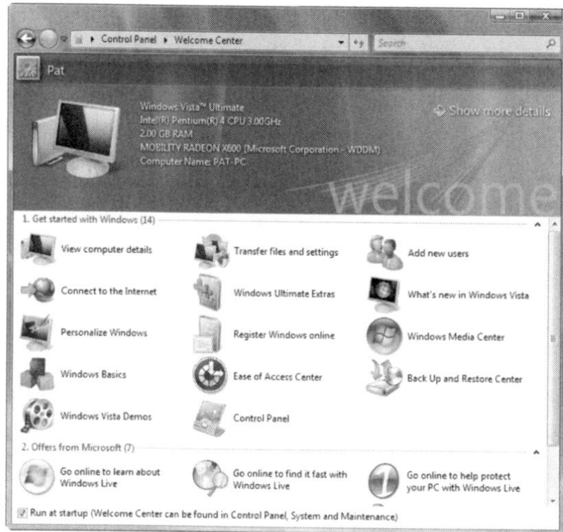

FIGURE 3.7 The Windows Welcome Center.

Managing Device Drivers

Device drivers are programs that control a device. They each act like a translator between the device and programs that use the device. Each device has its own set of specialized commands that only its drivers knows. Whereas most programs access devices by using generic commands, the driver accepts the generic commands from the program and translates them into specialized commands for the device.

Device drivers are needed for a device to work. These drivers can be retrieved from the following sources:

- Bundled with Windows Vista
- Supplied with a device
- Updated with Windows Update
- Updated from the manufacturer's website

Sometimes you might have to download an updated driver from Microsoft or the manufacturer's website to fix problems with device functionality caused by poorly written drivers or by changing technology.

Plug-and-Play Devices

Plug-and-play refers to the capability of a computer system to automatically configure expansion boards and other devices. You should be able to plug in a device and play with it, without worrying about setting DIP switches, jumpers, and other configuration elements. If you connect USB, IEEE 1394, and SCSI devices to a Windows Vista system, Windows Vista will automatically detect these devices. When you connect a PCI or AGP plug-and-play expansion card and turn on the computer, Windows Vista will detect these devices. If Windows Vista does not have a driver available on the device after detection, Windows Vista will prompt you to provide a media or path to the driver.

Signed Drivers

To ensure reliable drivers, Microsoft implemented signed drivers starting with Windows 2000. A *signed driver* is a device driver that includes a digital signature, which is an electronic security mark that can indicate the publisher of the software and information that can show whether a driver has been altered. When it is signed by Microsoft, the driver has been thoroughly tested to make sure that the driver will not cause problems with the system's reliability and not cause a security problem.

By default, if a driver is not signed, signed by a publisher that could not be properly identified, or has been altered since its release, Windows Vista will notify you. Of course, you should install only drivers that are properly signed.

Device drivers that are included on the Windows Vista installation DVD or downloaded from the Microsoft update website include a Microsoft digital signature (making it a signed driver). If you have problems installing a driver or device is not working properly, check with Microsoft's update website and visit the device manufacturer's support website to obtain an up-to-date digitally signed driver for your device.

EXAM ALERT

A driver that lacks a valid digital signature, or that was altered after it was signed, can't be installed on x64-based versions of Windows.

Device Manager

The *Device Manager* lists all hardware devices on your computer and allows you to change the properties for any device. Using the Device Manager, you can view a list of installed devices (see Figure 3.8). When a device is added to the system, the device list is re-created.

To access the Device Manager, you must be logged on to the system as an administrator. To Open Device Manager, click the Start button, click Control Panel, click System and Maintenance, and then click Device Manager. If you are prompted for an administrator password or confirmation, enter the password or provide confirmation.

FIGURE 3.8 Windows Vista Device Manager. The exclamation point indicates a problem with the Mass Storage Controller driver, and the down arrow indicates the Conexant AC-97 audio device is disabled.

If you locate and double-click a device, you will be able to do the following (see Figure 3.9):

- **Uninstall a device.** The Device Manager can be used to uninstall the device driver and remove the driver software from the computer.
- **Enable or disable devices.** Instead of uninstalling the driver installer, you can use the Device Manager to disable the device. The hardware configuration is not changed.

- **Update device drivers.** If you have an updated driver for a device, you can use the Device Manager to apply the updated driver.
- **Roll back drivers.** If you experience system problems after you update a driver, you can roll back to the previous driver by using Driver Rollback. This feature enables you to reinstall the last device driver that was functioning before the installation of the current device driver. If there's no previous version of the driver installed for the selected device, the Roll Back Driver button will be unavailable.
- **Troubleshoot devices.** If a device is not operating correctly, you can use the Device Manager as part of your troubleshooting process. For example, you might see a device listed as Unknown Device next to a yellow question mark.

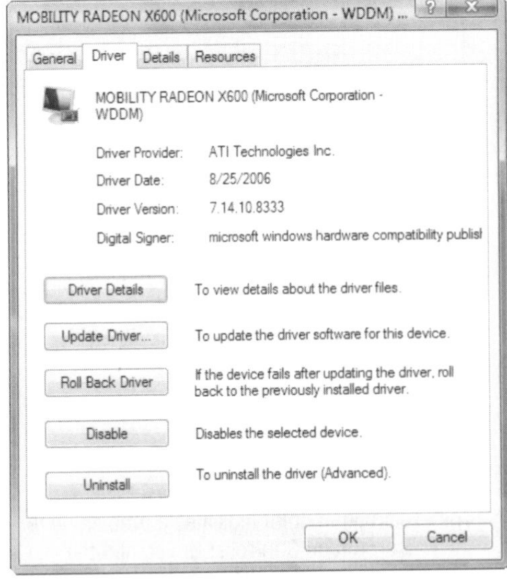

FIGURE 3.9 If you double-click a device in Device Manager, you can then update the driver, roll back the driver, disable the device, or uninstall the driver.

Display Settings

As a desktop technician, you will sometimes be tasked to adjust the look and feel of Windows, such as the background, the screen saver, and the display settings. These settings are found by clicking the Start button, clicking Control Panel, clicking Appearance and Personalization, and clicking Personalization (see Figure 3.10).

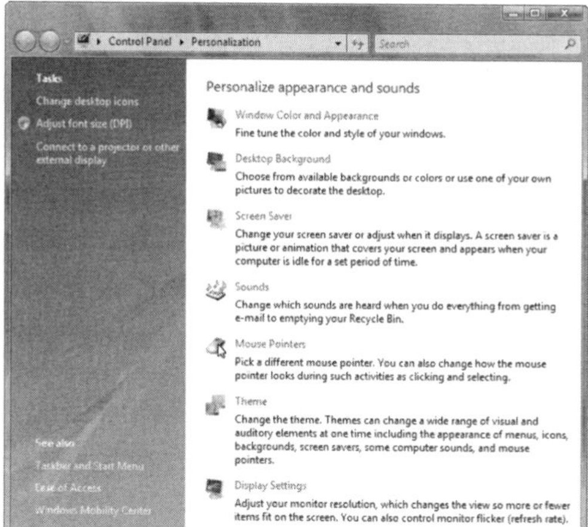

FIGURE 3.10 To configure the appearance and sound, open the Control Panel and select Personalize Appearance and Sounds.

Adjusting the Screen Settings

Screen resolution refers to the clarity of the text and images on your screen. At higher resolutions, items appear sharper because they use more pixels to form the images on the screen. Typically when you use a higher resolution, images will appear smaller, so more items fit on the screen. At lower resolutions, fewer items fit on the screen, but they are larger and easier to see. At very low resolutions, however, images might have jagged edges.

To change the resolution, follow these steps:

1. Open Display Settings by clicking the Start button, Control Panel, Appearance and Personalization, and Personalization. Then click Display Settings.
2. Under Resolution, move the slider to the resolution you want, and then click Apply (see Figure 3.11).

NOTE

When you change the screen resolution, it affects all users who log on to the computer.

FIGURE 3.11 The Display Settings dialog box enables you to select the resolution and color depth.

To set the *color depth* (the number of bits that determine the number of possible colors on the screen), follow these steps:

1. Open Display Settings by clicking the Start button, Control Panel, Appearance and Personalization, and Personalization. Then click Display Settings.
2. Under Colors, select the color depth. For the most possible colors, set to Highest (32 bit), and then click OK.

To set the monitor *refresh rate* (the frequency at which the screen is redrawn), follow these steps:

1. Open Display Settings by clicking the Start button, Control Panel, Appearance and Personalization, and Personalization. Then click Display Settings.
2. Click Advanced Settings.
3. Click the Monitor tab, and select a refresh rate.
4. Click Apply. The monitor might take a moment to adjust. If you get a message asking whether you want to keep the changes, click Yes. If you get this message and don't apply the changes within 15 seconds, the refresh rate will revert back to your original setting.
5. Click OK.

NOTE

Changes to the refresh rate affect all users who log on to the computer.

To change the desktop theme to Windows Vista, follow these steps:

1. Open Theme Settings by clicking the Start button, Control Panel, Appearance and Personalization, and Personalization. Then click Theme.
2. In the Theme list, click Windows Vista, and then click OK.

To change the color scheme to Windows Aero, follow these steps:

1. Open Appearance Settings by clicking the Start button, Control Panel, Appearance and Personalization, and Personalization. Then click Window Color and Appearance. If the Appearance Settings dialog box does not display, at the bottom of the page, click Open Classic Appearance Properties.
2. In the Color Scheme list, click Windows Aero, and then click OK.

To turn on window frame transparency, the color scheme must first be set to Windows Aero. Then you must do the following:

1. Open Personalization by clicking the Start button, Control Panel, Appearance and Personalization, and Personalization.
2. Click Window Color and Appearance.
3. Select the Enable Transparency check box.

If you sometimes have trouble seeing items on your screen, you can adjust the settings to make text and images on the screen appear larger, improve the contrast between items on the screen, and hear onscreen text read aloud. You can adjust these settings on the Make the Computer Easier to See page in the Ease of Access Center:

1. Open the Make the Computer Easier to See page by clicking the Start button, Control Panel, Ease of Access, Ease of Access Center, and then clicking Make the Computer Easier to See.
2. Select the options that you want to use:
   - **Choose a High Contrast Color Scheme.** This option enables you to set a high-contrast color scheme that heightens the color contrast

of some text and images on your computer screen, making those items more distinct and easier to identify.

- **Turn on Narrator.** This option sets Narrator to run when you log on to your computer. Narrator reads aloud onscreen text and describes some events (such as error messages appearing) that happen while you're using the computer.
- **Turn on Audio Description.** This option sets audio descriptions to run when you log on to your computer. Audio descriptions describe what's happening in videos.
- **Turn on Magnifier.** This option sets Magnifier to run when you log on to your computer. Magnifier enlarges the part of the screen where the cursor is pointing and can be especially useful for viewing objects that are difficult to see.
- **Adjust the Color and Transparency of the Window Borders.** This option enables you to change the appearance of window borders to make them easier to see.
- **Make the Focus Rectangle Thicker.** This option makes the rectangle around the currently selected item in dialog boxes thicker, which makes it easier to see.
- **Set the Thickness of the Blinking Cursor.** This option enables you to make the blinking cursor in dialog boxes and programs thicker and easier to see.
- **Turn Off All Unnecessary Animations.** This option turns off animation effects, such as fading effects, when windows and other elements are closed.
- **Remove Background Images.** This option turns off all unimportant, overlapped content and background images to help make the screen easier to see.

Windows Aero

Windows Aero is the premium visual experience of Windows Vista. It features a transparent glass design with subtle window animations and new window colors. Part of the Windows Aero experience is Windows Flip 3D, which is a way to arrange your open windows in a three-dimensional stack that you can quickly flip through without having to click the taskbar. Aero also includes taskbar previews for your open windows. When you point to a taskbar button, you'll see a thumbnail-size preview of the window, whether the content of the window is a document, a photo, or even a running video. Beyond the new graphics and visual polish, the Windows Aero desktop experience includes smoother window handling, increased graphics stability, and glitch-free visuals, all of which give you a simple, comfortable, and high-quality experience.

EXAM ALERT

Be sure to remember the minimum requirements and configuration for Windows Aero to function.

Remember that the following editions of Windows Vista support Aero:

- Windows Vista Business
- Windows Vista Enterprise
- Windows Vista Home Premium
- Windows Vista Ultimate

In addition, the display adapter must support the following:

- DirectX 9, with Pixel Shader 2.0
- Windows Vista Display Driver Model (WDDM)

Finally, the system must have the following graphics memory:

Graphics Memory	Support Single-Monitor Resolution
64 MB	Up to 1,310,720 pixels (equivalent to 1280x1024)
128 MB	Up to 2,304,000 pixels (equivalent to 1920x1200)
256 MB	Greater than 2,304,000 pixels

You must also configure the display system to the following:

- A color depth of 32 bits per pixel (bpp)
- A refresh rate higher than 10 hertz
- The theme set to Windows Vista
- The color scheme set to Windows Aero
- Window frame transparency on

If your system has a built-in graphics adapter based on the Unified Memory Architecture (UMA), you need 1 GB of dual-channel configured system memory, and your system must have 512 MB of RAM available for general system activities after graphics processing.

A *theme* is a collection of visual elements and sounds for your computer desktop. A theme determines the look of the various visual elements of your desktop, such as windows, icons, fonts, and colors, and it can include sounds. For Aero to work, you must configure Windows Vista to use the Windows Vista theme or a theme created by modifying the Windows Vista theme.

To set the theme, follow these steps:

1. Click the Start button, Control Panel, Appearance and Personalization, and Personalization. Then click Theme.
2. Under Theme, select the theme you want, and then click OK (see Figure 3.12).

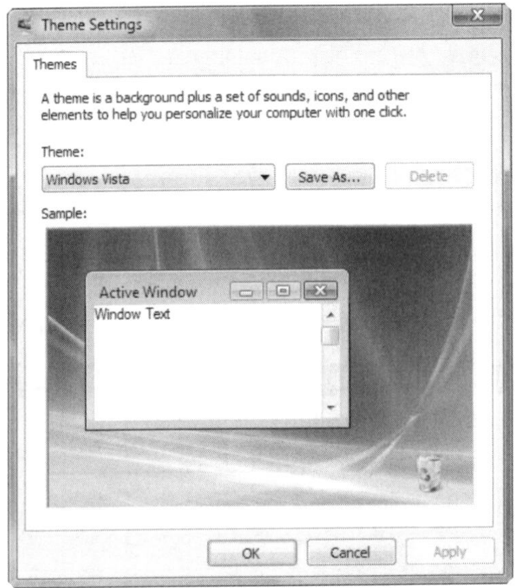

FIGURE 3.12 Selecting the Windows theme.

Windows Aero features windows that are truly translucent. This glass effect enables you to focus on the content of a window, while providing better context for the surrounding elements on your desktop. For added personalization and to get exactly the look and feel you want, you can change the

- Color of your windows
- Saturation of the screen colors
- Level of transparency

To configure Windows color and appearance, follow these steps:

1. Clicking the Start button, Control Panel, Appearance and Personalization, and Personalization. Then click Windows Color and Appearance.
2. You can then change the color of the windows, Start menu, and taskbar and enable or disable transparency (see Figure 3.13).

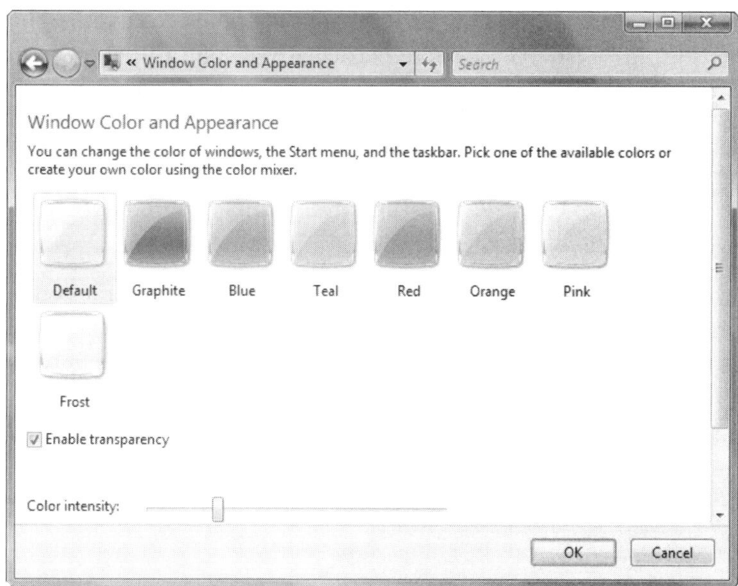

FIGURE 3.13 Configuring the color and appearance of windows.

If you have a program that is incompatible with the Windows Aero color scheme, one of the following may happen:

- Some of the visual elements, such as the window frame transparency, may be temporarily turned off.
- You might receive a message that the color scheme has been changed to Windows Vista Basic.
- Flip 3D does not function.

Verify that your hardware configuration, screen resolution, theme, color scheme, and color depths have not changed. Another cause could be because your computer does not have enough memory to run all the programs that you have open and also run the Windows Aero color scheme.

In this scenario, close some of the applications and retry the Flip 3D feature. If an application is incompatible with the Windows Aero color scheme, some of the visual elements will be automatically disabled and then reenabled after the incompatible application has been closed.

Configuring Accessibility

Windows Vista includes accessible technology that enables computer users to adjust their computers to make them easier to see, hear, and interact with. The accessibility settings in Windows Vista are particularly helpful to people with visual difficulties, hearing loss, pain in their hands or arms, or reasoning and cognitive issues.

Windows offers several programs and settings that can make the computer easier and more comfortable to use. Additional assistive technology products can be added to your computer if you need other accessibility features.

The *Ease of Access Center* is a central location that you can use to set up the accessibility settings and programs available in Windows (see Figure 3.14). In the Ease of Access Center, you'll find quick access for setting up the accessibility settings and programs included in Windows. You'll also find a link to a questionnaire that Windows can use to help suggest settings that you might find useful.

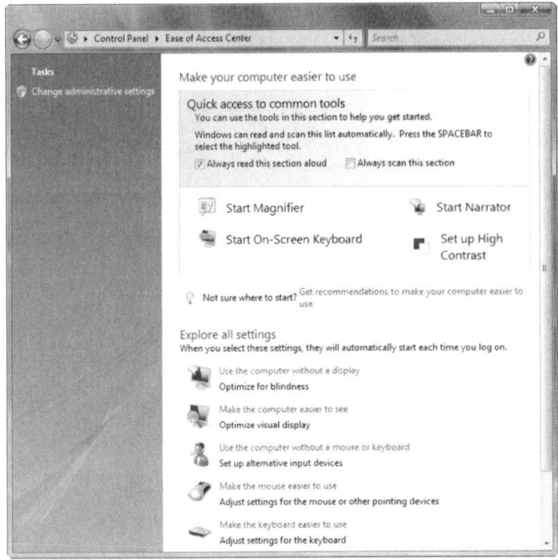

FIGURE 3.14 The Ease of Access Center.

To open the Ease of Access Center, click the Start button, Control Panel, Ease of Access, and then Ease of Access Center. Another way to access the Ease of Access Center is to press the Windows logo key + U. You can open a mini Ease of Access Center by clicking the Accessibility icon, located in the lower-left corner of the logon page.

You can adjust the following settings:

- **Use the Computer Without a Display.** Windows comes with a basic screen reader called Narrator that reads aloud text that displays on the screen. Windows also has settings for providing audio descriptions for videos and controlling how dialog boxes display. In addition, many other programs and hardware are compatible with Windows and available to help individuals who are blind, including screen readers, Braille output devices, and many other useful products.
- **Make the Computer Easier to See.** Several settings are available to help make the information on the screen easier to understand. For example, the screen can be magnified, screen colors can be adjusted to make the screen easier to see and read, and unnecessary animations and background images can be removed.
- **Use the Computer Without a Mouse of Keyboard.** Windows includes an onscreen keyboard that you can use to type. You can also use Speech Recognition to control your computer with voice commands and to dictate text into programs.
- **Make the Mouse Easier to Use.** You can change the size and color of the mouse cursor, and you can use the keyboard to control the mouse.
- **Make the Keyboard Easier to Use.** You can adjust the way Windows responds to mouse or keyboard input so that key combinations are easier to press, typing is easier, or inadvertent key presses are ignored.
- **Use Text and Visual Alternatives for Sounds.** Windows can replace two types of audio information with visual equivalents. You can replace system sounds with visual alerts, and you can display text captions for spoken dialog in multimedia programs.
- **Make It Easier to Focus On Reading and Typing Tasks.** A number of settings can help make it easier to focus on reading and typing. You can have Narrator read information on the screen, adjust how the keyboard responds to certain keystrokes, and control whether certain visual elements are displayed.

NOTE

For more information about assistive technology products, visit the Information for Assistive Technology Manufacturers website at http://www.microsoft.com/enable/at/atvinfo.aspx.

Parental Control

Concerned parents want to protect their children. Because the Internet opens a new world of information gathering, communication, commerce, productivity, and entertainment, it presents new risks for information disclosure, and easy access to inappropriate content in websites, messages, file downloads, games, and audio/video multimedia.

EXAM ALERT

Remember that parental control is not available if the computer is part of a domain. It also only applies to standard user accounts.

Parental controls are not available if your computer is connected to a domain. In addition, parental controls are applied only to standard user accounts, not administrative accounts. Of course, you will need an administrator user account to enable and configure parental controls.

To turn on parental controls for a standard user account, follow these steps:

1. Open parental controls by clicking the Start button, Control Panel, and then, under User Accounts, click Set Up Parental Controls. If you are prompted for an administrator password or confirmation, enter the password or provide confirmation.
2. Click the standard user account for which you want to set parental controls.
3. Under Parental Controls, click On.
4. After you have turned on parental controls for your child's standard user account, you can adjust the individual settings that you want to control (see Figure 3.15). You can control the following areas:

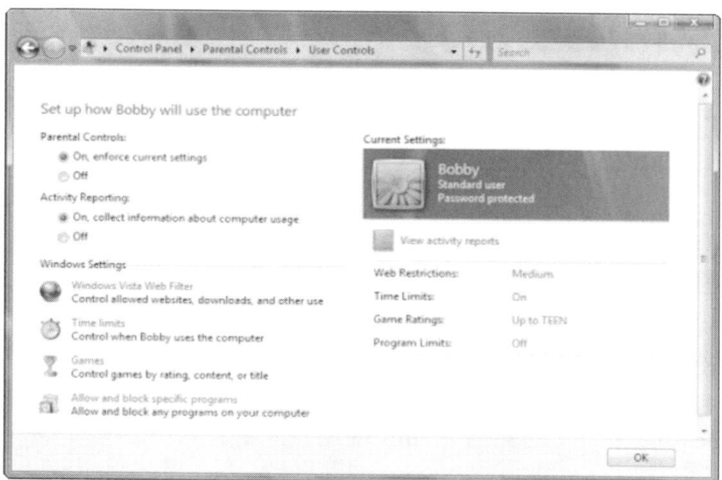

FIGURE 3.15 Parental controls.

- **Web restrictions.** You can restrict the websites that children can visit, make sure children visit only age-appropriate websites, indicate whether you want to allow file downloads, and set up which content you want the content filters to block and allow. You can also block or allow specific websites.
- **Time limits.** You can set time limits to control when children are allowed to log on to the computer. Time limits prevent children from logging on during the specified hours and, if they are already logged on, they will be automatically logged off. You can set different logon hours for every day of the week.
- **Games.** You can control access to games, choose an age rating level, choose the types of content you want to block, and decide whether you want to allow or block unrated or specific games.
- **Allow or block specific programs.** You can prevent children from running programs that you don't want them to run.

After you've set up parental controls, you can set up activity reports to keep a record of your child's computer activity.

Administrative Tools

Administrative Tools is a folder in Control Panel that contains tools for system administrators and advanced users. The tools in the folder might vary depending on which version of Windows you are using.

Many of the tools in this folder, such as Computer Management, are Microsoft Management Console (MMC) snap-ins that include their own Help topics. To view specific help for an MMC tool, or to search for an MMC snap-in that you do not see in the following list, open the tool, click the Help menu, and then click Help Topics.

Open Administrative Tools by clicking the Start button, Control Panel, System and Maintenance, and then clicking Administrative Tools.

Some common administrative tools in this folder are as follows:

- **Computer Management.** Manage local or remote computers by using a single, consolidated desktop tool. Using Computer Management, you can perform many tasks, such as monitoring system events, configuring hard disks, and managing system performance (see Figure 3.16).
- **Data Sources (ODBC).** Use Open Database Connectivity (ODBC) to move data from one type of database (a data source) to another.
- **Event Viewer.** View information that is recorded in event logs about significant events, such as a program starting or stopping, or a security errors.
- **iSCSI Initiator**. Configure advanced connections between storage devices on a network.
- **Local Security Policy.** View and edit Group Policy security settings.
- **Memory Diagnostics Tool.** Check your computer's memory to see whether it is functioning properly.
- **Print Management.** Manage printers and print servers on a network and perform other administrative tasks.
- **Reliability and Performance Monitor.** View advanced system information about the CPU, memory, hard disk, and network performance.
- **Services.** Manage the different services that run in the background on your computer.
- **System Configuration.** Identify problems that might be preventing Windows from running correctly.

- **Task Scheduler.** Schedule programs or other tasks to run automatically.
- **Windows Firewall with Advanced Security.** Configure advanced firewall settings on both this computer and remote computers on your network (see Figure 3.17).

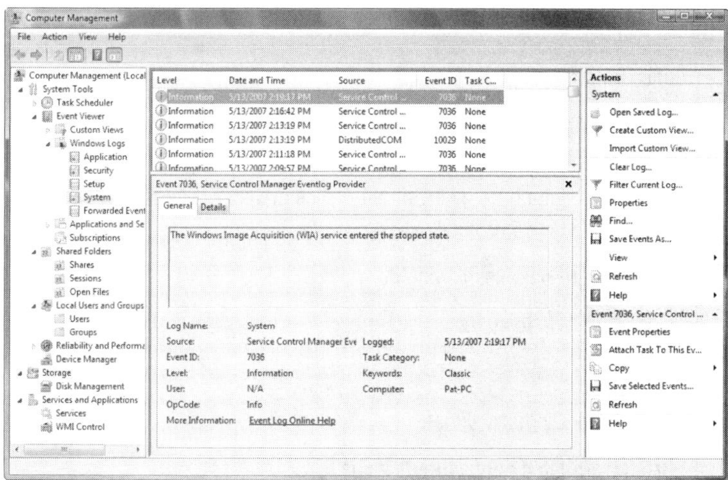

FIGURE 3.16 Computer Management Console.

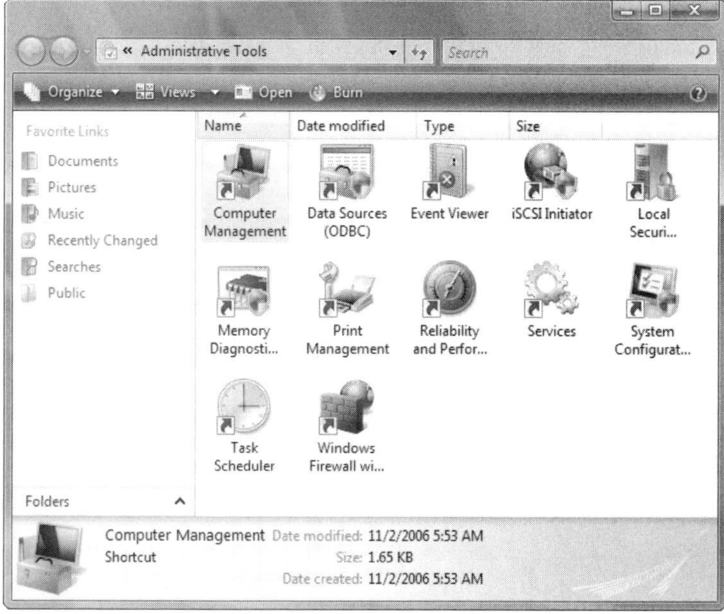

FIGURE 3.17 Administrative Tools.

Exam Prep Questions

1. What can you use to determine which edition of Windows Vista that you have? (Choose the best answer.)

   ❍ **A.** Task Manager

   ❍ **B.** Start menu

   ❍ **C.** Notification area

   ❍ **D.** Welcome Center

2. Which of the following is not a good place to get device drivers? (Choose the best answer.)

   ❍ **A.** Using a peer-to-peer search engine

   ❍ **B.** Bundled with Windows Vista

   ❍ **C.** Supplied with a device

   ❍ **D.** Updated with Windows Update

   ❍ **E.** Updated from the manufacturer's website

3. What are the advantages of using signed drivers? (Choose all that apply.)

   ❍ **A.** You can verify where the driver came from.

   ❍ **B.** You can verify that the driver has not been tampered with.

   ❍ **C.** You can limit who has access to the driver.

   ❍ **D.** The driver has been thoroughly tested.

4. In a Device Manager, how do you know whether there is a problem with a driver? (Choose the best answer.)

   ❍ **A.** There will be a red X.

   ❍ **B.** There will be an exclamation point.

   ❍ **C.** There is a down arrow.

   ❍ **D.** It is flashing.

5. What do you use to enable features so that disabled people can better use Windows Vista? (Choose the best answer.)

   ❍ **A.** Accessibility applet

   ❍ **B.** Ease of Access Center

   ❍ **C.** Administrative Tools

   ❍ **D.** System applet

6. You work as a desktop support technician at Acme.com. You are tasked to upgrade computers with Windows 2000 Pro with the Windows Vista Enterprise. You verified the video cards are Windows Vista Display Driver Model (WDDM) compatible. What else do you need to do to support Aero? (Each correct answer presents part of the solution. Choose four.)

   ❍ **A.** Set the monitor settings to a refresh rate higher than 10.

   ❍ **B.** Press the Windows logo key + Tab.

   ❍ **C.** Set the resolution to 1280x1024 or higher.

   ❍ **D.** Set the color to 32 bit.

   ❍ **E.** Set the theme to Windows Vista.

   ❍ **F.** Set the color scheme to Windows Aero.

7. You work as a desktop support technician at Acme.com. You receive a call from a user reporting that she has been using Flip 3D to allow her to work with several folders and applications for a large project. When she loaded a new program, Flip 3D stopped working. What should you do? (Choose the best answer.)

   ❍ **A.** Add more RAM to the computer.

   ❍ **B.** Close one application at a time and retry Flip 3D.

   ❍ **C.** Change the theme to Windows Vista.

   ❍ **D.** Replace the card with a card that supports Windows Vista Display Driver Model (WDDM).

8. You work as a support technician at Acme.com. There are both desktop and laptop workstations in operation at Acme.com. You are ready to configure the system, which should you configure? (Choose the best answer.)

❍ **A.** Ensure that the color depth is set to 16 bit.

❍ **B.** Ensure that the color depth is set to 32 bit.

❍ **C.** Ensure that the screen resolution is set to 800x600.

❍ **D.** Ensure that the screen resolution is set to 1280x1024.

❍ **E.** Ensure that the monitor refresh rate is greater than 10 hertz.

❍ **F.** Ensure that the theme is set to Windows Vista.

9. You work as a support technician at Acme.com. On your desktop, the user interface features of Windows Aero are not being displayed on a system that is running Windows Vista Ultimate edition. You have a 17-inch monitor that supports a refresh rate up to 100 hertz and a resolution of 1024x768. The video card has 32 MB of video memory. What do you need to enable the Windows Aero features? (Choose the best answer.)

❍ **A.** The operating system should be upgraded.

❍ **B.** The video card should be replaced.

❍ **C.** The monitor should be replaced.

❍ **D.** The display theme should be changed.

10. You work as a desktop support technician at Acme.com. The new systems are using Windows Vista Home Basic edition. At Acme.com, you must ensure that users do not use instant messaging applications. What can you do? (Choose the best answer.)

❍ **A.** Upgrade the systems to Windows Vista Business. Then configure parental controls to disable the use of instant messaging applications.

❍ **B.** Configure parental controls to only run allowed programs on each system.

❍ **C.** You should configure parental controls to enable the Windows Vista Web Filter.

❍ **D.** Make sure that the users do not have administrative accounts on these local systems.

11. You have a computer running Windows Vista Home Basic edition. When you use the system, you log on with an administrator account. You then use parental controls to restrict certain websites and only allow certain programs to run on the machine. You notice that when you log on, you can still access the restricted websites and run any software. What is the problem? (Choose the best answer.)

    ❍ **A.** The system must be part of the domain, so the option is not available.

    ❍ **B.** You just upgrade to the Windows Vista Ultimate edition.

    ❍ **C.** Parental control only applies to standard users, and not administrative accounts.

    ❍ **D.** Someone disabled the parental control on the system.

12. You work as the desktop support technician at Acme.com. A user is having problems logging on to the system. Every time that he logs on, he gets the following message:

    Your account has time restrictions that prevent you from logging on at this time. Please try again later.

    The system has Microsoft Windows Vista Home Premium. You need to identify the cause of this problem. What do you think the problem is? (Choose the best answer.)

    ❍ **A.** The Maximum Password Age local policy setting is set to 0 days.

    ❍ **B.** The Minimum Password Age local policy setting is set to 0 days.

    ❍ **C.** The parental controls settings for the user prevents him from logging on to the computer at specific times.

    ❍ **D.** A Group Policy set on the domain level is preventing him from logging on to the computer at specific times.

13. You work as a technician at Acme.com. You need to install a fingerprint reader. What should you do next? (Choose two answers.)

    ❍ **A.** Make sure that the application that uses the fingerprint reader is digitally signed.

    ❍ **B.** Make sure that the driver that you are installing is digitally signed.

    ❍ **C.** Connect the device before you load the driver.

    ❍ **D.** Load the driver before you connect the device.

Answers to Exam Prep Questions

1. **Answer D is correct.** You can quickly see what version of Windows Vista a system is running by looking at the Welcome Center. Answers B, C, and D are incorrect because none of them show what version you are using.

2. **Answer A is correct.** Answers B, C, D, and E are recommended places to get drivers. Answer A is not a good place because you cannot verify where the driver came from and whether it has been tampered with.

3. **Answers A, B, and D are correct.** It is always recommended to use signed drivers because you can verify where the driver came from, you can verify that the driver has not been tampered with, you can verify that the driver has been thoroughly tested to be reliable. Answer C is incorrect because you cannot control who can access a specific driver.

4. **Answer B is correct.** Problems with drivers are indicated by an exclamation point. Answer A is incorrect because a red X indicates a disabled device in Windows XP. Answer C is incorrect because a down arrow indicates a device is disabled. Answer D is incorrect because Device Manager does not flash.

5. **Answer B is correct.** To configure accessibility options, use the Ease of Access Center. Answer A is incorrect because the accessibility applet was the name used in Windows XP. Answers C and D are incorrect because the Administrative Tools and system applet are not used for any accessibility options.

6. **Answers A, D, E, and F are correct.** To enable Windows Aero, you must have set the monitor settings to a refresh rate higher than 10, set the color to 32 bit, set the theme to Windows Vista, and set the color scheme to Windows Aero. Answer B is incorrect because the key combination will not enable or disable Windows Aero. Answer C is incorrect because the resolution is not a direct factor for Windows Aero.

7. **Answer B is correct.** If an application is not compatible with Windows Aero, it might cause the Flip 3D to stop functioning. Answer A is a possible cause, but it is more likely that it is answer B. Answers C and D are incorrect because nothing else was changed on the system, and Flip 3D was functioning before the application was started.

8. **Answers B, E, and F are correct.** For Windows Aero to function, you must have the color depth set to 32 bit, the monitor refresh rate set to greater than 10 hertz, and the theme set to Windows Vista. Answer A is incorrect because Windows Aero requires 32 bits. Answers C and D are incorrect because resolution is not a direct factor for Windows Aero.

9. **Answer B is correct.** Because the video card only has 32 MB of video RAM, you need to upgrade the card that has at least 64 MB. More memory might be needed if you have a high resolution. Answers A, C, and D are incorrect because they all meet the minimum requirements to run Windows Aero.

10. **Answer B is correct.** You can use parental controls to run only allowed programs that you specify. Answer A is incorrect because the Windows Vista Home Basic edition has parental controls. Answer C is incorrect because Web Filter will not stop Messenger. Answer D is incorrect because you should not use administrative accounts to do daily tasks.

11. **Answer C is correct.** Parental controls only affect standard users, not administrative users. Answer A is incorrect because parental controls would not have been enabled if that computer was part of a domain. Answer B is incorrect because you don't need to upgrade (because parental controls are available in the Windows Vista Home Basic edition). Answer D would require an administrative account to disable parental control, and it is therefore unlikely that this is correct.

12. **Answer C is correct.** Because the computer is not part of a domain, which means no group policies, answers A, B, and D are incorrect. So, the only other way to control when someone can log on is by using parental controls.

13. **Answers B and C are correct.** To load drivers, you must have the device connected first. Then, it is always recommended to use signed drivers. Answer A is incorrect because applications do not have to be digitally signed. Answer D is incorrect because you must have the device connected before you load the driver.

Recommended Readings and Resources

Mitch Tulloch, Tony Northrup, Jerry Honeycutt, Ed Wilson, Ralph Ramos, and the Windows Vista Team, *Windows Vista Resource Kit (Pro - Resource Kit)* (Redmond, Washington: Microsoft Press, 2007).

William R. Stanek, *Introducing Microsoft Windows Vista* (Redmond, Washington: Microsoft Press, 2006).

Visit the Microsoft Accessibility website for solutions, tutorials, and case studies at http://www.microsoft.com/enable.

CHAPTER FOUR

Configuring Advanced Networking

Terms you'll need to understand:

- ✓ TCP/IP
- ✓ IP address
- ✓ IPv4
- ✓ IPv6
- ✓ Subnet mask
- ✓ Default gateway
- ✓ Domain Name System (DNS)
- ✓ HOSTS file
- ✓ LMHOSTS file
- ✓ Windows Internet Name Service (WINS)
- ✓ The **ping** command
- ✓ the **ipconfig** command
- ✓ Wireless network
- ✓ Ad hoc mode
- ✓ Infrastructure mode
- ✓ 802.11 standard
- ✓ Wireless Equivalency Protection (WEP)
- ✓ Wi-Fi Protected Access (WPA)
- ✓ Wi-Fi Protected Access Version 2 (WPA2)
- ✓ Temporal Key Integrity Protocol (TKIP)
- ✓ Advanced Encryption Standard (AES)
- ✓ Service set identifier (SSID)
- ✓ Dial-up connection
- ✓ Broadband connection
- ✓ Virtual private network (VPN)
- ✓ Internet service provider (ISP)

Techniques/concepts you'll need to master:

- ✓ Compare and differentiate IPv4 addressing and IPv6 addressing.
- ✓ List the private addresses used in an IPv4 addressing scheme.
- ✓ Configure a Windows Vista computer to use a giving IP address (IPv4 and IPv6), subnet mask, default gateway, and DNS server.
- ✓ Given a network connectivity problem, troubleshoot and correct the problem.
- ✓ Given a laptop running Windows Vista, connect the computer to a wireless network.
- ✓ Compare and differentiate between WEP, WPA-personal, WPA-enterprise, WPA2-personal, and WPA2-enterprise.
- ✓ Connect a computer running Windows Vista to an ISP using dial-up.
- ✓ Connect a computer running Windows Vista to a broadband connection such as DSL or cable modem.
- ✓ Connect a computer running Windows Vista to a network using a VPN.

A *network* is two or more computers connected to share resources such as files or printers. To function, a network requires a service to share (such as file or print sharing) and access a common medium or pathway. Today, most computers connect to a wired network using an Ethernet adapter, which in turn connects to a switch or set of switches via a twisted-pair cable, or the computers connect to a wireless network using a wireless adapter to connect to a wireless switch. To bring it all together, protocols give the entire system common communication rules. Today, virtually all networks use TCP/IP protocol suite, the same protocol on which the Internet runs.

Introduction to TCP/IP

TCP/IP (Transmission Control Protocol/Internet Protocol) is an industry suite of protocols on which the Internet is based. It is supported by most versions of Windows (including Windows NT, Windows 9x, Windows 2000, Windows XP, Windows Server 2003, and Windows Vista) and virtually all modern operating systems.

The lowest protocol within the TCP/IP suite is the Internet Protocol (IP), which is primarily responsible for addressing and routing packets between hosts. Each connection on a TCP/IP address is called a *host* (a computer or other network device that is connected to a TCP/IP network) and is assigned a unique *IP address*. A host is any network interface, including each network's interface cards or a network printer that connects directly onto the network. When you send or receive data, the data is divided into little chunks called *packets*. Each of these packets contains both the sender's TCP/IP address and the receiver's TCP/IP address.

Windows Vista supports both IPv4 and IPv6 through a dual-IP-layer architecture and enables both by default. This architecture enables you to tunnel IPv6 traffic across an IPv4 network in addition to IPv4 traffic across an IPv6 network.

IPv4 TCP/IP Addressing

The traditional version of the IP protocol is version 4: *IPv4*. Each connection on a TCP/IP address (logical address) is assigned a unique IP address. The format of the IP address is four 8-bit numbers (octet) divided by periods (.). Each number can be 0 to 255. For example, a TCP/IP address could be 131.107.3.1 or 2.0.0.1.

IP addresses are manually assigned and configured (static IP addresses) or dynamically assigned and configured by a Dynamic Host Configuration

Protocol (DHCP) server (dynamic IP addresses). Because the address is used to identify the computer, no two connections can use the same IP address. Otherwise, one or both of the computers would not be able to communicate, and will usually see a message stating "IP address conflict."

The TCP/IP address is broken down into a network number and a host number. The network number identifies the entire network, and the host number identifies the computer or connection on the specified network.

Usually when defining the TCP/IP for a network connection, IT managers also specify a *subnet mask*. A subnet mask is used to define which address bits describe the network number and which address bits describe the host address. Similar to the IP address, the format of the subnet mask is four 8-bit numbers (octet) divided by periods (.). Each number can be 0 to 255. For example, a subnet mask could be 255.0.0.0, 255.255.255.0, or 255.255.240.0.

For example, if you have an address of 15.2.3.6 and you define a subnet mask of 255.255.255.0, 15.2.3.0 defines the network address where every computer on that network must begin with 15.2.3. Then, each computer must have a unique host number, making the entire address unique. Because the first three octets are defined as the network ID, the last octet defines the host ID. Therefore, the one host (and only one host) would have a host ID of 0.0.0.6 located on the 15.2.3.0 network.

If an individual network is connected to another network and users must communicate with any computers on the other network, they must also define the *default gateway*, which specifies the local address of the router. If the default gateway is not specified, users will not be able to communicate with computers on other networks. If the LAN is connected to more than two networks, users must specify only one gateway, because when a data packet is sent, the gateway will first determine whether the data packet needs to go to a local computer or onto another network. If the data packet is meant to be sent to a computer on another network, the gateway forwards the data packet to the router. The router then determines the best direction that the data packet must go to reach its destination.

If you are connected to the Internet, you need a default gateway. Because the default gateway address is an address of a host, it also is a four 8-bit number (octet) divided by periods (.). Each number can be 0 to 255. Because it must be connected on the same network as the host, it must also have the same network address as the host address.

Because TCP/IP addresses are scarce for the Internet (based on the IPv4 and its 32-bit addresses), a series of addresses has been reserved to be used by the private networks. These addresses can be used by many organizations because these addresses are not seen from outside of the local network. The addresses are as follows:

- 10.*x*.*x*.*x* (1 Class A address range)
- 172.16.*x*.*x* to 172.31.*x*.*x* (16 Class B address ranges)
- 192.168.0.*x* and 192.168.255.*x* (256 Class C address ranges)

To enable these addresses to connect to the Internet, you use a router that supports Network Address Translation (NAT), also known as IP masquerading, which translates between the internal private addresses and the public Internet addresses.

IPv6 TCP/IP Addressing

Since the TCP/IP protocol and the Internet became popular, the Internet has grown and continues to grow at an exponential rate. Eventually, the Internet will run out of network numbers. Therefore, a new IP protocol called IPv6 is replacing IPv4.

IPv6 provides a number of benefits for TCP/IP-based networking connectivity, including the following:

- **Larger address space.** The 128-bit address space for IPv6 potentially provides every device on the Internet with a globally unique address.
- **Efficient routing.** The IPv6 network packet supports hierarchical routing infrastructures, which enables it to be more efficient routing than IPv4.
- **Straightforward configuration.** IPv6 can use both Dynamic Host Configuration Protocol for IPv6 (DHCPv6) and local routers for automatic IP configuration.
- **Enhanced security.** The IPv6 standard provides better protection against address and port scanning attacks, and all IPv6 implementations support IPSec for protection of IPv6 traffic.

IPv4 is based on 32-bit addresses (four 8-bit octets), which allows a little more than 4 billion hosts. IPv6 uses 128 bits for the addresses, which can have up to 3.4×10^{38} hosts. Thus, IPv6 can handle all of today's IP-based machines and allow for future growth while handling IP addresses for mobile devices such as personal digital assistants (PDAs) and cell phones.

An IPv6 address is usually divided into groups of 16 bits, written as 4 hex digits. Hex digits include 0, 1, 2, 3, 4, 5, 6, 7, 8, 9, A, B, C, D, E, and F. The groups are separated by colons (:). Here is an example of an IPv6 address:

FE80:0000:0000:0000:02A0:D2EF:FEA5:E9F5

Similar to IPv4, the IPv6 addresses are split in two parts, bits that identify the network and bits that define the host address. Different from IPv4, IPv6 has a fixed prefix that contains specific routing and subnet information. The first 64 bits (four groups of four hex digits) define the network address and the second 64 bits define the host address. For our FE80:0000:0000:0000:02A0:D2EF:FEA5:E9F5 address, FE80:0000:0000:0000 defines the network bits, and 02A0:D2EF:FEA5:E9F5 defines the host bits.

EXAM ALERT

If you need to assign a computer directly to the Internet, you need to configure the computer with an IPv6 address that is equivalent to a public IPv4 address, and you need to assign a global unicast IPv6. These addresses are globally routable and can be reached from the Internet.

Name Resolution

Most users will find the IPv4 and IPv6 addresses difficult to remember when communicating with other computers. Instead, a user specifies a recognizable name, and the name is translated into an address. For example, when a user opens Internet Explorer and specifies http://www.microsoft.com, the www.microsoft.com is translated into an IP address. The web page is then accessed from the server using the translated IP addresses.

Fully qualified domain names (FQDNs), sometimes referred to as just domain names, are used to identify computers on a TCP/IP network. Examples include the following:

- www.microsoft.com
- www.intel.com
- server1.acme.com

One way to translate the FQDN to the IP address is to use a *Domain Name System (DNS)* server. DNS is a distributed database (database is contained in multiple servers) that contains the host name and IP address information for all domains on the Internet. For every domain, a single authoritative name server contains all DNS-related information about the domain. When you configure IP, you must specify the address of a DNS server so that you can use the Internet or log on to a Windows Active Directory domain.

Besides the DNS server, a *HOSTS* file on each machine can also be used to translate domain/host names to IP addresses. The disadvantage of using HOSTS files is that you must add entries on every machine.

Another naming scheme used on TCP/IP networks is the NetBIOS names (such as that used to identify share names for file and printers, \\COMPUTERNAME\SHARENAME). To translate NetBIOS names to IP addresses, you use a *Windows Internet Name Service (WINS)* server or the *LMHOSTS* files.

NOTE

On Windows machines, the HOSTS and LMHOSTS files are located in the C:\Windows\System32\drivers\etc folder.

If you try to access a network resource by name rather than IP address and the device cannot be found, it is most likely a problem with the DNS server/HOSTS file or the WINS server/LMHOSTS file. Either the servers cannot be contacted, or the servers or files have the wrong address associated with the name. The failure of these servers or files can also affect network applications that need to access various services or resources.

IP Configuration on Windows Vista Machines

To configure the IP configuration in Windows Vista, follow these steps:

1. Open the Control Panel.
2. While in Category view, click Network and Internet, click Network and Sharing Center, and then click Manage Network Connection.
3. Right-click the connection that you want to change, and then click Properties. If you are prompted for an administrator password or confirmation, enter the password or provide confirmation.
4. Click the Networking tab. Under This Connection Uses the Following Items, click either Internet Protocol Version 4 (TCP/IPv4) or Internet Protocol Version 6 (TCP/IPv6), and then click Properties.

To specify IPv4 IP address settings, do one of the following:

- To obtain IP settings automatically from a DHCP server, click Obtain an IP Address Automatically, and then click OK.
- To specify an IP address, click Use the Following IP Address, and then, in the IP Address, Subnet Mask, and Default Gateway boxes, enter the IP address settings.

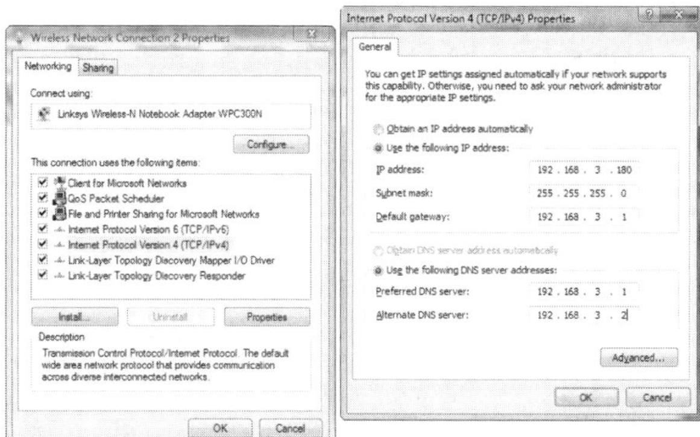

FIGURE 4.1 Configure IPv4 configuration in Windows Vista.

To specify IPv6 IP address settings, do one of the following:

- To obtain IP settings automatically, click Obtain an IPv6 Address Automatically, and then click OK.
- To specify an IP address, click Use the Following IPv6 Address, and then, in the IPv6 Address, Subnet Prefix Length, and Default Gateway boxes, enter the IP address settings.

Windows Vista provides the capability to configure alternate IP address settings to support connecting to different networks. Although static IP addresses can be used with workstations, most workstations use dynamic or alternate IP addressing, or both. You configure dynamic and alternate addressing by completing the following steps:

1. Click Start, and then click Network. In Network Explorer, click Network and Sharing Center on the toolbar.
2. In the Network and Sharing Center, click Manage Network Connections.
3. In Network Connections, right-click the connection you want to work with, and then select Properties.

4. In the Local Area Connection Status dialog box, click Properties. This displays the Local Area Connection Properties dialog box.
5. Double-click Internet Protocol Version 6 (TCP/IPv6) or Internet Protocol Version 4 (TCP/IPv4), as appropriate for the type of IP address you want to configure.
6. Select Obtain an IPv6 Address Automatically or Obtain an IP Address Automatically, as appropriate for the type of IP address you are configuring. If desired, select Obtain DNS Server Address Automatically. Or, select Use the Following DNS Server Addresses and then enter a preferred and alternate DNS server address in the text boxes provided.
7. When you use dynamic IPv4 addressing with desktop computers, you should configure an automatic alternate address. To use this configuration, on the Alternate Configuration tab, select Automatic Private IP Address (APIPA). Click OK twice, click Close, and then skip the remaining steps.
8. When you use dynamic IPv4 addressing with mobile computers, you might want to configure the alternate address manually. To use this configuration, on the Alternate Configuration tab, select User Configured. Then, in the IP Address text box, enter the IP address you want to use. The IP address that you assign to the computer should be a private IP address, and it must not be in use anywhere else when the settings are applied.
9. With dynamic IPv4 addressing, complete the alternate configuration by entering a subnet mask, default gateway, DNS, and WINS settings. When you have finished, click OK twice, and then click Close.

To specify DNS server address settings for IPv4 and IPv6, do one of the following:

- To obtain a DNS server address automatically, click Obtain DNS Server Address Automatically, and then click OK.
- To specify a DNS server address, click Use the Following DNS Server Addresses, and then, in the Preferred DNS server and Alternate DNS server boxes, type the addresses of the primary and secondary DNS servers.

Tools to Help Diagnose Network Problems

You can use several utilities to test and troubleshoot the TCP/IP network.

If you experience network connectivity problems while using Windows Vista, you can use Window Network Diagnostics to start the troubleshooting process. If there is a problem, Windows Network Diagnostics analyzes the problem and, if possible, presents a solution or a list of possible causes.

Windows Network Diagnostics may be able to complete the solution automatically or may require the user to perform steps in the resolution process.

If Windows Network Diagnostics cannot resolve the problem, you should follow a logical troubleshooting process using tools available in Windows Vista. Table 4.1 lists some of these tools.

TABLE 4.1 Troubleshooting Tools

Tool	Description
ipconfig	The **ipconfig** command displays current TCP/IP configuration. ▶ **ipconfig /all** command displays full TCP/IP configuration information. ▶ **ipconfig /release** releases the IPv4 address configured by a DHCP server. ▶ **ipconfig /release6** releases the IPv6 address configured by a DHCP server. ▶ **ipconfig /renew** renews the IPv4 address configured by a DHCP server. ▶ **ipconfig /renew6** renews the IPv6 address configured by a DHCP server. ▶ **ipconfig /flushdns** purges the DNS resolver cache. ▶ **ipconfig /registerdns** refreshes all DHCP leases and reregisters DNS names.
ping	By using the Internet Control Message Protocol (ICMP) protocol, the **ping** command verifies connections to a remote computer by verifying configurations and testing IP connectivity.
tracert	The **tracert** command traces the route that a packet takes to a destination and displays the series of IP routers that are used in delivering packets to the destination. If the packets are unable to be delivered to the destination, the **tracert** command displays the last router that successfully forwarded the packet. The **tracert** command also uses ICMP.
nslookup	The **nslookup** command displays information that you can use to diagnose your DNS infrastructure. You can use **nslookup** to confirm connection to the DNS server and the existence of required records.

A typical troubleshooting process follows:

1. Check local IP configuration (**ipconfig**).
2. Use the **ping** command to gather more information on the extent of the problem:
   - Ping the loopback address (127.0.0.1).
   - Ping the local IP address.
   - Ping the remote gateway.
   - Ping the remote computer.
3. Identify each hop (router) between two systems using the **tracert** command.
4. Verify DNS configuration using the **nslookup** command.

Using **ipconfig** with the **/all** switch will show you the IP configuration of the computer. If the IP address is invalid, communication may fail. If the subnet mask is incorrect, the computer will have an incorrect network ID, and therefore communication may fail, especially to remote subnets. If the default gateway is incorrect or missing, the computer will not be able to communicate with remote subnets. If the DNS server is incorrect or missing, the computer may not be able to resolve names, and communication may fail.

If the computer is set to accept a DHCP server and one does respond, the computer will use automatic private IP addressing, which generates an IP address in the form of 169.254.*xxx.xxx* and the subnet mask of 255.255.0.0. After the computer generates the address, it broadcasts this address until it can find a DHCP server. When you have an automatic private IP address, you can communicate with computers only on the same network/subnet that have an automatic private IP address.

If you can successfully ping the IP address but not the name, name resolution is failing. If you successfully ping the computer name but the response does not resolve the FQDN name, resolution has not used DNS. This means a process such as broadcasts or WINS has been used to resolve the name, and applications that require DNS may fail. A "Request timed out" message indicates that there is a known route to the destination computer but one or more computers or routers along the path, including the source and destination, are not configured correctly. "Destination host unreachable" indicates that the system cannot find a route to the destination system and therefore does not know where to send the packet on the next hop.

Wireless Connections

A quickly advancing field in networking is wireless technology. Today's computers can have a wireless network adapter to connect to other computers or to a wireless access point, which in turn allows the users to connect to the Internet or the rest of the internal network. Today's wireless adapters include PC cards for notebooks, Peripheral Component Interconnect (PCI) cards for desktops, and universal serial bus (USB) devices (which can be used with notebooks or desktops).

Wireless Technology

Wireless adapters can run in one of two operating modes:

- **Ad hoc.** Wireless adapter connects directly to other computers with wireless adapters.
- **Infrastructure.** Wireless adapter connects to an access point (AP).

The most widely used wireless network adapters and APs are based on the Institute of Electrical and Electronics Engineers (IEEE) *802.11* specification, as shown in Table 4.2. Most wireless networks used by companies are 802.11b 802.11g, or 802.11n networks. Wireless devices that are based on this specification can be Wi-Fi Certified to show they have been thoroughly tested for performance and compatibility.

NOTE

Because these devices use common public low-powered wireless frequencies, other wireless devices such as wireless phones or handsets may interfere with wireless adapters if they use the same frequency when they are used at the same time.

TABLE 4.2 Popular Wireless Standards

Wireless Standard	802.11a	802.11b	802.11g	802.11n
Speed	Up to 54 Mbps	Up to 11 Mbps	Up to 54 Mbps	Up to 240 Mbps
Transmission frequency	5 GHz	2.4 GHz	2.4 GHz	2.4 GHz
Effective indoor range	Approximately 25 to 75 feet	Approximately 100 to 150 feet	Approximately 100 to 150 feet	Approximately 300 to 450 feet

TABLE 4.2 *Continued*

Wireless Standard	802.11a	802.11b	802.11g	802.11n
Compatibility	Incompatible with 802.11b and 802.11g.	802.11b wireless devices can interoperate with 802.11g devices (at 11 Mbps); 802.11g wireless adapters can operate with 802.11b APs (at 11 Mbps).	802.11g wireless devices can operate with 802.11b devices (at 11 Mbps).	80.2.11n devices can interoperate with 802.11b and 802.11g devices.

Wireless Security

Because a wireless network signal can be captured by anyone within the range of the antennas, it is easy for someone to intercept the wireless signals that are being broadcast. Therefore, it is always recommended that you use some form of encryption.

The most basic wireless encryption scheme is *Wireless Equivalency Protection (WEP)*. With WEP, you encrypt data using 40-bit, 128-bit, 152-bit, or higher private key encryption. With WEP, all data is encrypted using a symmetric key derived from the WEP key or password before it is transmitted, and any computer that wants to read the data must be able to decrypt it using the key. However, it is easy for someone with a little knowledge or experience to break the shared key because it doesn't change automatically over time. Therefore, it is recommended to use a higher form of wireless encryption than WEP.

Today, it is recommended to use *Wi-Fi Protected Access (WPA)* and *Wi-Fi Protected Access Version 2 (WPA2)*. WPA was adopted by the Wi-Fi Alliance as an interim standard prior to the ratification of 802.11i. WPA2 is based on the official 802.11i standard and is fully backward compatible with WPA.

WPA provides strong data encryption via *Temporal Key Integrity Protocol (TKIP)*, whereas WPA2 provides enhanced data encryption via *Advanced Encryption Standard (AES)*, which meets the Federal Information Processing Standard

(FIPS) 140-2 requirement of some government agencies. To help prevent someone from hacking the key, WPA and WPA2 rotate the keys and change the way keys are derived.

WPA-compatible and WPA2-compatible devices can operate in Personal or Enterprise mode:

- Personal mode provides authentication via a preshared key or password.
- Enterprise mode provides authentication using IEEE 802.1X and Extensible Authentication Protocol (EAP).

In Personal mode, WPA or WPA2 uses a preshared encryption key rather than a changing encryption key. The preshared encryption key is programmed into the AP and all wireless devices, which is used as a starting point to mathematically generate session keys. The session keys are then changed regularly so that the same session key is never used twice. Because the key rotation is automatic, key management is handled in the background.

In Enterprise mode, wireless devices have two sets of keys: session keys and group keys. Session keys are unique to each association between an AP and a wireless client. They are used to create a private virtual port between the AP and the client. Group keys are shared among all clients connected to the same AP. Both sets of keys are generated dynamically and are rotated to help safeguard the integrity of keys over time. The encryption key can be supplied through a certificate or smart card.

Configuring a Wireless Connection

If you click View Status for the wireless connection, you'll see a status dialog box. You can use the Wireless Network Connection Status dialog box to check the status of the connection and to maintain the connection, in much the same way as you can for other types of connections. You'll also see the duration and speed of the connection (see Figure 4.2).

Any wireless AP broadcasting within range should be available to a computer with a wireless adapter. By default, Windows Vista is set to allow you to configure the network settings that should be used. This enables you to configure different authentication, encryption, and communication options as necessary.

FIGURE 4.2 The status of a wireless connection.

If you haven't previously connected to a wireless network, you can create a connection for the network by completing the following steps:

1. Click Start, and then click Network. In Network Explorer, click Network and Sharing Center on the toolbar.
2. In the Network and Sharing Center, click Set Up a Connection or Network. This starts the Set Up a Connection or Network Wizard.
3. Select Manually Connect to a Wireless Network, and then click Next.
4. Enter information about the wireless network to which you want to connect. Your network administrator should have this information.
5. In the Network Name box, enter the network name, also referred to as the network's *service set identifier (SSID)*.
6. Use the Security Type selection list to select the type of security being used. The encryption type is then filled in automatically for you.
7. With WEP and WPA-Personal, you must enter the required security key or password phrase in the Security Key/Passphrase box.
8. By default, the connection is started automatically whenever the user logs on. If you also want the computer to connect to the network regardless of whether it can be reached, such as when the computer is out of

range of the wireless base, select Connect Even if the Network Is Not Broadcasting.

9. Click Next to connect to the wireless network using the settings you've entered.

If you have multiple computers that need to be configured to connect to a wireless network, you can use a USB flash drive to carry the configuration from computer to computer. To save the USB information to a USB drive, follow these steps:

1. Click the Start button, and select the Control Panel.
2. Click Network and Internet, click Network and Sharing Center, and then, in the left pane, click Add a Wireless Device.
3. Follow the steps in the wizard to save your wireless network settings to the USB flash drive.

To add a wireless computer running Windows Vista by using a USB flash drive, follow these steps:

1. Log on to the computer.
2. Plug the USB flash drive into a USB port on the computer.
3. For a computer running Windows Vista, in the AutoPlay dialog box, click Wireless Network Setup Wizard.

You might be prompted to restart the computer. If you're previously connected to a wireless network, you can easily connect to it or disconnect from it by completing the following steps:

1. Click Start, and then click Network. In Network Explorer, click Network and Sharing Center on the toolbar.
2. In the Network and Sharing Center, click Connect to a Network. By default, all available networks are listed by name, status, and signal strength (see Figure 4.3). If a network that should be available isn't listed, try clicking the Refresh button.
3. Moving the cursor over a wireless network entry displays a message box that provides the network name, signal strength, security type, radio type (the wireless standard supported), and the link's security ID.

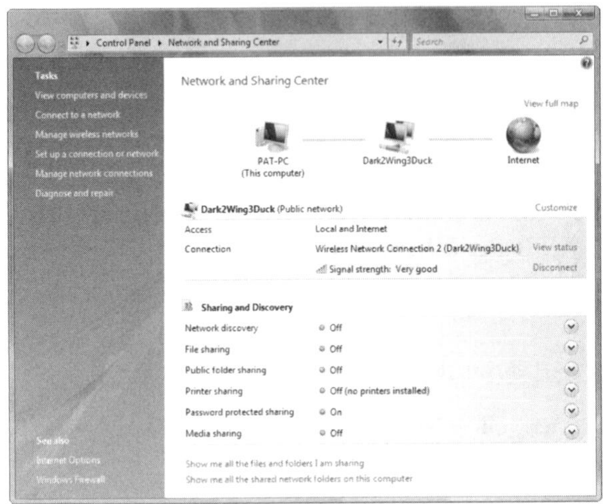

FIGURE 4.3 Network and Sharing Center.

4. You can now connect to or disconnect from wireless networks. To connect to a wireless network, click the network, and then click Connect. To disconnect from a wireless network, click the network, and then click Disconnect. Confirm the action by clicking Disconnect again.

You can manage wireless networks using Manage Wireless Networks. To access Manage Wireless Networks, follow these steps:

1. Click Start, and then click Network. In Network Explorer, click Network and Sharing Center on the toolbar.
2. In the Network and Sharing Center, click Manage Wireless Networks.

Manage Wireless Networks lists wireless networks in the order in which the computer should try to use the available networks. The network listed at the top of the list is tried before any others. If the computer fails to establish a connection over this network, the next network in the list is tried, and so on.

To change the preference order of a network, click it, and then use the Move Up or Move Down buttons to set the order in which the computer should try to use the network. As necessary, click Add to create a new wireless network that will be added to the wireless networks list, or select an existing network and click Remove to delete a listed wireless network.

Remote Access

As a Windows Vista Technology Specialist, you may be expected to support users in remote locations, including at their homes. Remote connections connect individuals or groups to a network from a remote location. Windows Vista supports the following remote connections:

- Dial-up
- Broadband
- Virtual private network (VPN)

Dial-Up Connections

A *dial-up connection* is a nonpermanent point-to-point connection typically using a modem and a phone line to connect to

- A modem pool at an *Internet service provider (ISP)* so that the computer can connect to the Internet.
- A modem pool on an internal network (such as work) to access network resources such as e-mail and data files.

Analog modems use dedicated telephone lines to connect users to the internal network at speeds up to 33.6 kilobits per second (kbps). Digital modems use channels of an ISDN line to connect users to the internal network at speeds up to 56 kbps. Communication is controlled by a remote access server (RAS), which authenticates the login ID and password and authorizes the user to connect to the Internet or internal network.

If you are using a modem, you need to configure dialing rules so that the modem knows how the phone lines are accessed, what the caller's area code is, and what additional features should be used when dialing connections. Sets of dialing rules are saved as dialing locations in the Phone and Modem Options tool.

To view and set the default dialing location, follow these steps:

1. Click Start, and then click Control Panel. In the Control Panel, click Hardware and Sound.
2. In the Hardware and Sound dialog box, click Set Up Dialing Rules under Phone and Modem Options. The first time you start this tool, you'll see the Location Information dialog box.

3. Specify the country/region you are in, the area code (or city code), a number to access an outside line, and whether the phone uses tone dialing or pulse dialing.

After you configure an initial location and click OK, you'll see the Phone and Modem Options dialog box. To create a dial-up Internet connection to an ISP, follow these steps:

1. Click Start, and then click Connect To. Then click Set Up a Connection or Network to start the Connect to a Network Wizard.
2. To make a dial-up connection to an ISP, select Set Up a Dial-Up Connection, and then click Next.
3. Enter the phone number to dial for this connection using the Dial-Up Phone Number text box.
4. Enter the account information, including the username and password.
5. In the Connection Name field, enter the name for the connection, such as Service Provider. Keep in mind that the name should be fewer than 50 characters, but should be descriptive.
6. If you want (although not recommended), you can check the Remember This Password check box.
7. If you want the connection to be available to all users of the computer, select Allow Other People to Use This Connection.
8. Click Create to create the dial-up connection, and then click Close.

Dial-up uses a telephone line to establish connections between two modems. To establish a dial-up connection, follow these steps:

1. Click Start, and then click Connect To. In the Connect to a Network dialog box, click the dial-up connection you want to use, and then click Connect.
2. Confirm that the username is correct, and enter the password for the account if it doesn't already appear.
3. To use the username and password whenever you attempt to establish this connection, select Save This User Name and Password for the Following Users, and then select Me Only. To use the username and password when any user attempts to establish this connection, select Save This User Name and Password for the Following Users, and then select Anyone Who Uses This Computer.

4. The Dial drop-down list shows the number that will be dialed. The primary number is selected by default. To choose an alternate number, click the drop-down list, and then select the number you want to use.
5. Click Dial. When the modem connects to the ISP or office network, you'll see a connection speed. The connection speed is negotiated on a per-call basis and depends on the maximum speed of the calling modem and the modem being called, the compression algorithms available, and the quality of the connection.

Broadband Connections

Today, many connections are *broadband connections*, typically using a cable or Digital Subscriber Line (DSL) connection. Because these connections are always on, you don't need to set up dial-up rules or locations, and you don't have to worry about ISP access numbers. Most broadband providers give users a router or modem, which users need to connect to the service provider. In most scenarios, a network adapter on the user's computer is used to connect to the router or modem. In this configuration, the necessary connection is established over the local area network (LAN) rather than a specific broadband connection. Therefore, it is the local area connection that must be properly configured to gain access to the Internet. You won't need to create a broadband connection.

You can, however, create a specific broadband connection if needed. In some cases, you need to do this to set specific configuration options required by the ISP, such as secure authentication, or you might want to use this technique to set the username and password required by the broadband provider.

Virtual Private Networking

Virtual private networking (VPN) is the creation of secured, point-to-point connections across a private network or a public network such as the Internet. A virtual private networking client uses special TCP/IP-based protocols, called *tunneling protocols*, to make a virtual call to a virtual port on a virtual private networking service. Encryption technology is used to secure the communication channel.

Windows Vista supports VPN tunnels that use Point-to-Point Tunneling Protocol (PPTP) for tunneling and Microsoft Point-to-Point Encryption (MPPE) for encryption. In addition, Windows Vista also supports VPN tunnels that use Layer 2 Tunneling Protocol (L2TP) for tunneling and IP security (IPSec) for encryption. The VPN client authenticates to the remote-access server, at which time they negotiate the tunneling and encryption technologies.

VPNs are used to establish secure communications channels over an existing dial-up or broadband connection. You must know the IP address or FQDN of the remote-access server to which you are connecting. If the necessary connection is available and you know the host information, you can create the connection by following these steps:

1. Click Start, and then click Connect To. Click Set Up a Connection or Network to start the Set Up a Connection or Network Wizard.
2. To make a VPN connection, scroll down, select Connect to a Workplace, and then click Next.
3. Select No, Create a New Connection, and then click Next.
4. The user will need to establish a connection to the Internet—via either dial-up or broadband—before attempting to use the VPN. Therefore, click Use My Internet Connection (VPN). On the Before You Connect page, select the previously created connection to use, and then click Next. This connection can be a dial-up or broadband connection.
5. Enter the IP address or FQDN of the computer to which you are connecting, such as 131.5.27.14 or www.external.acme.com. In most cases, this is the remote-access server you've configured for the office network.
6. Enter a name for the connection in the Destination Name field.
7. If the computer is configured to use a smart card for authentication, select Use a Smart Card.
8. If you want the connection to be available to all users of the computer, select Allow Other People to Use This Connection. This option is best when you plan to assign the connection through Group Policy and have not provided user logon information. Click Next.
9. A user is prompted by default for her name and password when she makes a connection. If you're creating a connection for an individual user and don't want the user to be prompted for logon information, you can enter the username and password in the fields provided.
10. If you want to ensure that password will be remembered, you can select Remember This Password. If you don't select Remember This Password, the user is prompted for the password.
11. Specify the logon domain in the Domain field, and then click Connect. Of course, to connect to a VPN connection, you must first be connected to the dial-up or broadband connection specified previously.

Exam Prep Questions

1. What command would you use to renew DHCP IPv4 addresses?

   ❍ **A. ipconfig**

   ❍ **B. ipconfig /renew**

   ❍ **C. ipconfig /renew6**

   ❍ **D. ipconfig /release_and_renew**

   ❍ **E. ipconfig /registerdns**

2. What command would you use to flush the DNS cache stored on an individual Windows Vista machine?

   ❍ **A. ipconfig**

   ❍ **B. ipconfig /renew**

   ❍ **C. ipconfig /renew6**

   ❍ **D. ipconfig /registerdns**

   ❍ **E. ipconfig /flushdns**

3. What command can be used to show network connectivity to a computer?

   ❍ **A. ipconfig**

   ❍ **B. arp**

   ❍ **C. ping**

   ❍ **D. traceroute**

4. If you want to show IP addresses and their corresponding MAC addresses, what command would you use?

   ❍ **A. ipconfig**

   ❍ **B. ipconfig /all**

   ❍ **C. arp**

   ❍ **D. ping**

   ❍ **E. tracert**

5. You are trying to figure out why a computer cannot connect to a file server. You type in **ipconfig /all**, and you get the following output:

```
C:\Users\User>ipconfig
Windows IP Configuration
Ethernet adapter Local Area Connection:
  Connection-specific DNS Suffix . : acme.com.
  Link-local IPv6 Address . . . . . : fe80::35d3:1958:365b:380a%13
  IPv4 Address. . . . . . . . . . . : 169.254.3.103
  Subnet Mask . . . . . . . . . . . : 255.255.0.0
  Default Gateway . . . . . . . . . :
```

What is the problem?

- ❍ **A.** The computer cannot connect to the DHCP server to get an address.
- ❍ **B.** The server was not assigned a default gateway.
- ❍ **C.** The subnet mask is wrong.
- ❍ **D.** You cannot determine the problem from this screen shot.

6. You can ping a PC using an address but not by name. What is the problem?

- ❍ **A.** You are not in the same subnet as the computer.
- ❍ **B.** A firewall is blocking access to the computer by name.
- ❍ **C.** You need to start the DHCP client service on your PC.
- ❍ **D.** You have a DNS name-resolution problem.

7. You have a laptop with an 802.11a wireless network card. When you boot the Windows Vista machine and you double-checked the SSID, you cannot connect to your company's wireless network. What is the problem?

- ❍ **A.** Your company is most likely using an 802.11b or 802.11g wireless network, which 802.11a is incompatible with.
- ❍ **B.** The 802.11a network card is too slow, which is preventing a connection.
- ❍ **C.** You need to change the SSID because it expired.
- ❍ **D.** You need to assign an IP address to the wireless card.

8. You work as the desktop support technician at Acme.com. Your company just purchased 20 new laptops with wireless adapters. You have to configure each computer with the least amount of administrative effort. What should you do?

❍ **A.** Manually configure each computer's wireless adapters.

❍ **B.** Save the wireless network settings to a USB device and apply it to each computer.

❍ **C.** Copy the wireless network settings to a shared folder and access the configuration from the share folder on each laptop.

❍ **D.** Copy the wireless network settings to the hard disk of each of the new computers.

9. You work as the desktop support technician at Acme.com. You want to assign an address to a computer that will be available on the Internet and will have the same address for both IPv4 and IPv6. What kind of address is this?

❍ **A.** A unique private address

❍ **B.** A multicast local address

❍ **C.** A site-local address

❍ **D.** A global unicast address

10. You work as the desktop support technician at Acme.com. You have a user who works between the Sacramento and New York offices. She currently has a static IP address assigned to her computer. When she is at the Sacramento office, her system has no problem connecting to the network. When she travels to New York, her system cannot connect to the network. What is the problem?

❍ **A.** You need to update the drivers for the network card.

❍ **B.** You need to assign a public IPv4 address.

❍ **C.** You need to run the Troubleshooting Wizard.

❍ **D.** Within the TCP/IPv4 Properties dialog box, you need to select the Obtain an IP Address Automatically option.

11. You work as the network administrator at Acme.com. Your company just purchased 20 new laptop computers, which are going to connect to the new wireless network. You want the computers to connect to the network using the Temporal Key Integrity Protocol (TKIP) without requiring the use of any security key or passphrase. Which option would you select in the Wireless Network dialog box?

❍ **A.** The WEP option

❍ **B.** The WPA-Personal option

❍ **C.** The WPA2-Personal option

❍ **D.** WPA-Enterprise option

❍ **E.** WPA2-Enterprise option

12. You are a desktop support technician for Acme.com. You are configuring several new laptops with Microsoft Windows Vista Enterprise. You need to configure a connection so that the users can connect to the Acme.com internal network while working from home. How can you set this up?

❍ **A.** Open the Network and Sharing Center in the Control Panel. Click Set Up Connection or Network from the Tasks list. Choose Connect to a Workplace under the Choose a Connection option. Choose VPN under How Do You Want to Connect. Enter the Internet address of the server to which you want to connect.

❍ **B.** Click Manage Network Connections from the Start menu. Click Set Up Connection or Network from the Tasks list. Choose Connect to a Workplace under the Choose a Connection option. Choose Dial-Up Connection under How Do You Want to Connect. Enter the Internet address of the server to which you want to connect.

❍ **C.** Open the network connection's interface. Click Set Up Connection or Network from the Tasks list. Choose Connect to a Workplace under the Choose a Connection option. Enter the Internet address of the server to which you want to connect.

❍ **D.** Open the Network and Sharing Center in the Control Panel. Click Set Up Connection or Network from the Tasks list. Choose Connect to a Workplace under the Choose a Connection option. Choose VPN under How Do You Want to Connect. Enter the Internet address of the server to which you want to connect.

Answers to Exam Prep Questions

1. **Answer B is correct**. To renew IPv4, you have to use the **ipconfig /renew** command. Answer A is incorrect because the **ipconfig** command without any options will only display basic IP configuration information. Answer C is incorrect because the **/renew6** option will renew IPv6 IP addresses. Answer D is incorrect because the **/release_and_renew** option does not exist. Answer E is incorrect because the **/registerdns** option is how to get the computer to register itself with the DNS server.

2. **Answer E is correct**. To flush local cached DNS information, you use the **ipconfig /flushdns** command. Answer A is incorrect because the **ipconfig** command without any options will only display basic IP configuration information. Answer B is incorrect because the **/renew** option will renew the IPv4 IP addresses. Answer C is incorrect because the **/renew6** option will renew IPv6 IP addresses. Answer D is incorrect because the **/registerdns** option is how to get the computer to register itself with the DNS server.

3. **Answer C is correct**. The two commands that will show network connectivity to another computer are the **ping** command and the **tracert** command. Answer A is incorrect because the **ipconfig** command without any options will only display basic IP configuration information. Answer B is incorrect because the **arp** command is used to view and manage IP address-to-MAC address mappings. The **traceroute** command would be found on UNIX and Linux machines. Windows machines use **tracert**.

4. **Answer B is correct**. To show all IP configuration information, you must use the **ipconfig /all** command. Answer A is incorrect because the **ipconfig** command without any options will only display basic IP configuration information. Answer C is incorrect because the **arp** command is used to view and manage IP address-to-MAC address mappings. Answer D and E are commands used to test network connectivity.

5. **Answer A is correct**. According to this output, the address assigned to the computer is 169.254.3.103, which is an automatic private IP address. Automatic private IP addresses are assigned to Windows computers when they cannot find a DHCP server to get an address from. Automatic private IP addresses begin with 169.254. Answer B is incorrect because although a gateway address might be needed to communicate with computers on another network, the gateway was not assigned because it could not find a DHCP server. Answer C is incorrect because the subnet mask was assigned because it could not find a DHCP server. Answer D is incorrect because the problem does not describe any kind of name-resolution problem.

6. **Answer D is correct**. If you have a name resolution, the problem has to be with a DNS or WINS server, or you have incorrect entries in your HOSTS or LMHOST files. Answer A is incorrect because if you can ping it by address, you have network connectivity to the server. So, it does not matter whether the server is on the same subnet or a different subnet. Answer B is incorrect because you cannot block access to a computer by name but keep access by address. Answer C is incorrect because if the DHCP client service was not on, you would not be able to get any address from a DHCP server and not able to connect to the network.

7. **Answer A is correct**. In corporations, most networks use 802.11b or 802.11a networks. Because 802.11a is not compatible with 802.11b/g, it is most likely the problem. Answer B is incorrect because 802.11b and 802.11g can operate at lower speeds. Answer C is incorrect because although having the wrong SSID will cause problems, the SSID does not expire. Answer D is incorrect because most networks will have DHCP service to assign IP addresses.

8. **Answer B is correct**. You can save the information to a USB device and then use that device to copy the configuration to each computer. Answer A is incorrect because although this would work, it would require a lot more administrative effort. Answer C is incorrect because these computers do not have wired network cards to connect to a shared drive. Answer D is incorrect because copying the network settings would also require a lot more administrative effort.

9. **Answer D is correct**. If you want an address to be available from the Internet and be the same address for both IPv4 and IPv6, it must have a global address that can be seen on the Internet. Answer A is incorrect because private addresses cannot be used on the public network such as the Internet. Answer B is incorrect because it has to be a single address assigned to a single computer, not a multicast that is used to broadcast to multiple addresses at the same time. Answer C is incorrect because a local address cannot be seen on the outside.

10. **Answer D is correct**. Because this person is traveling between two sites, the user needs to have a local address on each site. Therefore, you should let the local DHCP server hand out the addresses when she connects to each network. Answer A is incorrect because she can connect to one network. Therefore, the driver is working fine. Answer B is incorrect because this means that you are putting this computer directly on the Internet. Answer C is incorrect because running a Troubleshooting Wizard could be a lengthy process (when the solution is, in fact, simple).

11. **Answer D is correct**. WPA uses Temporal Key Integrity Protocol (TKIP), and Enterprise does not require a security key or passphrase. Instead, a certificate or similar technology is used to provide the initial key. Answer A is incorrect because WEP does not use TKIP and requires a key to be supplied. Answer B is incorrect because Personal means that you have to enter a security key or passphrase. Answers C and E are incorrect because they use AES rather than TKIP.

12. **Answer A is correct**. To connect to the office over the Internet, you need to set up a VPN connection. The correct order to set up a VPN connection is as follows:

    1. Click Set Up a Connection or Network from the Tasks list. This is the option that enables you to create new connections, such as dial-up, wireless, or VPN connections.

    2. Under the Choose a Connection option, choose Connect to a Workplace. This is the section that allows for VPN connections to be set up. The other options, such as Set Up a Dial-Up Connection, will not allow you to connect to an office over the Internet.

3. Under How Do You Want to Connect, choose VPN. A VPN connection will allow you to tunnel over the Internet to a VPN server in at the office.
4. Enter the Internet address of the server to which you want to connect. To connect to a VPN server, you need to provide a name and IP address for the connection.

Answer B is incorrect because you do not click Manage Network Connections from the Start menu. Answer C is incorrect because to set up a VPN, you do not open a network connection's interface. Answer D is incorrect because you do not choose VPN; instead, you choose Connect to a Workplace.

Recommended Readings and Resources

Mitch Tulloch, Tony Northrup, Jerry Honeycutt, Ed Wilson, Ralph Ramos, and the Windows Vista Team, *Windows Vista Resource Kit (Pro - Resource Kit)* (Redmond, Washington: Microsoft Press, 2007).

William R. Stanek, *Introducing Microsoft Windows Vista* (Redmond, Washington: Microsoft Press, 2006).

Patrick Regan, *Working with Windows 2000 and 2003* (Upper Saddle River, New Jersey: Prentice Hall, 2004).

Patrick Regan, *Wide Area Networks* (Upper Saddle River, New Jersey: Prentice Hall, 2004).

3Com, "Understanding IP Addressing: Everything You Ever Wanted to Know," white paper located at http://www.3com.com/other/pdfs/infra/corpinfo/en_US/501302.pdf.

CHAPTER FIVE

NTFS Security Features and File Sharing

Terms you'll need to understand:

- ✓ File system
- ✓ NT File System (NTFS)
- ✓ File Allocation Table (FAT)
- ✓ FAT32
- ✓ Access control list (ACL)
- ✓ Access control entry (ACE)
- ✓ Permission
- ✓ Explicit permission
- ✓ Inherited permission
- ✓ Shared folder
- ✓ Server message block (SMB)
- ✓ Universal Naming Convention (UNC)
- ✓ Link Layer Topology Discovery (LLTD)
- ✓ Public folder sharing
- ✓ Standard file sharing
- ✓ Encryption
- ✓ Encrypting File System (EFS)
- ✓ BitLocker Drive Encryption
- ✓ Trusted Platform Module (TPM)
- ✓ Compression

Techniques/concepts you'll need to master:

- ✓ List the advantages of NTFS over FAT or FAT32.
- ✓ List and describe the NTFS file permissions.
- ✓ Using Windows Explorer, configure NTFS permissions.
- ✓ List and describe the share permissions.
- ✓ Using Windows Explorer, share a folder.
- ✓ Using Windows Explorer, encrypt a file using EFS.
- ✓ Encrypt a drive with BitLocker Drive Encryption.
- ✓ Using Windows Explorer, compress a folder.

Now that you have installed Windows and configured it to communicate on the network, you are now ready to look at some of the services and features that Windows Vista offers. The primary file system used in Windows Vista is *NT File System (NTFS)*, which offers a secure and reliable environment to store files. After you have placed your files in a secure environment, you can then share those files so that they can be available over the network. This chapter focuses on sharing files so that users can access files from a Windows Vista computer directly or over the network, and it explains how to control such access so that the folders remain secure using share permissions, NTFS permissions, and encryption.

File Systems

The disk structure does not describe how a hard drive or floppy disk physically works, but how it stores files on the disk. In other words, it describes the formatting of the disk (file system, partitions, the root directory, and the directories). A *file system* is the overall structure in which files are named, stored, and organized. File systems used in Windows Vista include FAT, FAT32, and NTFS. Whereas FAT and FAT32 were primarily used in older operating systems, NTFS is the preferred file system.

An older file system used by DOS was the *File Allocation Table (FAT)*. FAT is a simple file system that uses minimum memory. Although it is based on filenames of 11 characters, which include the 8 characters for the filename and 3 characters for the file extension, it has been expanded to support long filenames. Early DOS used FAT12, which used a 12-bit number for each cluster, but was later expanded to FAT16, which would recognize volumes up to 2 GB.

FAT32, which was introduced in the second major release of Windows 95, is an enhancement to the FAT file system. It uses 32-bit FAT entries, which support hard drives up to 2 TB, although Windows 2000, Windows XP, Windows Vista, and Windows Server 2003 support volumes up to 32 GB. FAT32 does not have the security that NTFS provides; so, if you have a FAT32 partition or volume on your computer, any user who has access to your computer can read any file on it. The main reason to use FAT32 is because you have a computer that will sometimes run Windows 95, Windows 98, or Windows Millennium edition and at other times run this version of Windows, known as a multiboot configuration.

NTFS is the preferred file system for this version of Windows. It has many benefits over the earlier FAT32 file system, including the following:

- Improved support for much larger hard disks.
- Because NTFS is a journaling file system that keeps track of its transactions to make sure that that entire transaction is completed before being recognized, it can recover from some disk-related errors automatically.
- Better security because you can use permissions and encryption to restrict access to specific files to approved users.

NTFS File Permissions

A primary advantage of NTFS over FAT and FAT32 is that NTFS volumes have the capability to apply NTFS permissions to secure folders and files. By setting the permissions, you specify the level of access for groups and users for accessing files or directories. For example, to one user or group of users, you can specify that they can only read the file; another user or group of users can read and write to the file; and others have no access. No matter if you are logged on locally at the computer or accessing a computer through a network, NTFS permissions always apply.

The NTFS permissions that are granted are stored in an *access control list (ACL)* with every file or folder on an NTFS volume. The ACL contains an *access control entry (ACE)* for each user account and group that has been granted access for the file or folder and the permissions granted to each user and group. To simplify the task of administration, the NTFS permissions have been logically grouped into the standard folder and file NTFS permissions as shown in Table 5.1. If you need finer control, you need to use special permissions.

NOTE

Remember that when you manage your folders and files and when you open up a drive or folder, you are using Windows Explorer.

TABLE 5.1 Standard NTFS Folder and File Permissions

Permission Level	Description
Full control	Users can read files and folders; execute files; write, modify, and delete files; change attributes of files and folders; change permissions; and take ownership of files.
Modify	Users can read files and folders, execute files, write and modify files, delete files and folders, and change attributes of files and folders.
List folder contents	Users can view the names of folders and subfolders in the folder. This permission is available only at the folder level and is not available at the file level.
Read and execute	Users can see the contents of existing files and folders and can run programs in a folder.
Read	Users can see the contents of a folder and open files and folders.
Write	Users can create new files and folders and make changes to existing files and folders. Users cannot create new files or folders.

To set, view, change, or remove permissions on files and folders, follow these steps:

1. Right-click the file or folder for which you want to set permissions and click Properties.
2. Click the Security tab to display the Data Properties dialog box shown in Figure 5.1.
3. Click Edit to open the Permissions for *name of file or folder* dialog box.

Then do one of the following:

- To set permissions for a group or user that does not appear in the Group or User Names box, click Add. Enter the name of the group or user you want to set permissions for, and then click OK.
- To change or remove permissions from an existing group or user, click the name of the group or user. To allow or deny a permission, in the Permissions for *User or Group* box, select the Allow or Deny check box. To remove the group or user from the *User or Group* box, click Remove.

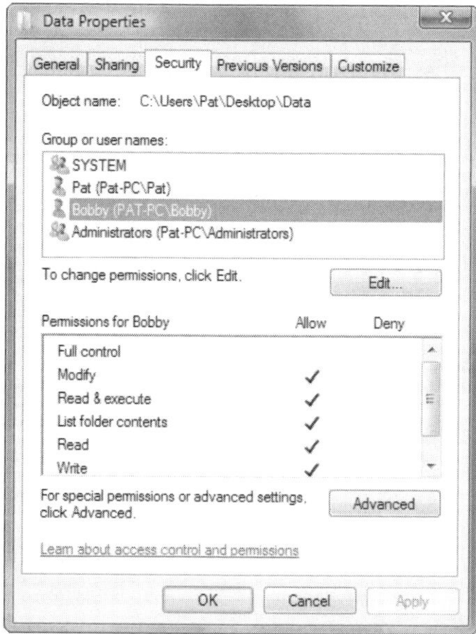

FIGURE 5.1 You can use the Properties dialog box to configure NTFS permissions.

Permissions are given to a folder or file as either *explicit permissions* or *inherited permissions*. Explicit permissions are those granted directly to the folder or file. Some of these permissions are granted automatically, such as when a file or folder is created, whereas others have to be assigned manually.

Windows offers the ability to deny individual permissions. The Deny permission always overrides the permissions that have been granted, including when a user or group has been given full control. For example, if the group has been granted read and write, yet a person has been denied the write permission, the user's effective rights would be the read permission.

When you set permissions to a folder (explicit permission), the files and subfolders in the folder inherit these permissions (inherited permissions). In other words, the permissions flow down from the folder into the subfolders and files, indirectly giving permissions to a user or group. Inherited permissions ease the task of managing permissions and ensure consistency of permissions among the subfolders and files within the folder.

Because users can be members of several groups, it is possible for them to have several sets of explicit permissions to a folder or file. When this occurs, the permissions are combined to form the effective permissions, which are the actual permissions when logging on and accessing a file or folder. They consist of explicit permissions plus any inherited permissions.

When you are managing NTFS permissions, remember the following:

- You can set only file and folder permissions on drives formatted to use NTFS.
- Performing this procedure might require you to elevate permissions through the User Account Control. Chapter 6, "Configuring User Account Security," covers the User Account Control.
- To change permissions, you must be the owner or have been granted permission to do so by the owner.
- Groups or users that are granted full control for a folder can delete files and subfolders within that folder, regardless of the permissions that protect the files and subfolders.
- If the check boxes under Permissions for *User or Group* are shaded or if the Remove button is unavailable, the file or folder has inherited permissions from the parent folder.
- When adding a new user or group, by default, this user or group will have read and execute, list folder contents, and read permissions.

Sharing Files and Folders

A *shared folder* on a computer makes the folder available for others to use on the network. A shared drive on a computer makes the entire drive available for others to use on the network. Shared drives and folders can be used on FAT/FAT32 and NTFS volumes. If used on an NTFS volume, the user will still need NTFS permissions before accessing the share.

When you share a folder with Microsoft Windows, file sharing is based on the network basic input/output system (NetBIOS) protocol and *server message block (SMB)*. NetBIOS, which runs on top of TCP/IP, was created for IBM for its early PC networks, but it was adopted by Microsoft and has since become a de facto industry standard. It is responsible for establishing logical names (computer names) on the network, establishing a logical connection between the two computers, and supporting reliable data transfer between computers that established a session.

After a logical connection is established, computers can exchange data in the form of NetBIOS requests or in the form of SMBs. The SMB protocol, which was jointly developed by Microsoft, Intel, and IBM, allows shared access to files, printers, serial ports, and miscellaneous communications between nodes on a network.

SMB 2.0, introduced with Windows Vista, can compound multiple actions into a single request, which significantly reduces the number of round trips the client needs to make to the server, improving performance as a result. Larger buffer sizes are supported, also increasing performance with large file transfers. In addition, durable file handles were introduced, which allow a connection to an SMB server to survive brief network outages, such as with a wireless network, without having to construct a new session.

When using the SMB protocol to share a directory or drive, these resources are accessed using the *Uniform Naming Convention (UNC)*:

*servername**sharedname*

The *servername* could be a NetBIOS name (computer name) or an IP address.

Network Discovery and Browsing

With earlier versions of Windows, you could use Network Neighborhood to browse network resources such as shared folders and printers. However, this system was inefficient because it relied on network broadcasts to gather such information.

To fix this problem, Windows Vista introduced *Link Layer Topology Discovery (LLTD)*, which queries each device that supports Plug and Play Extensions (PnP-X) or web services for devices to determine its capabilities and to determine the topology of the network. It also uses version control to keep the information current. It also describes the quality of service (QoS) extensions that enable stream prioritization and quality media streaming experiences, even on networks with limited bandwidth.

The information that is gathered to create the network map and which information the computer will give out to other Windows Vista computers will depend on which network services that you have enabled or configured using the Network and Sharing Center (see Table 5.2 and Figure 5.2).

TABLE 5.2 Network Services Managed with the Network and Sharing Center

Feature	Settings	Result
Network Discovery. Allows this computer to see other network computers and devices and is visible to other network computers.	On	Turns on Network Discovery.
	Off	Turns off Network Discovery.
File sharing. Files and printers that you have shared from this computer can be accessed by people on the network.	On	Shares created on this computer can be accessed from the network.
	Off	Shares created on this computer cannot be accessed from the network.
Public folder sharing. People on the network can access files in the public folder.	Off	Only local users can access the Public folder.
	On (read)	Local and network users can read the contents of the Public folder, but cannot change them.
	On (change)	Local and network users can change the contents of the Public folder.
Printer sharing. Allows users to access shared printers.	On	Printers directly connected to this computer can be shared.
	Off	Printers directly connected to this computer cannot be shared.
Password-protected sharing. Gives access to shared folders, including the Public folder, to users who don't have a username and password that corresponds to a user account on the computer with the shared folder.	On (recommended)	People who access shared folders must have corresponding local user account and password.
	Off	Computer sharing the folder does not require a user account or password.

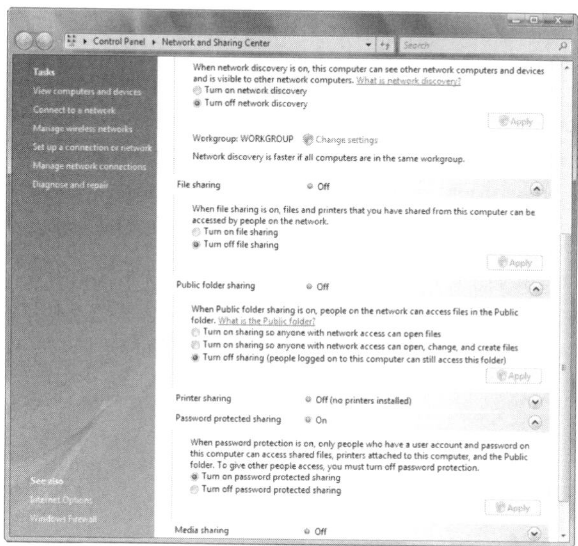

FIGURE 5.2 Managing network services with the Network and Sharing Center.

To view the topology or to view the network resources, you open a network folder or the Network and Sharing Center. However, a Windows Vista computer will not be visible on the network map, and it will not be able to map other hardware devices on the network until you enable Network Discovery service. To see the full map, click the View Full Map link in the Network and Sharing Center (see Figure 5.3).

EXAM ALERT

LLTD is installed by default, but it will only function if you enable Network Discovery.

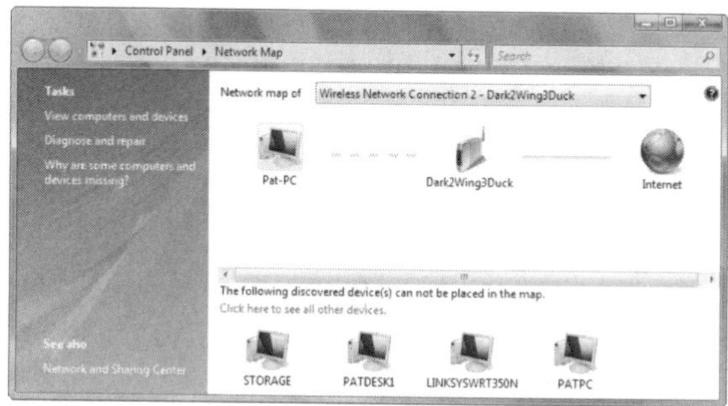

FIGURE 5.3 A sample of a network map.

Public Folder

Windows Vista supports two ways to share folders: *public file sharing* and *standard file sharing*. Of these two models, standard file sharing is preferred because it is more secure than public file sharing. However, public folder sharing is designed to enable users to share files and folders from a single location quickly and easily.

Windows Vista supports the use of only one Public folder for each computer. Any files that you want to make available publicly can be copied or moved to an appropriate folder inside the Public folder. The Public folder is located at C:\Users\Public and contains the following subfolders:

- Public Documents
- Public Downloads
- Public Music
- Public Pictures
- Public Videos
- Recorded TV

Another folder worth mentioning is the Public Desktop folder, which is used for shared desktop items. Any files and program shortcuts placed in the Public Desktop folder appear on the desktop of all users who log on to the computer (and to all network users if network access has been granted to the Public folder).

To access public folders using Windows Explorer, follow these steps:

1. Click the Start button, and then click Computer.
2. In Windows Explorer, click the leftmost option button in the address list and then click Public.

Public folder sharing settings are set on a per-computer basis. If you want to share a file, you just need to copy or move the file into the C:\Users\Public folder. When the file is copied or moved to the Public folder, access permissions are changed to match that of the Public folder so that all users who log on to the computer and all network users (if network access has been granted to the Public folder) can access the file.

By default, files stored in the Public folder hierarchy are available to all users who have an account on this computer and can log on to it locally. You cannot access the Public folder from the network. To enable and configure public folder sharing, follow these steps:

1. Click Start, and then click Computer. In Windows Explorer, click the leftmost option button in the address list, and then click Public.
2. On the Windows Explorer toolbar, click Sharing Settings.
3. Open the Network and Sharing Center.
4. Expand the Public Folder Sharing Panel by clicking the Expand button.
5. Under Public Folder Sharing, select the public folder sharing option you want to use. The options available are as follows:
    - Turn On Sharing So Anyone with Network Access Can Open Files
    - Turn On Sharing So Anyone with Network Access Can Open, Change, and Create Files
    - Turn Off Sharing

    Permissions are shown in Table 5.3.
6. Click Apply to save the changes.

NOTE

Windows Firewall settings might prevent external access.

TABLE 5.3 Share and NTFS Permissions for the Public Folder

Access Type	Share Permission	NTFS Permissions
Open files	Read	Read and execute, list folder contents, read
Open, change, and create files	Full control	All (full control, modify, read and execute, list folder contents, read/write)

Standard Sharing

Creating and managing a shared folder is a little bit more of a manual process than the public sharing model, but allows you to share any folder on the Windows Vista computer, and it gives you more fine-tuned control over sharing the folders.

Standard file sharing enables you to use a standard set of permissions to allow or deny initial access to files and folders over the network. Standard file sharing settings are enabled or disabled on a per-computer basis. To enable file sharing, follow these steps:

1. Click Start, and then click Network.
2. On the Explorer toolbar, click Network and Sharing Center.
3. Expand the File Sharing Panel by clicking the related Expand button.
4. To enable file sharing, select Turn On File Sharing. To disable file sharing, select Turn Off File Sharing.
5. Click Apply.

When a user accesses a file or folder in a share over the network, the two levels of permissions are used: share permissions and NTFS permissions (if it is on an NTFS volume). The three share permissions are as follows:

- **Owner/co-owner.** Users allowed this permission have read and change permissions and the additional capabilities to change file and folder permissions and take ownership of files and folders. If you have owner/co-owner permissions on a shared resource, you have full access to the shared resource.
- **Contributor.** Users allowed this permission have read permissions and the additional capability to create files and subfolders, modify files, change attributes on files and subfolders, and delete files and subfolders. If you have contributor permissions on a shared resource, the most you can do is perform read operations and change operations.
- **Reader.** Users with this permission can view file and subfolder names, access the subfolders of the share, read file data and attributes, and run program files. If you have reader permissions on a shared resource, the most you can do is perform read operations.

NOTE

If the user accesses the computer directly where the share folder is located and accesses the folder directly without going through the share, share permissions do not apply.

Because a user can be member of several groups, it is possible for the user to have several sets of permissions to a shared drive or folder. The effective permissions are the combination of all user and group permissions. For example, if a user has the contributor permissions to the user and a reader permission to the group, of which the user is a member, the effective permissions would be the contributor permission. Like NTFS permissions, deny permissions override the granted permission.

To create a shared folder using the shared folder model, you have to complete a multipart process:

1. Share the folder so that it can be accessed.
2. Set the share permissions.
3. Check and modify the NTFS file system permissions.

There are two methods to set permissions on a shared resource, depending on the resource type:

- **Using the File Sharing Wizard to set permissions of a file or folder.** You can start the File Sharing Wizard by right-clicking the file or folder, and then clicking Share. The wizard enables you to select the user and group that can share the file or folder, and allows you to set permissions on the file or folder for each user or group.
- **Using Windows Explorer to set permissions on a resource.** You can use Windows Explorer to set permissions through the Share option or through the Properties page on a resource. When you right-click the object, selecting the Share or Properties option displays the Properties dialog box. Permissions can be set or modified by using the Advanced Sharing button on the Sharing tab.

When a folder is shared, a symbol of two users is added at the bottom left of the folder icon (see Figure 5.4). If you click Show Me All the Files and Folders I Am Sharing in Network and Sharing Center, you can view all shared folders on the system (see Figure 5.5).

When accessing a shared folder on an NTFS volume, the effective permissions that a person can use in the share folder are calculated by combining the shared folder permissions with the NTFS permissions. When combining the two, first determine the cumulative NTFS permissions and the cumulative shared permissions and apply the more restrictive permissions, the one that gives the least permission.

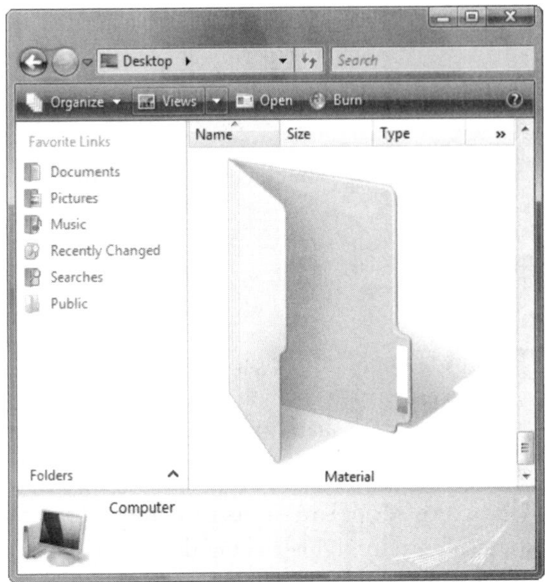

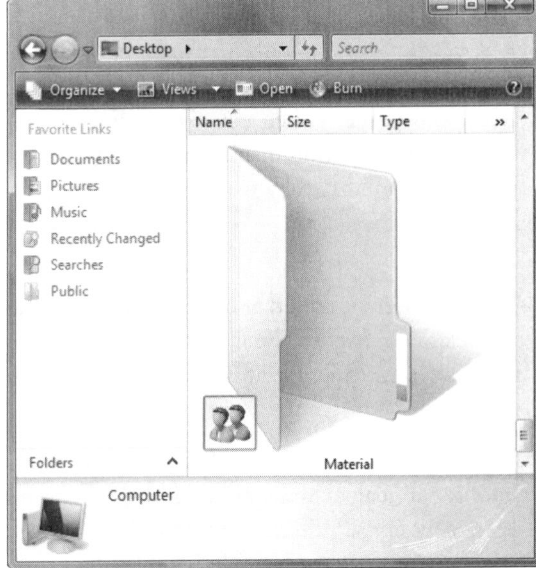

FIGURE 5.4 A nonshared and shared folder.

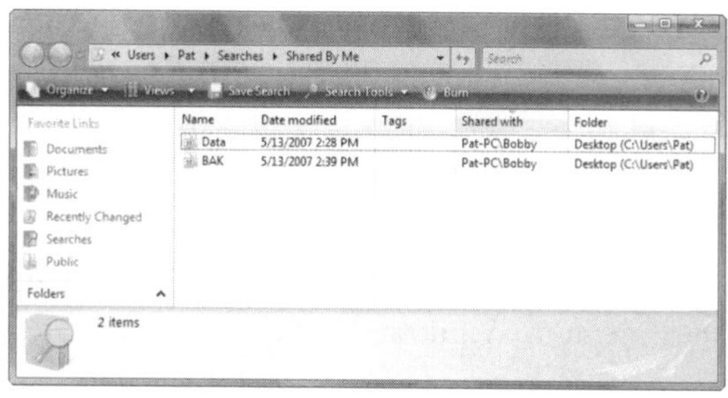

FIGURE 5.5 Using the Show Me All the Files and Folders I Am Sharing option in the Network and Sharing Center.

Accessing a Shared Folder

After you share a file or folder, users can connect to it as a network resource or map to it by using a driver letter on their machines. After a network drive has been mapped, users can access it just as they would a local drive on their computer.

To map a network drive to a shared file or folder, follow these steps:

1. Click Start, and then click Computer.
2. In Windows Explorer, click the Map Network Drive button on the toolbar. This displays the Map Network Drive dialog box.
3. Use the Drive field to select a free drive letter to use, and then click the Browse button to the right of the Folder field.
4. In the Browse for Folder dialog box, expand the Network folders until you can select the name of the workgroup or the domain with which you want to work. When you expand the name of a computer in a workgroup or a domain, you'll see a list of shared folders. Select the shared folder you want to work with, and then click OK.
5. Select Reconnect at Logon if you want Windows Vista to connect to the shared folder automatically at the start of each session.
6. If your current logon doesn't have appropriate access permissions for the share, click the Different User Name link. You can then enter the username and password of the account with which you want to connect to the shared folder. Typically, this feature is used by administrators who log on to their computers with a limited account and also have an administrator account for managing the network.
7. Click Finish.

If you later decide you don't want to map the network drive, click Start, and then click Computer. In Windows Explorer, under Network Location, right-click the network drive icon and choose Disconnect.

You can also type in a UNC in the Run box or the address bar in Windows Explorer. To display the Run box quickly, use the Windows logo key + R shortcut. If you don't have a Windows logo key or if you prefer to use the mouse, you can add the Run option to the Start menu in Windows Vista, as follows:

1. Right-click the Start button and choose Properties.
2. On the Start Menu tab, click the Customize button to the right of the Start Menu option.
3. In the Customize Start Menu dialog box, scroll down and place a check mark next to the Run option.
4. Click OK to save your changes.

File Encryption

If someone has administrative privilege on a Windows Vista computer or has unauthorized physical access to the device, including if the computer/hard drive was stolen, that person can take ownership of files and folder, change permissions of a file, and access the file. Data can be secured against these risks by using encryption.

Encryption is the process of converting data into a format that cannot be read by another user. After a user has encrypted a file, it automatically remains encrypted when the file is stored on disk. Decryption is the process of converting data from encrypted format back to its original format. After a user has decrypted a file, the file remains decrypted when stored on disk.

Windows Vista offers two file encrypting technologies: *Encrypting File System (EFS)* and *BitLocker Drive Encryption*. EFS is used to help protect individual files on any drive on a per-user basis. BitLocker is designed to help protect all the personal and systems files on the drive Windows is installed on if your computer is stolen, or if unauthorized users try to access the computer. You can use BitLocker Drive Encryption and EFS together to get the protection offered by both features. Table 5.4 shows the main differences between BitLocker Drive Encryption and EFS.

TABLE 5.4 A Comparison Between EFS and BitLocker Drive Encryption

Encrypting File System (EFS)	BitLocker Drive Encryption
EFS encrypts individual files on any drive.	BitLocker encrypts all personal and system files on the drive where Windows is installed.
EFS encrypts files based on the user account associated with it. If a computer has multiple users or groups, each can encrypt their own files independently.	BitLocker does not depend on the individual user accounts associated with files. BitLocker is either on or off, for all users or groups.
EFS does not require or use any special hardware.	BitLocker uses the Trusted Platform Module (TPM), a special microchip in some newer computers that supports advanced security features.
You do not have to be an administrator to use EFS.	You must be an administrator to turn BitLocker encryption on or off after it has been enabled.

Encryption File System

Windows Vista includes EFS, which allows a user to encrypt and decrypt files that are stored on an NTFS volume. When you use EFS, folders and files are still kept secure against those intruders who might gain unauthorized physical access to the device (for example, as by stealing a notebook computer or a removable drive).

EFS is used to encrypt data in files and folders with a key. This key is stored in protected storage as part of your user profile, and it provides transparent access to the encrypted data.

Several improvements have been made to EFS in Windows Vista. Smart cards are now supported for storing user EFS keys in addition to administrative recovery keys. If you use smart cards for logon, EFS can operate as a single sign-on service that gives transparent access to your encrypted files. The System Page file can also be protected by EFS when you configure it by using Group Policy.

When you are using encrypted files on a network, client-side cached copies of network files can also be encrypted, providing security for these files even if the portable computer is lost or stolen. When you use Windows Vista in conjunction with a supported server platform, encrypted files can be transmitted over the network, and the receiving Windows Vista client will decrypt them.

NOTE

EFS is available only in the Windows Vista Business, Enterprise, and Ultimate versions. EFS is not fully supported on Windows Vista Starter, Windows Vista Home Basic, and Windows Vista Home Premium.

To encrypt a folder or file, follow these steps:

1. Right-click the folder or file you want to encrypt, and then click Properties.
2. Click the General tab, and then click Advanced.
3. Select the Encrypt Contents to Secure Data check box, and then click OK.

After you encrypt the file, encrypted files are colored green in Windows Explorer.

NOTE

You cannot encrypt files or folders that are compressed.

To decrypt a folder or file, follow these steps:

1. Right-click the folder or file you want to decrypt, and then click Properties.
2. Click the General tab, and then click Advanced.
3. Clear the Encrypt Contents to Secure Data check box, and then click OK.

The first time you encrypt a folder or file, you should back up your encryption certificate. If your certificate and key are lost or damaged and you do not have a backup, you won't be able to use the files that you have encrypted. To back up your EFS certificate, follow these steps:

1. Open Certificate Manager by clicking the Start button, typing **certmgr.msc** into the Search box, and then pressing Enter.
2. Click the arrow next to the Personal folder to expand it.
3. Click Certificates.

4. Click the certificate that lists Encrypting File System under Intended Purposes. (You might need to scroll to the right to see this.) If there is more than one EFS certificate, you should back up all of them.
5. Click the Action menu, point to All Tasks, and then click Export.
6. In the Export Wizard, click Next, click Yes, export the private key, and then click Next.
7. Click Personal Information Exchange, and then click Next.
8. Type the password you want to use, confirm it, and then click Next. The export process will create a file to store the certificate.
9. Enter a name for the file and the location (include the whole path) or click Browse and navigate to the location, and then enter the filename.
10. Click Finish.
11. Store the backup copy of your EFS certificate in a safe place.

If the encrypted file needs to be shared with another user on the same computer, you need to do the following:

1. Export the EFS certificate.
2. Import the EFS certificate.
3. Add EFS certificate to the shared file.

The person with whom you want to share files needs to export his EFS certificate and give it to you by doing the following:

1. Open Certificate Manager by clicking the Start button, typing **certmgr.msc** into the Search box, and then pressing Enter.
2. Click the arrow next to the Personal folder to expand it, and then click the EFS certificate that you want to export.
3. Click the Action menu, point to All Tasks, and then click Export.
4. In the Certificate Export Wizard, click Next.
5. Click No, Do Not Export the Private Key, and then click Next.
6. On the Export File Format page, click Next to accept the default format.
7. The export process creates a file to store the certificate in. Type a name for the file and the location (include the whole path), or click Browse, navigate to the location, and then type the filename.
8. Click Finish.

After you get the EFS certificate from the person you want to share the file with, you need to import the certificate:

1. Open Certificate Manager by clicking the Start button, typing **certmgr.msc** into the Search box, and then pressing Enter.
2. Select the Personal folder.
3. Click the Action menu, point to All Tasks, and click Import.
4. In the Certificate Import Wizard, click Next.
5. Type the location of the file that contains the certificate, or click Browse, navigate to the file's location, and then click Next.
6. Click Place All Certificates in the Following Store, click Browse, click Trusted People, and then click Next.
7. Click Finish.

To add the EFS certificate to the shared file, follow these steps:

1. Right-click the file you want to share, and then click Properties.
2. Click the General tab, and then click Advanced.
3. In the Advanced Attributes dialog box, click Details.
4. In the Encryption Details dialog box that displays, click Add.
5. In the Select User dialog box, click the certificate, and then click OK.

BitLocker Drive Encryption

A new feature that was added to Windows Vista is BitLocker Drive Encryption, which is designed to protect computers from attackers who have physical access to a computer. Without BitLocker Drive Encryption, an attacker can start the computer with a boot disk and then reset the administrator password to gain full control of the computer, or the attacker can access the computer's hard disk directly by using a different operating system to bypass file permissions.

Workings of BitLocker Drive Encryption

BitLocker Drive Encryption is the feature in Windows Vista that makes use of a computer's TPM. A *Trusted Platform Module (TPM)* is a microchip that is built in to a computer. It is used to store cryptographic information, such as encryption keys. Information stored on the TPM can be more secure from external software attacks and physical theft. BitLocker Drive Encryption can use a TPM to validate the integrity of a computer's boot manager and boot files at startup, and to guarantee that a computer's hard disk has not been tampered with while the operating system is offline. BitLocker Drive Encryption also stores measurements of core operating system files in the TPM.

If the computer is equipped with a compatible TPM, BitLocker uses the TPM to lock the encryption keys that protect the data. As a result, the keys cannot be accessed until the TPM has verified the state of the computer. Encrypting the entire volume protects all the data, including the operating system itself, the Windows registry, temporary files, and the hibernation file. Because the keys needed to decrypt data remain locked by the TPM, an attacker cannot read the data just by removing your hard disk and installing it in another computer.

During the startup process, the TPM releases the key that unlocks the encrypted partition only after comparing a hash of important operating system configuration values with a snapshot taken earlier. This verifies the integrity of the Windows startup process. During computer startup, if BitLocker detects a system condition that can represent a security risk (for example, disk errors, a change to the BIOS, or changes to any startup files), it will lock the drive, go into Recovery mode, and require a special BitLocker recovery password (48-digit key is entered with the function keys in 6 groups of 6 digits) to unlock it. Make sure that you create this recovery password when you turn on BitLocker for the first time; otherwise, you could permanently lose access to your files. Recovery mode is also used if a disk drive is transferred to another system.

On computers with a compatible TPM, BitLocker can be used in three ways:

- **TPM-only.** This is transparent to the user, and the user logon experience is unchanged. If the TPM is missing or changed, or if the TPM detects changes to critical operating system startup files, BitLocker enters its Recovery mode, and you need a recovery password to regain access to the data.
- **TPM with startup key.** In addition to the protection provided by the TPM, a part of the encryption key is stored on a USB flash drive. This is referred to as a startup key. Data on the encrypted volume cannot be accessed without the startup key.
- **TPM with PIN.** In addition to the protection provided by the TPM, BitLocker requires a personal identification number (PIN) to be entered by the user. Data on the encrypted volume cannot be accessed without entering the PIN.

By default, the BitLocker Setup Wizard is configured to work seamlessly with the TPM. An administrator can use Group Policy or a script to enable additional features and options.

On computers without a compatible TPM, BitLocker can provide encryption, but not the added security of locking keys with the TPM. In this case, the user is required to create a startup key that is stored on a USB flash drive.

On computers with a compatible TPM, BitLocker Drive Encryption can use one of two TPM modes:

- **TPM-only.** In this mode, only the TPM is used for validation. When the computer starts up, the TPM is used to validate the boot files, the operating system files, and any encrypted volumes. Because the user doesn't need to provide an additional startup key, this mode is transparent to the user, and the user logon experience is unchanged. However, if the TPM is missing or the integrity of files or volumes has changed, BitLocker will enter Recovery mode and require a recovery key or password to regain access to the boot volume.
- **Startup key.** In this mode, both the TPM and a startup key are used for validation. When the computer starts up, the TPM is used to validate the boot files, the operating system files, and any encrypted volumes. The user must have a startup key to log on to the computer. A startup key can be either physical, such as a USB flash drive with a machine-readable key written to it, or personal, such as a PIN set by the user. If the user doesn't have the startup key or is unable to provide the correct startup key, BitLocker will enter Recovery mode. As before, BitLocker will also enter Recovery mode if the TPM is missing or the integrity of boot files or encrypted volumes has changed.

System Requirements of BitLocker

The system requirements of BitLocker are as follows:

- Because BitLocker stores its own encryption and decryption key in a hardware device that is separate from your hard disk, you must have one of the following:
  - **A computer with TPM.** If your computer was manufactured with TPM version 1.2 or higher, BitLocker will store its key in the TPM.

- **A removable USB memory device, such as a USB flash drive.** If your computer doesn't have TPM version 1.2 or higher, BitLocker will store its key on the flash drive.
- Your computer must have at least two partitions. One partition must include the drive Windows is installed on. This is the drive that BitLocker will encrypt. The other partition is the active partition, which must remain unencrypted so that the computer can be started. Partitions must be formatted with the NTFS file system.
- Your computer must have a BIOS that is compatible with TPM and supports USB devices during computer startup. If this is not the case, you must update the BIOS before using BitLocker.

To find out whether your computer has TPM security hardware, follow these steps:

1. Open BitLocker Drive Encryption by clicking the Start button, Control Panel, Security, and then clicking BitLocker Drive Encryption. If you are prompted for an administrator password or confirmation, enter the password or provide confirmation.
2. If the TPM administration link appears in the left pane, your computer has the TPM security hardware. If this link is not present, you will need a removable USB memory device to turn on BitLocker and store the BitLocker startup key that you'll need whenever you restart your computer.

Enabling and Disabling BitLocker

To turn on BitLocker, follow these steps:

1. Open BitLocker Drive Encryption by clicking the Start button, Control Panel, Security, and then clicking BitLocker Drive Encryption. If you are prompted for an administrator password or confirmation, enter the password or provide confirmation.
2. Click Turn On BitLocker. This opens the BitLocker Setup Wizard. Follow the instructions in the wizard.

To turn off or temporarily disable BitLocker, follow these steps:

1. Open BitLocker Drive Encryption by clicking the Start button, Control Panel, Security, and then clicking BitLocker Drive Encryption. If you are prompted for an administrator password or confirmation, enter the password or provide confirmation.
2. Click Turn Off BitLocker. This opens the BitLocker Drive Encryption dialog box.
3. To decrypt the drive, click Decrypt the Volume. To temporarily disable BitLocker, click Disable BitLocker Drive Encryption.

The BitLocker Control Panel applet enables you to recover the encryption key and recovery password at will. You should consider carefully how to store this information, because it will allow access to the encrypted data. It is also possible to escrow this information into Active Directory.

Compression

NTFS *compression* provides the capability to selectively compress the contents of individual files, entire directories, or entire drives on an NTFS volume. NTFS compression uses file compression that works by substitution. It starts by locating repetitive data with another pattern, which is shorter. Windows tracks which files and folders are compressed via a file attribute. As far as the user is concerned, the compressed drive, folder, or file is simply another drive, folder, or file that works like any other. Although you expand the amount of space for volume, the performance of the PC will be slower because it has to process the compression and decompression of files. Therefore, do not use compression unless you are compressing files that are rarely used or when disk space is critical. If disk space is critical, use this as a temporary solution until you can delete or move files from the drive or you can extend the volume.

To compress a file or folder on an NTFS drive, follow these steps:

1. Open Windows Explorer.
2. Right-click the file or folder that you want to compress, and select the Properties option.
3. Click the Advanced button.
4. Select the Compress Contents to Save Disk Space check box.
5. Click OK or Apply button.

6. If you select to compress a drive or folder, select Apply Changes to This Folder Only (or Apply Changes to the Folder, Subfolder, and Files), and then click the OK button.

To compress an NTFS drive, follow these steps:

1. Click the Start button, and then click Computers.
2. Right-click the drive that you want to compress.
3. Select the Compress Drive to Save Disk Space check box.
4. Click the OK or Apply button.

To uncompress a drive, folder, or file, uncheck the Compress Contents to Save Disk Space box or the Compress Drive to Save Disk Space box.

NOTE

You cannot compress encrypted files or folders.

Exam Prep Questions

1. You want to control the permissions of files and directories on an NTFS drive on the network. Which application must you use?

   ❍ **A.** Windows Explorer

   ❍ **B.** Active Directory Users and Computers

   ❍ **C.** Computer Management Console

   ❍ **D.** Disk Administrator

2. Which of the following file systems is the most secure and the most reliable used by Windows Vista?

   ❍ **A.** FAT

   ❍ **B.** FAT32

   ❍ **C.** NTFS

   ❍ **D.** VFAT

   ❍ **E.** NFS

3. You work as the desktop support technician at Acme.com. A Windows Vista computer contains a shared folder on an NTFS partition. Which one of the following statements concerning access to the folder is correct?

   ❍ **A.** A user who is accessing the folder remotely has the same or more restrictive access permissions than when she accesses the folder locally.

   ❍ **B.** A user who is accessing the folder remotely has less-restrictive access permissions than when she accesses the folder locally.

   ❍ **C.** A user who is accessing the folder remotely has the same access permissions as when she accesses the folder locally.

   ❍ **D.** A user who is accessing the folder remotely has more restrictive access permissions than when she accesses the folder locally.

4. You work as the desktop support technician at Acme.com. Pat is a member of the Manager group. There is a shared folder called DATA on an NTFS partition on a remote Windows Vista computer. Pat is given the write NTFS permission, the Manager group is given the read and execute NTFS permissions, and the Everyone group has the read NTFS permission to the DATA folder. In addition, Pat, Manager, and Everyone are assigned the shared contributor permission to the DATA folder. When Pat logs on to the Windows Vista computer that has the DATA folder and accesses the DATA folder directly, what would be Pat's permissions? (Choose all that apply.)

   ❍ **A.** Read the files in the folder

   ❍ **B.** Write to the files in the folder

   ❍ **C.** Execute the files in the folder

   ❍ **D.** Delete the files in the folder

   ❍ **E.** No access to the files in the folder

5. You work as the desktop support technician at Acme.com. Pat is a member of the Manager group. There is a shared folder called DATA on an NTFS partition on a remote Windows Vista computer. Pat is given the write NTFS permission, the Manager group is given the read and execute NTFS permissions, and the Everyone group has the read NTFS permission to the DATA folder. In addition, Pat, Manager, and Everyone are assigned the shared read permission to the DATA folder. When Pat logs on his client computer and accesses the DATA folder, what would be Pat's permissions? (Choose all that apply.)

   ❍ **A.** Read the files in the folder

   ❍ **B.** Write to the files in the folder

   ❍ **C.** Execute the files in the folder

   ❍ **D.** Delete the files in the folder

   ❍ **E.** No access to the files in the folder

6. You work as the desktop support technician at Acme.com. Pat is a member of the Manager group. There is a shared folder called DATA on an NTFS partition on a remote Windows Vista computer. Pat is given the write NTFS permission, the Manager group is given the deny all NTFS permissions, and the Everyone group has the read NTFS permission to the DATA folder. In addition, Pat, Manager, and Everyone are assigned the shared contributor permission to the DATA folder. When Pat logs on his client computer and accesses the DATA folder, what would be Pat's permissions? (Choose all that apply.)

   ❍ **A.** Read the files in the folder

   ❍ **B.** Write to the files in the folder

   ❍ **C.** Execute the files in the folder

   ❍ **D.** Delete the files in the folder

   ❍ **E.** No access to the files in the folder

7. You work as the desktop support technician at Acme.com. You have configured BitLocker Drive Encryption on a computer, which has a Trusted Platform Module (TPM) installed. Unfortunately, when Windows Vista starts, a TPM error displays, and the user cannot access the data on her computer because it is encrypted. What should you do?

   ❍ **A.** Restart the computer and enter the recovery password at the BitLocker Driver Encryption Recovery Console.

   ❍ **B.** Restart the computer and log on as the local administrator.

   ❍ **C.** Disable the TPM component in the BIOS and reboot the computer.

   ❍ **D.** Open the TPM Management Console.

8. You work as the desktop support technician at Acme.com. You have a laptop that has several shared folders. You configure the network location type on the Windows Vista computer as Private to enable you to connect to the main office where you work. You want to ensure that only users with a user account and password on your computer can access your shared folders, including the Public folder. What should you do?

   ❍ **A.** You need to create a DNS Public entry for Windows Vista computer.

   ❍ **B.** The Public Folder Sharing option should be turned on in the Network and Sharing Center.

   ❍ **C.** The Password Protected Sharing option should be turned on in the Network and Sharing Center.

   ❍ **D.** Network Discovery should be turned off in the Network and Sharing Center.

9. You work as the desktop support technician at Acme.com. You have two users who share a computer running Windows Vista Business edition. Both users are working on a major report, but you don't want one user to access the other user's files data files. What should you do?

   ❍ **A.** Give the appropriate NTFS permissions to each other's My Documents folder.

   ❍ **B.** Have the users log on with the same account.

   ❍ **C.** Instruct these users to store the report in the Public folder.

   ❍ **D.** Instruct these users to log off as themselves and log on as the other user to access the report.

10. You work as the desktop support technician at Acme.com. Your boss wants to protect the laptops if they get stolen. What would you do? (Choose the best answer.)

   ❍ **A.** Make sure that all volumes are using NTFS file system.

   ❍ **B.** Implement BitLocker.

   ❍ **C.** Implement IP Security (IPSec) for all network communications.

   ❍ **D.** Implement Encrypted File System (EFS) on key data files.

11. You have shared a couple of folders on your Windows Vista computer. Unfortunately, they are not visible on anyone's network map so that users can find the shares easily. What is most likely the problem?

   ❍ **A.** You need to enable the Network Discovery service.

   ❍ **B.** You did not give the appropriate share permissions to the Everyone group.

   ❍ **C.** You did not give the appropriate NTFS permissions to the Everyone group.

   ❍ **D.** You need to make sure there is a DNS entry in the DNS server for the Windows Vista computer.

12. Which of the following is not a requirement for BitLocker?

   ❍ **A.** A computer with a TPM

   ❍ **B.** A computer with only one large NTFS volume

   ❍ **C.** A computer that has a compatible BIOS with TPM

   ❍ **D.** A USB flash drive if your system does not have TPM

Answers to Exam Prep Questions

1. **Answer A is correct**. To manage folders and files and their NTFS permissions, you use Windows Explorer. Answer B is incorrect because Active Directory Users and Computers is used to manage the user and computer accounts within Active Directory, not NTFS permissions. Answer C is incorrect because the Computer Management Console, which includes the Disk Administrator, can be used to look at the Event Viewer and status of the disks and to manage the file system volumes, but has nothing to do with NTFS permissions. Answer D is incorrect because the Disk Administrator has nothing to do with NTFS permissions.

2. **Answer C is correct**. NTFS is the only one that provides security features such as encryption and NTFS permissions and the ability to use transaction tracking to keep the file system reliable. Answers A and B are incorrect because they do not offer the features just mentioned for NTFS. Answer D is incorrect because this was the name given to the FAT file system that supported long filenames. Answer E is incorrect because NFS is a file system used in UNIX/Linux machines and is not supported by Windows Vista as a file system.

3. **Answer A is correct**. When you access a computer remotely through the share, you include the share permissions and the NTFS permissions (which can both restrict access). When you access the local folder directly, only the NTFS permissions apply. Therefore, they could have the same or more restrictive access if both are applied. Answers B and C are incorrect because if the user is accessing it remotely, the share permissions may further restrict. Answer D is incorrect because the share and NTFS permissions combined may also give the same access rather than just more restrictive.

4. **Answers A, B, C, and D are correct**. When you combine the NTFS permissions assigned to Pat and to the Manager group that Pat is a member of, Pat can read, write, execute, and delete the files in the folder. When you access a folder directly on a local computer, share permissions do not apply. Because answers A, B, C, and D are correct answers, answer E cannot be correct.

5. **Answers A and C are correct**. When you combine the NTFS permissions assigned to Pat and to the Manager group that Pat is a member of, Pat can read, write, execute, and delete the files in the folder. However, the read share permission only allows you to read and execute the files, blocking writing and delete when going through the shared folder. Answer B and D are incorrect because the read permission blocked the write and delete permissions. Because answers A and C are correct answers, answer E cannot be correct.

6. **Answer E is correct**. Pat is a member of the Managers group. Because deny all NTFS permissions has been granted to the Managers group, it blocks all permissions for Pat. Answers A, B, C, and D are incorrect because no access permissions always wins.

7. **Answer A is correct**. When you get a TPM error, you need to restart the computer and enter the recovery password in the recovery console. Answer B is incorrect because you cannot log on as any user because of the TPM error. Answer C is incorrect

because disabling the feature in BIOS will not decrypt the disk. Answer D is incorrect because it will not be able to open the TPM Management Console.

8. **Answer C is correct**. For other users to access your shared folders, including the Public folder, you need to enable the Password Protected Sharing option. Answer A is incorrect because this scenario does not mention any problem with name resolution. Answer B is incorrect because the Public Folder Sharing option would not affect the other shared folders. Answer D is incorrect because it is needed for Link Layer Topology Discovery (LLTD).

9. **Answer C is correct**. One place to store the report is in the Public folder where they both can have access to it. Answers A, B, and D are not the best answers because they do not provide a secure environment where one user cannot look at the data files of another user.

10. **Answer B is correct**. Because BitLocker encrypts the entire drive, BitLocker is the best solution. Answer A is incorrect because you can connect a stolen hard drive to another system that has another operating system and bypass much of the security on the drive, including security set by NTFS permissions. Answer C is incorrect because IPSec is used to encrypt data being transmitted over the network. Answer D is incorrect because EFS is used to encrypt data files only, not system files.

11. **Answer A is correct**. To view the computer using the network map, you need to have the Link Layer Topology Discovery (LLTD) operational. Therefore, you need to have the Network Discovery service. Answers B and C are incorrect because share and NTFS permissions have nothing to do with a computer showing on the network map. Answer D is incorrect because there is no indication that there is a name-resolution problem.

12. **Answer B is correct**. You need to have two NTFS volumes, not one. Answers A, C, and D are incorrect because they are requirements for BitLocker.

Recommended Readings and Resources

Mitch Tulloch, Tony Northrup, Jerry Honeycutt, Ed Wilson, Ralph Ramos, and the Windows Vista Team, *Windows Vista Resource Kit (Pro - Resource Kit)* (Redmond, Washington: Microsoft Press, 2007).

William R. Stanek, *Introducing Microsoft Windows Vista* (Redmond, Washington: Microsoft Press, 2006).

Patrick Regan, *Working with Windows 2000 and 2003* (Upper Saddle River, New Jersey: Prentice Hall, 2004).

CHAPTER SIX

Configuring User Account Security

Terms you'll need to understand:

- ✓ User account
- ✓ Local user
- ✓ Domain user
- ✓ Administrator account
- ✓ Guest account
- ✓ Standard account
- ✓ User Account Control (UAC)

Techniques/concepts you'll need to master:

- ✓ Describe the differences between standard, administrator, and guest accounts.
- ✓ Using the User Accounts console, create and manage users.
- ✓ Describe the purpose of UAC and how it affects users using the computer.
- ✓ Using the Control Panel, enable or disable UAC.
- ✓ Using local policies, configure UAC.
- ✓ Configure legacy software to work with Windows Vista.

To keep a system secure, you need to use user accounts, which provide accountability and the ability to give rights and permissions to individuals. If your computer has many users, you can then use groups to simplify the assigning of rights and permissions by assigning users to groups and assign the rights and permissions to those groups. To make your system secure, Windows Vista introduced User Account Control (UAC) to help protect against malware that may attack your system at any time by expanding what a standard user can do on a system without becoming an administrator.

User Accounts and Groups

Microsoft Windows Vista workstations can be configured as a member of a workgroup or domain. When a workstation is configured as a member of a workgroup, user access and security are configured on the workstation itself. Each computer maintains its own security database, which includes its own local user accounts and groups. If a user on one computer needs to access resources on other computers, a user account must be created on each computer. The user and group information is not shared with other computers.

A domain is a logical group of computers that define a security boundary. A domain uses one database known as Active Directory, which is stored on one or more domain controllers. It gives the ability to share its common security and user and group account information for all computers with the domain. When a user logs on to the domain, that user can access resources throughout the domain with the same logon (single sign-on). The domain allows for centralized network administration of all users, groups, and resources on the network.

A *user account* enables a user to log on to a computer or domain with an identity that can be authenticated and authorized for access to the resources of the computer or domain. Because the user account is meant to be assigned to one and only one user, it allows you to assign rights and permissions to a single user and enables you to track what users are doing (accountability).

NOTE

It is highly recommended that all users who log on to the network should have their own unique user account and password.

Two general types of user accounts are defined in Windows Vista:

- **Local user accounts.** User accounts defined on a local computer, which have access to the local computer only. You add or remove local user accounts with the Control Panel's User Accounts options or the Local Users and Groups utility. Local Users and Groups is accessible through the Computer Management console, a Microsoft Management Console (MMC) tool, which is found in Administrative Tools.

- **Domain user accounts.** User accounts defined in the Active Directory. Through single sign-on, these accounts can access resources throughout a domain/forest. When a computer is a member of an Active Directory domain, you can create domain user accounts using Active Directory Users and Computers. This MMC tool is available on the Administrative Tools menu when you install the Windows Server Administrator Tools (Adminpak.msi) on your Windows Vista computer.

A local user account allows users to log on at and gain resources on only the computer where they create such an account. The user account tells Windows which files and folders the user can access, which changes the user can make to the computer, and the user's personal preferences, such as desktop background or color theme. User accounts enable the sharing a computer between several people, with each user having personal files and settings. Each person accesses his user account with a username and password.

Default User Accounts

Every Windows Vista computer has local computer accounts, regardless of whether the computer is a member of a workgroup or a domain. When you install Windows Vista, the operating system installs default user accounts, which are managed using the Local Users and Groups console. The key accounts you'll see are the following:

- **Administrator.** Administrator is a predefined account that provides complete access to files, directories, services, and other facilities on the computer. You can't delete this account.
- **Guest.** Guest is designed for users who need one-time or occasional access. Although guests have only limited system privileges, you should be careful about using this account because it opens the system up to potential security problems. The risk is so great that the account is initially disabled when you install Windows Vista.

The built-in administrator account is disabled by default in Windows Vista on new installations. If Windows Vista determines during an upgrade from

Windows XP that the built-in administrator is the only active local administrator account, Windows Vista leaves the account enabled and places the account in Admin Approval mode. The built-in administrator account, by default, cannot log on to the computer in Safe mode.

Windows Vista also provides groups, which you use to grant permissions to similar types of users and to simplify account administration. If a user is a member of a group that can access a resource, that particular user can access the same resource. Therefore, you can give a user access to various work-related resources just by making the user a member of the correct group.

Windows Vista Local Accounts

When you create additional accounts in Windows Vista using the Control Panel, you choose between three different kinds of accounts:

- Standard
- Administrator
- Guest

Each account type gives the user a different level of control over the computer.

The standard account is the account to use for everyday computing. A standard user account lets you use most of the capabilities of the computer, but permission from an administrator is required if you want to make changes that affect other users or the security of the computer. You can use most programs that are installed on the computer, but you can't install or uninstall software and hardware, delete files that are required for the computer to work, or change settings on the computer that affect other users. If you're using a standard account, some programs might require you to provide an administrator password before you can perform certain tasks.

The administrator account provides the most control over the computer, and should only be used when necessary. It lets you make changes that will affect other users. Administrators can change security settings, install software and hardware, and access all files on the computer. Administrators can also make changes to other local user accounts.

NOTE

When you create an administrator user, it adds the user to the Administrators group. When you create a standard user, it adds the user to the Users group.

When you set up Windows, you'll be required to create a user account. This account is an administrator account that enables you to set up your computer and install any programs that you would like to use. After you have finished setting up your computer, we recommend that you use a standard user account for your day-to-day computing.

EXAM ALERT

Because the administrator account has access to all network resources on the computer, it is always more secure to use a standard user account rather than an administrator account.

The guest account is primarily for people who need temporary access to the computer. It is for users who don't have a permanent account on your computer or domain. It enables people to use your computer without having access to your personal files. People using the guest account can't install software or hardware, change settings, or create a password.

NOTE

By default, the guest account is disabled. Therefore, you must turn on the guest account before it can be used.

All user accounts are identified with a logon name. In Windows Vista, this logon name has two parts: the username and the user computer or domain in which the user account exists. If you have a computer called PC1 and the username is User1, the full logon name for Windows Vista is PC\User1. Of course, User1 can log on to his local workstation and access local resources, but would not be able to access domain resources.

When working with domains, the full logon name can be expressed in two different ways:

- The user account name and the full domain name separated by the at (@) symbol. For example, the full logon name for User1 in the Acme.com domain is User1@Acme.com.
- The user account name and the domain separated by the backslash symbol (\). For example, the full logon name for User1 in the Acme domain is Acme\User1.

While Windows Vista represents a user with an user account, administrators as well as users see the user account represented by a user name for easy identification. Windows Vista identifies the user account by using the user account's security identifier (SID). A SID is a unique identifier that is automatically generated when a user account is created and consists of a computer or domain security ID prefix combined with a unique relative ID for the user. Having a unique identifier allows administrators to change a user's username while keeping all settings, permissions, and rights associated with the account. Because each user account has a unique security identify, an administrator can delete an account without worrying that someone might gain access to resources just by re-creating an account.

To provide security, user accounts should have passwords. Passwords are authentication strings for an account and may consist of upper- and lowercase characters, digits, and special characters.

EXAM ALERT

It is recommended that all local computer accounts have passwords. If an account is created without a password, anyone can log on to the account from the console, and there is no protection for the account. However, a local account without a password cannot be used to remotely access a computer.

Managing Local Logon Accounts

The User Accounts console accessed through the Control Panel provides an easy way to manage user accounts. If you want more advanced control, use the Users and Groups console (which is also part of the Computer Management console).

Creating a New Local Account

For a computer that is a member of a workgroup, you can create a local user account on a computer by following these steps:

1. In the Control Panel, click Add or Remove User Accounts under the User Accounts heading. This displays the Manage Accounts page. The Manage Accounts page lists all configurable user accounts on the local computer by account type and with configuration details. If an account has a password, it is listed as being password protected. If an account is disabled, it is listed as being off.
2. Click Create a New Account to display the Create New Account page.

3. Enter the name of the local account. This name is displayed on the Welcome screen and Start menu.
4. Set the type of account as either Standard User or Administrator. To give the user full permissions on the local computer, select Administrator (see Figure 6.1).

FIGURE 6.1 Selecting the account type.

Giving Domain Accounts Local Access

If a user needs to be able to log on locally to a computer and has an existing domain account, you can grant the user permission to log on locally by completing the following steps:

1. In the Control Panel, click User Accounts. On the User Accounts page, click the Give Other Users Access to This Computer link. This displays the User Accounts dialog box (see Figure 6.2). The User Accounts dialog box lists all configurable user accounts on the local computer by account type and with group membership details.
2. Click Add. This starts the Add New User Wizard.

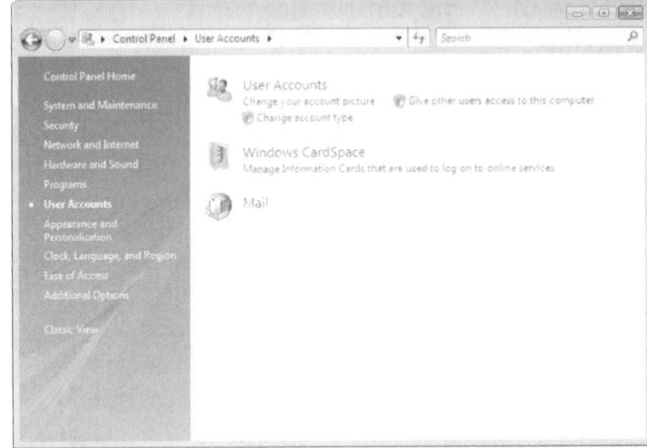

FIGURE 6.2 Users Account dialog box.

3. You are creating a local computer account for a user with an existing domain account. Enter the user's domain account name and domain in the fields provided.
4. Using the options provided, select the type of user account: Administrator, Standard User, or Other. An other account is created as a member of the specific group you choose. To give the user the permissions of a specific group, select Other, and then select the desired group.
5. Click Finish.

Changing Accounts

To change the account type for a local computer user, follow these steps:

1. In the Control Panel, click Add or Remove User Accounts under the User Accounts heading. This displays the Manage Accounts page.
2. Click the account you want to change and then click Change the Account Type.
3. On the Change the Account Type page, set the level of access for the user as either Standard User or Administrator and then click Change the Account Type.

In a domain, you can change the account type for a local computer user by completing the following steps:

1. In the Control Panel, click User Accounts. On the User Accounts page, click the Change the Account Type link. This displays the User Accounts dialog box.

2. On the Users tab, click the user account you want to work with and then click Properties.
3. In the Properties dialog box, select the Group Membership tab.
4. Select the type of account as Standard User or Administrator. Or select Other and then select the desired other group.
5. Click OK twice.

When the computer is not part of a domain (workgroup configuration), local users are created without passwords by default. Therefore, if you click the account name on the Welcome screen on an account that does not have a password, you will automatically be logged in.

Creating and Changing Passwords

To create a password for a local user account, follow these steps:

1. Log on as the user whose password you want to create. In the Control Panel, click Add or Remove User Accounts under the User Accounts heading, to display the Manage Accounts page.
2. All user accounts available on the machine are shown, and you must click the account you want to work with. To prevent possible data loss, this should be the same as the account under which you are currently logged on. Any account that has a current password is listed as password protected. Any account without this label doesn't have a password.
3. Click Create a Password. Enter a password, and then confirm it. Afterward, enter a unique password hint. The password hint is a word or phrase that can be used to obtain the password if it is lost. This hint is visible to anyone who uses the computer.
4. Click Change Password.

Removing Local User Accounts

In a workgroup, you can remove a user's local account and effectively deny logon by completing these steps:

1. Log on as a user with local administrator privileges. In the Control Panel, click Add or Remove User Accounts under the User Accounts heading, to display the Manage Accounts page.
2. Click the account you want to remove.

3. Click Delete the Account.
4. Before deleting the account, you have the opportunity to save the contents of the user's desktop and Documents folder to a folder on the current user's desktop. To save the user's documents, click Keep Files. To delete the files, click Delete Files.
5. Confirm the account deletion by clicking Delete Account. Keep in mind that in a domain, unless further restrictions apply with regard to logon workstations, a user might still be able to gain access to the workstation by logging on with a domain account.

Local User Accounts and Groups in the Computer Management Console

To access the Users and Groups in the Computer Management console, follow these steps:

1. Click the Start button.
2. Click Control Panel.
3. Click System and Maintenance.
4. Click Administrative Tools.
5. Click Computer Management.
6. Double-click Local Users and Groups.
7. Select either Users or Groups (see Figures 6.3 and 6.4).

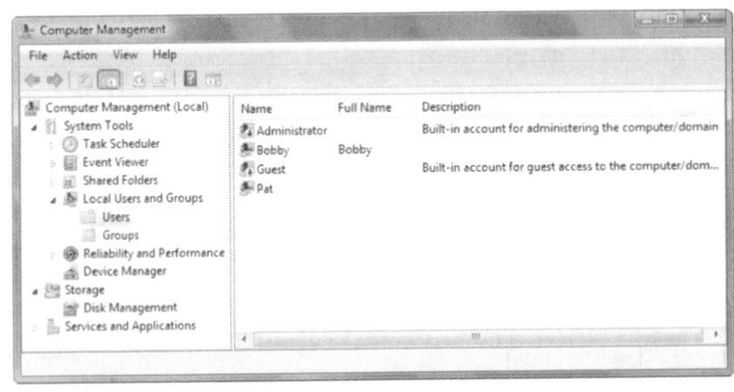

FIGURE 6.3 Managing users with the Computer Management console.

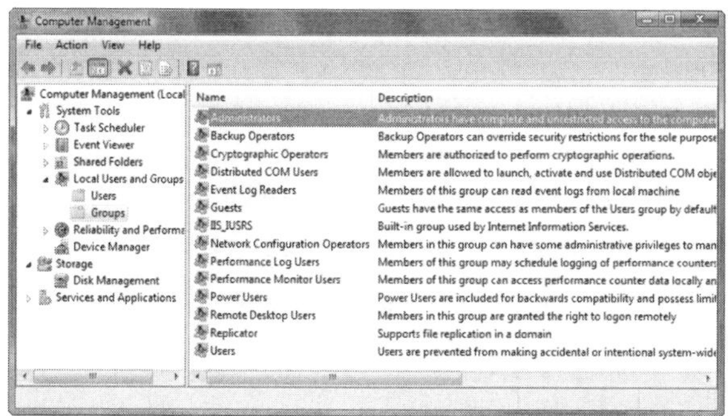

FIGURE 6.4 Managing groups with the Computer Management console.

User Account Control

"Need to know" is a basic security concept that says information should be limited to only those individuals who require it. When planning for how you assign the rights and permissions to the network resources, follow these two main rules:

- Give the rights and permissions for the user to do his job.
- Don't give any additional rights and permissions that a user does not need.

Although you want to keep these resources secure, you want to make sure that users can easily get what they need. For example, give users access to the necessary files, and give them only the permissions they need. If they need to read a document but don't need to make changes to it, they need to have only the read permission. Apply the rule of least privilege; that is, give a person or group only the required amount of access and nothing more.

When you run earlier versions of Windows, including Windows XP, and you log on with an administrative account, every task that you execute and every process that runs in the account's session run as an as administrator with elevated privileges. Because the elevated privileges give access to everything, it opens the possibility of human error, which can cause problems in Windows functionality or data loss and may allow malicious software to access any part of the computer. Unfortunately, most legacy applications (and even new applications) were not (or are not) designed to work without full administrator privileges.

User Account Control (UAC) is a feature in Windows that can help prevent unauthorized changes to your computer. If you are logged on as an administrator, UAC asks you for permission (see Figure 6.5); if you are logged on as a standard user, UAC will ask you for an administrator password before performing actions that could potentially affect your computer's operation or change settings that affect other users (see Figure 6.6). When you see a UAC message, read it carefully, and then make sure the name of the action or program that's about to start is one that you intended to start.

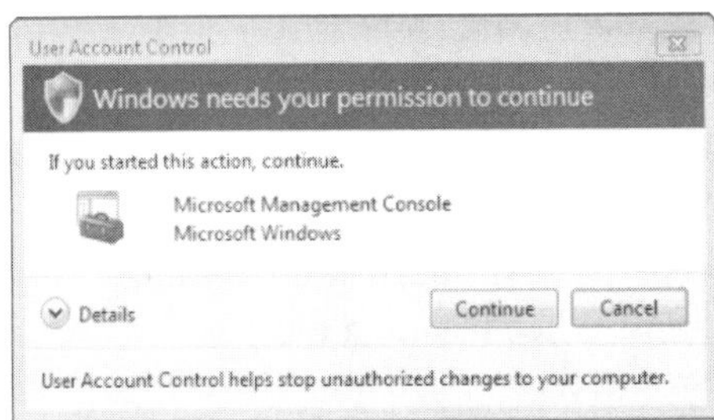

FIGURE 6.5 UAC asking for permission to continue.

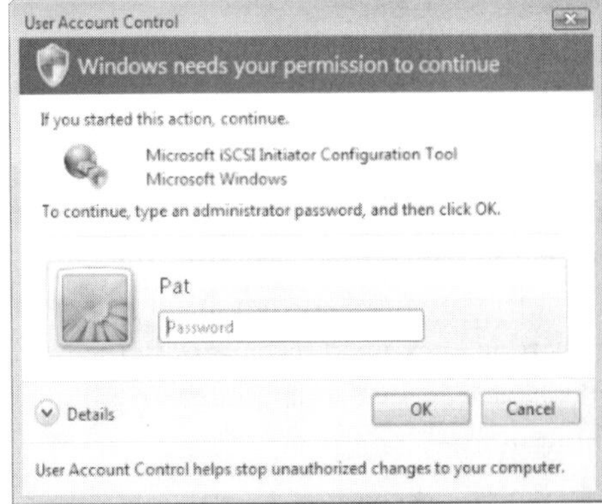

FIGURE 6.6 UAC asking for administrative credentials when logged in as a standard user.

To keep track of a user's access, when a standard user logs in to Windows Vista, a token is created that contains only the most basic privileges assigned. When an administrator logs in, two separate tokens are assigned. The first token contains all privileges typically awarded to an administrator, and the second is a restricted token similar to what a standard user would receive. User applications, including the Windows shell, are then started with the restricted token, resulting in a reduced-privilege environment even under an administrator account. When an application requests elevation or is run as administrator, UAC prompts for confirmation and, if consent is given, starts the process using the unrestricted token.

The following additional privileges have been granted to standard user accounts so that users can carry out more tasks without requiring administrative permissions or rights:

- View system clock and calendar
- Change time zone
- Install Wired Equivalent Privacy (WEP) to connect to secure wireless networks
- Change display settings
- Change power management settings
- Install fonts
- Add printers and other devices that have the required drivers installed on computer or are provided by an IT administrator
- Create and configure a virtual private network connection
- Download and install updates using UAC-compatible installer

In addition, extra services have been created to automate certain tasks. They include an ActiveX installer, which administrators can use to pre-approve sites from which users can install ActiveX controls, and a disk defragmenter, which runs as a scheduled process to optimize disk performance.

Tasks that will trigger a UAC prompt, if UAC is enabled, include the following:

- Changes to files in %SystemRoot% or %ProgramFiles%
- Installing and uninstalling applications
- Installing device drivers
- Installing ActiveX controls
- Installing Windows Updates
- Changing settings for Windows Firewall
- Changing UAC settings
- Configuring Windows Update
- Adding/removing user accounts
- Changing a user's account type
- Configuring parental controls

- Running Task Scheduler
- Restoring backed-up system files
- Viewing/changing another user's folders and files

When your permission or password is needed to complete a task, UAC will alert you with one of the following messages:

- **Windows needs your permission to continue.** A Windows function or program that can affect other users of this computer needs your permission to start. Check the name of the action to ensure that it's a function or program you want to run.
- **A program needs your permission to continue.** A program that's not part of Windows needs your permission to start. It has a valid digital signature indicating its name and its publisher, which helps to ensure that the program is what it claims to be. Make sure that this is a program that you intended to run.
- **An unidentified program wants access to your computer.** An unidentified program is one that doesn't have a valid digital signature from its publisher to ensure that the program is what it claims to be. This doesn't necessarily indicate danger (because many older, legitimate programs lack signatures). However, use extra caution and only allow this program to run if you obtained it from a trusted source, such as the original CD or a publisher's website.
- **This program has been blocked.** This is a program that your administrator has specifically blocked from running on your computer. To run this program, you must contact your administrator and ask to have the program unblocked. Of course, it is recommended that you log on to your computer with a standard user account most of the time. With a standard user account, you can run standard business applications such as a word processor or spreadsheet, surf the Internet, or send e-mail. When you want to perform an administrative task, such as installing a new program or changing a setting that will affect other users, you don't have to switch to an administrator account. Windows will prompt you for permission or an administrator password before performing the task.

To help protect your computer, you can create standard user accounts for all the users who share the computer. When someone who has a standard account tries to install software, Windows will ask for an administrator account's password so that software can't be installed without your knowledge and permission.

Program Compatibility

Some legacy applications will not run on Windows Vista because of some compatibility problems. Starting with Windows XP, Windows includes a Program Compatibility Wizard to configure Windows to run a program under an older Windows environment. For example, if you have a program that will run under only Windows 9x, you can configure Windows to run that program under the Windows 95 environment. This means that when Windows XP is running this application, it will pretend to be a Windows 95 system. The wizard also allows you to try different settings, such as switching the display to 256 colors and the screen resolution to 640x480 pixels.

To start the Program Compatibility Wizard, right-click the executable file that you are using to start the program, select Properties, and select the Compatibility tab. Enable the Run This Program in Compatibility Mode option and select the appropriate operating system environment.

An application that is made to be 100 percent compatible with Windows Vista is designed to work with UAC to keep the system secure by requesting privilege elevation as necessary. If you have an older application that requires administrative permissions to run, you can use the Application Compatibility tab to select the Run This Program as an Administrator option, which will allow the application to use the UAC system to request privilege escalation. This setting applies only to the account of the currently logged-on user, and no other users are affected by it. You can only configure this option if you have administrator privileges. If you need to have an application run as an administrator for all users, you can use the Show Settings for All Users option on the Application Compatibility tab.

EXAM ALERT

Use the Properties dialog box for an executable to make a legacy application run on a Windows Vista machine, including running under an administrator account.

Controlling UAC

UAC can be enabled or disabled for any individual user account. If you disable UAC for a user account, you lose the additional security protections UAC offers and put the computer at risk. To enable or disable UAC for a particular user account, follow these steps:

1. In the Control Panel, click User Accounts.

2. On the User Accounts page, click the Turn User Account Control On or Off link.
3. You can now enable or disable UAC for the currently logged-on user account. Disable UAC by clearing the Use User Account Control (UAC) to Help Protect Your Computer check box. Enable UAC by selecting the Use User Account Control (UAC) to Help Protect Your Computer check box.
4. Click OK.
5. When prompted to restart the computer, click Restart Now or Restart Later, as appropriate, for the changes to take effect.

Besides enabling or disabling UAC, you can control the behavior of the UAC by using local or group policies. Local policies are managed from each local computer, whereas group policies are managed as part of Active Directory. Table 6.1 shows the settings found in local and group policies.

TABLE 6.1 UAC Policy Settings Available in the Policy Editor Snap-In

Policy	Security Settings
Admin Approval Mode for the Built-In Administrator Account	Enabled Disabled (Default)
Behavior of the Elevation Prompt for Administrators in Admin Approval Mode	Elevate without prompting Prompt for credentials Prompt for consent (Default)
Behavior of the Elevation Prompt for Standard Users	Automatically deny elevation requests Prompt for credentials (Default)
Detect Application Installations and Prompt for Elevation	Enabled (Default) Disabled
Only Elevate Executables That Are Signed and Validated	Enabled Disabled (Default)
Only Elevate UIAccess Applications That Are Installed in Secure Applications	Enabled (Default) Disabled
Run All Administrators in Admin Approval Mode	Enabled (Default) Disabled
Switch to the Secure Desktop When Prompting for Elevation	Enabled (Default) Disabled
Virtualize File and Registry Write Failures to Per-User Locations	Enabled (Default) Disabled

To change the behavior of the UAC message for administrators in Admin Approval mode, follow these steps:

1. Click Start, All Programs, Accessories, Run. Then, enter **secpol.msc** in the Open box and click OK.
2. If UAC is currently configured in Admin Approval mode, the UAC message will appear. Click Continue.
3. From the Local Security Policy tree, click Local Policies, and then double-click Security Options.
4. Scroll down and double-click User Account Control: Behavior of the Elevation Prompt for Administrators in Admin Approval Mode.
5. From the drop-down menu, select one of the following settings:
    - **Elevate without Prompting.** In this case, applications that have been marked as administrator applications, and applications detected as setup applications, will automatically run with the full administrator access token. All other applications will automatically run with the standard user token.
    - **Prompt for Credentials.** In this case, to give consent for an application to run with the full administrator access token, the user must enter administrator credentials. This setting supports compliance with Common Criteria or corporate policies.
    - **Prompt for Consent.** This is the default setting.
6. Click Apply.

To change the UAC message behavior for standard users, follow these steps:

1. Click Start, All Programs, Accessories, Run. Then, enter **secpol.msc** in the Open text box and click OK.
2. If UAC is currently configured to prompt for administrator credentials, the UAC message will appear. Click Continue.
3. From the Local Security Policy tree, click Local Policies, and then double-click Security Options (see Figure 6.7).
4. Scroll down and double-click User Account Control: Behavior of the Elevation Prompt for Standard Users.

5. From the drop-down menu, select one of the following settings:
   - **Automatically Deny Elevation Requests.** In this case, administrator applications will not be able to run. The user should see an error message from the application that indicates a policy has prevented the application from running.
   - **Prompt for Credentials.** This is the default setting. In this case, for an application to run with the full administrator access token, the user must enter administrator credentials.
6. Click Apply.

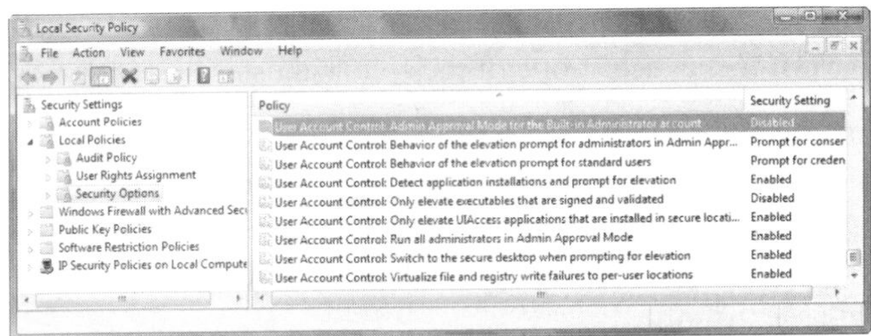

FIGURE 6.7 Using local policies to change UAC settings.

Exam Prep Questions

1. Which of the following will UAC prompt for permission or administrative credentials?

   ❍ **A.** Change time zone

   ❍ **B.** Change power management settings

   ❍ **C.** Install fonts

   ❍ **D.** Install a device driver

   ❍ **E.** Install an application

2. Which of the following is used to prevent unauthorized changes to your computer?

   ❍ **A.** Computer Management console

   ❍ **B.** User Account Control (UAC)

   ❍ **C.** Windows Firewall

   ❍ **D.** Event Viewer

3. You receive a message asking permission to continue. What is causing this?

   ❍ **A.** Windows Firewall

   ❍ **B.** NTFS permissions

   ❍ **C.** User Account Control (UAC)

   ❍ **D.** Internet Sharing console

4. You work as part of the IT support staff at Acme.com. You have upgraded several computers from Windows 2000 Professional to Microsoft Windows Vista Enterprise. You had an accounting application that worked fine in Windows 2000 but does not run fine on Windows Vista. After further research, you find when the user tries to run the application, a login is requested. When the user enters the username and password, the application still fails, but when you use an administrator user account and password, the application works. What is the best solution to fix this problem?

   ❍ **A.** Add the user accounts to the local administrator group.

   ❍ **B.** Add the user accounts to the domain administrator group.

   ❍ **C.** Use parental control for the users to access the applications.

   ❍ **D.** Right-click the executable and select Properties. Use the application's Properties dialog box to run this program as an administrator.

5. You work as the desktop support technician at Acme.com. You have many computers running Windows Vista that are part of a Windows domain. Your company decides to have only applications that have been approved by the IT department. You have a handful of users who need to make configuration changes to these applications. However, when they try to make the appropriate changes, they always receive the following error message:

   You need to ensure that *username* is able to make configuration changes to *computer name*.

   After verifying that these users have administrative access to their computer, how do you make sure that they no longer receive these messages?

   ❍ **A.** Add all users to the Power Users group.

   ❍ **B.** Add all users to the Users group.

   ❍ **C.** Turn off the Windows Firewall.

   ❍ **D.** Change the elevation prompt for administrators in User Account Control (UAC) to Admin Approval mode.

6. You work as the desktop support technician at Acme.com. You need to assign a handful of users the ability to install applications without giving them administrative permissions. What do you do?

   ❍ **A.** Make these users part of the local administrator group.

   ❍ **B.** Turn UAC off in the User Accounts Control Panel tool.

   ❍ **C.** You should configure parental controls to block each user from downloading unapproved software.

   ❍ **D.** Configure the UAC not to prompt during software installation in the Security Options section of the Local Security Policy.

7. You work as the desktop support technician at Acme.com. You have certain users who have to make configuration changes to a handful of applications on several computers. Some of the users are reporting that they are getting the following error message, whereas others users do not see this message:

   You need to ensure that *username* is able to make configuration changes to *computer name*.

   What is most likely the cause of the problem?

   ❍ **A.** You need to add the users to the local administrators group on the computer.

   ❍ **B.** The users have been entering the wrong username and password.

   ❍ **C.** The application has been configured to run as a standard user rather than an administrator.

   ❍ **D.** You need to start the Application service on the systems that have the problem.

8. To create local user accounts, you should use ____________. (Choose two answers.)

   ❍ **A.** User Accounts in the Control Panel

   ❍ **B.** Computer Management console

   ❍ **C.** Active Directory Users and Computers console

   ❍ **D.** Users and Groups Administrator console

9. A logical unit of computers that defines a security boundary and that allows single sign-on is known as a what?

   ❍ **A.** Active Directory

   ❍ **B.** Workgroup

   ❍ **C.** Domain

   ❍ **D.** Domain controller

10. Which account is disabled by default on a Windows Vista computer?

    ❍ **A.** Administrator

    ❍ **B.** Guest

    ❍ **C.** Sysadmin

    ❍ **D.** Admin

Answers to Exam Prep Questions

1. **Answers D and E are correct.** Installing a device driver and installing an application require administrative permission. Therefore, UAC will prompt you to make sure it is something that you want done. Answers A, B, and C are incorrect because standard users can do these.

2. **Answer B is correct.** UAC is used to prevent unauthorized changes to the computer. Answer A is incorrect because the Computer Management console is used to manage the computer, including managing volumes, using the Event Viewer, and managing local users and groups. Answer C is incorrect because the Windows Firewall will help block unwanted packets from getting to your computer. Answer D is incorrect because the Event Viewer is used to look at warning and error messages and the security logs.

3. **Answer C is correct.** The UAC will ask for permission to continue when you are performing tasks that require you to be an administrator, to make sure that they are tasks that you really want completed. Answer A is incorrect because the Windows Firewall prevents unwanted packets from the outside. Answer B is incorrect because NT File System (NTFS) permissions help protect the files on an NTFS volume. Answer D is incorrect because the Internet Sharing console does not exist.

4. **Answer D is correct.** To configure legacy applications to run under Windows Vista, you can right-click an executable and open the Properties dialog box. From there, you can specify what environment to run under and if necessary specify whether the application can run under an administrator account.

5. **Answer D is correct.** The message is generated by the User Account Control, which you can configure by using local or group policies. Answer A is incorrect because the Power Users group is left behind from Windows 2000 and XP for backward compatibility. Answer B is incorrect because all standard user accounts should already be a member of the Users group. Answer C is incorrect because turning off the firewall would not get rid of the message.

6. **Answer D is correct.** You need to edit the Local Security Policy to not prompt during installs by disabling the Detect Application Installations and Prompt for Elevation Setting. This will allow applications to be installed without prompting for the administrative credentials. Answer A is incorrect because you don't want to give administrative permission. Answer B is incorrect because turning off UAC will stop protecting the system. Answer C is also incorrect because parental controls cannot be used when a computer is connected to a domain.

7. **Answer A is correct.** Some users are not having the problem, whereas others are. Therefore, you need to focus on what is different from those accounts; in this case, you need to add those users to the administrator group. Answer B is incorrect because they would not get logged on to the system with the wrong username and password. Answer C is incorrect because all users would be affected if the application runs as a standard user. Answer D is incorrect because the Application service does not exist.

8. **Answers A and B are correct.** The Control Panel user accounts and the Computer Management console, specifically under Users and Groups, are used to add and manage user accounts. Answer C is incorrect because Active Directory Users and Computers console is used to manage domain user accounts. Answer D is incorrect because the Users and Groups Administrator console does not exist.
9. **Answer C is correct.** A domain is a logical unit group of computers and network that define a security boundary and which use one database known as Active Directory to store relevant security information. Answer A is incorrect because the Active Directory is the directory service. Answer B is incorrect because a workgroup is only used to easily access other computers within the workgroup. Each computer contains its own database of user accounts and does not provide single sign-on. Answer D is incorrect because the domain controller is used to provide Active Directory.
10. **Answer B is correct.** The only account disabled by default is the guest account. Answer A is incorrect because the administrator account is not disabled by default. Answers C and D are incorrect because these accounts are not found on a Windows Vista machine unless they are created.

Recommended Readings and Resources

Stanek, William R., *Introducing Microsoft Windows Vista* (Redmond, Washington: Microsoft Press, 2006).

Tulloch, Mitch, Tony Northrup, Jerry Honeycutt, Ed Wilson, Ralph Ramos, and the Windows Vista Team, *Windows Vista Resource Kit (Pro. Resource Kit)* (Redmond, Washington: Microsoft Press, 2007).

For more information about UAC, visit http://technet.microsoft.com/en-us/windowsvista/aa905108.aspx.

7

CHAPTER SEVEN

Configuring Network Security

Terms you'll need to understand:

- ✓ Spyware
- ✓ End user license agreement (EULA)
- ✓ Antivirus software
- ✓ Windows Defender
- ✓ Windows Firewall
- ✓ Stateful firewall
- ✓ Packet filter
- ✓ Port

Techniques/concepts you'll need to master:

- ✓ List the symptoms of a system infected with spyware.
- ✓ Configure a computer to resist spyware.
- ✓ Given a computer with spyware, use Windows Defender to remove the spyware.
- ✓ Use Software Explorer to configure items not loaded during startup.
- ✓ Configure and use Windows Firewall to protect your computer from unauthorized access.

In today's world, users often need to share data with other users. This chapter focuses on sharing files so those users can access files from a Windows Vista computer over the network and how to control such access so that it remains secure. Because these files will access the files over the network, this chapter also discusses how to configure Windows Vista to connect to the network.

Spyware

A common threat to computers that can cause problems similar to a virus is *spyware*. Spyware (including adware) programs are more like Trojan horse viruses. Some machines are infected with spyware when it is bundled with other software, often without the user's knowledge, or is slipped into the fine print of an *end user license agreement (EULA)*. A EULA is a type of license used for most software, and represents a legal contract between the manufacturer or the author and the end user of an application. The EULA details how the software can and cannot be used and any restrictions that the manufacturer imposes. Spyware can also be picked up by simply visiting various websites, where they are often hidden as ActiveX controls.

After it has been installed, spyware can monitor user activity on the Internet and transmit information such as e-mail addresses, passwords, and credit card numbers without the user's knowledge. This information can be used for advertising or marketing purposes, to send the information to other parties, or to use the information for illegal purposes. Spyware can do the following:

- Generate annoying pop-ups
- Monitor keystrokes
- Scan files on the hard drive
- Snoop other applications such as chat programs or word processors
- Install other spyware programs
- Read cookies
- Change the default home page on the web browsers other links or default pages
- Open your computer to be accessed by others

EXAM ALERT

It is important that you know the symptoms of spyware so that when presented with a troubleshooting question you will know what steps to take next.

Spyware can also use network bandwidth and computer memory and can lead to system crashes or general system instability.

To reduce your chance of being affected by spyware, you should do the following:

- Use a good antivirus package such as Norton Antivirus, McAfee Viruscan, or Microsoft Windows Live OneCare.
- Use spyware-detecting and -removal programs such as Windows Defender if it is not included in the antivirus software.
- Be sure that your machine has all security patches and fixes loaded.
- Install software only from sources and websites you trust.
- Be careful about what software you install on your system. Be sure to read the EULA for any piece of shareware or file-sharing package you plan to install.
- Keep your web browser security settings to Medium or higher.
- Install or enable a personal firewall such as the one included in Windows Vista.
- Use pop-up blockers.

Windows Defender

Windows Defender, included with Windows Vista, helps users detect and remove known spyware and other potentially unwanted software. Windows Defender protects your computer with automated and real-time scanning and software removal.

Because spyware and other potentially unwanted software can try to install itself on your computer any time you connect to the Internet or when you install some programs, it is recommended that you have Windows Defender running whenever you use your computer.

Windows Defender offers three ways to help keep spyware and other potentially unwanted software from infecting your computer:

- **Real-time protection.** Running in the background, Windows Defender alerts you when spyware or potentially unwanted software attempts to install itself or to run on your computer. It also alerts you when programs attempt to change important Windows settings.

- **Scanning options.** You can use Windows Defender to actively scan your disks for spyware and other potentially unwanted software that might be installed on your computer and to automatically remove any malicious software that is detected during a scan (see Figure 7.1). Windows Defender can be set up to scan automatically according to a schedule or manually.

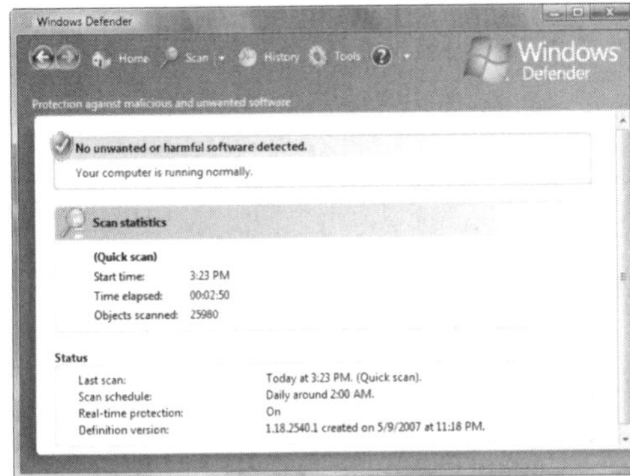

FIGURE 7.1 Windows Defender.

- **SpyNet community.** The online Microsoft SpyNet community helps you see how other people respond to software that has not yet been classified for risks.

You can also use Windows Defender to constantly monitor your system to offer real-time protection. The real-time protection uses nine security agents to monitor the critical areas of your computer that spyware may attack. Then, an agent detects potential spyware activity, it stops the activity, and raises an alert. The agents include the following:

- **Microsoft Internet Explorer Configuration.** Monitors browser security settings so that they do not get changed by spyware.
- **Internet Explorer Downloads.** Monitors files and applications that work within Internet Explorer, such as ActiveX controls and software installation applications to make sure spyware is not being installed with the files and applications.
- **Internet Explorer Add-Ons (Browser Helper Objects).** Monitors browser applications that automatically run when you start Internet Explorer to make sure that these programs are not spyware.
- **Auto Start.** Monitors applications that start when Windows starts to verify that these applications are not spyware.

- **System Configuration.** Monitors Windows hardware and security settings to make sure they do not get changed by spyware.
- **Services and Drivers.** Monitors services and drivers to make sure that spyware does not use them to access the computer.
- **Windows Add-Ons.** Monitors add-on applications, also known as software utilities, that integrate with Windows.
- **Application Execution.** Monitors applications to make sure that spyware does not use software application vulnerabilities to access a computer.
- **Application Registration (API Hooks).** Monitors files and tools in the operating system to make sure that they do not open up applications or other files that contain spyware.

When you choose automatic scanning, you can choose the type of scan that you would like to perform:

- **Quick Scan.** Checks areas on a hard disk that spyware is most likely to infect.
- **Full Scan.** Checks all critical areas, all files, the registry, and all currently running applications.
- **Custom Scan.** Allows you to scan specific drives and folders.

EXAM ALERT

A quick scan will check locations where spyware is normally found.

When you perform a scan, you can configure what Windows Defender will do when it identifies unwanted software (see Figure 7.2). The actions include the following:

- **Ignore.** Windows Defender does not take any action, and the next scan will detect the item again.
- **Quarantine.** Windows Defender places identified unwanted software in quarantine, which allows you to determine whether it is spyware.
- **Remove.** Windows Defender removes the item from the system.
- **Always Allow.** Windows Defender will not take any action and will stop detecting the item in future scans.

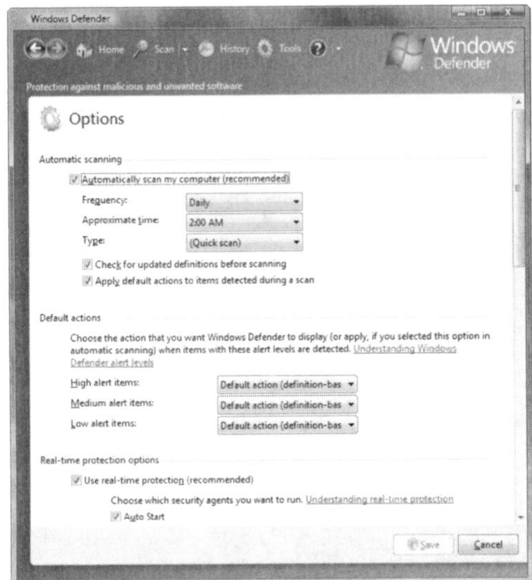

FIGURE 7.2 Configuring Windows Defender options.

To prevent Windows Defender from automatically taking the recommended action, such as quarantining or removing software, you need to clear the Apply Default Actions to Items Detected During a Scan option. As a result, Windows Defender will recommend an action to take for detected malicious software.

Similar to antivirus software, Windows Defender uses a definition database that lists and details the characteristics of known spyware. When software is identified as spyware, it removes the software. Like antivirus software, the definition database becomes out of data as new spyware is introduced. Therefore, you must update the database regularly for it to be effective.

To help keep your system from being compromised, Windows Defender will scan all startup items, including those specified in the following registry key:

HKEY_LOCAL_MACHINE\SOFTWARE\Microsoft\Windows\CurrentVersion\Run

EXAM ALERT

You can use Windows Defender to view which items load during startup and easily disable any programs that you don't recognize.

To view all programs that are set to run at startup, click the Tools button, and then click the Software Explorer option to view all programs that are set to run at startup (see Figure 7.3). This enables you to view several categories of software, including what is running at that time and what is set to run at startup. For each application set to run at startup, there is additional information, including the startup type, so you can identify the mechanism used to start it, such as the registry.

FIGURE 7.3 Using Software Explorer in Windows Defender.

By deleting the correct program in Windows Defender, you prevent the program from starting whenever Windows starts. Therefore, you should open Windows Defender and remove any unfamiliar programs whose startup type is set to Registry: Local Machine.

Windows Defender in Windows Vista automatically blocks all startup items that require administrator privileges to run. Because this feature is related to the User Account Control (UAC) functionality in Windows Vista, and requires the user to manually run each of these startup items each time he logs in, if you cannot get an update to the software that allows a startup item to run without being an administrator, you need to disable UAC altogether.

EXAM ALERT

Windows Defender automatically blocks all startup items that require administrator privileges.

To turn Windows Defender on or off, follow these steps:

1. Open Windows Defender by clicking the Start button, All Programs, and then clicking Windows Defender.
2. Click Tools, Options.
3. Under Administrator options, select or clear the Use Windows Defender check box, and then click Save. If you are prompted for an administrator password or confirmation, enter the password or provide confirmation.

To turn Windows Defender real-time protection on or off, follow these steps:

1. Open Windows Defender by clicking the Start button, All Programs, and then clicking Windows Defender.
2. Click Tools, Options.
3. Under Real-time Protection options, select the Use Real-Time Protection (Recommended) check box.
4. Select the options you want. To help protect your privacy and your computer, we recommend that you select all real-time protection options.
5. Under Choose If Windows Defender Should Notify You About, select the options you want, and then click Save. If you are prompted for an administrator password or confirmation, enter the password or provide confirmation.

If you trust software that Windows Defender has detected, you can stop Windows Defender from alerting you to risks that the software might pose to your privacy or your computer. To stop being alerted, you need to add the software to the Windows Defender allowed list. If you decide that you want to monitor the software again later, you can remove it from the Windows Defender allowed list at any time.

To add an item to the allowed list, follow these steps:

1. The next time Windows Defender alerts you about the software, on the Action menu in the Alert dialog box, click Always Allow.
2. If you are prompted for an administrator password or confirmation, enter the password or provide confirmation.

To remove an item from the allowed list, follow these steps:

1. Open Windows Defender by clicking the Start button, All Programs, and then clicking Windows Defender.
2. Click Tools, Allowed Items.
3. Select the item that you want to monitor again, and then click Remove From List.
4. If you are prompted for an administrator password or confirmation, enter the password or provide confirmation.

Windows Firewall Settings

Because most computers are connected to the Internet through dialup, broadband (such as Digital Subscriber Line [DSL] or cable modems), or through a local area network, computers are vulnerable to attack or unauthorized access. To help protect your system, you should have a firewall between you and the outside world that will monitor all traffic going in and out and prevent such access.

Windows Firewall is a packet filter and stateful host-based firewall that allows or blocks network traffic according to the configuration. A *packet filter* protects the computer by using an access control list (ACL), which specifies which packets are allowed through the firewall based on IP address and protocol (specifically the port number). A *stateful firewall* monitors the state of active connections and uses the information gained to determine which network packets are allowed through the firewall. Typically, if the user starts communicating with an outside computer, it will remember the conversation and allow the appropriate packets back in. If an outside computer tries to start communicating with a computer protected by a stateful firewall, those packets will automatically be dropped unless it was granted by the ACL.

EXAM ALERT

Remember that any program or service that needs to communicate on a network must be able to pass through a firewall. This includes file sharing.

The rules that can be defined include the following:

- **Inbound rules.** Prevents other computers from making an unsolicited or unexpected connection to your computer from other computers making an unsolicited connection to it.
- **Outbound rules.** Prevents your computer from making unsolicited connections to other computers.
- **Connection-specific rules.** Allows you to create and apply custom rules based on a specific connection.

Compared to Windows Firewall introduced with Windows XP SP2, the Windows Firewall used in Windows Vista has been improved. Some of the improvements are as follows:

- IPv6 connection filtering.
- Outbound packet filtering.
- Rules can be configured for individual services chosen from a list without needing to specify the full path filename.
- Internet Protocol Security (IPSec) is fully integrated with Windows Firewall to make sure there is not a conflict between IPSec and firewall settings.
- Capability to have separate firewall profiles when computers communicating on a Windows domain are connected to the Internet (public) or private network.

Basic Configuration

Windows Firewall is on by default. When Windows Firewall is on, most programs are blocked from communicating through the firewall. If you want to unblock a program, you can add it to the Exceptions list (on the Exceptions tab). For example, you might not be able to send photos in an instant message until you add the instant messaging program to the Exceptions list.

To turn on or off Windows Firewall, follow these steps:

1. Open Windows Firewall by clicking the Start button, Control Panel, Security, and then clicking Windows Firewall.

2. Click Turn Windows Firewall on or off shown in the left pane (see Figure 7.4). If you are prompted for an administrator password or confirmation, enter the password or provide confirmation.

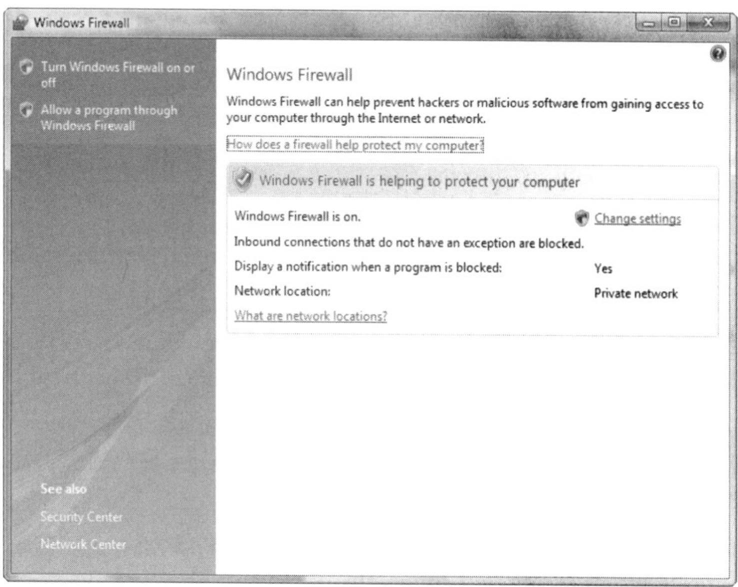

FIGURE 7.4 Windows Firewall options in the Control Panel.

3. Click On (recommended) or Off (not recommended), and then click OK (see Figure 7.5).

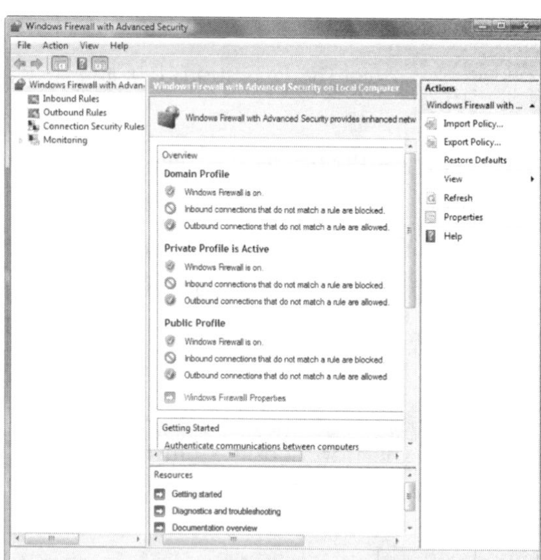

FIGURE 7.5 Enabling or disabling Windows Firewall using the Control Panel.

If you want the firewall to block everything, including the programs selected on the Exceptions tab, select the Block All Incoming Connections check box (which blocks all unsolicited attempts to connect to your computer). Use this setting when you need maximum protection for your computer, such as when you connect to a public network in a hotel or airport, or when a computer worm is spreading over the Internet. With this setting, you are not notified when Windows Firewall blocks programs, and programs on the Exceptions list are ignored.

The Windows Firewall Settings interface has three tabs:

- **General.** Allows you to turn Windows Firewall on and off and temporarily block all incoming connections.
- **Exceptions.** Allows you to specify which programs and services are allowed through the firewall or not. Of course, you should never create an exception for a program when you are unsure of the functionality of that program.
- **Advanced.** Allows you to select which network interfaces that Windows Firewall will protect.

To configure programs as exceptions, follow these steps:

1. Open Windows Firewall by clicking the Start button, Control Panel, Security, and then clicking Windows Firewall.
2. Click Allow a Program Through Windows Firewall. If you are prompted for an administrator password or confirmation, enter the password or provide confirmation.
3. In the Windows Firewall dialog box, select the Exceptions tab, and then click Add Program.
4. In the Add a Program dialog box, select the program in the Programs list or click Browse to use the Browse dialog box to find the program.
5. By default, any computer, including those on the Internet, can access this program remotely. To restrict access further, click Change Scope.
6. Click OK three times to close all open dialog boxes.

To open a port in Windows Firewall, follow these steps:

1. Open Windows Firewall by clicking the Start button, Control Panel, Security, and then click Windows Firewall.

2. Click Allow a Program Through Windows Firewall. If you are prompted for an administrator password or confirmation, enter the password or provide confirmation.
3. Click Add Port.
4. In the Name box, enter a name that will help you remember what the port is used for.
5. In the Port Number box, enter the port number.
6. Click TCP or UDP, depending on the protocol.
7. By default, any computer, including those on the Internet, can access this program remotely. To change scope for the port, click Change Scope, and then click the option that you want to use. (*Scope* refers to the set of computers that can use this port opening.)
8. Click OK two times to close all open dialog boxes.

Advanced Configuration

The new Windows Firewall with Advanced Security is a Microsoft Management Console (MMC) snap-in that provides more advanced options for IT professionals. With this firewall, you can set up and view detailed inbound and outbound rules and integrate with IPSec. To access the Windows Firewall with Advanced Security, follow these steps:

1. Open Administrative Tools by clicking the Start button, Control Panel, System and Maintenance, and then click Administrative Tools.
2. Double-click Windows Firewall with Advanced Security. If you are prompted for an administrator password or confirmation, enter the password or provide confirmation.

Of course, you must be a member of the Administrators group or the Network Operators group to use Windows Firewall with Advanced Security.

The Windows Firewall with Advanced Security management console enables you to configure the following (see Figure 7.6):

- **Inbound rules.** Windows Firewall will block all unsolicited incoming traffic unless allowed by a rule.
- **Outbound rules.** Windows Firewall will allow all outbound traffic unless blocked by a rule.

- **Connection security rules.** Forces two computers to authenticate to each other and to secure or encrypt data using IPSec.
- **Monitoring.** Display information about current firewall rules, connection security rules, and security associations.

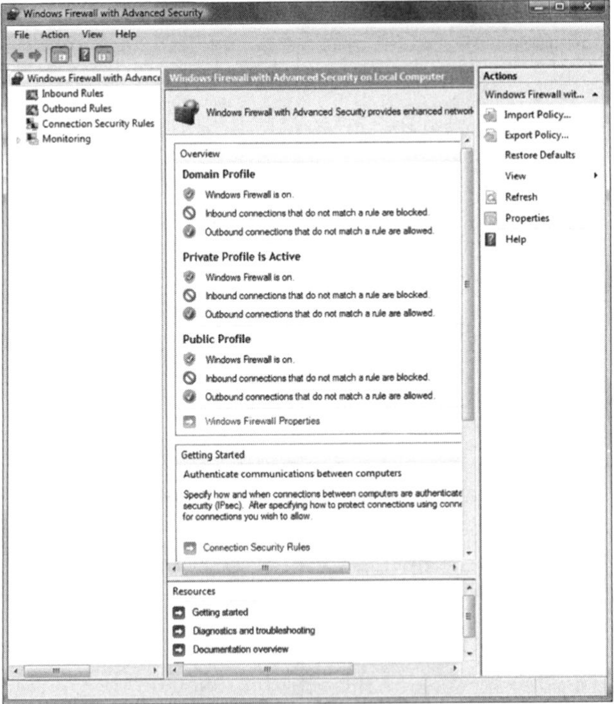

FIGURE 7.6 Windows Firewall with Advanced Security console.

You create inbound rules to control access to your computer from the network. Inbound rules can prevent the following:

- Unwanted software being copied to your computer
- Unknown or unsolicited access to data on your computer
- Unwanted configuration of your computer

To configure advanced properties for a rule using the Windows Firewall with Advanced Security, follow these steps:

1. Right-click the name of the inbound rule, and click Properties.
2. From the Properties dialog box for an inbound rule, configure settings on the following tabs:
   - **General.** The rule's name, the program to which the rule applies, and the rule's action (allow all connections, allow only secure connections, or block).
   - **Programs and Services.** The programs or services to which the rule applies.
   - **Users and Computers.** If the rule allows only secure connections, you can specify which computer accounts are allowed to make the connection.
   - **Protocols and Ports.** The rule's IP protocol, source and destination TCP or UDP ports, and ICMP or ICMPv6 settings.
   - **Scope.** The rule's source and destination addresses.
   - **Advanced.** The profiles or types of interfaces to which the rule applies.

You can also use the Windows Firewall with Advanced Security to create outbound rules to control access to network resources from your computer. Outbound rules can prevent the following:

- Programs including malware from accessing network resources without your knowledge
- Programs including malware from downloading software without your knowledge
- Users downloading software without your knowledge

Computer Connection Security Rules

Because the Internet is inherently insecure, businesses still need to preserve the privacy of data travelling over the network. IPSec creates a standard platform to develop secure networks and electronic tunnels between two machines. The two machines are known as endpoints. After the tunnel has been defined and both endpoints agree on the same parameters, the data will be encrypted on one end, encapsulated in a packet, and sent to the other endpoint (where the data is decrypted).

In Windows XP and Windows Server 2003, you configure the Windows Firewall and IPSec separately. Unfortunately, because both can block or allow incoming traffic, it is possible that the firewall and IPSec rules can conflict with each other. In Windows Vista, Windows Firewall with Advanced Security provides a single, simplified interface for managing both firewall filters and IPSec rules.

Windows Firewall with Advanced Security uses authentication rules to define IPSec policies. No authentication rules are defined by default. To create a new authentication rule, follow these steps:

1. In Windows Firewall with Advanced Security, select the Computer Connection Security node.
2. Right-click the Computer Connection Security node in the console tree, and then click New Rule to start the New Connection Security Rule Wizard.
3. From the Rule Type page of the New Authentication Rule Wizard, you can select the following:
   - **Isolation.** Used to specify that computers are isolated from other computers based on membership in a common Active Directory domain or current health status. You must specify when you want authentication to occur (for example, for incoming or outgoing traffic and whether you want to require or only request protection), the authentication method for protected traffic, and a name for the rule.
   - **Authentication exemption.** Used to specify computers that do not have to authenticate or protect traffic by their IP addresses.
   - **Server to server.** Used to specify traffic protection between specific computers, typically servers. You must specify the set of endpoints that will exchange protected traffic by IP address, when you want authentication to occur, the authentication method for protected traffic, and a name for the rule.
   - **Tunnel.** Used to specify traffic protection that is tunneled, typically used when sending packets across the Internet between two security gateway computers. You must specify the tunnel endpoints by IP address, the authentication method, and a name for the rule.

- **Custom.** Used to create a rule that does not specify a protection behavior. You would select this option when you want to manually configure a rule, perhaps based on advanced properties that cannot be configured through the pages of the New Authentication Rule Wizard. You must specify a name for the rule.

To configure advanced properties for the rule, follow these steps:

1. Right-click the name of the rule, and then click Properties.
2. From the Properties dialog box for a rule, you can configure settings on the following tabs:
   - **General.** The rule's name and description and whether the rule is enabled.
   - **Computers.** The set of computers, by IP address, for which traffic is protected.
   - **Authentication.** When you want authentication for traffic protection to occur (for example, for incoming or outgoing traffic and whether you want to require or only request protection) and the authentication method for protected traffic.
   - **Advanced.** The profiles and types of interfaces to which the rule applies and IPSec tunneling behavior.

Exam Prep Questions

1. Which of the following does spyware *not* do?

   ❍ **A.** Monitors keystrokes in an attempt to retrieve passwords and other private information

   ❍ **B.** Changes the default home page to another site

   ❍ **C.** Makes pop-up windows open frequently

   ❍ **D.** Changes the polarity of your monitor, causing physical damage

   ❍ **E.** Slows your machine

2. You work as a desktop technician at Acme.com. You have configured Windows Defender on all Microsoft Windows Vista machines on your domain. One user has an accounting application (which comes from a reputable company) that interacts with Microsoft Excel. When the application runs, an alert window opens up giving a medium-level warning stating that the software may be spyware. Because you are sure that the application is not spyware, what do you need to do to stop these warnings from appearing? (Select the best answer.)

   ❍ **A.** Open Windows Defender. Click Tools, Options, and configure Windows Defender to ignore Medium alert items.

   ❍ **B.** Configure parental controls to allow this application to run.

   ❍ **C.** Open Windows Defender. Click Tools, Options. Then, under the Advanced options, click Add in the Do Not Scan These Files or Locations. Then browse to the application executable. Click OK.

   ❍ **D.** When the warning appears again, click Always Allow.

3. You work as a desktop technician at Acme.com. Every time a user opens Internet Explorer, the home page changes even after it has been manually set to the corporate home page. What should you do?

   ❍ **A.** Open the Control Panel and remove any programs that do not have any assigned publisher.

   ❍ **B.** Remove any unfamiliar programs on the Exceptions tab in the Windows Firewall.

   ❍ **C.** Change the security level for the Internet zone to High in the Internet Options.

   ❍ **D.** Remove any unfamiliar programs whose startup type is set to Registry: Local Machine.

4. You work as the client support technician at Acme.com. You have a user who is reporting that her machine is extremely slow, even after she reboots the computer. You suspect it is either a virus or spyware. You need to view all programs during startup. What do you do?

   ❍ **A.** Open the Control Panel, double-click Services, and view all services that are set to start automatically.

   ❍ **B.** In Windows Explorer, browse to the Startup folder.

   ❍ **C.** Open Task Manager and view all applications that are currently running.

   ❍ **D.** Use Software Explorer to check what programs are loaded at startup.

5. You work as the desktop support technician at Acme.com. You want to use the fastest scan that checks the most common locations where spyware is normally found. Which type of scan would you do?

   ❍ **A.** Quick Scan

   ❍ **B.** Fast Scan

   ❍ **C.** Full Scan

   ❍ **D.** Custom Scan

6. You work as the desktop support technician at Acme.com. You are looking at the current settings in Windows Defender, which are shown in the figure.

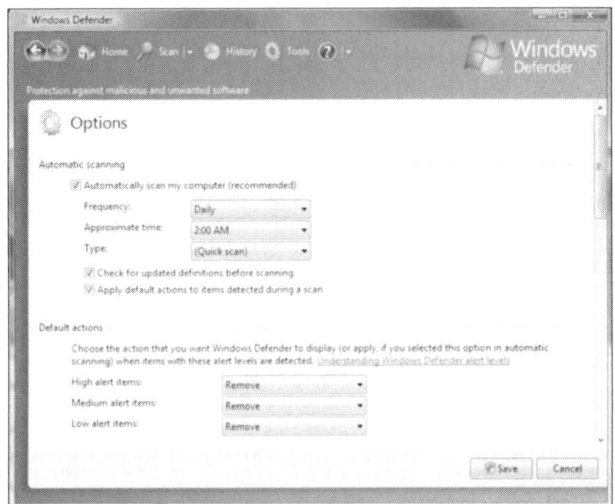

Windows Defender screenshot.

What do you need to do to make sure it that it will recommend an action to take when it detects malicious software?

- ❍ **A.** Change the High alert, Medium alert, and Low alert items to "default recommended."
- ❍ **B.** Change the type to Full Scan.
- ❍ **C.** Uncheck the Apply Default Actions to Items Detected During a Scan check box.
- ❍ **D.** Uncheck the Check for Updated Definitions Before Scanning check box.

7. You work as the desktop support technician at Acme.com. You have a user who travels a lot when working. Therefore, you have set up three sets of Windows Firewall rules for when he is at work, at home, and when traveling. The user wants to share files at home. What do you do?

❍ **A.** Using the Windows Firewall with Advanced Security console, create a rule for file sharing. Change the public profile settings to allow for incoming connections.

❍ **B.** Using the Windows Firewall with Advanced Security console, make a rule for file sharing. Change the private profile settings to allow for incoming connections.

❍ **C.** Configure Windows Firewall in the Control Panel to allow file sharing.

❍ **D.** Using the Windows Firewall with Advanced Security console, make a rule for file sharing. Change the domain profile settings to allow for incoming connections.

8. You work as part of the IT support staff at Acme.com. You have a payroll application (PAY.EXE) that requires you to send data to the check-printing company using TCP port 8787. What do you need to make this application able to function?

❍ **A.** Open Windows Firewall and ensure that it is enabled. Add PAY.EXE to the Exceptions list on the Exceptions tab.

❍ **B.** Open Windows Firewall and ensure that it is enabled. Add port 8787 to the Exceptions list on the Exceptions tab.

❍ **C.** Open Windows Defender. Add PAY.EXE to the Exceptions tab.

❍ **D.** Open Windows Defender. In the Software Explorer, click the Disable button for PAY.EXE.

9. What protocol is used to encrypt data being sent over the network?

❍ **A.** AES

❍ **B.** Stateful firewall

❍ **C.** EFS

❍ **D.** IPSec

10. You are have a mobile computer that has Windows Vista Ultimate edition. You take your computer to work and you need to get some files from the laptop computer. So, you connect the computer to your network and you try to access the shared folder, but you cannot connect to it. What do you need to do?

    ❍ **A.** You need to configure the firewall to allow file sharing.

    ❍ **B.** You need to configure Windows Defender to allow file sharing.

    ❍ **C.** You need to configure parental controls to allow file sharing.

    ❍ **D.** You need to configure Ease of Use to allow file sharing.

Answers to Exam Prep Questions

1. **Answer D is correct.** Spyware cannot physically damage a computer. It can, however, capture information as you type, change the default home page, generate pop-up windows, and slow your machine. Therefore, answers A, B, C, and E are incorrect.

2. **Answer D is correct.** When you know that a program is not spyware, click Always Allow so that it stops thinking the software is spyware. Answer A is incorrect because you don't want to ignore the other programs. Answer B is incorrect because parental controls do not function on domains. Answer C could be a correct answer, but when taking Microsoft exams where you are to choose the best answer, answer B is a better answer.

3. **Answer D is correct.** If you use Software Explorer, you can remove any program that executes during startup. Many spyware programs, including those that change home pages, load themselves automatically during startup. Therefore, you should remove any programs that you don't recognize. Answer A is incorrect because not all programs will be shown in the Add/Remove Programs. Answer B is incorrect because there is no indication it is communicating with the outside world, and using the firewall would not stop the spyware program from changing the home page. Answer C is incorrect because changing the security level would do nothing because the spyware program is already on the machine.

4. **Answer D is correct.** Because the computer is slow even after reboot, the spyware program must load every time the computer is rebooted. Therefore, it has to be loaded during startup. Answer A is incorrect because spyware is not typically loaded as a service. Answer B is not the best answer because most startup programs are specified in the registry, not the startup folder. Answer C is incorrect because if you stop the program using Task Manager, the program will still reload when you restart the computer.

5. **Answer A is correct.** Quick Scan will check all places that you normally would find spyware, including those that execute during startup. Answer B is incorrect because a Fast Scan does not exist. Answer C is incorrect because a Full Scan is much more thorough but takes much longer. Answer D is incorrect because you would then need to manually specify where to search for spyware.

6. **Answer C is correct.** By default, all suspected spyware will be removed. If you uncheck the Apply Default Actions to Items During a Scan, it will prompt you for each item on what action to take. Answer A is incorrect because there is no default recommended option. Answer B is incorrect because the same actions will be taken. A Full Scan checks all drives instead of checking where spyware is typically found. Answer D is incorrect because checking for updates is important to keep updated, but it will not change Windows Defender from automatically removing any spyware that it finds.

7. **Answer B is correct.** If you want full control of the firewall, you would use the Windows Firewall with Advanced Security. By using the Windows Firewall with Advanced Security, you can enable and configure firewall rules depending on its connection. Answer A is incorrect because you only want it enabled for private connection (home). Answer C is incorrect because if you use the Windows Firewall settings in the Control Panel, it will open up file sharing for all connections. Answer D is incorrect also because it would be for all incoming connections.

8. **Answer A is correct.** Because you want the PAY.EXE to communicate through the firewall, you can use an exception, where you can specify that PAY.EXE can communicate out port 8787. Answer B is incorrect because you want to specify that only PAY.EXE can communicate through port 8787, not any other programs. Answer C is incorrect because you don't want the PAY.EXE to communicate through any other port. Answer D is incorrect because the PAY.EXE is not a program that executes during startup.

9. **Answer D is correct.** IPSec, short for IP Security, is a protocol that encrypts data packets sent over the network. Answer A is incorrect because the AES is an encryption scheme used to encrypt data. Answer B is incorrect because stateful firewall is used to keep track of all conversations going through a firewall so that it determine which outside packets can come into the network. Answer C is incorrect because EFS is used to encrypt files and folders on an NTFS volume.

10. **Answer A is correct.** Windows Firewall is configured to block packets, including accessed shared folders. Answer B, C, and D are incorrect because you do not need to configure any of these to allow communications.

Recommended Readings and Resources

Mitch Tulloch, Tony Northrup, Jerry Honeycutt, Ed Wilson, Ralph Ramos, and the Windows Vista Team, *Windows Vista Resource Kit (Pro - Resource Kit)* (Redmond, Washington: Microsoft Press, 2007).

William R. Stanek, *Introducing Microsoft Windows Vista* (Redmond, Washington: Microsoft Press, 2006).

For more information about Windows Defender, visit http://www.microsoft.com/athome/security/spyware/software/default.mspx.

CHAPTER EIGHT

Configuring Internet Explorer 7.0

Terms you'll need to understand:

- ✓ Internet Explorer
- ✓ Add-on
- ✓ Phishing
- ✓ Protected mode
- ✓ Cookie
- ✓ ActiveX controls
- ✓ Dynamic Security
- ✓ RSS Feeds

Techniques/concepts you'll need to master:

- ✓ Demonstrate how to zoom in and out within Internet Explorer
- ✓ Configure common Internet Explorer options
- ✓ Configure Internet Explorer security
- ✓ Enable Protected mode in Internet Explorer
- ✓ Configure RSS feeds for Internet Explorer

A web browser is the client program or software that you run on your local machine to gain access to a web server. It receives commands, interprets the commands, and displays the results. It is strictly a user-interface/document presentation tool. It knows nothing about the application it is attached to, and only knows how to take the information from the server and present it to the user. It also able to capture data entry made into a form and gets the information back to the server for processing. Because these browsers are used to search and access web pages on the Internet and can be used by an organization's website or provide interface to a program, you need to understand how to configure, customize, and troubleshoot browser issues.

By far, Microsoft *Internet Explorer (IE)* is the most common browser available (because it comes with every version of Windows). Windows Vista includes IE 7.0, which has new functionality while reducing online risks.

New Features of IE 7.0

Compared to older versions of IE, the most obvious difference is its redesigned streamlined interface, which is simpler and less cluttered. As a result, IE 7.0 maximizes the space available for displaying web pages. In addition to a simpler interface, IE 7.0 introduced tabs that enable you to open multiple web pages in a single browser window. If you have a lot of tabs, you can use Quick Tabs to easily switch between open tabs.

Other features in IE 7.0 include the following:

- The new Instant Search box lets you search the web from the address bar. You can also search using different search providers to get better results.
- IE now lets you delete your temporary files, cookies, web page history, saved passwords, and form information from one place. Delete selected categories, or everything at once.
- Click the Favorites Center button to open the Favorites Center to manage favorites, feeds, and history in one place.
- Printing now scales web pages to fit the paper you're using. Print Preview gives more control when printing, with manual scaling and an accurate view of what you're about to print.
- By subscribing to a feed, you can get updated content, such as breaking news or your favorite blog, without having to visit the website.

- The Zoom feature lets you enlarge or reduce text, images, and some controls. IE Zoom lets you enlarge or reduce the view of a web page. Unlike changing font size, Zoom enlarges or reduces everything on the page, including text and images. You can zoom from 10 percent to 1,000 percent.

To zoom a web page, follow these steps:

1. On the bottom right of the IE screen, click the arrow to the right of the Change Zoom Level button.
2. Do one of the following:
    - To go to a predefined zoom level, click the percentage of enlargement or reduction you want.
    - To specify a custom level, click Custom. In the Percentage Zoom box, enter a zoom value, and then click OK.

If you have a mouse with a wheel, hold down the Ctrl key, and then scroll the wheel to zoom in or out. If you click the Change Zoom Level button, it will cycle through 100%, 125%, and 150%, giving you a quick enlargement of the web page. From the keyboard, you can increase or decrease the zoom value in 10 percent increments. To zoom in, press Ctrl + the plus sign key (Ctrl++). To zoom out, press Ctrl + the hyphen (Ctrl+-). To restore the zoom to 100 percent, press Ctrl+0.

Common IE Settings

Most of the configuration options for IE are accessed by starting IE, clicking the Tools button, and selecting Internet Options. It can also be accessed from the Internet Options applet in the Control Panel. The Internet Options dialog box has several tabs, including General, Security, Privacy, Content, Connections, Programs, and Advanced (see Figure 8.1).

At the top of the General tab, you can configure the home page or the default page that is loaded when you start IE. This enables you to have your favorite search engine, news, website, portal, or an organization's internal website load automatically when you start IE. By going to a web page and then clicking the Use Current button, you make the page that is currently being displayed your home page. You can also configure it to show a blank page. Of course, to make the change go into effect, you have to click the Apply or OK button.

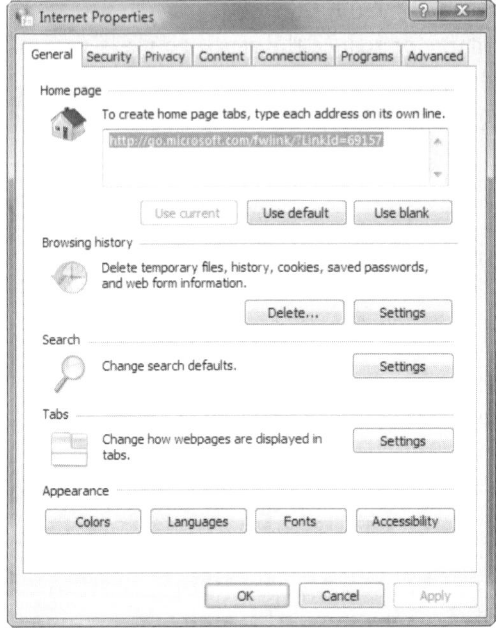

FIGURE 8.1 IE options.

Some organizations may configure the organization's home page as the default home page so that users cannot make changes to IE using group policies. Other times, if you experience an unexpected change in the home page, it was most likely caused by visiting a particular website (usually you have to click Yes to change the website, but that is not always the case), installing a program that changes the IE home page, or being infected by a virus or spyware.

Below the home page, you will find the section to configure browsing history, including how IE uses temporary Internet files, which are used as a disk cache for Internet browsing. When you visit a website, parts of the web page (such as pictures, sound, and video files) are copied on the system as a temporary Internet file so that on future visits to that site, it will load faster. If you click the Settings button, you can configure the browser to check for newer versions of the saved page on every visit, every time you start IE, automatically, or never. If you need to force IE to reload a fresh web page, you can hold down on the Shift key while you click Refresh, or press Shift+F5. You can also click the View Files button to view the temporary Internet files.

You can determine how much disk space you want to use as a cache and where the folder is located that stores the temporary files. If you click View Files, you will open the folder that stores the temporary files so that you can inspect them directly.

History specifies the number of days that IE should keep track of your viewed pages in the History list. IE creates shortcuts to pages you viewed in this and previous browsing sessions. If you are low on disk space, you might want to decrease the number. You can also clear your history from here.

The AutoComplete feature remembers previous entries that you made for web addresses, forms, and passwords. When you type information in one of these fields, AutoComplete suggests possible matches. These matches can include folder and program names you type into the address bar; the matches can also include search queries, stock quotes, or other information that you type in forms on web pages. To use AutoComplete, start typing the information in the address bar, in a field on a web page, or in a box for a username or password. If you have typed a similar entry before, AutoComplete lists possible matches as you type. If a suggestion in the list matches what you want to enter in that field, click the suggestion. If no suggestion matches what you are typing, continue typing.

To select AutoComplete settings in IE, click Tools, Internet Options. On the Content tab, click AutoComplete. You can specify whether you want to use AutoComplete for web addresses, forms, usernames, and passwords. You can also clear the history of previous AutoComplete entries. When typing information in web forms, and when typing passwords, you can remove an item from the list of suggestions by clicking the item and then pressing the Delete key.

If you click the Advanced options, you can configure a wide range of configuration options, including disabling script debugging, enabling Folder view for FTP sites, enabling personalized favorites menu, notifying when downloads are complete, enabling automatic image resizing, and playing sounds and videos in web pages. It also has several security features such as emptying temporary Internet files when the browser is closed, enabling Profile Assisting, using Secure Sockets Layer (SSL) 2.0 or 3.0 (needed to connect to secure web pages as indicated by https://), warning about invalid site certificates, and warning if a form is being redirected (see Figure 8.2).

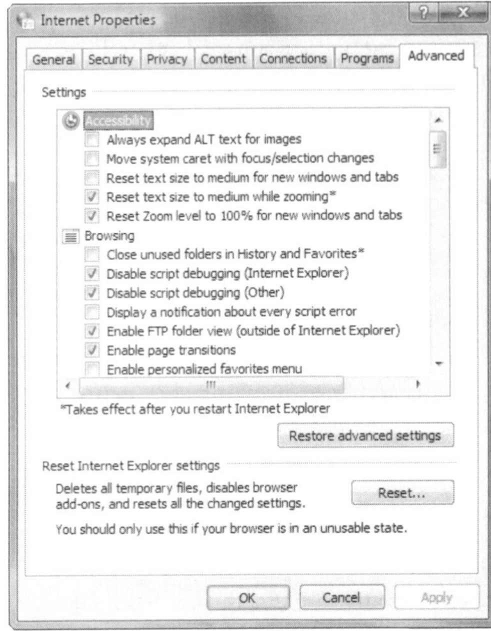

FIGURE 8.2 Advanced options in IE.

Plug-Ins, Add-Ons, and Scripting Languages

To make IE more powerful and more flexible and by adding additional functionality, IE has the capability to use add-ons and scripting languages. A *plug-in* is a software module that adds a specific feature or service to the browser to display or play different types of audio or video messages. The most common plug-ins are Shockwave, RealMedia (RealAudio and RealVideo), and Adobe Reader (used to read Portable Document Format [PDF]).

In an effort to make browsing more functional, web developers create and enable active content. Active content uses small executable or script code that is executed and shown within the client's web browser. Unfortunately, like a Trojan horse virus, this feature is an added security risk; some scripts could be used to perform harmful actions on a client machine. Some of the most popular types of active content are VBScript, JavaScript, and ActiveX components.

To view current add-ons, follow these steps:

1. Click the Tools button, Manage Add-Ons, Enable or Disable Add-Ons.
2. In the Show box, select one of the following options:
    - To display a complete list of the add-ons that reside on your computer, click Add-Ons That Have Been Used by Internet Explorer.
    - To display only those add-ons that were needed for the current web page or a recently viewed web page, click Add-Ons Currently Loaded in Internet Explorer.
    - To display add-ons that were preapproved by Microsoft, your computer manufacturer, or a service provider, click Add-Ons That Run Without Requiring Permission.
    - To display only 32-bit ActiveX controls, click Downloaded ActiveX Controls (32-bit).

When you run an add-on for the first time, IE will ask permission, which should notify you if a website is secretly trying to run malicious code. IE has a list of preapproved add-ons that have been checked and digitally signed. The add-on list can come from Microsoft, your computer manufacturer, your Internet service provider (if you are using a private branded version of IE), or your corporation's network administrator. These add-ons in this list are run without displaying the permissions dialog.

Add-ons are typically fine to use, but sometimes they force IE to shut down unexpectedly. This can happen if the add-on was created for an earlier version of IE or has a programming error. When you encounter a problematic add-on, you can disable it or report it to Microsoft. If disabling add-ons doesn't solve the problem, try resetting IE back to its default settings.

To permanently disable add-ons, follow these steps:

1. Click the Tools button, Manage Add-Ons, Enable or Disable Add-Ons.
2. In the Show list, click Add-Ons That Have Been Used by Internet Explorer to display all add-ons.
3. Click the add-on you want to disable, and then click Disable. Repeat for every add-on you want to disable.
4. When you have finished, click OK.

To reenable an add-on, follow these steps:

1. Click the Tools button, Manage Add-Ons, Enable or Disable Add-Ons.
2. In the Show list, click Add-Ons That Have Been Used by Internet Explorer to display all add-ons.
3. Click the add-on you want to enable, and then click Enable. Repeat for every add-on you want to enable.
4. When you have finished, click OK.

To temporarily disable all add-ons, follow these steps:

1. Click the Start button, All Programs.
2. Click Accessories.
3. Click System Tools.
4. Click Internet Explorer (No Add-ons).

You can delete only ActiveX controls that you have downloaded and installed. You cannot delete ActiveX controls that were preinstalled or add-ons of any kind, but you can disable them. To delete an ActiveX control that you have installed, use the Remove Programs tool in the Windows Control Panel, as follows:

1. Click the Start button and select Control Panel.
2. Under Programs, click Uninstall a Program.
3. Select the program that has ActiveX and click the Uninstall button.
4. If it asks whether you are sure, click the Yes button.

IE Security Features

IE offers a number of features to help protect your security and privacy when you browse the web, including the following:

- **Phishing Filter.** Helps protect you from online phishing attacks, fraud, and spoofed websites.
- **Protected mode.** Helps protect you from websites that try to save files or install programs on your computer.
- **Pop-up Blocker.** Helps block most pop-up windows.

- **Add-on Manager.** Lets you disable or enable web browser add-ons and delete unwanted ActiveX controls.
- **Notification.** Notifies you when a website is trying to download files or software to your computer.
- **Digital signatures.** Tells you who published a file and whether it has been altered since it was digitally signed.
- **128-bit secure (SSL) connection for using secure websites.** Helps IE create an encrypted connection with websites such as banks and online stores.

Cookies and Privacy Settings

A *cookie* is a message given to a web browser by a web server, and is typically stored in a text file on the PC's hard drive. The message is then sent back to the server each time the browser requests a page from the server. The main purpose of cookies is to identify users and possibly prepare customized web pages for the user. When you enter a website using cookies, you may be asked to fill out a form providing some information as your name and interests. This information is packaged into a cookie and sent to your web browser, which stores it for later use. The next time you go the same website, your browser will send the cookie to the web server. The server can use this information to present you with custom web pages. So, for example, instead of seeing just a generic welcome page, you might see a welcome page with your name on it.

Among other things, cookies are used to keep track of what a person buys, personalize online ordering, personalize a website, store a person's profile, store IDs, and provide support to older web browsers that do not support host header names. A cookie cannot be used to get data from your hard drive, get your e-mail addresses, or steal sensitive information about you.

From the General tab, you can delete the cookies that are stored on your hard drive. By clicking the Privacy tab, you can determine how much of your personal information can be accessed by websites and whether a website can save cookies on your computer by adjusting the tab slider on the privacy scale.

To view privacy settings, select the Privacy tab on the Internet Options dialog box. To adjust your privacy settings, adjust the tab slider to a new position on the privacy scale. A description of the privacy settings that you select displays on the right side of the tab slider. The default level is Medium; it is recommended to configure Medium or higher. You can also override the default for cookies in each security zone. In addition, you can override certain settings (automatic cookie handling and session cookies) by clicking the Advanced button, or you can allow or block cookies from individual websites by clicking the Edit button.

Many websites provide privacy statements that you can view. A site's privacy policy tells you what kind of information the site collects and stores and what it does with the information. Information that you should be mostly concerned with is how the websites uses personally identifiable information such as your name, e-mail addresses, address, and telephone number. Websites also might provide a Platform for Privacy Preferences (P3P) privacy policy, which can be used by browsers to filter cookie transactions on the basis of the cookie's content and purpose. To view the privacy report, open the View menu and click Privacy Report. To view a site's privacy statement, select the website and click the Summary button.

Content Zones

To help manage IE security when visiting sites, IE divides the network connection into four content types:

- **Internet zone.** Anything that is not assigned to any other zone and anything that is not on your computer, or your organization's network (intranet). The default security level of the Internet zone is Medium.
- **Local intranet zone.** Computers that are part of the organization's network (intranet) that do not require a proxy server, as defined by the system administrator. These include sites specified on the Connections' tab, network, paths such as *computername**foldername*, and local intranet sites such as http://internal. You can add sites to this zone. The default security level for the local intranet zone is Medium=Low, which means IE will allow all cookies from websites in this zone to be saved on your computer and read by the website that created them.
- **Trusted sites zone.** Contains trusted sites that you believe you can download or run files from without damaging your computer or data or that you consider are not a security risk. You can assign sites to this zone. The default security level for the trusted sites zone is Low, which means IE will allow all cookies from websites in this zone to be saved on your computer and read by the website that created them.
- **Restricted sites zone.** Contains sites that you do not trust and from which downloading or running files may damage your computer or data, or you just consider them a security risk. You can assign sites to this zone. The default security level for the restricted sites zone is High, which means IE will block all cookies from websites in this zone.

For each of the web content zones, there is a default security level. The security levels available in IE are as follows:

- **High.** Excludes any content that can damage your computer.
- **Medium.** Warns you before running potentially damaging content.
- **Low.** Does not warn you before running potentially damaging content.
- **Custom.** A security setting of your own design. Use this level to customize the behavior and Active Data Object (ADO) and Remote Data Services (RDS) objects in a specific zone.

Whenever you access a website, IE checks the security settings for zone of the website. To tell which zones the current web page falls into, you look at the right side of the IE status bar. Besides adjusting the zones or assigning the zones or assigning a website to a zone, you can also customize settings for a zone by importing a privacy settings file from a certificate authority.

To modify the security level for a web content zone, follow these steps:

1. Click the Tools button, Internet Options.
2. In the Internet Options dialog box, on the Security tab, click the zone on which you want to set the security level.
3. Drag the slider to set the security level to High, Medium, or Low. IE describes each option to help you decide which level to choose. You are prompted to confirm any reduction in security level. You can also choose the Custom Level button for more detailed control (see Figure 8.3).
4. Click OK to close the Internet Options dialog box.

Software publisher certificates (third-party digital certificates) are used to validate software code such as Java or ActiveX controls or plug-ins. Depending on the security settings for a zone, when software code is accessed from a website, you will automatically download the software code, disable the software code, or prompt to download the software code via a security warning. If you open the Tools menu and select Internet Options, select the Security tab, and click the Custom Level button, you can select to enable, disable, or prompt to download ActiveX controls (signed and unsigned) and scripting of Java applets.

To view the certificates for IE, open the Internet Options dialog box, click the Content tab, and then click the Certificates button. To see list of certificates, click the appropriate certificates. From here, you can also import and export individual certificates.

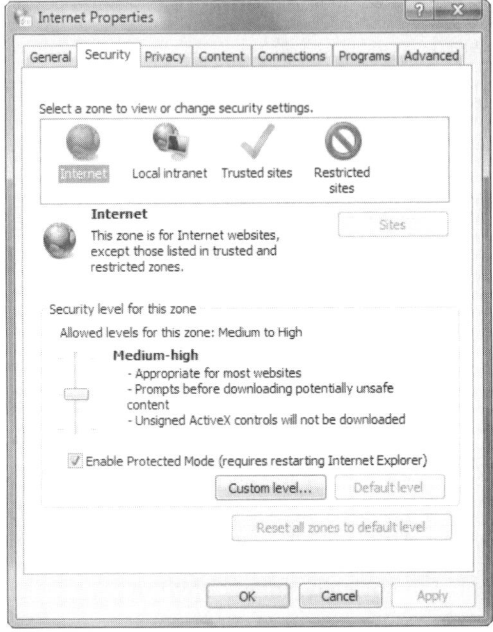

FIGURE 8.3 Security options within IE.

Dynamic Security and Protected Mode

Dynamic Security options for IE 7.0 offer multiple security features to defend your computer against malware and data theft. The Security status bar keeps you notified of the website security and privacy settings by using color-coded notifications next to the address bar. Some of these features are as follows:

- Address bar turns green to indicate that a website is bearing new High Assurance certificates, indicating the site owner has completed extensive identity verification checks.
- Phishing Filter notifications, certificate names, and the gold padlock icon are now also adjacent to the address bar for better visibility.
- Certificate and privacy detail information can easily be displayed with a single click in the Security status bar.
- The address bar is displayed to the user for every window, whether it's a pop-up or standard window, which helps to block malicious sites from emulating trusted sites.

- To help protect you against phishing sites, IE warns you when visiting potential or known fraudulent sites and blocks the site if appropriate. The opt-in filter is updated several times per hour with the latest security information from Microsoft and several industry partners.
- International Domain Name Anti-Spoofing notifies you when visually similar characters in the URL are not expressed in the same language.

To protect your system even further, IE includes the following features:

- **ActiveX opt-in.** Disables nearly all pre-installed ActiveX controls to prevent potentially vulnerable controls from being exposed to attack. You can easily enable or disable ActiveX controls as needed through the Information Bar and the Add-on Manager.
- **Cross-domain barriers.** Limit scripts on web pages from interacting with content from other domains or windows. This enhanced safeguard will help to protect against malicious software by limiting the potential for malicious websites to manipulate flaws in other websites or cause you to download undesired content or software.

If IE is still using its original settings, you'll see the Information bar in the following circumstances:

- If a website tries to install an ActiveX control on your computer or run an ActiveX control in an unsafe manner
- If a website tries to open a pop-up window
- If a website tries to download a file to your computer
- If a website tries to run active content on your computer
- If your security settings are below recommended levels
- If you access an intranet web page, but have not turned on intranet address checking
- If you started IE with add-ons disabled
- If you need to install an updated ActiveX control or add-on program
- If the web page address can be displayed with native language letters or symbols, but you don't have the language installed

When you see a message in the information bar, click the message to see more information or to take action.

To stop the information bar from blocking file and software downloads, follow these steps:

1. Click to open IE.
2. Click the Tools button, Internet Options.
3. Click the Security tab, and then click Custom Level.
4. Do one or both of the following:
    - To turn off the information bar for file downloads, scroll to the Downloads section of the list, and then, under Automatic Prompting for File Downloads, click Enable.
    - To turn off the information bar for ActiveX controls, scroll to the ActiveX Controls and Plug-Ins section of the list, and then, under Automatic Prompting for ActiveX Controls, click Enable.
5. Click OK, click Yes to confirm that you want to make the change, and then click OK again.

Table 8.1 lists some of the more common messages that might appear in the information bar, along with a description of what each message means.

TABLE 8.1 Information Bar Messages

Message	What It Means
To help protect your security, Internet Explorer stopped this site from installing an ActiveX control on your computer. Click here for options.	The web page tried to install an ActiveX control, and IE blocked it. If you want to install the ActiveX control and you trust the publisher of the ActiveX control, right-click the information and select Install Software.
Pop-up blocked. To see this pop-up or additional options click here.	Pop-up Blocker has blocked a pop-up window. You can turn Pop-up Blocker off or allow pop-ups temporarily by clicking the information bar.
This website is using a scripted window to ask you for information. If you trust this website, click here to allow scripted windows.	IE has blocked a website that tried to display a separate window such as a logon screen in an attempt to gather confidential information. If you trust the website, click the information bar and click select Temporarily Allow Scripted Windows or Allow Websites to Prompt for Information Using the Scripted Windows customer security setting.

TABLE 8.1 *Continued*

Message	What It Means
To help protect your security, Internet Explorer blocked this site from downloading files to your computer. Click here for options.	A web page tried to download a file that you might not have requested. If you want to download the file, click the information bar, and then click Download File.
Your security settings do not allow websites to use ActiveX controls installed on your computer. This page may not display correctly. Click here for options.	The website tried to install an ActiveX control, but your security settings did not allow it. This is usually caused when a website is listed in the restricted site list. If you trust the site, remove the site from the restricted site zone. If the problem still exists, try adding the site to the trusted sites list. To access the trusted sites, click the Tools button and select Internet Options. Then select the Security tab, select Trusted Sites, and click the Sites button.
Internet Explorer has blocked this site from using an ActiveX control in an unsafe manner. As a result, this page may not display correctly.	A website tried to access an ActiveX control on your computer without your permission.

IE's *Protected mode* is a feature that makes it more difficult for malicious software to be installed on your computer. In addition, it allows users to install wanted software when they are logged on as a standard user rather than an administrator. Protected mode is turned on by default, and an icon appears on the status bar to let you know that it's running. When you try to install software, Protected mode will warn you when web pages try to install software or if a software program runs outside of Protected mode. If you trust the program and want to allow it to run on any website, select the Always Allow Websites to Use This Program to Open Web Content check box.

EXAM ALERT

Protected mode makes it more difficult for malicious software to be installed on your machine.

NOTE

As mentioned in Chapter 3, "Using Windows Vista," Windows Vista offers parental controls to help keep children safer online (by allowing parents to control browsing behavior). A child's browsing session can even be examined by a parent afterward, and cannot be removed without the parent's permission. Parental controls can be configured from the User Accounts and Family Safety section of the Control Panel.

RSS Feeds

RSS, short for RDF Site Summary or Rich Site Summary, is an Extended Markup Language (XML) format for syndicating web content. A website that wants to allow other sites to publish some of its content creates an RSS document and registers the document with an RSS publisher. A user that can read RSS-distributed content can use the content on a different site. Syndicated content includes such data as news feeds, events listings, news stories, headlines, project updates, and excerpts from discussion forums or even corporate information.

A feed can have the same content as a web page, but it's often formatted differently. When you subscribe, IE automatically checks the website and downloads new content so that you can see what is new since you last visited the feed.

To indicate whether a web page has a feed, the Feeds button will change color, letting you know that feeds are available on the web page. To subscribe to a feed, follow these steps:

1. Open IE.
2. Go to the website that has the feed you want to subscribe to.
3. Click the Feeds button to discover feeds on the web page.
4. Click a feed (if more than one is available). If only one feed is available, you will go directly to that page.
5. Click the Subscribe to This Feed button, and then click Subscribe to This Feed.
6. Type a name for the feed and select the folder to create the feed in.
7. Click Subscribe.

To view feeds, go to the Feed tab in the Favorites Center. To view your feeds, click the Favorites Center button, and then click Feeds. You can also use other programs such as e-mail clients such as Microsoft Outlook and Windows Sidebar to read the feeds set up with IE.

Reset IE to Default Settings

To reset IE settings and to help troubleshoot problems, you can remove all changes that have been made to IE since it was installed, without deleting your favorites or feeds. To reset IE, follow these steps:

1. Close all IE or Windows Explorer windows.
2. Click to open IE.
3. Click the Tools button, Internet Options.
4. Click the Advanced tab, and then click Reset.
5. Click Reset.
6. When you have finished, click Close, and then click OK.
7. Close IE and reopen it for the changes to take effect.

You can also restore the options in the Advanced tab of the Internet Options dialog box by clicking the Restore Advanced Settings button on the Advanced tab.

EXAM ALERT

To reset Windows Explorer, click the Reset button within the Advanced tab. If you want to reset only the advanced options, click the Restore Advanced Settings button.

Exam Prep Questions

1. You work as the desktop support technician at Acme.com. How do you reset IE to its original settings?

   ❍ **A.** Reinstall IE 7.0.

   ❍ **B.** Navigate to the Security tab in Internet Options and click Reset all zones to default level.

   ❍ **C.** Navigate to the Advanced tab in Internet Options and click Restore Advanced Settings.

   ❍ **D.** Navigate to the Advanced tab and click Reset.

2. You work as the desktop support technician at Acme.com. How do you remove the stored passwords from a computer?

   ❍ **A.** On the Security tab in Internet Options, set the Internet zone security to High.

   ❍ **B.** On the Privacy tab in Internet Options, set the level to Medium.

   ❍ **C.** On the Privacy tab in Internet Options, set the level to High.

   ❍ **D.** Navigate to the Advanced tab in Internet Options and click Restore advanced settings.

   ❍ **E.** Click Tools in the IE, and then click Delete Browsing History. Click Delete passwords.

3. How do you prevent passwords from being stored locally when visiting websites that require usernames and passwords?

   ❍ **A.** On the Security tab in Internet Options, set the Internet zone security to High.

   ❍ **B.** On the Privacy tab in Internet Options, set the level to Medium.

   ❍ **C.** On the Privacy tab in Internet Options, set the level to High.

   ❍ **D.** On the Content tab in Internet Options, click the AutoComplete Settings button and clear the User Names and Passwords on Forms check box.

   ❍ **E.** Click Tools in the IE, and then click Delete Browsing History. Click Delete passwords.

4. You have a user who is complaining that the images shown in IE are too small. What do you need to do?

   ❍ **A.** You need to decrease the screen resolution.

   ❍ **B.** You need to increase the screen resolution.

   ❍ **C.** You need to decrease the zoom level for the tab.

   ❍ **D.** You need to increase the zoom level for the tab.

5. You work as part of the IT support staff at Acme.com. You have a user who saves files that she downloads from various websites. You want to make sure that when she visits these websites those websites don't modify the files that she saved previously. What do you need to do?

   ❍ **A.** Disable all ActiveX controls that are currently loaded.

   ❍ **B.** Enable the Phishing Filter.

   ❍ **C.** Change the security level for the Internet zone to High.

   ❍ **D.** Enable the Protected mode option.

6. You work as the desktop support technician at Acme.com. When a user clicks a link in a website, nothing happens. What do you think the problem is?

   ❍ **A.** You need to enable an add-on that the link points to.

   ❍ **B.** Open the Internet Options dialog box. On the Security tab, add the URL to the trusted sites list.

   ❍ **C.** Open the Pop-up Blocker Settings dialog box. Add the URL to the allowed sites list.

   ❍ **D.** Open the Internet Options dialog box. On the Privacy tab, add the URL to the allowed sites list.

   ❍ **E.** Open the Internet Options dialog box. On the Advanced tab, choose the Disable Phishing Filter option.

7. What technology in IE is used to protect you from spoofed sites that might try to trick you into divulging confidential information?

   ❍ **A.** Protected mode

   ❍ **B.** Phishing Filter

   ❍ **C.** Junk Mail Filter

   ❍ **D.** Fake Site Filter

8. What can be done to notify you when a website has changed?

   ❍ **A.** Configure Auto-Update within IIS.

   ❍ **B.** Configure Dynamic Update within IIS.

   ❍ **C.** If a website supports RSS, you can configure an RSS feed.

   ❍ **D.** Close IE and restart it.

Answers to Exam Prep Questions

1. **Answer D is correct.** To reset IE to its original settings, you have to open Internet Options, select the Security tab, and click Reset. Answer A is incorrect because reinstalling IE does not generally overwrite the settings that are already configured. Answer B is incorrect because resetting zones will affect only information specified in the security zones. Answer C is incorrect because this will only reset the advanced options.

2. **Answer E is correct.** To delete saved passwords in IE, you must delete the browsing history. Answers A, B, and C are incorrect because these methods will not affect any saved passwords. Answer D is incorrect because passwords are not affected by the advanced settings.

3. **Answer D is correct.** To prevent passwords from beings stored, you have to configure the AutoComplete feature. Answer A, B, and C do not affect AutoComplete and passwords. Answer E is used to delete saved passwords.

4. **Answer D is correct.** When you have trouble seeing an image, you can use the Zoom feature. Answers A and B are incorrect because they affect all programs. Answer C is incorrect because decreasing the zoom makes the image smaller.

5. **Answer D is correct.** Protected mode helps protect you from websites that try to save files or install programs on your computer. Answer A is incorrect because disabling all ActiveX components may disable functionality that you might use for other websites. Answer B is incorrect because the Phishing Filter is used to stop users from being tricked into fake sites that emulate corporate sites in an attempt to steal confidential information. Answer C is incorrect because it was never stated what level the website is. Therefore, changing the level may or may not affect the controls.

6. **Answer C is correct.** When you click some links, the link is supposed to open a separate window. If you have a pop-up blocker set up, the site might be blocked. Answer A is incorrect because add-ons are designed to run within a website, not as a stand-alone application. Anwer B is incorrect because adding a URL to a trusted site might have some effect on functionality but it would not allow or disallow the entire window for opening. Answers D and E are incorrect because none of these affect whether a website opens.

7. **Answer B is correct.** Some sites are created to look like other sites and are used to lure people to divulge confidential information. Because these sites are "fishing" for information, these sites are referred to as phishing. Answer A is incorrect because Protected mode tries to secure the IE by securing other files. Answer C is incorrect because Junk Mail Filter is used in e-mail. Answer D is incorrect because there is no such thing as Fake Site Filter.

8. **Answer C is correct.** RSS feeds are used to get automatic updates and notifications when a website posts something new. Answer A is incorrect because auto updates are used to automatically update Windows security patches and fixes. Answer B is incorrect because dynamic updates provide application and device compatibility updates, driver updates, and emergency fixes for setup or security issues (when you run Windows Setup). Answer D is incorrect because closing IE and restarting it will open up the home page again. It will not notify when other websites get updated.

Recommended Readings and Resources

Mitch Tulloch, Tony Northrup, Jerry Honeycutt, Ed Wilson, Ralph Ramos, and the Windows Vista Team, *Windows Vista Resource Kit (Pro. Resource Kit)* (Redmond, Washington: Microsoft Press, 2007).

William R. Stanek, *Introducing Microsoft Windows Vista* (Redmond, Washington: Microsoft Press, 2006).

For more information about Internet Explorer, visit http://www.microsoft.com/windows/products/winfamily/ie/default.mspx.

CHAPTER NINE

Maintaining and Optimizing Windows Vista Systems

Terms you'll need to understand:

- ✓ Performance
- ✓ Reliability
- ✓ Task Manager
- ✓ Data Collector Set (DCS)
- ✓ Windows Reliability and Performance Monitor
- ✓ Chkdsk
- ✓ Defragmentation
- ✓ ReadyBoost
- ✓ ReadyDrive
- ✓ Memory Diagnostic tool
- ✓ Startup Repair tool (StR)
- ✓ Safe mode

Techniques/concepts you'll need to master:

- ✓ Use the Windows Reliability and Performance Monitor and Task Manager to identify bottlenecks.
- ✓ Run Chkdsk to verify the integrity of the drive.
- ✓ Run Disk Defragmenter to optimize your drive.
- ✓ Configure the paging file for optimum performance.
- ✓ Describe, enable, and configure ReadyBoost and ReadyDrive.
- ✓ Run multiple troubleshooting tools, including the Memory Diagnostic tool, Network Diagnostic tool, Startup Repair tool, System Configuration tool, and the Problems Reports and Solutions tool.
- ✓ Troubleshoot various computer problems in Safe mode.
- ✓ Use Event Viewer to view errors and warnings when troubleshooting a problem.

Performance is the overall effectiveness of how data moves through the system. To be able to improve performance, you must determine the part of the system that is slowing down the throughput. Processor speed, the amount of RAM on the machine, the speed of the disk system, the speed of the network adapter card, or another factor can affect performance. This limiting factor is referred to as the bottleneck of the system.

Reliability is a measure of how often a system deviates from configured, expected behavior. Reliability problems occur as the result of application crashes, service freezes and restarts, driver initialization failures, and operating system failures.

Hardware, memory, and performance diagnostics are the heart of the Windows Vista self-correcting architecture. Hardware diagnostics can detect error conditions and either repair the problem automatically or guide the user through a recovery process. With potential disk failures, hardware diagnostics guide users through the backup procedure to minimize downtime and data loss.

Windows Reliability and Performance Monitor and Task Manager

Windows Reliability and Performance Monitor is a Microsoft Management Console (MMC) snap-in that provides tools for analyzing system performance. From a single console, you can monitor application and hardware performance in real time, customize what data you want to collect in logs, define thresholds for alerts and automatic actions, generate reports, and view past performance data in a variety of ways.

An important feature in Windows Reliability and Performance Monitor is the *Data Collector Set (DCS)*, which groups data collectors into reusable elements. After a Data Collector Set is defined, you can schedule the collection of data using the DCS or see it in real time.

Windows Reliability and Performance Monitor consists of three monitoring tools:

- Resource View
- Performance Monitor
- Reliability Monitor

To start the Reliability and Performance Monitor, follow these steps:

1. Click Start, right-click Computer, and click Manage.
2. Expand System Tools and click Reliability and Performance.

NOTE

To be able to view the performance counters, a user needs to be in the Performance Monitor Users group or an administrator.

Windows Reliability and Performance Monitor will start with the Resource view display, which enables you to monitor the usage and performance of the major system subcomponents: processors, disks, network, and memory resources in real time (see Figure 9.1). You can then click the Detail button to see which processes are using which resources.

NOTE

If Resource view does not display real-time data when Windows Reliability and Performance Monitor starts, click the green Start button in the toolbar.

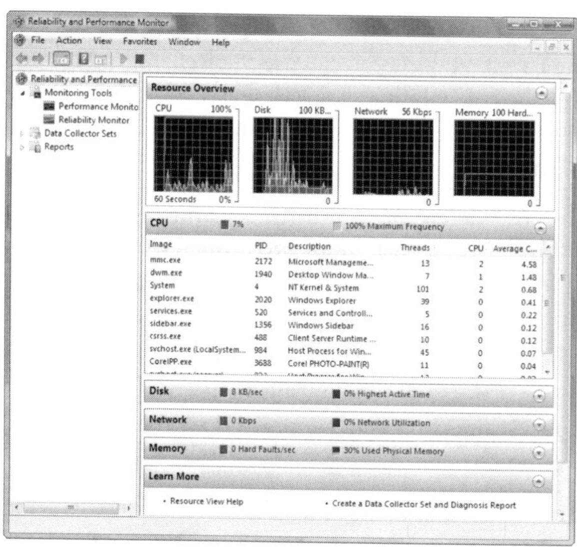

FIGURE 9.1 Reliability and Performance Monitor showing the Resource view.

Performance Monitor provides a visual display of built-in Windows performance counters, either in real time or as a way to review historical data (see Figure 9.2).

You can add performance counters to Performance Monitor by dragging and dropping, or by creating custom DCSs. It features multiple graph views that enable you to visually review performance log data. You can create custom views in Performance Monitor that can be exported as DCSs for use with performance and logging features.

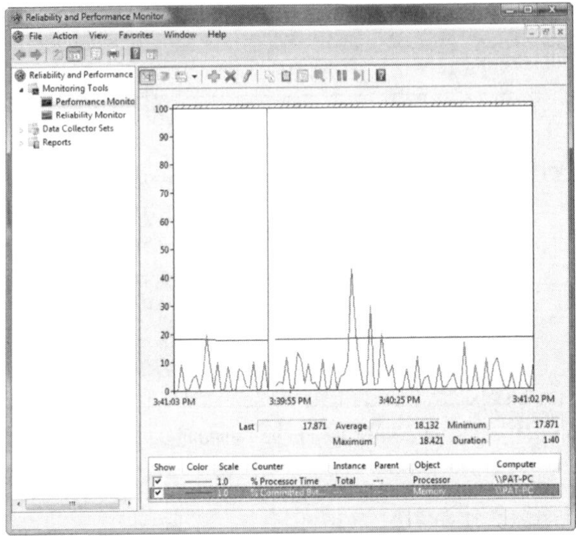

FIGURE 9.2 Performance Monitor.

Besides combing through the Event Viewer, you can use the Reliability Monitor to give you an overview of the system stability and to view individual events that affect overall stability. Some of the events shown are software installation, operating system updates, and hardware failures (see Figure 9.3).

Another tool that you can use to view system performance is the Windows *Task Manager*. The Performance tab includes four graphs (see Figure 9.4). The top two graphs show how much CPU is being used, both at the moment, and for the past few minutes. (If the CPU Usage History graph appears split, your computer either has multiple CPUs, a single dual-core CPU, or both.) A high percentage means that programs or processes are requiring a lot of CPU resources, which can slow your computer. If the percentage appears frozen at or near 100 percent, a program might not be responding.

The bottom two graphs display how much RAM, or physical memory, is being used in megabytes (MB), both at the current moment and for the past few minutes. The percentage of memory being used is listed at the bottom of the Task Manager window. If memory use seems consistently high or slows your computer's performance noticeably, try reducing the number of programs you have open at one time or install more RAM.

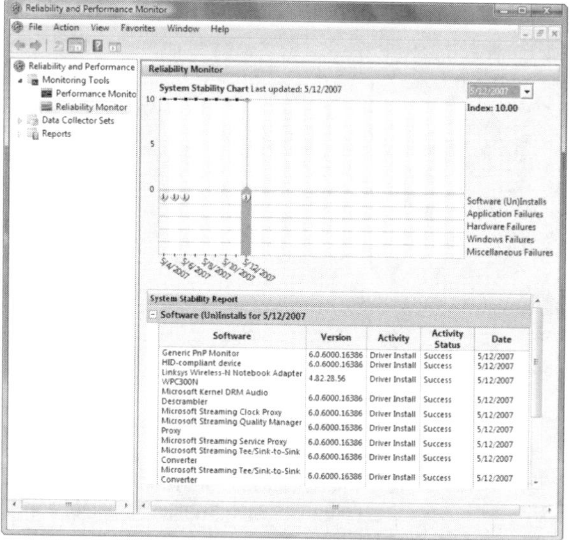

FIGURE 9.3 Reliability Monitor.

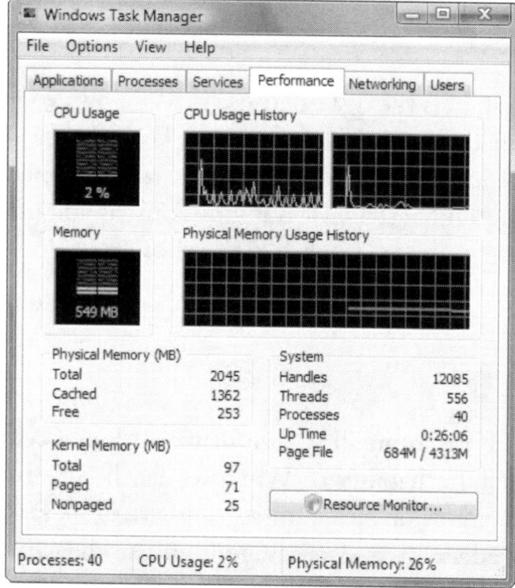

FIGURE 9.4 Window Task manager showing the Performance tab.

To get a list of all individual processes or programs running in memory and how much processor utilization and memory use each application is using, click the Processes tab. You can also manually end any process here, which comes in handy when a process stops responding (see Figure 9.5).

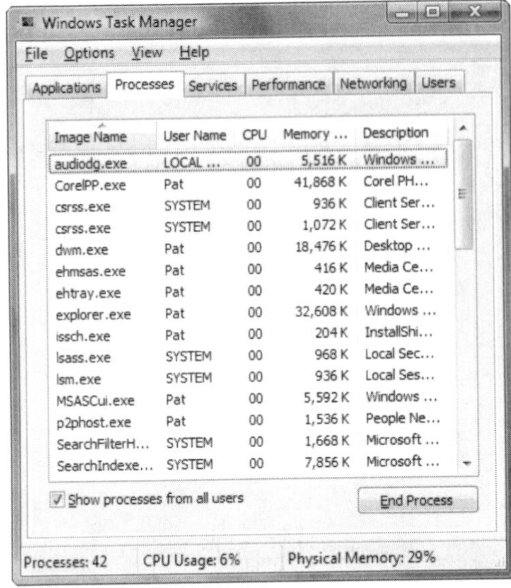

FIGURE 9.5 The Process tab in Windows Task Manager can show you what processes are running, how much resources each process is using, and enable you to end a process.

Optimizing the Disk

One of the key components to the system is the disk. Because in Windows your applications and the data come from the hard drive, you must keep the hard drive optimized to keep your system performing well. Of course, as mentioned in Chapter 6, "Configuring User Account Security," it is important that you use the NTFS file system. You should then monitor free disk space, check your drive for errors, and defrag your hard drive on a regular basis.

Monitoring Disk Space

You should closely monitor disk space usage on all system drives. When a system drive fills up, the performance and reliability of Windows can be greatly reduced, particularly if the system runs low on space for storing virtual memory or temporary files. One way to reduce disk space usage is to use the Disk Cleanup tool to remove unnecessary files and compress old files.

Running Check Disk

You should periodically use the Check Disk tool (Chkdsk.exe) to check the integrity of disks. *Chkdsk* examines and corrects many types of common errors. It cannot fix a corrupt file, however. You can run Chkdsk from the command line or through a graphical user interface (GUI).

If you open an elevated command prompt, you can test the C: drive by entering the following:

```
chkdsk C:
```

Without the **/f** option, Chkdsk will report only the status of the C: drive and any problems that it finds. To fix the problems, you need to enter the following:

```
chkdsk C: /f
```

EXAM ALERT

To fix errors, you must include the /f option with the chkdsk command.

To run the graphical interface of Chkdsk, follow these steps:

1. Click Start, and then click Computer. Under Hard Disk Drives, right-click a drive, and then select Properties.
2. On the Tools tab, click Check Now.

If you are using the command prompt or the graphical interface and Chkdsk is in use, Chkdsk displays a prompt to schedule the disk to be checked the next time you restart the system.

Defragging the Hard Drive

When a file is created, it is assigned the number of clusters needed to hold the amount of data. After the file is saved to the disk, other information is usually saved to the clusters following those assigned to the saved file. Therefore, if the original file is changed or more information is added to it, the bigger file doesn't fit within the allocated clusters when it is saved back to the disk. Part of the file will be saved in the original clusters, and the remaining amount will be placed elsewhere on the disk. Over time, files become fragmented as they are spread across the disk. The fragmented files are still complete when they are opened, but it takes longer for the computer to read them, and opening them causes more wear and tear on the hard disk.

To reduce fragmentation, Windows Vista automatically defragments disks periodically using Disk Defragmenter. By default, Windows Vista runs Disk Defragmenter automatically at 4 a.m. every Sunday. As long as the computer is on at the scheduled run time, automatic *defragmentation* will occur. You can cancel automated defragmentation or modify the defragmentation schedule by following these steps:

1. Click Start, and then click Computer.
2. Under Hard Disk Drives, right-click a drive, and then select Properties.
3. On the Tools tab, click Defragment Now to open the Disk Defragmenter dialog box.
4. To cancel automated defragmentation, clear Run Automatically, and then click OK twice. To modify the defragmentation schedule, click Modify Schedule. Use the Modify Schedule dialog box to set the desired run schedule.
5. Click OK twice to save your settings.

To manually defragment a disk, follow these steps:

1. Click Start, and then click Computer.
2. Under Hard Disk Drives, right-click a drive, and then select Properties.
3. On the Tools tab, click Defragment Now.

NOTE

Depending on the size of the disk, defragmentation can take several hours. You can click Cancel Defragmentation at any time to stop defragmentation.

Memory Usage and the Paging File

When your computer does not have enough memory to perform all of its functions, Windows and your programs can stop working. To help prevent data loss, Windows will notify you when your computer is low on memory. Other signs of low memory include poor performance and screen problems. You can also check the Event Viewer and the Windows Reliability and Performance Monitor.

Your computer has two types of memory: random access memory (RAM), also known as physical memory; and virtual memory, also known as a paging file. All programs use RAM, but when there is not enough RAM for the program you're trying to run, Windows temporarily moves information that would normally be stored in RAM to the virtual memory.

Virtual memory is disk space that acts like RAM, which allows the operating system to load more programs and data. Parts of all the programs and data to be accessed are constantly swapped back and forth between RAM and disk so that the virtual memory looks and acts like regular RAM. This is beneficial to the user because disk memory is much cheaper than RAM.

The RAM and virtual memory are broken down into chucks called *pages*, which are monitored by the operating system. When the RAM becomes full, the virtual memory system copies the least recently used programs and data to the virtual memory. Because this frees part of the RAM, it then has room to copy something else from virtual memory, load another program, or load more data. Windows Vista calls the virtual memory a paging file.

If you have low memory, you should consider

- Installing more memory
- Increasing the size of the paging file
- Determining whether a program overuses memory

To determine how much RAM your system has, you can use the Welcome Center, Task Manager, or the System Information. Open System Information, and then follow these steps:

1. Click the Start button and select All Programs
2. Select Accessories, and then select System Tools.
3. Select System Information. The total amount of RAM is listed under Total Physical Memory.

Windows Vista does a much better job of managing virtual memory than earlier versions of Windows. Windows Vista will set the minimum size of the paging file at the amount of RAM installed on your computer plus 300 MB and the maximum size at three times the amount of RAM installed on your computer. If you want to manually manage virtual memory, use a fixed virtual memory size in most cases. To do this, set the initial size and the maximum size to the same value. This ensures that the paging file is consistent and can be written to a single contiguous file (if possible, given the amount of space on the volume).

EXAM ALERT

A high value for pages/sec counter in Performance Monitor most likely means that you are low on physical memory because pages/sec shows how often it has to access the paging file.

To manually configure virtual memory, follow these steps:

1. Click Start, and then click Control Panel.
2. In the Control Panel, click the System and Maintenance category heading link.
3. Click System.
4. In the System Console, click Change Settings under Computer Name, Domain, and Workgroup Settings. Or, click Advanced System Settings in the left pane.
5. Click the Advanced tab in the System Properties dialog box.
6. Click Settings in the Performance section to display the Performance Options dialog box.
7. Click the Advanced tab, and then click Change to display the Virtual Memory dialog box.
8. Clear the Automatically Manage Paging File Size for All Drives check box.
9. Under Drive *Volume Label*, click the drive that contains the paging file you want to change.
10. Click Custom Size, enter a new size in megabytes in the Initial Size (MB) or Maximum Size (MB) box, click Set, and then click OK.

Increases in size usually do not require a restart, but if you decrease the size, you must restart your computer for the changes to take effect. We recommend that you don't disable or delete the paging file.

ReadyBoost and ReadyDrive

Windows Vista has several features that affect how disks are used, including the following:

- Windows *ReadyBoost* boosts system performance by using USB flash devices as additional sources for caching.
- Windows *ReadyDrive* boosts system performance on mobile computers equipped with hybrid drives.

With Windows ReadyBoost, USB flash devices with sufficiently fast memory (flash devices can be read up to 10 times faster than physical disk drives) are used to extend the disk caching capabilities of the computer's main memory. Using flash devices for caching enables Windows Vista to make random reads faster by caching data on the USB flash device rather than on a disk drive. Because this caching is applied to all disk content, not just the page file or system dynamic link libraries (DLLs), the computer's overall performance is boosted.

USB flash devices that can be used with Windows ReadyBoost include USB 2.0 flash drives, Secure Digital (SD) cards, and CompactFlash cards. These devices must have sufficiently fast flash memory and be at least 512 MB or larger in size. Windows Vista can use an amount of flash memory equal to twice the amount of physical memory (RAM) on the computer.

When you insert a USB flash device into a USB 2.0 or later port, Windows Vista analyzes the speed of the flash memory on the device. When you click Speed Up My System Using Windows ReadyBoost, Windows Vista extends the computer's physical memory to the device. The default configuration enables Windows ReadyBoost to reserve all available space on the device for boosting system speed.

To use Windows ReadyBoost with a USB flash device that you either already inserted or that you previously declined to use with Windows ReadyBoost, follow these steps:

1. Click Start, and then click Computer.
2. Right-click the USB flash device in the Devices with Removable Storage list, and then choose Properties.
3. On the ReadyBoost tab, select Use This Device, and then click OK.
4. For USB flash devices that do not support ReadyBoost, you cannot enable the device. The only option you'll have is to stop retesting the device when you plug it in. The Stop Retesting This Device When I Plug It In option is selected by default.

If the USB flash drive has both slow and fast flash memory, you will not be able to use the slow flash memory portion of the USB storage device to speed up the computer performance. As a result, you might not see all the memory of the USB device when it is added to your physical memory.

Windows ReadyDrive improves performance on mobile computers equipped with hybrid drives. A hybrid drive is a drive that uses both flash RAM and a physical drive for storage. Because flash RAM is much faster than a physical disk, mobile computers running Windows Vista write data and changes to data to the flash memory first and periodically sync these writes and changes to the physical disk. This approach reduces the spinning of the physical drive and thus saves battery power.

The flash RAM on hybrid drives can be used to provide faster startup and resume from sleep or hibernation. In this case, the information needed for starting or resuming the operating system is written to the flash RAM prior to shutting down, entering sleep, or going into hibernation. When you start or wake the computer, this information is read from the flash RAM.

You do not need to enable ReadyDrive. ReadyDrive is enabled for use automatically on mobile computers with hybrid drives.

Diagnostic Tools

Windows Vista has multiple tools for diagnosing and resolving problems. To proactively and automatically identify potential problems, Windows Vista includes built-in diagnostics that can automatically detect and diagnose common support problems. The Windows Vista built-in diagnostics can automatically identify and help users resolve the following problems:

- Hardware error conditions
- Failing disks
- Degraded performance
- Failure to shut down properly
- Memory problems
- Problems related to installing drivers and applications
- Problems related to using drivers and applications

In most cases, the built-in diagnostics prompt users to make them aware of any problems as they occur and then help to guide users through resolving the problem.

Memory Diagnostic Tool

Bad memory can cause a wide assortment of problems with your system, including causing Windows not to be reliable. The *Memory Diagnostic tool* is used to diagnose physical memory problems, including memory leaks and failing memory. The tool also works with the Microsoft Online Crash Analysis tool to detect system crashes possibly caused by failing memory, which then prompts the user to schedule a memory test the next time the computer is restarted.

If you suspect that a computer has a memory problem that is not being automatically detected, you can run Windows Memory Diagnostic manually by completing the following steps:

1. Click Start, point to All Programs, and then click Accessories.
2. Right-click Command Prompt, and then select Run As Administrator.
3. At the command prompt, enter **mdsched.exe**.
4. You can choose to restart the computer and run the tool immediately or schedule the tool to run at the next restart.

The Windows Memory Diagnostic tool can also be run manually from Administrative Tools in the Control Panel or from the boot menu before Windows loads.

If you choose to run the tool at the next restart, Windows Memory Diagnostic runs automatically after the computer restart, allowing you to choose the type of testing to perform. When the computer restarts and the memory is tested, you are provided with an easy-to-understand report detailing the problem. Information is also written to the event log for future analysis.

While the test is running, you can press F1 to access advanced diagnostic options, including the following:

- **Test Mix.** Choose what type of test you want to run.
- **Cache.** Choose the cache setting you want for each test.
- **Pass Count.** Type the number of times you want to repeat the tests.

Press the Tab key to move between the different advanced options. When you have selected your options, press F10 to start the test.

Network Diagnostic Tool

The Windows Network Diagnostic Tool, discussed in Chapter 4, "Configuring Advanced Networking," helps resolve network-related issues. When a user is unable to connect to a network resource, the user is presented with a repair option, which will run the Windows Network Diagnostic Tool. You can also choose to run the tool manually by using the Diagnose option on the Local Area Connections Status property sheet.

System Configuration

System Configuration is an advanced tool that can help identify problems that might prevent Windows from starting correctly. You can start Windows with common services and startup programs turned off and then turn them back on, one at a time. If a problem does not occur when a service is turned off, but does occur when turned on, the service could be the cause of the problem. System Configuration is intended to find and isolate problems, but it is not meant as a startup management program.

The System Configuration tool can be loaded from the Administrative Tools. The tabs found in the System Configuration tool include those listed in Table 9.1.

TABLE 9.1 System Configuration Tabs

Tab	Description
General	Lists choices for startup configuration modes: ▶ **Normal Startup.** Starts Windows in its normal mode. ▶ **Diagnostic Startup.** Starts Windows with basic services and drivers only. If Diagnostic Startup starts without a problem, it verifies that the problem is not the basic Windows files. ▶ **Selective Startup.** Starts Windows with basic services and drivers and allows you to select individual services and startup programs. Selective Startup is used to isolate problematic services and startup programs.
Boot	Shows configuration options for the operating system and advanced debugging settings, including the following: ▶ **Safe Boot: Minimal.** Boots Windows into Safe mode with a GUI, which runs only essential system services. Networking is disabled. ▶ **Safe Boot: Alternate Shell.** Boots to the Safe mode (command prompt). Networking and the GUI are disabled. ▶ **Safe Boot: Active Directory Repair.** Starts Windows in Directory Services Restore mode so that you can restore or repair Active Directory. ▶ **Safe Boot: Network.** Boots Windows into Safe mode, which runs only essential system services but also enables networking. ▶ **Boot Log.** Lists all the drivers that are installed during startup in the ntbtlog.txt file. The ntbtlog.txt file can be used to determine which driver failed if Windows cannot start properly. ▶ **Base Video.** Boots to the Windows GUI in minimal VGA mode using the standard VGA drivers (640x480 resolution and 16 colors).

TABLE 9.1 *Continued*

Tab	Description
	▶ **OS Boot Information.** Shows driver names as the drivers are loaded during the boot process. ▶ **Make All Settings Permanent.** Does not track changes made in System Configuration. Options can be changed later using System Configuration, but must be changed manually. When this option is selected, you cannot roll back your changes by selecting Normal Startup on the General tab.
Services	Lists all services that are registered with Windows and displays their current status (running or stopped). You can use the Services tab to enable or disable individual services so that you can isolate a problematic service that loads during boot up. You can select Hide all Microsoft Services to show only third-party applications in the services list.
Startup	Lists applications that start when the computer boots, including the name of their publisher, the path to the executable file, and the location of the registry key or shortcut that causes the application to run. This option is used to isolate problematic programs that load during boot.
Tools	Provides a list of diagnostic tools.

Advanced Startup Options

The Advanced Boot Options menu lets you start Windows in advanced troubleshooting modes. To access the advanced startup options, do the following:

- If your computer has a single operating system installed, repeatedly press the F8 key as your computer restarts. You need to press F8 before the Windows logo appears. If the Windows logo appears, you will need to try again.
- If your computer has more than one operating system, use the arrow keys to highlight the operating system you want to start in Safe mode, and then press F8.

On the Advanced Boot Options screen, use the arrow keys to highlight the Safe mode option you want, and then press Enter. Log on to your computer with a user account that has administrator rights. When your computer is in Safe mode, you'll see the words *Safe Mode* in the corners of the display. To exit Safe mode, restart your computer and let Windows start normally.

Some options, such as Safe mode, start Windows in a limited state, where only the bare essentials are started. If a problem does not reappear when you start in Safe mode, you can eliminate the default settings and basic device drivers as possible causes. Other options start Windows with advanced features intended for use by system administrators and IT professionals.

The options that are available are as follows:

- **Repair Your Computer.** Shows a list of system recovery tools (Startup Repair tool) you can use to repair startup problems, run diagnostics, or restore your system. This option is available only if you install the tools onto the computer. If they are not installed, the system recovery tools are located on the Windows installation disc.
- **Safe Mode.** Starts Windows with a minimal set of drivers and services.
- **Safe Mode with Networking.** Starts Windows in Safe mode but also enables networking.
- **Safe Mode with Command Prompt.** Starts Windows in Safe mode with a command prompt window rather than the Windows GUI. This option is intended for IT professionals and administrators.
- **Enable Boot Logging.** Lists all the drivers that are installed during startup in the ntbtlog.txt file. The ntbtlog.txt file can be used to determine which driver failed if Windows cannot start properly.
- **Enable Low-Resolution Video (640x480).** Boots to the Windows GUI in minimal VGA mode using the standard VGA drivers (640x480 resolution and 16 colors).
- **Last Known Good Configuration (advanced).** Starts Windows with the last registry and driver configuration that worked when the last user logged on successfully.
- **Directory Services Restore Mode.** Starts Windows in Directory Services Restore mode so that you can restore or repair Active Directory.
- **Debugging Mode.** Shows driver names as the drivers are loaded during the boot process.
- **Disable Automatic Restart on System Failure.** Prevents Windows from automatically restarting if an error occurs during boot. Use this option if Windows constantly fails and reboots.
- **Disable Driver Signature Enforcement.** Allows drivers containing improper signatures to be installed.
- **Start Windows Normally.** Starts Windows in its normal mode.

Startup Repair Tool

In earlier versions of Windows, corrupted system files were one of the most common causes of startup failure. Some of these problems would be fixed by replacing the corrupted files, whereas others would be fixed using the Recovery Console. At other times, the system could be recovered only by attempting to repair the installation or reinstalling the operating system.

Windows Vista includes the *Startup Repair tool (StR)* to automatically fix many common problems, including incompatible drivers, missing or corrupted startup configuration settings, and corrupted startup files. Once started, StR performs diagnostics and attempts to determine the cause of the startup failure by analyzing startup logs and error reports. If the problem cannot be corrected, StR will restore the system to its last known good working state, and then provides diagnostic information and support options to make further troubleshooting easier for the user or administrator.

StR is included on the Windows Vista installation disc and can be preinstalled so that it shows on the Windows Advanced Startup Options menu. To launch the StR from the installation CD, follow these steps:

1. Insert the Windows Vista installation disc, and then restart the computer.
2. Click View System Recovery Options (Advanced).
3. Enter the name and password for an account on the computer.
4. Click Startup Repair in the list of recovery tools.
5. Follow the Startup Repair prompts to recover the system.

Event Viewer

The Event Viewer is a useful tool for viewing and managing logs of system, program, and security events on your computer. Event Viewer gathers information about hardware and software problems and monitors Windows security events. The Event Viewer can be found in Administrative Tools, and it is contained within the Computer Management Console (see Figure 9.6).

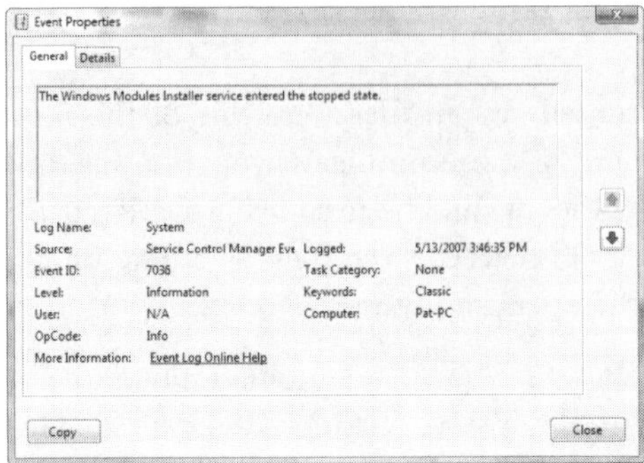

FIGURE 9.6 Event Viewer.

Problem Reports and Solutions Tool

The Problems Reports and Solutions tool works with the Windows Error Reporting services to provide a history of attempts to diagnose problems on your computer. It also prompts users if they want to send error information to Microsoft over the Internet. It can also check for solutions over the Internet. You can view a list of current problems at any time by following these steps:

1. Click Start, and then click Control Panel.
2. In the Control Panel, click System and Maintenance, and then click Problem Reports and Solutions.
3. In the Problem Reports and Solutions dialog box, click See Problems to Check in the left pane.

Restore a Driver to Its Previous Version

If you install driver and you encounter problems with the driver, you can roll back the driver. To roll back a device driver, open the Device Manager from within the Control Panel. If you are prompted for an administrator password or confirmation, enter the password or provide confirmation. Double-click the category containing your device driver, and then double-click the name of the device you want to restore to a previous driver version. Click the Driver tab, and then click Roll Back Driver. If there's no previous version of the driver software installed for the selected device, the Roll Back Driver button will be unavailable. If the machine does not boot, you can try loading Safe mode before accessing Device Manager.

System Restore

System Restore helps you restore your computer's system files to an earlier point in time. It's a way to undo system changes to your computer without affecting your personal files, such as e-mail, documents, or photos. This comes in handy when you install a program or a drive that causes Windows to behave unpredictable. If uninstalling does not fix the problem, you can try restoring your computer's system to an earlier date when everything worked correctly.

System Restore uses a feature called System Protection to regularly create and save restore points on your computer. These restore points contain information about registry settings and other system information that Windows uses. You can also create restore points manually.

System Restore is not intended for backing up personal files, so it cannot help you recover a personal file that has been deleted or damaged. You should regularly back up your personal files and important data using a backup program.

Restore points are created automatically every day, and just before significant system events, such as the installation of a program or device driver. You can also create a restore point manually.

System Restore automatically recommends the most recent restore point created before a significant change, such as installing a program. You can also choose from a list of restore points. Try using restore points created just before the date and time you started noticing problems.

To access the System Restore utility, follow these steps:

1. Click the Start button and select Programs.
2. Select Accessories.
3. Select System Tools
4. Select System Restore.
5. If you are prompted for an administrator password or confirmation, enter the password or provide confirmation.

Remote Desktop and Remote Assistance

Starting with Windows XP, Microsoft introduced Remote Desktop and Remote Assistance. Similar to Terminal Services used in Windows 2000 servers, you can have access to a Windows session that is running on your computer when at another computer. This means, for example, that you can connect your work computer from home and have access to all of your applications, files, and network resources as though you are in front of your computer at work. You can leave programs running at work, and when you get home you can see your desktop at work displayed on your home computer, with the same programs running. Another example of using Remote Desktop and Remote Assistance is to remotely troubleshoot or administer a computer that is not nearby.

You would use Remote Desktop to access one computer from another remotely. With Remote Desktop Connection, you can access a computer running Windows from another computer running Windows that is connected to the same network or to the Internet. For example, you can use all of your work computer's programs, files, and network resources from your home computer, and it's just like you're sitting in front of your computer at work.

EXAM ALERT

You cannot use Remote Desktop Connection to connect to computers running Windows Vista Starter, Windows Vista Home Basic, Windows Vista Home Basic N, or Windows Vista Home Premium. You can create outgoing connections *only* from those editions of Windows Vista. Windows Vista Business, Ultimate, and Enterprise editions offer full Remote Desktop Connection capability.

NOTE

You cannot use Remote Desktop Connection to connect to computers running Windows XP Home edition.

To connect to a remote computer, that computer must be turned on, it must have a network connection, Remote Desktop must be enabled, you must have network access to the remote computer (this could be through the Internet), and you must have permission to connect (a member of the Administrators group or the Remote Desktop Users group). For permission to connect, you must be on the list of users. The steps that follow include adding names to that list.

EXAM ALERT

To use Remote Desktop, the computer that you are trying to connect to must be on, Remote Desktop must be enabled, and you must have the proper permissions.

To allow remote connections on the computer you want to connect to, follow these steps:

1. Click the Start button. Right-click Computer, and select Properties.
2. Click Remote Settings, and then select one of the three options under Remote Desktop. If you are prompted for an administrator password or confirmation, enter the password or provide confirmation.
3. Click Select Users. If you are enabling Remote Desktop for your current user account, your name will automatically be added to this list of remote users, and you can skip the next two steps.
4. In the Remote Desktop Users dialog box, click Add. This will add users to the Remote Desktop Users group.
5. In the Select Users dialog box, do the following:
    - To specify the search location, click Locations, and then select the location you want to search.
    - In Enter the Object Names to Select, type the name of the user who you want to add, and then click OK.
    - The name will be displayed in the list of users in the Remote Desktop Users dialog box.

To start Remote Desktop on the computer you want to work from, follow these steps:

1. Open Remote Desktop Connection by clicking the Start button, selecting Accessories, and selecting Remote Desktop Connection.
2. In the Computer box, enter the name of the computer that you want to connect to, and then click Connect. (You can also type the IP address rather than the computer name if you want.)

For more advanced options before the connection, click the Options button.

Remote Assistance is used to give or receive assistance remotely. For example, a friend or a technical support person can access your computer to help you with a computer problem or show you how to do something. You can help someone else the same way. In either case, both you and the other person see the same computer screen. If you decide to share control of your computer with your helper, you will both be able to control the mouse cursor.

To use Remote Assistance, first you invite a person to help you, using e-mail or an instant message. You can also reuse an invitation that you have sent before.

After the person accepts the invitation, Windows Remote Assistance creates an encrypted connection between the two computers over the Internet or the network that both computers are connected to. You give the other person a password so that he or she can connect. You can also offer assistance to someone else, and when that person accepts your offer, Windows Remote Assistance creates an encrypted connection between the two computers. To start a Remote Assistance session and to create invitations, click All Programs, Maintenance, and then click Windows Remote Assistance.

EXAM ALERT

To allow a user to remotely access a Windows Vista computer, you need to enable Remote Desktop or Remote Assistance through the firewall.

Exam Prep Questions

1. You work as the desktop support technician at Acme.com. You have a computer with 1 GB RAM with Windows Vista Ultimate. You want to add a fast removable flash drive to improve performance. What should you use?

   ❍ **A.** Windows SuperFetch

   ❍ **B.** Windows ReadyBoost

   ❍ **C.** Windows ReadyDrive

   ❍ **D.** Windows Memory Diagnostic tool

2. You work as the desktop support technician at Acme.com. You have a user who loaded a drive, but now Windows does not boot properly. You want to display the driver names while they are being loaded during startup. What should you do?

   ❍ **A.** Start System Configuration. On the Boot tab, select the Base Video check box.

   ❍ **B.** Start System Configuration. On the Boot tab, select the Boot Log check box.

   ❍ **C.** Start System Configuration. On the Boot tab, select the No GUI Boot check box.

   ❍ **D.** Start System Configuration. On the Boot tab, select the OS Boot Information check box.

3. You insert a flash drive and discover that you cannot make use of all the memory on the USB flash device when configuring ReadyBoost. What do you think the problem is?

   ❍ **A.** The USB flash drive has slow flash memory.

   ❍ **B.** The USB flash drive has fast flash memory.

   ❍ **C.** The USB flash drive has both slow and fast flash memory.

   ❍ **D.** The USB flash drive does not meet the minimum requirement to configure ReadyBoost.

4. You work as the desktop support technician at Acme.com. You suspect an application is not releasing memory. You would like a user who is using the Windows Vista machine to run Performance Monitor. What do you need to do so that the user has access to Performance Monitor?

  ❍ **A.** Add the user to the Power Users group.

  ❍ **B.** Add the user to the Performance Log Users group.

  ❍ **C.** Add the user to the Performance Monitor Users group.

  ❍ **D.** Add the user to the Administrators group.

5. If you want to see whether you are running out of physical memory, which counter should you use?

  ❍ **A.** CPU utilization

  ❍ **B.** Pages\sec

  ❍ **C.** Network utilization

  ❍ **D.** Interrupts\sec

6. You work as the desktop support technician at Acme.com. You have a user who called and states that he has had problems over the past few weeks. You need to identify the cause of the failures. Therefore, you want to look at a historical view of workstation performance and see when the failures first started. What should you do?

  ❍ **A.** You should use Performance Monitor.

  ❍ **B.** You should use the Reliability Monitor.

  ❍ **C.** You should use a System Diagnostics Data Collector Set.

  ❍ **D.** You should use the Resource Overview tool.

7. You work as the help desk technician at Acme.com. You have a user who is getting a Stop error and then the computer is started in Normal mode or Safe mode. What should you do to troubleshoot this problem further?

  ❍ **A.** Uninstall Windows Vista and reinstall Windows XP.

  ❍ **B.** Reboot the computer using the Windows Vista installation DVD and run the Startup Repair tool.

  ❍ **C.** Run Software Explorer.

  ❍ **D.** You should disable startup items by running msconfig.exe.

8. You made changes to the video refresh rate on your computer, but now the display does not work properly. What should you do?

   ❍ **A.** Run the SYSEDIT tool.

   ❍ **B.** Reinstall Windows.

   ❍ **C.** Reboot the system with the emergency repair disk.

   ❍ **D.** Press F8 during the boot sequence and select Last Known Good Configuration.

9. Your machine will not boot properly. You suspect a faulty driver that you just installed. Unfortunately, you cannot access the Device Manager because the system does not complete the boot process. What should you do next?

   ❍ **A.** Restart the computer with another Windows version.

   ❍ **B.** Insert a DOS bootable disk into the drive and boot the system.

   ❍ **C.** Reboot the computer in Safe mode.

   ❍ **D.** Start the System Configuration tool.

10. What tool would you use to temporarily disable a service that starts during the boot process?

   ❍ **A.** Device Manager

   ❍ **B.** System Configuration

   ❍ **C.** Boot.ini tool

   ❍ **D.** Last Known Good Configuration option

11. You just loaded a new application. Now your computer has gotten slow and sometimes causes Stop errors. Even after reinstalling the application, you still have the same problems. What can you try next?

   ❍ **A.** Roll back the latest driver using Device Manager.

   ❍ **B.** Reboot the computer in Safe mode.

   ❍ **C.** Press F8 during the boot sequence and select Last Known Good Configuration.

   ❍ **D.** Use the System Restore tool to restore to a known good working restore point.

12. Which of the following does support Remote Desktop?

❍ **A.** Windows Vista Home Basic

❍ **B.** Windows Vista Home Premium

❍ **C.** Windows Vista Ultimate

❍ **D.** Windows Vista Starter

13. To use Windows Remote Desktop, a user must be added to one of two groups. What are the two groups?

❍ **A.** Administrator

❍ **B.** Power Users

❍ **C.** Remote Desktop Administrators

❍ **D.** Remote Desktop Users

Answers to Exam Prep Questions

1. **Answer B is correct**. Windows ReadyBoost boosts system performance by using USB flash devices as additional sources for caching. Answer A is incorrect because SuperFetch utilizes machine-learning techniques to analyze usage patterns to allow Windows Vista to make intelligent decisions about what content should be present in system memory at any given time. Answer C is incorrect because ReadyDrive boosts system performance on mobile computers equipped with hybrid drives. Answer D is incorrect because the Memory Diagnostic tool is used to test memory and not to increase performance.
2. **Answer D is correct**. If you open System Configuration, select the Boot tab, and you select OS Boot Information, it will show you the driver names that are loaded during startup. Answers A, B, and C are incorrect because those options do not provide that information. Base Video starts the monitor with a 640x480 resolution. The Boot Log generates a log that can be accessed after it boots. The No GUI Boot check box starts in with a command prompt.
3. **Answer C is correct**. To get the benefit of ReadyBoost, your USB device needs to use fast flash memory. Therefore, if you insert a USB flash device that consists of slow and fast flash memory, ReadyBoost will only use the fast flash memory. Therefore, answers A and B are incorrect. Because ReadyBoost recognizes some of the memory, you can assume that the USB flash device meets the minimum requirements. Therefore, answer D is incorrect.
4. **Answer C is correct**. For standard users to run the Performance Monitor, you must add them to the Performance Monitor Users group or make them administrators.

Because there is no need to make them administrators, it is best to only add them to the Performance Monitor Users group. Therefore, answer D is incorrect. Answer A is incorrect because Power Users groups are only there for backward compatibility. Answer B is incorrect because there is no such group.

5. **Answer B is correct**. To see how much paging takes place between RAM and the paging file, you use the pages\sec counter. A high value indicates that you need to use paging often, which means you are running out of physical memory. Answer A is incorrect because CPU utilization shows how hard the processor is working. Answer C is incorrect because network utilization indicates how much bandwidth is being used on the network. Answer D is incorrect because a high value for interrupts\sec might indicate a faulty device or device driver.

6. **Answer B is correct**. The two places to look for a history of problems are the Event Viewer and the Reliability Monitor. Answer A is incorrect because Performance Monitor is used to measure performance. Answer C is incorrect because the Data Collector Set is used to group counters together so that you can call them up as needed or schedule them to be measured. Answer D is incorrect because the Resource Overview tool shows the performance of the major subcomponents, including CPU, memory, network, and disk.

7. **Answer B is correct**. Because you cannot start the computer, there might be a problem with the startup files. Therefore, you need to run the Startup Repair tool. Answer A is incorrect because you don't want to go back to an old operating system. Answers C and D are incorrect because you cannot start Windows to get to the Software Explorer or msconfig.exe (System Configuration tool).

8. **Answer D is correct**. If you load a driver and your machine does not boot properly, you can access the Advanced Boot menu and try Last Known Good Configuration. Answer A is incorrect because you cannot access SYSEDIT because you cannot get the Windows GUI to load. Answer B is incorrect because reinstalling Windows takes a lot of effort and may not correct the problem. Answer C is incorrect because there is no emergency repair disk to use with Windows Vista; everything is included with the Windows Vista installation disc.

9. **Answer C is correct**. If you cannot boot the computer, the next logical step is to boot Windows in Safe mode. In Safe mode, minimum drivers are loaded. Answer A is not a viable option because most systems do not have another hard drive with another Windows version. This solution can also become very messy. Answer B is incorrect because you cannot use DOS to correct most Windows problems. Answer D is incorrect because you need to first load Windows before you can use the System Configuration tool.

10. **Answer B is correct**. The System Configuration tool is a diagnostic tool that can help you isolate startup programs and services that prevent Windows from booting. Answer A is incorrect because Device Manager manages devices, not services. Answer C is incorrect because the boot.ini file (used in Windows 2000 and Windows XP) is used to select certain drive parameters and to provide a boot menu so that you can choose

which operating system to boot on a multiboot system. Answer D is used to revert back when you load a driver, service, or program that prevents Windows from loading. It does not disable a service.

11. **Answer D is correct**. System Restore can reconfigure Windows back to its original settings before the problem occurred. Answer A is incorrect because this is not a device problem. Answer B is incorrect because you can load Windows, so you don't need to use Safe mode. Answer C is incorrect because if you log on to Windows successfully, it will overwrite the last known good configuration.

12. **Answer C is correct**. Windows Vista Ultimate does support Remote Desktop. You cannot connect to computers with Remote Desktop that have Windows Vista Home Basic, Windows Vista Home Premium, or Windows Vista Starter. Therefore, answers A, B, and D are incorrect.

13. **Answers A and D are correct**. All administrators are automatically given the necessary permission to use Windows Remote Desktop. For other users, you must add them to the Remote Desktop Users group. Answer B is incorrect because the Power Users group is mostly used for backward compatibility. Answer C is incorrect because there is no Remote Desktop Administrators group.

Recommended Readings and Resources

Mitch Tulloch, Tony Northrup, Jerry Honeycutt, Ed Wilson, Ralph Ramos, and the Windows Vista Team, *Windows Vista Resource Kit (Pro - Resource Kit)* (Redmond, Washington: Microsoft Press, 2007).

William R. Stanek, *Introducing Microsoft Windows Vista* (Redmond, Washington: Microsoft Press, 2006).

Patrick Regan, *Working with Windows 2000 and 2003* (Upper Saddle River, New Jersey: Prentice Hall, 2004).

Patrick Regan, *Troubleshooting the PC with A+ Preparation, 3rd Edition* (Upper Saddle River, New Jersey: Prentice Hall, 2006).

CHAPTER TEN

Configuring Windows Vista Media Applications

Terms you'll need to understand:

- ✓ Windows Media Player
- ✓ Codec
- ✓ MPEG-2
- ✓ Region
- ✓ Windows Media Center

Techniques/concepts you'll need to master:

- ✓ Configure your system, Windows Media Player, and Windows Media Center to be as secure as possible.
- ✓ Describe what a codec is and how it relates to Windows Media Player.
- ✓ Describe what a region is and how it relates to Windows Media Player.

This chapter introduces you to Windows Media Player and Windows Media Center. We discuss how to secure each of these media devices. We also discuss Windows Media Player codecs and regions.

Windows Media Player

Windows Media Player 11 is an all-in-one media player that enables you to play most media files with an easy-to-use, intuitive interface. It can also be used to synchronize your files with a wide variety of portable devices and organize your digital media collection.

Security Options

To enhance the media experience, media files can contain script commands to open related websites while Media Player plays back content. However, as with any scripting language used in Windows, scripts can be used in a harmful way that can cause some serious problems. As a desktop technician, you must understand the security options found in Windows Media Player so that you can keep your system secure and maintain your privacy.

To access the Security tab, click the arrow under the Now Playing tab, click More Options, and then click the Security tab (see Figure 10.1). You will find the options in Table 10.1.

TABLE 10.1 Windows Media Security Options

This Setting	Does This
Run Script Commands When Present check box	If your media contains a script, the script that includes malicious scripts will run when you play the media.
Run Script Commands and Rich Media Streams If the Player Is in a Web Page check box	If the Media Player is embedded or playing within a web page, this option enables the script or rich media streams (such as a slide show or a movie) to run.
Play Enhanced Content That Uses Web Pages Without Prompting check box	If you select this option, you will be not be warned if the player tries to open a web page with enhanced content.
Show Local Captions When Present check box	Synchronized Accessible Media Interchange (SAMI) gives the ability to provide closed captioning to a wide range of multimedia products. If the check box is cleared, captions do not display.

TABLE 10.1 *Continued*

This Setting	Does This
Zone Settings button	Opens the Internet Explorer's Security dialog box so that you can configure security zones and related security settings. Enables you to safely view online stores; find, view, and update media information such as album art and information about CDs and DVDs; download codecs; and gather media usage rights for protected files.

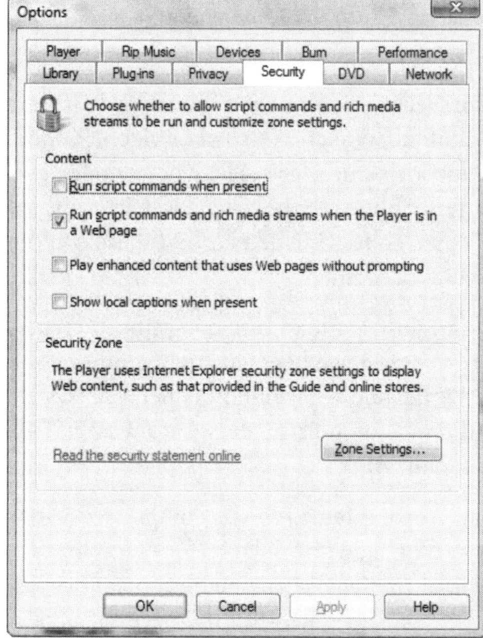

FIGURE 10.1 Windows Media Player Security options.

Of course, to keep your computer safe when using Media Player, you need to follow these basic guidelines:

- Keep your computer up-to-date with the latest security patches, fixes, and service packs.
- Install virus-scanning software on your computer and keep it current with the latest security updates.
- Understand the options for configuring Windows Media Player security.
- Only play and download files and programs from websites that you trust.
- Read and understand a website privacy policy before you provide any personal information.

- Log on with a user account with limited privileges.
- If possible, work offline when using Windows Media Player.
- Use file format validation so that you are not tricked into downloading and installing files that you do not want. File format validation is enabled by default and it verifies that the filename extension matches the format of the file. If a discrepancy is found, Windows Media Player asks you to confirm that the file should be played.

Codecs

Codecs, an abbreviation for compressor/decompressor, are software or hardware used to compress and decompress digital media such as a song or video. A codec can consist of two components: an encoder and a decoder. The encoder performs the compression (encoding) function, and the decoder performs the decompression (decoding) function. Some codecs include both of these components, and some codecs only include one of them.

Hundreds of audio and video codecs are in use today. Some have been created by Microsoft, but the vast majority of codecs have been created by other companies, organizations, or individuals. By default, the Windows operating system and the Player include a number of the most popular codecs, such as Windows Media Audio, Windows Media Video, and MP3.

Sometimes, however, you will want to play content that was compressed with a codec that Windows or the Player doesn't include by default (for example, a file compressed with the DivX video codec or the Ogg Vorbis audio codec). Because the Player is extensible, in many cases you can download the necessary codec from the Web for free or for a fee. In some cases, the Player can automatically use the codecs installed by other digital media playback and creation programs on your computer. Some codecs are available for download from the WMPlugins.com codec web page, http://go.microsoft.com/fwlink/?linkid=40931.

Codecs can be written for 32-bit or 64-bit operating systems. If you are running a 64-bit version of Windows, you need to install 64-bit codecs. If you install a 32-bit codec on a 64-bit operating system, for example, the Player might not be able to play any files that require that codec. Many older codecs are only available in 32-bit versions. If the codec provider does not specify whether its codec is 32-bit or 64-bit, the codec is likely 32-bit. For more information, contact the codec provider.

The Moving Pictures Experts Group (MPEG) is an organization that creates video formats used on computers. MPEG is not a single file type or a single kind of video format. There are actually several different kinds of MPEG video, such as MPEG-1 and MPEG-2. The main difference between different versions of MPEG video (such as MPEG-1 and MPEG-2, for example) is image quality. MPEG-1 is an older format that plays video at low resolution and is often compared to the quality of a VHS videotape. MPEG-2 is the most common format because it is the format used on most video DVDs. MPEG-2 uses a much higher resolution and looks much sharper on computer screens and televisions.

If you want to play a DVD, you need a DVD decoder, also known as a MPEG-2 decoder. The content on DVD-Video discs is encoded in the MPEG-2 format, as is the content in DVR-MS files (Microsoft Digital Video Recording) and some AVI (Audio Video Interleave) files. To play these items in the Player, you need a compatible DVD decoder installed on your computer. Only Windows Vista Home Premium and Windows Vista Ultimate ship with an MPEG-2 decoder. So, if you are using other versions of Windows Vista, you will need to upgrade to Windows Vista Home Premium or Vista Ultimate; otherwise, you will need to purchase an MPEG-2 decoder and install it on the computer.

Regions

The commercial DVD video player specification dictates that DVD players must be coded to play discs that contain the region code for the country in which they were sold. By law, all new DVD players shipped in the United States are set to Region 1. All DVD players and PCs with DVD drives must implement region coding, which specifies which country code the DVD player is sold in.

In Windows Vista, to change the region assigned to the drive, follow these steps:

1. Click the Start button and click Computer.
2. Right-click the DVD drive and select Properties.
3. Click the Hardware tab.
4. Double-click the DVD drive.
5. Click the DVD Region tab (see Figure 10.2).
6. Select the geographic area and click the OK button.

NOTE

You can only change the region a set number of times (five).

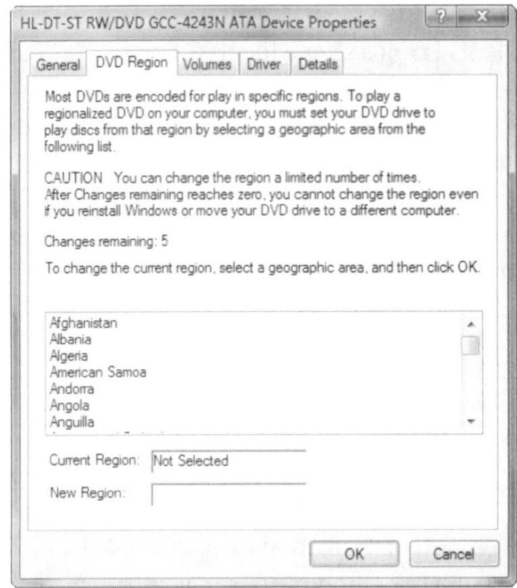

FIGURE 10.2 DVD drive's Properties dialog box showing DVD region.

Windows Media Center

The Windows Media Center enables you to manage and play back all of your digital media through one interface, including live and recorded TV, movies, music, and pictures. The Windows Media Center in Windows Vista includes enhancements for expanded support of digital and high-definition cable TV and for FM and Internet radio stations; it also includes options for multiroom access to your entertainment through Media Center Extenders, including Xbox 360. Windows Media Center incorporates Online Media, a portal to a wide range of free, premium, and subscription-based products and services. Online Media gives you access to the wealth of media available online, from music and radio programming to movie downloads, on-demand services, and customized sports, news, and entertainment programming.

If your computer has no TV tuner, an optional analog or digital TV tuner is required to play and record TV in Windows Media Center. Before you add one or more TV tuners to your Windows Media Center computer, you should know that the TV signals and programming that you can receive and watch on your Windows Media Center computer depend on the following:

- The system resources available on your Windows Media Center computer. This includes system resources such as a processor speed, memory, and video graphics card capabilities, and available card slots and Universal Serial Bus (USB) ports.
- The type of TV signal that you can receive in your location.

- The type of antenna that you have connected to your Windows Media Center computer.
- If you want to receive over-the-air high-definition TV signals, such as Advanced Television Systems Committee (ATSC) or Digital Video Broadcasting Terrestrial television (DVB-T), you must have a TV tuner installed on your computer that can receive a digital TV signal.
- If you want to receive standard TV signals, such as National Television Standards Committee (NTSC), Phase Alternating Line (PAL), or Sequential Color with Memory (SECAM), you must have a tuner installed on your computer that can receive a standard TV signal. The tuner must support Moving Picture Experts Group-2 (MPEG-2) video hardware or software video decoding.
- Your TV cable or satellite provider.
- An analog or digital TV tuner is required to watch or record live TV in Windows Media Center. If you have one TV tuner installed on your Windows Media Center computer, you can do the following when watching and recording TV in Windows Media Center:
  - Watch live TV on one channel
  - Record live TV on one channel
  - Watch a previously recorded show while you record another show

If you add an additional TV tuner, you can expand the capabilities of your Windows Media Center computer when watching TV in Windows Media Center. For example, with two TV tuners, you can do the following:

- Watch live TV on one channel while recording a show on a different channel.
- Record two different TV shows that are on two different channels at the same time.
- Watch a show that you have previously recorded while two shows are recording at the same time on two different channels.

For users in the United States, here are some guidelines and considerations to make before adding multiple TV tuners to your Windows Media Center computer:

- You can install multiple tuners that let you receive both standard and digital TV signals. For example, you can have two TV tuners installed that let you receive a standard TV signal, in addition to two TV tuners that let you receive a digital TV signal.

- A Digital Cable Tuner cannot be installed and used on a Windows Media Center computer that has a tuner that is used to receive a standard TV signal. Before installing a Digital Cable Tuner, uninstall the TV tuner that is used to receive a standard TV signal using the Device Manager.
- You can install multiple TV tuner hardware devices that let you receive high-definition TV. For example, you can have two TV tuners that support a digital signal, such as ATSC, in addition to two Digital Cable Tuners.

Like the Windows Media Player, the Windows Media Center can play media that has harmful scripts. Therefore, as with the Windows Media Player, you should follow the same security guidelines.

Exam Prep Questions

1. What version of Media Player does Windows Vista include?

   ❍ **A.** 7

   ❍ **B.** 10

   ❍ **C.** 11

   ❍ **D.** 15

2. You work as the desktop support technician at Acme.com. You have a user who is running Windows Vista Home Basic and cannot view movies when he tries to play DVDs. What is the problem?

   ❍ **A.** You must purchase and install a MPEG-2 decoder on the computer.

   ❍ **B.** You must configure Windows Media Player to automatically play DVD movies.

   ❍ **C.** You must associate DVD movies with Windows Media Player.

   ❍ **D.** You must configure Windows Media Player to automatically download codecs.

3. You work as part of the IT support staff at Acme.com. You want to set up a Windows Vista workstation that can record two movies and play back a movie at the same time. What do you need?

   ❍ **A.** Microsoft Windows Vista Enterprise and two TV tuners

   ❍ **B.** Internet connection and two TV tuners

   ❍ **C.** Microsoft Windows Vista Home Basic and three TV tuners

   ❍ **D.** Microsoft Windows Vista Home Premium and two TV tuners

4. You have a user who is trying to watch a DVD that came from the office in Paris. Your computer was made in the United States. You test the DVD player, and you have no problem playing other movies. What should you do?

   ❍ **A.** On the Location tab of Regional and Language Options (Control Panel), change the current location to France.

   ❍ **B.** Associate all Movie Clip file types with Windows Media Player.

   ❍ **C.** On the DVD Region tab of DVD drive's Properties dialog box, change the region to France.

   ❍ **D.** Change the DVD Language settings in Windows Media Center.

5. Which of the following is not a recommendation in keeping Windows Media Player secure?

   ❍ **A.** Keep your system up-to-date with the latest security patches.

   ❍ **B.** Keep an up-to-date virus scanner running on your computer.

   ❍ **C.** Log on with the administrator account.

   ❍ **D.** Use file format validation.

6. What software or hardware is used to compress and decompress digital media?

   ❍ **A.** Media translator

   ❍ **B.** MTran

   ❍ **C.** Codec

   ❍ **D.** Encryptor/decryptor

7. What region is the United States in for DVD players?

   ❍ **A.** 0

   ❍ **B.** 1

   ❍ **C.** 2

   ❍ **D.** 5

Answers to Exam Prep Questions

1. **Answer C is correct.** The initial release of Windows Vista includes Windows Media Player 11. Therefore, answers A, B, and D are wrong.

2. **Answer A is correct.** The MPEG-2 decoder is included in the Windows Home Premium version and Windows Vista Ultimate version. Because the MPEG-2 decoder is not included, one will have to be purchased and installed. Answer B is incorrect because Windows Media Player will automatically play DVD movies when they are inserted. Answer C is incorrect because the Windows Media Player is associated with DVD movies by default. Answer D is incorrect because you cannot automatically download a codec from Microsoft.

3. **Answer D is correct.** To record two movies at the same time, you need Microsoft Windows Vista Home Premium (or Windows Vista Ultimate) and two TV tuners. Therefore, answers A, B, and C are incorrect.

4. **Answer C is correct.** You need to change the region of the DVD player to the region used by France. Answer A would change languages and currency used on the computer, not DVD regions. Answer B is incorrect because Windows Media Player plays most movie types by default. Answer D is incorrect because this is not a language problem.

5. **Answer C is correct.** You should log in as a standard user. Answers A, B, and D are incorrect because these are recommending things you should do to keep your system secure.

6. **Answer C is correct.** A codec, short for compressor/decompressor, is the software or hardware that is used to compress or decompress digital media. Therefore, answers A, B, and D are incorrect.

7. **Answer B is correct.** The United States is in region 1. Therefore, answers A, C, and D are incorrect.

Recommended Readings and Resources

Stanek, William R., *Introducing Microsoft Windows Vista* (Redmond, Washington: Microsoft Press, 2006).

Tulloch, Mitch, Tony Northrup, Jerry Honeycutt, Ed Wilson, Ralph Ramos, and the Windows Vista Team, *Windows Vista Resource Kit (Pro. Resource Kit)* (Redmond, Washington: Microsoft Press, 2007).

For more information about Windows Media Player, visit www.microsoft.com/windows/windowsmedia/default.mspx.

11

CHAPTER ELEVEN

Configuring Windows Vista Productivity Applications

Terms you'll need to understand:

- ✓ WordPad
- ✓ Notepad
- ✓ Text file
- ✓ Rich Text Format
- ✓ Windows Mail
- ✓ E-mail
- ✓ Junk e-mail
- ✓ Phishing
- ✓ Windows Calendar
- ✓ Windows Fax and Scan
- ✓ Meeting Space
- ✓ Windows Sidebar
- ✓ Gadget

Techniques/concepts you'll need to master:

- ✓ Use WordPad and Notepad to create and modify files.
- ✓ Use Windows Mail to access e-mail.
- ✓ Secure Windows Mail.
- ✓ Use Windows Calendar to organize appointments, set reminders, and set tasks.
- ✓ Create multiple calendars and group them together.
- ✓ Use Windows Fax and Scan to fax and scan documents.
- ✓ Use Windows Meeting Space to conduct meetings and share documents during the meeting.
- ✓ Configure the Windows Sidebar and its gadgets.

Windows Vista includes a number of productivity applications to help users communicate, collaborate, and manage business and personal information. Although many organizations use Microsoft Office 2007 as their primary set of applications, and although Microsoft Office has far more capability, it is important to know what functionality the built-in tools provide and how to configure and support them to perform tasks that other applications do not support. Some of these applications include Windows WordPad, Windows Mail, Windows Calendar, Windows Meeting Space, and Windows Fax and Scan.

Windows WordPad and Notepad

Windows *WordPad* is a simple word processor that enables you to create more complex documents by changing fonts, adding bullets, adding color, adding pictures, and aligning text. All of this formatting is saved with your document using RTF format (*RTF* is short for Rich Text Format), so no matter who opens it, it will appear as if you created it.

Windows *Notepad* is a simple text editor that enables you to create and edit text documents. Because many configuration files are written in as text files, Notepad becomes a commonly used application for desktop support technicians.

Windows Mail

E-mail, short for electronic mail, is a fast and convenient way to communicate with others by transmitting and sending text messages with file attachments (documents, pictures, sound, and movies) over a network, including the Internet. You can send a single message to groups of people and forward messages that you receive to other people. Because e-mail messages are created and sent electronically, they can be easily stored and retrieved. Organizations that are fully computerized and have many users make extensive use of e-mail because it is fast, flexible, and reliable.

To use e-mail, you need the following:

- A network and/or Internet connection
- An e-mail program or web-based service
- An e-mail address that consists of a username, the at symbol (@), and the name of your Internet service provider (ISP) or web-based e-mail provider.

Windows Mail is an e-mail and newsgroup client software package that replaced Outlook Expressed, which came with Windows XP. It enables you to exchange e-mail with others, and it enables you to organize, manage, and protect your e-mail.

Using Windows Mail

To use e-mail in Windows Mail, you must set up an e-mail account. You need the following information from your network administrator or ISP:

- Your e-mail address
- Password
- Names of your incoming and outgoing e-mail servers

To add an account, you run the Add User Account Wizard, which can be started by doing the following:

1. Open Windows Mail.
2. On the Tools menu, click Accounts.
3. Click Add.
4. Select E-mail Account and click Next.

You then follow the instructions through the wizard. If you do not know the names of your services, your address, or your password, contact your ISP or network administrator.

If you do not receive e-mail, check the following:

- Make sure your computer is properly connected to the Internet by opening a web page on the Internet.
- If this is your first time trying to receive e-mail from this e-mail account on this computer, verify that the account/server information is set up properly. If you don't know your account information, check with your system administrator or your ISP. Account information can be accessed by opening the Tools menu and selecting Accounts.
- Click Send/Receive to retrieve your e-mail again.

After you have added an account, Windows Mail checks for new e-mail messages when you first start it. E-mail you receive is stored in your Inbox.

By default, it then checks every 30 minutes after that. To change how often it checks for new e-mail, open the Tools menu and select Options. Then, change the Check for New Messages Every *x* Minute option.

The Inbox is one of several folders that hold e-mail. To see a list of e-mail you've received, click the Inbox in the Folders list. Your e-mail messages display in the Message list. The list shows who sent the mail, the subject, and when it was received. To read a message, click it in the Message list. The contents of the message display below the Message list in the Preview pane. To read the message in a separate window, double-click it in the Message list. To reply to a message, click the Reply button.

To create a new e-mail message in Windows Mail, click the Create Mail button. A new message window opens. In the To box, enter the e-mail address of at least one recipient. If you are sending the message to multiple recipients, enter a semicolon (;) between e-mail address. You can also specify recipients in the CC box, short for carbon copy. CC is typically used when you want to send informational e-mails to a person and you don't expect action from them. In the Subject box, type a title for your message.

To attach a file to the message, click the Attach File to Message button on the toolbar (located just below the menu bar). Locate the file, select it, and then click Open. The file displays in the Attach box in the message header.

To send the message, click the Send button. If you are connected to a network, the e-mail will be received by the recipients.

Configuring Windows Mail

To configure the settings for Windows Mail, open the Tools menu and select Options. An Options dialog box displays with multiple tabs, as shown in Figure 11.1. The options include the following:

- General settings for configuring newsgroup behavior, send and receive timings and behavior, and default messaging programs
- Read settings for configuring how messages appear, how newsgroups messages are downloaded, and how fonts are used in Windows Mail
- Receipts settings for configuring how read receipts behave
- Send settings for configuring the format to send e-mail and news messages, and general settings for actions to take when mail is sent
- Compose settings for configuring fonts and stationery used in e-mail and news messages, and settings for using business cards

- Signatures settings for configuring a personalized signature to add to your outgoing e-mail
- Spelling settings for configuring your spelling checker preferences
- Security settings for configuring secure e-mail by using certificates, for using virus protection for your e-mail, and whether to allow image downloads
- Connection settings for configuring how the connection to the mail server behaves
- Advanced settings for configuring maintenance and troubleshooting

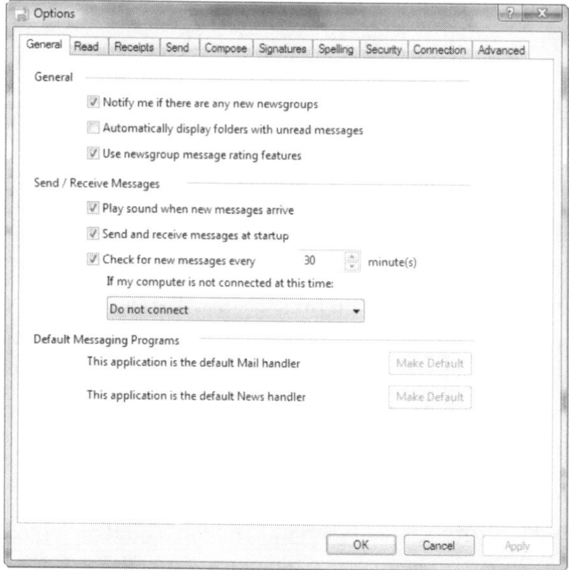

FIGURE 11.1 Windows Mail options.

Dealing with Junk E-Mail

With the popularity of e-mail and because of its low cost, users have to deal with junk e-mail. *Junk e-mail* is unsolicited e-mail that usually contains advertisements, flyers, and catalogs that may or may not contain fraudulent schemes and pornography. In addition, viruses are often spread through junk e-mail.

Windows Mail includes a Junk E-Mail Filter that analyzes the content of messages sent to you and moves suspicious messages to a special Junk E-Mail folder, where you can view or delete them at any time. And if a junk e-mail message slips past the filter into your Inbox, you can specify that any future messages from the sender be automatically moved to the Junk E-Mail folder.

Windows Mail automatically screens junk e-mail. However, you can customize how junk e-mail is filtered by opening the Tools menu, selecting Junk E-mail options, and selecting one of the following protection levels:

- **No Automatic Filtering.** Use this option if you want to stop blocking junk e-mail messages altogether. Windows Mail will continue to block messages from domain names and e-mail addresses on your Blocked Senders list.
- **Low.** Use this option if you don't receive many junk e-mail messages and want to block only the most obvious junk e-mail messages. This is the default setting.
- **High.** Use this option if you receive a large number of junk e-mail messages and want to block as many as possible.
- **Safe List Only.** Use this option if you want to receive only messages from people or domain names on your Safe Senders list. E-mail messages from people or domain names not on your Safe Senders list will be treated as junk e-mail messages, so you should choose this option only if you are certain that every person or domain name that you want to receive messages from is on your Safe Senders list.

Of course, you can take the following steps to reduce your junk e-mail:

- Use caution in giving out your e-mail address. Avoid publishing your real e-mail address in websites, newsgroups, or in other public areas of the Internet.
- Before you give your e-mail address to a website, check the site's privacy statement to be sure it does not permit the disclosure of your e-mail address to other companies.
- Never reply to a junk e-mail message. The sender will know that your e-mail address is valid and might sell it to other companies. You are then likely to receive even more junk e-mail.

If you are getting junk mail from a specific e-mail address, you can add that address to the Blocked Senders list. If you have e-mail that is getting flagged as junk e-mail, you can prevent the blocking of the messages from a specific e-mail address by adding them to the Safe Senders list. If an address is on both the Safe Senders list and the Blocked Senders list, the Safe Senders list has a higher priority than the Blocked Senders list; therefore, the message will be received rather than blocked. To add addresses to the Blocked Sender's list, follow these steps:

1. Open Windows Mail.
2. Click a message from the sender that you want to add to the Blocked Senders list.
3. Click the Message menu, point to Junk E-mail, and then do one of the following:
    - To block all future messages from that specific sender, click Add Sender to Blocked Senders List.
    - To block all messages from any sender whose domain name (the portion of the e-mail address after the @) is the same as the sender's, click Add Sender's Domain (@example.com) to Blocked Senders List.

To move a message from the Junk E-mail folder to your Inbox, follow these steps:

1. Open Windows Mail.
2. Click the Junk E-mail folder.
3. Click the message that you want to move to your Inbox.
4. Click the Message menu, point to Junk E-mail, and then click Mark as Not Junk. The message is moved to your Inbox.

NOTE

Although marking a message as not junk will move that message to your Inbox, future messages from that sender might still end up in the Junk E-mail folder. To prevent this from happening, add the sender to the Safe Senders list.

Phishing Options

Phishing Filter is a Windows Mail feature that helps detect phishing websites. The Phishing Filter uses the following methods to help protect you from phishing scams:

- It compares the addresses of websites you visit against a list of legitimate sites reported to Microsoft. This list is stored on your computer.
- It helps analyze the sites you visit to see whether they have the characteristics common to a phishing website.
- With your consent, Phishing Filter sends some website addresses to Microsoft to be further checked against a frequently updated list of reported phishing websites.

If you visit a website that has been reported as a phishing website, Internet Explorer will display a warning web page and a notification on the address bar. You can then choose to continue or close the page. If the website contains characteristics common to phishing sites, Internet Explorer will notify you in the address bar that it may possibly be a phishing website.

Securing Windows Mail

To keep Windows Mail secure, follow these guidelines:

- Use an up-to-date antivirus program.
- Make sure that virus protection is enabled for Windows Mail security options, including warning when an application tries to send mail and not to open attachments that could be potentially have a virus. You should also consider blocking images within HTML e-mail.
- Use caution when opening e-mail attachments.
- Be careful when clicking links in messages.
- Always use a secure password. Passwords that use a combination of uppercase, lowercase, and alphanumeric characters are harder to guess than passwords that can be found in a dictionary.
- If more than one user uses a computer, create a different profile for each user with its own e-mail account.

Windows Calendar

Calendar programs enable a user to organize appointments, set reminders, organize tasks, and share calendars with other users. *Windows Calendar* enables you to manage your schedule, let others view your schedule, and subscribe to web-based calendars.

Windows Calendar provides an individual calendar for each user account on a computer so that each user can maintain a private schedule (see Figure 11.2). You can also have one user have multiple calendars so that he can keep personal events separate from work-related events, or you can have multiple work-related calendars if you are involved with multiple projects.

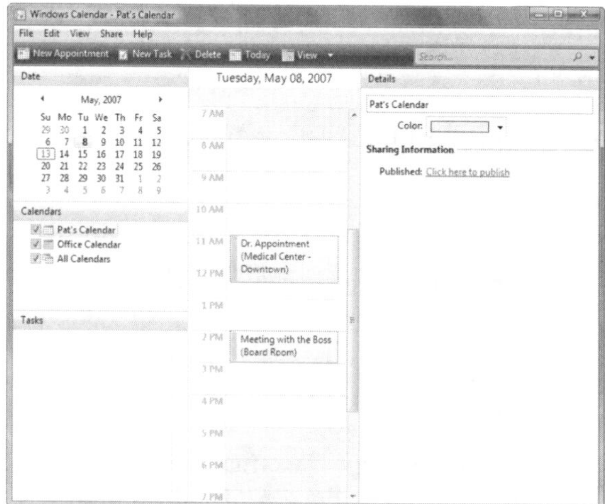

FIGURE 11.2 Windows Calendar.

To view several calendars together, you can create a calendar group, which then enables you to view the appointments in each calendar individually, or together. Although you cannot add new appointments directly to a calendar group, you can edit existing appointments. Appointments from each calendar display in a different color, making it easy to tell which schedule each item belongs to.

To create a calendar, follow these steps:

1. Click the File menu, and then click New Calendar.
2. In the New Calendar box, enter the name you want for the calendar, and then press Enter.
3. To choose the color of your appointments, in the Details pane, click Color, and then click the color you want.

You can view your calendar by day, work week, week, or month. Just click the View menu, and then click the view you want. A check mark displays next to the view you select.

To create an appointment, follow these steps:

1. On the toolbar, click New Appointment.
2. In the New Appointment box, enter a description of the appointment.
3. In the Location box on the Details pane, type the location of the appointment.
4. In the Calendar list, click the calendar where you want the appointment to display.
5. To make an all-day appointment, select the All-Day Appointment check box.
6. Enter start and end times.
7. To make the appointment recur, in the Recurrence list, click the type of recurrence you want.
8. To set a reminder, in the Reminder list, click how long before the appointment you want to be reminded.
9. To invite someone, in the Attendees list, type the e-mail address of the person you want to invite, press Enter, click the e-mail address in the Invite list, and then click Invite.

To edit an appointment, double-click the appointment, and then type over the existing text with your changes. Finally, you can have Windows Calendar use e-mail to send and receive appointments and invitations to friends and family members.

To help manage your time, you can create tasks. To create a task, follow these steps:

1. On the toolbar, click New Task.
2. In the New Task box, enter a description of the task.
3. In the Calendar list on the Details pane, click the calendar where you want the task to appear.
4. In the Priority list, click the priority you want: Low, Medium, or High.
5. Enter the start and due dates.
6. To set a reminder, in the Reminder list, click On Date, and enter the date and time you want to be reminded.

To search for appointments or tasks based on letters, words, or other text, in the Search box, type letters or words from the appointment you want to find. The results display as you type. The more you type, the more precise the results.

You can print your calendar by day, work week, week, or month. To print the calendar, click Print on the toolbar. Under Print Style, click one of the following: Day, Work Week, Week, or Month, and then click OK.

Many organizations publish their calendars on the Internet. If these calendars are published using the iCalendar format (ICS), you can subscribe to these calendars by clicking subscribe on the toolbar and then following the instructions.

You can publish your own calendar on the Internet through a web host so that others can see and share it. If you want, you can publish your personal schedule with password protection, which means you can choose who can access and view it:

1. Click the Share menu, and then click Publish.
2. In the Calendar Name box, enter the calendar name that you want to share.
3. In the Location to Publish Calendar box, enter the location (such as a website) where you want to publish the calendar.
4. Select any other options you want, and then click Publish.

Because Windows Calendar is compatible with the iCalendar format, you can import and export calendar information to and from other applications and websites.

Windows Fax and Scan

The *Windows Fax and Scan* program enables users to use a scanner to scan a document or picture into the system. Then, the same users can use e-mail to send the document to other users or a fax modem or fax server to fax the document or picture to another fax machine. It can also be configured to receive faxes from other fax machines.

Before you can send or receive faxes, you must configure a fax account. A fax account contains all the settings necessary for you to use a specified analog modem or fax server. You can create fax accounts for both an analog modem and a fax server on the same computer. You can configure a fax account to use either an internal or an external modem. To create a fax account, run the Fax Setup Wizard by selecting Fax Accounts under the Tools menu.

To scan a document, follow these steps:

1. Make sure that your scanner is connected to your computer and turned on.
2. Place a document on the scanner, or, if the scanner has a document feeder, place one or more pages in the feeder. If your scanner offers both options, use the option that you prefer.
3. Click the Start button, click All Programs, and then click Windows Fax and Scan.
4. To use Scan view, at the bottom of the left pane, click Scan.
5. On the toolbar, click New Scan.
6. In the New Scan dialog box, click the Profile list, and then click Documents. The default settings for scanning a document, which you can use or change, are automatically displayed.
7. To see how a document will appear when scanned, click Preview. If needed, change your scan settings, and then preview the document again. Repeat this step until you are satisfied with the preview results.
8. Click Scan. When the scan is complete, Windows Fax and Scan automatically displays the document so that you can view and manage it.

If you need to crop (cut the outside part of image that you do not desire to keep) an image before scanning it, click Preview in the New Scan dialog box, and then, in the preview area, drag the handles of the cropping tool to resize the image.

If a page that you're scanning contains more than one picture, you can save each picture as a separate file by selecting the Preview or Scan Images as Separate Files check box. You can automatically forward scanned documents to an e-mail address or a network folder. To choose a forwarding option, click Tools, and then click Scan Routing.

To send a fax using your computer, you can use Windows Fax and Scan or other programs that you run on Windows. Before you try sending a fax, however, make sure that your computer is connected to a fax modem or fax server, and then follow these steps:

1. Click the Start button, click All Programs, and then click Windows Fax and Scan.
2. To use Fax view, at the bottom of the left pane, click Fax.

3. On the toolbar, click New Fax.
4. Using the options provided in the New Fax window, create a new fax, and then click Send.

To fax directly from an application without going through the Windows Fax and Scan tool, open the File menu, select Print, and select Fax as the printer.

To send a fax to more than one recipient, in the To box, type the fax numbers, separated by semicolons. You can also select recipients from your Windows Contacts folder by clicking To, and then, in the list of contacts, double-clicking each contact. Make sure that you've saved your recipients' fax numbers in the contact information.

A cover page, which usually contains who the fax is being sent to and from including fax numbers, is used to help prevent people other than your intended recipients from seeing the contents of the fax, especially if the fax contains personal or confidential information. Therefore, it is recommended that the first page of each fax should be the cover page.

When working within Fax view, you can easily attach a file or insert text and pictures from other faxes by using the toolbar. When you attach a file, the file will be converted into a TIF image so that it can be received by any fax device. You can also drag the file from the desktop or any folder to the new Fax windows.

To ensure that a fax has been sent, you can configure the Windows Fax and Scan to send you a receipt. To enable receipts, navigate to the Receipts tab of Fax Options on a Windows Vista computer. Then, choose the E-mail To option and specify the user's e-mail address.

Received faxes are automatically stored in your Windows Fax and Scan Inbox. To save a copy to your Documents folder or any other folder, right-click the fax and click Save As, browse to the location, and save the fax.

To e-mail a scanned document or picture, follow these steps:

1. Click the Start button, click All Programs, and then click Windows Fax and Scan.
2. Click Scan.
3. Click the document or picture in the list of scanned files, and then click Forward as E-mail on the toolbar.
4. In the new e-mail message, enter the appropriate e-mail address for each recipient in the To and CC boxes. If you are sending to more than one recipient, separate the addresses with semicolons.

5. Enter the subject of the e-mail message in the Subject box and type the appropriate message.
6. Click Send.

You can also route all scans to an e-mail address by opening the Tools menu and selecting the Scan Routing option.

To receive faxes automatically, follow these steps:

1. Click the Start button, click All Programs, and then click Windows Fax and Scan.
2. To use Fax view, at the bottom of the left pane, click Fax.
3. Click Tools, and then click Fax Settings. If you are prompted for an administrator password or confirmation, enter the password or provide confirmation.
4. Click the General tab, and then, under Send/Receive options, select the Allow Device to Receive Fax Calls check box.
5. Click Automatically Answer After *x* Rings, and then select the number of rings after which the modem can answer incoming phone calls to try to receive a fax.

If you choose to receive faxes automatically, the modem will answer all incoming phone calls. To answer calls using your phone, you need to answer before the modem answers them.

To manually receive a fax, follow these steps:

1. Click the Start button, click All Programs, and then click Windows Fax and Scan.
2. To use Fax view, at the bottom of the left pane, click Fax.
3. On the toolbar, click Receive a Fax Now. The Fax Monitor dialog box appears and displays the progress of the fax.

To automatically save a copy of each fax that you receive, follow these steps:

1. Click the Start button, click All Programs, and then click Windows Fax and Scan.
2. To use Fax view, at the bottom of the left pane, click Fax.

3. Click the Tools menu, and then click Fax Settings. If you are prompted for an administrator password or confirmation, type the password or provide confirmation.
4. Click the General tab, and then click More options.
5. Under When a Fax Is Received, select the Save a Copy To check box, and then browse to the folder where you want to save copies.

To preview a fax, click the fax; it will display in the Preview pane below the list of faxes in your Inbox. To open a fax, double-click the fax in your list of faxes.

Meeting Space

Windows *Meeting Space*, which is a replacement for NetMeeting, enables you to share documents, programs, or your entire desktop with other people (see Figure 11.3). One of the advantages of using Windows Meeting Space is that it uses peer-to-peer technology that automatically sets up an ad hoc network if it can't find an existing network. So, you can use it in a conference room, a favorite hotspot, or a place where no network exists. You can join a meeting that someone else sets up, or you can start a new meeting and invite other people to join it.

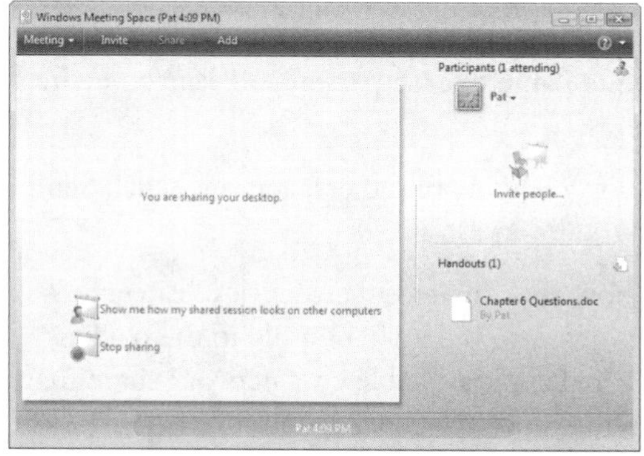

FIGURE 11.3 Windows Meeting Space.

After you have a method for users to connect to your computer, to start a new meeting, follow these steps:

1. Click Start a New Meeting, and then enter a name and password for the meeting. The password must be at least eight characters long.
2. If you want to change visibility or network options for the meeting, click Options.
3. Click the right-arrow button.

When you start Windows Meeting Space for the first time on a computer, you are prompted to turn on some services and sign in to People Near Me. If you are prompted for an administrator password or confirmation, enter the password or provide confirmation.

People Near Me identifies people using computers near you so that you can use Windows Meeting Space and other programs. When you sign in to People Near Me and then use a collaborative program such as Windows Meeting Space, a list of available people appears. Display names, computers names, and IP addresses are visible to everyone signed in to People Near Me.

You can configure People Near Me to accept invitations from anyone, no one, or trusted contacts only. A trusted contact is someone who supplies a digital certificate that you trust. The invitation can be dismissed, declined, or viewed and accepted.

TIP

Users must be on the same subnet to see available Windows Meeting Space Meetings in the People Near Me list.

There are three ways to invite people in a meeting. Either way, you first click the Invite People button. You then do one of the following:

- Select the check box beside the name of each person you want to invite, and then click Send invitations.
- In the Invite people dialog box, click Invite Others, and then click Send an Invitation in E-mail.
- In the Invite People dialog box, click Invite Others, click Create an Invitation File, and save the file. Give the invitation file to the person you want to invite, either by making it available on a network share that the person can access, e-mailing it, or providing it on removable media.

You can join a meeting by double-clicking the invitation file that you receive from someone in the meeting. You can also join a meeting by following these steps:

1. Open Windows Meeting Space.
2. Click Join a Meeting Near Me, enter the password for the meeting, and then click the right-arrow button.

If you have trouble connecting to a meeting, confirm the meeting password. You also need to make sure that the person who is offering the meeting has the correct firewall ports open.

After people have joined the meeting, you can share documents and programs. You can also add handouts, which will be copied to the participants' computers as they join the meeting.

Windows Sidebar

The *Windows Sidebar* is a pane that keeps your gadgets organized and always available. Gadgets are easy-to-use mini programs (tools) that give you information at a glance for frequently performed tasks such as checking the weather, checking the time (via a digital clock), and checking email (without opening other programs).

To remove the Sidebar from the desktop, right-click the Sidebar and select Close. To reopen the Sidebar, right-click the Sidebar icon in the notification area and select Open. To close the Sidebar program, right-click the Sidebar, and select Close. Then, right-click the Sidebar icon in the notification area and select Exit. To start the Sidebar, select All Programs, Accessories, and then click Windows Sidebar.

You can keep Sidebar and any detached gadgets that are on your desktop on top of your open windows. If open windows are maximized, they will automatically lock against Sidebar. To make the Sidebar always be on top, follow these steps:

1. Right-click the Windows Sidebar and select Properties.
2. Select the Sidebar Is Always on Top of Other Windows check box, and then click Apply.

To place a gadget on the desktop, follow these steps:

1. Right-click the gadget you want to detach, and then click Detach from Sidebar.
2. Drag the gadget to the location you want on the desktop.

You can add any installed gadget to the Sidebar. If you want, you can add multiple instances of a gadget. For example, if you are keeping track of time in two time zones, you can add two instances of the Clock and set each accordingly.

1. Right-click the Sidebar, and then click Add Gadgets.
2. Double-click a gadget to add it.

You can find additional gadgets from the following website:

http://gallery.microsoft.com/vista/sidebar.aspx

To configure a gadget, you can do the following:

- To configure a gadget to always be on top, right-click a detached gadget, and then click Always on Top.
- To move the gadget back to the Sidebar, right-click the gadget, and then click Attach to Sidebar.
- To remove a gadget from the Sidebar, right-click the gadget, and then click Close Gadget.
- To change an individual gadget's options, right-click the gadget you want to change, and then click Options.
- To change the opacity of a gadget, right-click the gadget and select Opacity. Then, select the percentage of opacity.

Exam Prep Questions

1. You work as the desktop support technician at Acme.com. A user was on a business trip when he decided to connect to the external mail server via POP3 using Microsoft Mail. He most likely did not select the option to leave a copy of messages on the server. Now that he is back in the office, he wants the messages that he already received to be seen in his Microsoft Outlook that connects directly to the Microsoft Exchange Server. What do you do?

   ❍ **A.** You should open Windows Mail and then change the message store location.

   ❍ **B.** You should open Windows Mail and then choose the menu option to export messages from the Inbox folder to Exchange.

   ❍ **C.** You should open Windows Mail and then choose the menu option to import messages from Exchange.

   ❍ **D.** You should open Outlook and then choose the menu option to import messages from the Outlook Web Access server.

2. You work as the desktop support technician at Acme.com. One user is getting junk mail from an online store. You want to block that e-mail as junk mail, but you do not want to block any other junk mail. What two steps do you need to complete for that to happen? (Choose two answers.)

   ❍ **A.** Block all @*.COM sites.

   ❍ **B.** Add the address of the online store to the Blocked Senders list.

   ❍ **C.** Add the address of the online store to the Safe Senders list.

   ❍ **D.** The junk e-mail protection level should be configured to No Automatic Filtering.

   ❍ **E.** The junk e-mail protection level should be configured to Low.

3. You work as the desktop support technician at Acme.com. You have two offices, one in Sacramento and one in Cleveland. Both sites are connected together through a WAN link. Pat, a user in the Sacramento office, wants to have a meeting using Windows Meeting Space. The users in the Sacramento office have no problem seeing the meeting and so join the meeting. However, the Cleveland users cannot see the meeting. What should you do?

   ❍ **A.** Instruct Pat to change his IP address because there is apparently a duplicate address in the other office.

   ❍ **B.** Check firewall settings between the two sites.

   ❍ **C.** Create invitations and send them to the Cleveland office.

   ❍ **D.** Re-create the meeting and choose the Allow People Near Me to See This Meeting option.

4. You work as the desktop support technician at Acme.com. You want to create a meeting using Windows Meeting space, but you do not want people to see the meeting. Instead, you will send out invitations to those people who you want to come to the meeting. What should you do?

   ❍ **A.** Select the Create a Private Ad Hoc Wireless Network option.

   ❍ **B.** Select the Do Not Allow People Near Me to See This Session option.

   ❍ **C.** Select the Allow People to Send Me Invitations option on the Settings tab.

   ❍ **D.** Select the Sign Out of People Near Me option on the Sign In tab.

5. You work as the desktop support technician at Acme.com. Pat wants to combine several calendars so that he can see them as one. What can he do?

   ❍ **A.** Create a calendar group and add those calendars to the group.

   ❍ **B.** Select the Merge option with the calendars highlighted.

   ❍ **C.** Import the information from the calendars into the one master calendar.

   ❍ **D.** Export the information from the calendars into the one master calendar.

6. You work as the desktop support technician at Acme.com. You have two users who share the same computer. Both of these users make use of Windows Calendar under their own profile. You need to enable both of these users to see each other's calendar without reducing security. What should you do?

❍ **A.** Add a Microsoft Exchange server to enable you to give other users the ability to see another's calendar.

❍ **B.** Instruct these users to share an account so that they have a common calendar.

❍ **C.** Instruct these users to publish their calendars to the Publish folder.

❍ **D.** Instruct these users to log out as themselves and log in as the other user so that they can access the other user's calendar.

7. You work as the desktop support technician at Acme.com. How do you set up a notification when a user sends a fax so that the user knows when a fax has been delivered?

❍ **A.** Navigate to the Tracking tab of Fax Settings on the Windows Vista computer. Then, select the Notify of Success and Failure for Outgoing Faxes option.

❍ **B.** Navigate to the Receipts tab of Fax Options on the Windows Vista computer. Then, choose the E-mail To option and specify the user's e-mail address.

❍ **C.** Navigate to the Additional Settings dialog box of Fax Settings on the Windows Vista computer. Specify the user's e-mail address in the CSID field.

❍ **D.** Navigate to the Additional Settings dialog box of Fax Settings on the Windows Vista computer. Specify the user's e-mail address in the TSID field.

8. You work as the desktop support technician at Acme.com. You have added a scanner to a newly installed Windows Vista computer. You want to configure all scanned images to go to a user's e-mail inbox. What do you need to do?

❍ **A.** You should use the Tools, Scan Settings option to configure new faxes to be forwarded to an e-mail address.

❍ **B.** You should use the Tools, Scan Routing option to configure new faxes to be forwarded to an e-mail address option.

❍ **C.** You should select all the scanned images on a regular basis, and click the Forward as E-mail button on the toolbar.

❍ **D.** You should use the Document, Forward as E-mail option to configure new faxes to be forwarded to an e-mail address.

9. You work as the desktop support technician at Acme.com. You just created a new report using Microsoft Word. You want to fax this document to your boss, who is at another office. What is the easiest way to do this?

❍ **A.** Print the report and place the document on the scanner. Choose File, New, Fax from Scanner from Windows Fax and Scan.

❍ **B.** Open the report in Microsoft Word. Choose File, Print. When prompted to select the printer, choose Fax as the printer.

❍ **C.** Save the report. Create a new fax. Browse to and attach the Word document file in the new fax in Windows Fax and Scan.

❍ **D.** Print the document. Then, scan the document using the scanner and fax it to your boss.

10. You work as the desktop support technician at Acme.com. How do you close the Sidebar?

❍ **A.** Right-click each gadget on the Sidebar and choose Close Gadget from the context menu.

❍ **B.** Right-click each gadget and choose Detach from Sidebar from the context menu.

❍ **C.** Right-click the Windows Sidebar and choose Close Sidebar from the context menu.

❍ **D.** Open the Control Panel, select the Sidebar applet, and select Do Not Load Sidebar.

11. You work as a desktop support technician at Acme.com. A user only wants the Weather gadget on his desktop. Before you remove the Windows Sidebar, how do you place the Weather gadget on the desktop?

❍ **A.** Right-click each gadget on the Sidebar except the Weather gadget, and then choose Close Gadget from the context menu.

❍ **B.** Right-click each gadget except the Weather gadget, and then choose Detach from Sidebar from the context menu.

❍ **C.** Right-click the Weather gadget, and then choose Detach from Sidebar from the context menu.

❍ **D.** Open the Control Panel and select the Sidebar applet. Deselect all gadgets except the Weather gadget.

12. You work as the desktop support technician at Acme.com. A user has the Clock gadget activated but has problem seeing it because it is too dim. What do you need to do so that the user can see it better?

 ❍ **A.** Right-click the Clock gadget and increase the clock's opacity.

 ❍ **B.** Right-click the Windows Sidebar and choose Bring Gadgets to Front.

 ❍ **C.** Ensure that the Windows Sidebar Is Always on Top of the Other Windows option is selected in the Windows Sidebar Properties window.

 ❍ **D.** Ensure that the Clock gadget is checked under the Select which System Icons to Always Show section in the Task and Start menu Properties.

Answers to Exam Prep Questions

1. **Answer B is correct.** Apparently, the user did not configure to leave the messages on the Exchange box when configuring Microsoft Mail. Therefore, you need to export messages from the Inbox folder to Exchange. Answer A is incorrect because changing the store in Windows will not change the messages on the Exchange Server that the user accesses using Microsoft Outlook. Answer C is incorrect because Microsoft Outlook is the user's primary mail client. Therefore, importing into Windows Mail will not fix the problem. Answer D is incorrect because Outlook Web Access server provides only a web interface to e-mails that are already on the Exchange server. Therefore, no e-mails will be recovered to the Exchange server.

2. **Answers B and D are correct.** To shut off the junk e-mail protection, you need to configure to No Automatic Filtering. You then need to add the address on the online store to the Blocked Senders list so that messages sent from that address will be blocked. Answer A is incorrect because you don't want to block all .com addresses. Answer C is incorrect because if you add the address to the Safe Senders list, Microsoft Mail will not block messages from this address. Answer E is incorrect because setting junk e-mail protection to Low will still block some messages that it thinks is junk mail.

3. **Answer C is correct.** Because the People Near Me will list only people who are on the same subnet, you must create invitations for the remote users. Answer A is incorrect because Pat not seeing the meeting is not an IP address problem. Answer B is incorrect because Pat not seeing the meeting is less likely compared to answer C. Answer D is incorrect the real problem is that the People Near Me will list only people who are on the same subnet.

4. **Answer B is correct.** If you don't want your meeting sessions listed, select the Do Not Allow People Near Me to See This Session. Answer A is incorrect because this option would be used when you are out of the office with no formal network available. Answer C is incorrect because just sending invitations will not change whether a person can see the available sessions. Answer D is incorrect because signing out people will not affect whether they can see the session listed.

5. **Answer A is correct.** To combine several calendars together so that they can be seen as one is done using groups. Answer B is incorrect because the Merge option would physically combine calendars. Answers C and D are incorrect because importing and exporting calendars do not keep the calendars separate.

6. **Answer C is correct.** If you share the folders in a Publish folder, both users can access each other's calendars while keeping all other personal files secure. Answer A is incorrect because delegation only works with Microsoft Outlook. Answers B and D are incorrect because these solutions give access to personal files.

7. **Answer B is correct.** To set up electronic receipts when faxes are delivered, open the Fax Options, select the Receipts tab, and choose the E-mail To option. Answer A is not used for user notification; instead it is used for logging of fax activities. Answers C and D are incorrect because these settings have nothing to do with user notifications of faxes sent.

8. **Answer B is correct.** To forward scanned images to an e-mail address, use the Scan Routing option. Answer A is incorrect because the Scan Settings option does not exist. Answers C and D are more difficult ways because you have to do them manually.

9. **Answer B is correct.** You can fax a document from any application that can print directly to the fax. Answers A, C, and D would take much longer and more effort to complete.

10. **Answer C is correct.** To close a Sidebar, right-click the Windows Sidebar and select Close Sidebar. Answers A and B are incorrect because they will affect the individual gadgets and not the Sidebar itself. Answer D is incorrect because the Sidebar applet does not exist in the Control Panel.

11. **Answer C is correct.** You can detach individual gadgets to be kept on the desktop by right-clicking the gadget and selecting Detach. Answer A would remove the gadget from the Sidebar. Answer B is incorrect because this would detach all of the gadgets except the Weather gadget. Answer D is incorrect because there is no Sidebar applet in the Control Panel.

12. **Answer A is correct.** The user cannot see it because the opacity was set too low. Answers B and C are incorrect because the gadget is not being blocked by another application or gadget. Answer D does not affect the Sidebar.

Recommended Readings and Resources

Tulloch, Mitch, Tony Northrup, Jerry Honeycutt, Ed Wilson, Ralph Ramos, and the Windows Vista Team, *Windows Vista Resource Kit (Pro. Resource Kit)* (Redmond, Washington: Microsoft Press, 2007).

Stanek, William R., *Introducing Microsoft Windows Vista* (Redmond, Washington: Microsoft Press, 2006).

CHAPTER TWELVE

Configuring Mobile Computers

Terms you'll need to understand:

- ✓ Windows Mobility Center
- ✓ Power plans
- ✓ Hibernate mode
- ✓ Sleep mode
- ✓ Hybrid Sleep
- ✓ Battery meter
- ✓ Sync Center
- ✓ Offline folder
- ✓ Bluetooth
- ✓ Windows Mobility Device Center
- ✓ Presentation mode
- ✓ Windows SideShow
- ✓ Tablet PC
- ✓ Flicks

Techniques/concepts you'll need to master:

- ✓ Configure Power Management to balance performance and battery life.
- ✓ Compare and differentiate Sleep, Hybrid Sleep, Hibernate, and Shutdown.
- ✓ Use the battery meter to monitor power levels.
- ✓ Use the Sync Center to synchronize offline files.
- ✓ Use the Sync Center to connect mobile devices.
- ✓ List the features of Presentation mode.
- ✓ Use Windows SideShow to check e-mail or access Windows Media Player.
- ✓ Configure Windows Vista to support Tablet PCs, including configuring flicks.

Mobile computers are computers that are meant to be mobile. Just like desktop computers, mobile computers (including laptops, notebook computers, Tablet PCs and Ultra-Mobile computers) can come in various sizes and configurations. In any case, mobile computers bring a set of challenges because they are not always connected to the Internet or corporate office, and they are designed to be portable, conserve power for a longer battery life, and run cooler.

A mobile device is a computing device that has been optimized for specific mobile computing tasks. Mobile device types include the following:

- Personal digital assistants (PDAs)
- Windows Mobile devices
- Portable media players
- Mobile phones

Mobile devices offer their own challenges because they are often configured to synchronize with a desktop or mobile computer to obtain data.

Control Panel and Windows Mobility Center

All mobile and power settings are configured within the Control Panel. After you open the Control Panel, click Mobile PC (see Figure 12.1).

To make finding these settings quick and easy, Windows Vista includes the *Windows Mobility Center*, which provides a single location that enables you to quickly adjust mobile PC settings. Depending on your system, the Mobility Center window has some, but perhaps not all, of the following tiles (see Figure 12.2):

- **Brightness.** Move the slider to temporarily adjust the brightness of your display. To adjust the display brightness settings for your power plan, click the icon on the tile to open Power Options in Control Panel.
- **Volume.** Move the slider to adjust the speaker volume of your mobile PC or select the Mute check box.
- **Battery Status.** View how much charge remains on your battery or select a power plan from the list.
- **Wireless Network.** View the status of your wireless network connection or turn your wireless adapter on or off.

- **External Display.** Connect an additional monitor to your mobile PC or customize the display settings.
- **Sync Center.** View the status of an in-progress file sync, start a new sync or set up a sync partnership, and adjust your settings in Sync Center.
- **Presentation Settings.** Adjust settings, such as the speaker volume and the desktop background image, for giving a presentation.
- **Screen Rotation.** Change the orientation of your Tablet PC screen, from portrait to landscape, or vice versa.

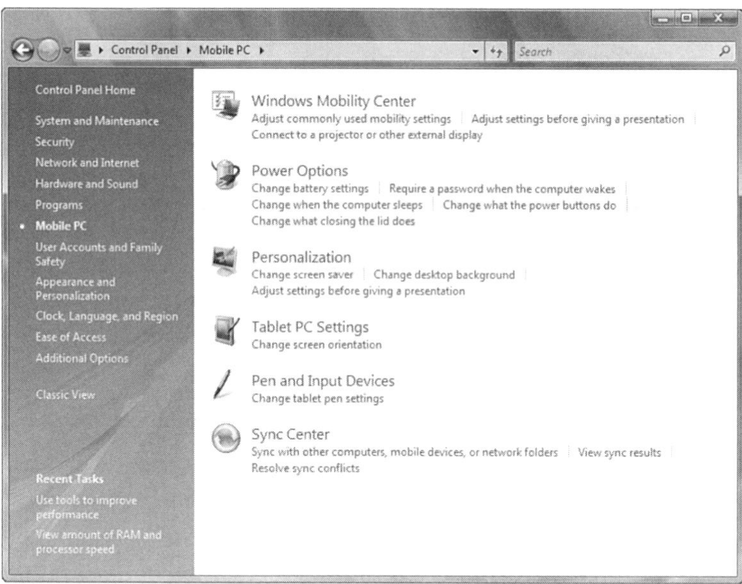

FIGURE 12.1 Mobile PC options in the Control Panel.

If a tile doesn't display, it may be because the required hardware, such as a wireless network adapter, or drivers are missing.

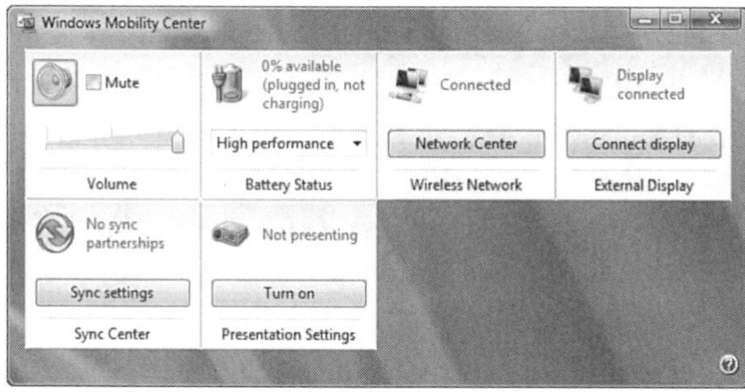

FIGURE 12.2 Windows Mobility Center.

If you need to make additional adjustments to your mobile PC settings that require you to access Control Panel, click the icon on a tile to open the Control Panel for that setting. For example, you can select an existing power plan from the Battery Status tile, or you can click the icon on the tile to open Power Options in the Control Panel to create a power plan.

The Mobility Center can be opened using any one of the following methods:

- Click the Start button, click Control Panel, click Mobile PC, and then click Windows Mobility Center.
- Click the battery meter icon in the notification area in the Windows taskbar, and then click Windows Mobility Center.
- Press the Windows logo key + X.

Power Management

One of the goals of mobile computers is to run off the battery for as long as possible. Therefore, the mobile computers use components that typically use less power than components that you would find in a desktop computer. Consider the following:

- Mobile computers use processors that run on a lower voltage and consume less power.
- Mobile processors, including Intel SpeedStep and AMD PowerNow, have the ability to adjust voltage and the ability to throttle—temporarily run at a slower clock speed—to use even less power when running off the battery.
- LCD monitor can be dimmed so that it consumes less power.
- Hard drives can be spun down when not in use.

Power Plans

A *power plan* (formerly known as power schemes in earlier versions of Windows) is a collection of hardware and system settings that manages how your computer uses and conserves power. You can use power plans to save energy, maximize system performance, and balance energy conservation with performance.

Windows Vista includes three default power plans (see Figure 12.3):

- **Balanced.** Offers full performance when you need it and saves power during periods of inactivity.
- **Power saver.** Saves power by reducing system performance. This plan can help mobile PC users get the most from a single battery charge.
- **High performance.** Maximizes system performance and responsiveness. Mobile PC users may notice that their batteries don't last as long when using this plan.

If a default plan doesn't meet your needs (even if you change some settings), you can create your own plan by using a default plan as a starting point.

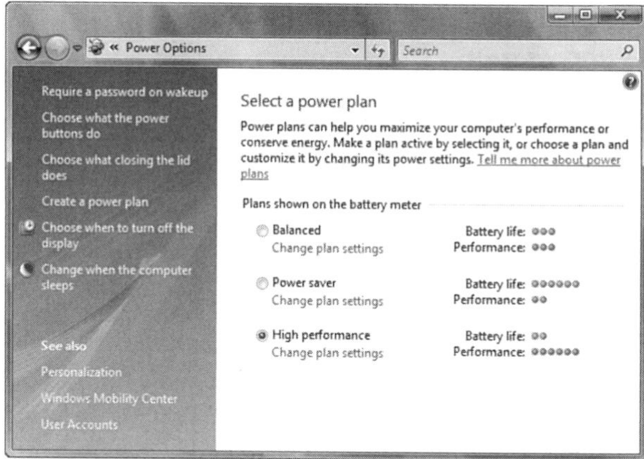

FIGURE 12.3 Configuring power plans using the Control Panel.

To change an existing plan, follow these steps:

1. Open Power Options by clicking the Start button, clicking Control Panel, clicking System and Maintenance, and then clicking Power Options.
2. On the Select a Power Plan page, click Change Plan Settings under the plan that you want to change.
3. On the Change Settings for the Plan page, choose the display and sleep settings that you want to use when your computer is running off the battery and when it's plugged in.
4. If you don't want to change any more settings, click Save Changes. To change additional power settings, click Change Advanced Power Settings.

5. On the Advanced Settings tab, expand the category that you want to customize, expand each setting that you want to change, and then choose the values that you want to use when your computer is running on battery and when it's plugged in.
6. Click OK to save the changes, and then click the Close button on the Change Settings for the Plan page.

To create your own plan, follow these steps:

1. Open Power Options by clicking the Start button, clicking Control Panel, clicking System and Maintenance, and then clicking Power Options.
2. On the Select a Power Plan page, in the task pane, click Create a Plan.
3. On the Create a Power Plan page, select the plan that's closest to the type of plan that you want to create.
4. In the Plan Name box, enter a name for the plan, and then click Next.
5. On the Change Settings for the Plan page, choose the display and sleep settings that you want to use when your computer is running on battery and when it's plugged in, and then click Create.

If you created power plans that you no longer use or need, you can delete them. To delete a plan, follow these steps:

1. Open Power Options by clicking the Start button, clicking Control Panel, clicking System and Maintenance, and then clicking Power Options.
2. If the active plan is the one that you want to delete, make a different plan the active plan.
3. On the Select a Power Plan page, click Change Plan settings under the plan that you want to delete.
4. On the Change Settings for the Plan page, click Delete this Plan.
5. When prompted, click OK.

NOTE

You can't delete any of the three default power plans (Balanced, Power saver, or High performance).

Shutdown Options

When you shut down your computer, all open files are saved to the hard disk, the contents of the memory are saved to the hard disk or discarded as appropriate, the page file is cleared, and all open applications are closed. The active user is then logged out of Windows and the computer is turned off. Of course, this may take a minute or two depending on the computer and the applications that the computer was running at the time of shutdown.

Windows Vista offers two other modes besides shutdown. When you *hibernate* your computer, the system state, along with the contents of the system memory, is saved to a file (Hiberfil.sys) on the hard disk and the computer is shut down. The Hiberfil.sys file will be the same size as the amount of physical memory (RAM). No power is required to maintain this state because the data is stored on the hard disk. You can then continue where you left off within a short time.

Sleep is a power-saving state that saves work and open programs to memory. To maintain the contents of memory while the computer is in Sleep mode, the system still consumes a small amount of power. The advantage of Sleep mode is that you can continue where you left off, typically within a few seconds.

Hybrid Sleep, a combination of Sleep and Hibernate, saves your work to your hard disk and puts your mobile PC into a power-saving state. If you suffer a power failure on a computer when it is in a Hybrid Sleep state, your data will not be lost. Hybrid Sleep is turned off by default on mobile PCs.

When you click the power button on the Start menu, Windows Vista automatically goes into Sleep mode. If your battery power is low, Windows Vista hibernates the computer.

In addition to power plans, you can configure what the computer does when you press the power button or when you close the lid (on a laptop computer). You can also tell Windows Vista whether to prompt for a user password when returning to its power-on state. You can also control button actions depending on whether the computer is plugged in or running on battery power (see Figure 12.4).

Battery Meter

Displayed in the notification area of the Windows taskbar, the *battery meter* helps you manage your computer's power consumption by indicating how much charge is remaining on your battery and which power plan your computer is using.

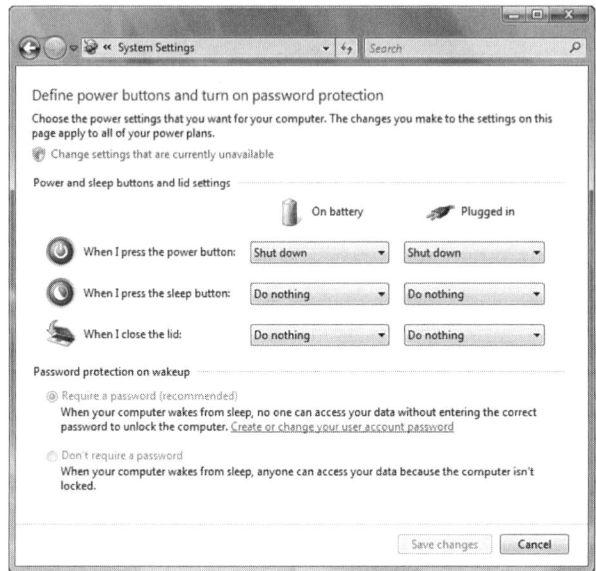

FIGURE 12.4 System settings for power, sleep buttons, and lid settings.

Windows continuously monitors the power level of your battery and warns you when the battery power reaches low and critical levels. When your battery charge gets low, the battery icon on the Windows taskbar indicates a low-battery power level. Make sure that you have sufficient time to install a fully charged battery, find an AC power outlet, or save your work and turn off the mobile PC. When your battery is almost out of power, the battery icon changes to indicate a critical-battery level.

To choose low and critical power levels, follow these steps:

1. Open Power Options by clicking the Start button, clicking Control Panel, clicking System and Maintenance, and then clicking Power Options.
2. On the Select a power plan page, click Change plan settings under the selected plan.
3. On the Change settings for the plan page, click Change Advanced Power Settings.
4. On the Advanced Settings tab, expand Battery, expand Low Battery Level and Critical Battery Level, and then choose the percentage that you want for each level.
5. Click OK to save the changes, and then click the Close button on the Change Settings for the Plan page.

File and Data Synchronization

While using mobile computers, sometimes you are connected to a corporate network and other times you are not. Sometimes you might want to work on the files stored on a network server even when you are not connected to the network that holds the network server. You might also want to connect mobile devices such as phones and PDAs to your mobile computer or desktop computer so that information can be copied back and forth.

The new Windows Vista *Sync Center* provides a single easy-to-use interface to manage data synchronization between multiple computers, including network servers, and with mobile devices you connect to your computer. To start the Sync Center, click the Start button, click All Programs, click Accessories, and then click Sync Center.

To set up synchronization between two computers, you create a sync partnership between two or more sync locations, which specifies what files and folders to sync, where to sync them, and when (see Figure 12.5). You can schedule an automatic sync on a daily, weekly, or monthly basis, or when a specific event occurs, such as every time you log on to your computer. You can also perform a manual sync at any time, such as when you are getting ready to disconnect a mobile PC from the network and want to make sure you have the latest copies of files on a network server.

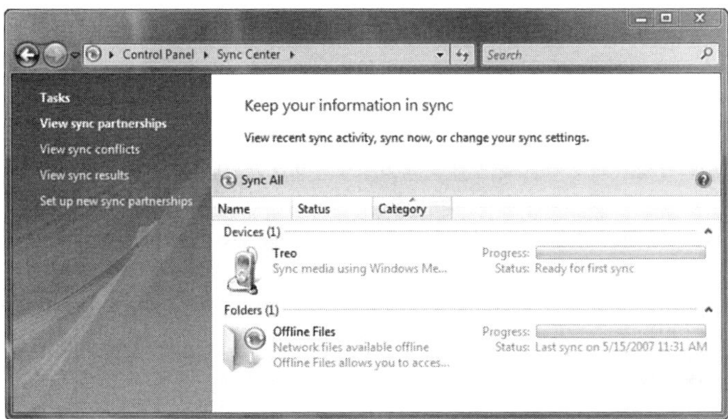

FIGURE 12.5 Sync Center.

NOTE

The ability to sync with network folders is not included in Windows Vista Starter, Windows Vista Home Basic, and Windows Vista Home Premium.

Every time you sync files between two locations (such as between a computer and a mobile device), Sync Center compares the files in both locations to determine whether they still match or whether any have changed. It determines whether any files need to be updated to stay in sync.

If the files differ, Sync Center determines which version of each file to keep and copies that version to the other location, overwriting the other version there. It selects the most recent version to keep, unless you have set up the sync partnership to sync differently. Sometimes Sync Center will prompt you to choose which version of a file to keep. This usually occurs when a file has changed in both locations since the last sync. When this happens, Sync Center will notify you of a sync conflict, which you must resolve before it can sync the items in conflict.

When you set up the synchronization, you may set up a one-way or two-way synchronization. In one-way sync, files are copied from a primary location to a secondary location, but no files are ever copied back to the primary location. In two-way sync, Sync Center copies files in both directions, keeping the two locations in sync with each other. Most sync partnerships are automatically set up to perform either one-way or two-way sync, although some sync partnerships let you choose.

You might set up two-way sync between a network folder and your computer, where you instruct Sync Center to copy the newest version of any file it finds to the other location, overwriting any older versions of the same file. This is a good way to sync if you work with the same files on both the network folder and your computer, and you want to make sure you always have the most recent version of every file you've worked on.

You might set up one-way sync for a portable music player, for example, where you instruct Sync Center to copy every new music file from your computer to the mobile device but never to copy music files in the other direction (from the device to your computer).

Offline Folders

To create an *offline folder*, open a network folder, right-click a file or folder, and select Always Available Offline. Windows automatically creates a copy of that file or folder on your computer. Anytime you reconnect to that network folder, Windows will sync the files between your computer and the network folder. You can also sync them manually at any time.

In addition, you can encrypt your offline files to help secure private information. Of course, when you encrypt offline files, only your user account can access the cached data.

To configure offline files, click Control Panel, then click Network and Internet, and then click Offline Files. From the General tab in the Offline Files dialog box, you can enable or disable offline files by clicking the top button. You can also use the General tab to open Sync Center and view your offline files (see Figure 12.6).

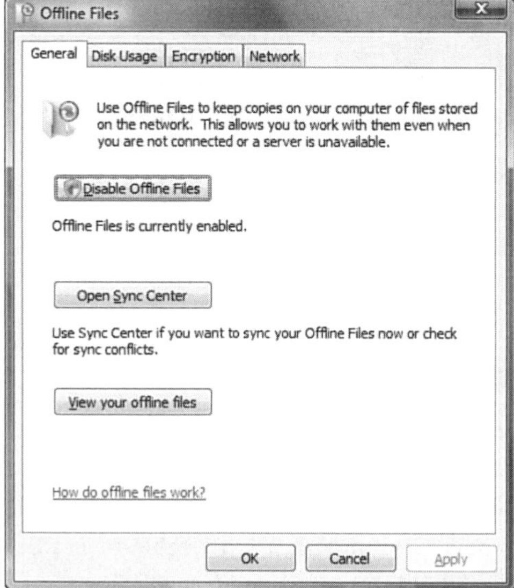

FIGURE 12.6 Offline files options.

The Disk Usage tab enables you to see how much disk space is currently being used by offline files and enables you to change the limits of storage that offline files will use. The Encryption tab enables you to encrypt or unencrypt your offline files.

The Network tab enables you to choose to automatically work on any locally cached offline files when your connection to the network is slow. You can also choose how often to check for a slow network connection.

When a shared resource is made available on a network, you can control the cache settings for that shared resource. This enables you to determine how remote users access files inside each of your shares. The cache settings are defined on the computer on which the shared resource resides.

The Caching settings for shared folders are configured by clicking Advanced Sharing, on the Sharing tab of the folder's Properties sheet. The options are as following:

- **Only the files and programs that users specify will be available offline.** This setting is the default and enables any files or programs in the share to be available offline to users but users must make the decision.
- **All files and programs that users open from the share will be automatically available offline.** This setting ensures that any files a user accesses from this share while online will be available offline.
- **Optimized for performance.** This check box enables the caching to take place in the background therefore helping to optimize network performance.
- **Files or programs from the share will not be available offline.** This setting disables caching from the share.

Connecting Mobile Devices

Many mobile devices can connect to your Windows Vista computer and synchronize data and files between the two. Typically, you connect your device to your computer either using a USB cable or cradle, or through a wireless signal (infrared, Bluetooth, or WiFi). Most devices ship with a USB cable or cradle, and most modern computers are equipped with infrared or *Bluetooth*.

If you connect a mobile device using Bluetooth technology, you need to configure the device as discoverable. You also need to set up the passkey to associate the device with the Bluetooth signal. This ensures that each device is connected to the device to which it is intended to connect.

NOTE

You can use the *Windows Mobility Device Center* to disable USB connections and Bluetooth connections. To access the Mobility Device Center, open the Control Panel, click Mobile PC, and select Mobility Device Center.

Before you can synchronize information with devices, you must set up sync partnerships. To create a sync partnership with a portable media player, you just need to do the following:

1. Connect your device to a computer running Windows Vista and open Sync Center. Windows Vista includes drivers for many common devices, but you can also obtain drivers from the CD that came with your device or from Windows Update.
2. Set up a sync partnership. Clicking Set Up for a Media Device Sync Partnership opens Windows Media Player 11.
3. Select some media files or a playlist to synchronize to the device. To select media, just drag it onto the Sync dialog box on the right side of Windows Media Player.
4. Click Start Sync. When your chosen media has transferred to the device, you can disconnect it from your computer and close Windows Media Player.

You can sync your contacts with some mobile devices, allowing you to take your contacts with you wherever you go. To sync contacts with a mobile device, the device must be able to read the contact file that Windows creates for each individual contact. The device must also be compatible with Sync Center, which Windows uses to sync files between a computer and a mobile device.

If you have Exchange Server 2003 or later deployed in your organization, take advantage of its integration with Windows Mobile, which provides direct push e-mail using ActiveSync technology, Global Address List lookup, and numerous security features.

Giving Presentations

Presentation settings are options on your mobile PC that you can apply when giving a presentation. If you've ever had your display screen turn black during a presentation, you'll appreciate that you can automatically turn off your screen saver every time that you give a presentation.

When presentation settings are turned on (often referred to as presentation mode), your mobile PC stays awake, and system notifications are turned off. You can also choose to turn off the screen saver, adjust the speaker volume, and change your desktop background image. Your settings are automatically saved and applied every time that you give a presentation, unless you manually turn them off.

You can turn on presentation settings by using one of the following methods:

- Open Windows Mobility Center by clicking the Start button, clicking Control Panel, clicking Mobile PC, and then clicking Windows Mobility Center.
- On the Presentation Settings tile, click Turn On. Click OK.

To turn presentation settings on or off for the current monitor or projector that the mobile PC is connected to, follow these steps:

1. Open Windows Mobility Center by clicking the Start button, clicking Control Panel, clicking Mobile PC, and then clicking Windows Mobility Center.
2. On the Presentation Settings tile, click the Change Presentation Settings icon.
3. In the Presentation Settings dialog box, click Connected Displays.
4. In the Current Displays dialog box, select or clear the I Always Give a Presentation When I Use This Display Configuration check box, and then click OK.

Presentation settings automatically turn off when you disconnect your mobile PC from a network projector or additional monitor, and when you shut down or log off from your mobile PC. Or, you can manually turn off presentation settings:

1. Open Windows Mobility Center by clicking the Start button, clicking Control Panel, clicking Mobile PC, and then clicking Windows Mobility Center.
2. On the Presentation Settings tile, click Turn Off.

To customize presentation settings, follow these steps:

1. Open Windows Mobility Center by clicking the Start button, clicking Control Panel, clicking Mobile PC, and then clicking Windows Mobility Center.
2. On the Presentation Settings tile, click the Change Presentation Settings icon.
3. In the Presentation Settings dialog box, adjust settings for giving a presentation, and then click OK.

To keep the display on during presentations, follow these steps:

1. Open Windows Mobility Center by clicking the Start button, clicking Control Panel, clicking Mobile PC, and then clicking Windows Mobility Center.
2. On the Presentation Settings tile, click the Change Presentation Settings icon.
3. Expand Display, expand Turn Off Display After, click On Battery or Plugged In, and then click the arrow to change the setting to Never. You can also type the word **Never** in the box.
4. Click OK, and then click Save Changes.

To prevent the mobile PC from going to sleep during presentations, follow these steps:

1. Open Windows Mobility Center by clicking the Start button, clicking Control Panel, clicking Mobile PC, and then clicking Windows Mobility Center.
2. On the Presentation Settings tile, click the Change Presentation Settings icon.
3. Expand Sleep, expand Sleep After, click On Battery or Plugged In, and then click the arrow to change the setting to Never. You can also type the word **Never** in the box.
4. Click OK, and then click Save Changes.

Windows SideShow

Windows SideShow is a new technology in Windows Vista that supports a secondary screen on your mobile PC. By viewing the second monitor or display, you can run Windows Media Player or check e-mail whether your laptop is on, off, or in Sleep mode. Windows SideShow is available in Windows Vista Home Premium, Windows Vista Business, Windows Vista Enterprise, and Windows Vista Ultimate.

Windows SideShow uses gadgets, which are convenient mini programs, to extend information from your computer to other devices. Gadgets can run on a Windows SideShow–compatible device and update that device with information from your computer. Using a gadget, you can view information from your computer regardless of whether your mobile PC is on, off, or in the Sleep power state, which can save you both time and battery life.

To configure Windows SideShow, open the Control Panel, click Hardware and Sound, and click Windows SideShow, where you can turn gadgets on or off for each of your devices. From the Control Panel, you can also set your computer to wake periodically (such as every hour) so that all gadgets that are turned on can update your devices with the latest information.

Windows SideShow–compatible devices can take many forms. Hardware manufacturers are already including secondary displays in their designs for mobile PCs and devices such as keyboards, mobile phones, and remote controls.

Configuring Tablet PCs

A *Tablet PC* is a fully functioning compact PC. Different from most desktop computers, Tablet PCs tools are available to make handwritten notes and sketches. The tools include the following:

- Integrated digital pen support
- A touchscreen
- Digital ink input
- Handwriting-recognition technologies

All Tablet PCs have several hardware buttons for common tasks, which can be programmed as needed. In addition, you can program the digital pen by assigning key commands or actions to simple pen gestures called *flicks*. The Handwriting Recognition Personalization Tool enables you to tailor recognition results to your own personal handwriting style. Finally, Windows Touch Technology provides support for touchscreens, including accessing context menus and accessing small components with your finger.

To configure a Tablet PC, you use the Tablet PC Settings tool, which is found under Mobile PC in the Control Panel. The tabs shown in the Tablet PC Setting tool are as follows:

- **General tab.** Enables you to configure on-screen menus for left-handed or right-handed users and to calibrate the effectiveness of your tablet pen.
- **Handwriting Recognition tab.** Allows you to configure Tablet PC handwriting recognition, which can adapt to your particular style of handwriting, resulting in a more productive end-user experience.

- **Display tab.** Allows you to manually change screen orientation (portrait versus landscape). Most Tablet PCs have hardware buttons for changing screen orientation, so this tab also allows you to change the order in which screen orientation is changed when this button is used.
- **Pen Options tab.** Allows you to tell Windows Vista what it should do for actions that you perform with your pen. For example, if you tap twice on an icon on the screen, Windows Vista responds as if you had double-clicked the icon. You can also configure pen button options in this pane. The Dynamic Feedback area allows you to configure visual feedback for pen actions as a way of confirming that Windows Vista has recognized your pen input correctly.

Exam Prep Questions

1. You work as the desktop support technician at Acme.com. You need to give a presentation using your mobile computer. So, you take the computer to the conference room and connect the projector to the computer with an S-Video cable. You want the desktop and Start menu to be displayed on the projector. What should you do in Windows Vista?

   ❍ **A.** Open Display Settings. Select the icon that represents the project. Then, select the This Is My Main Monitor option.

   ❍ **B.** Open Display Settings. Select the icon that represents the laptop display. Then clear the Extend the Desktop onto This Monitor option.

   ❍ **C.** Clear the Lock the Taskbar option of the taskbar's context menu. Drag the taskbar as far to the right as possible.

   ❍ **D.** Clear the Lock the Taskbar option of the taskbar's context menu. Drag the taskbar as far to the left as possible.

2. You work as the desktop support technician at Acme.com. You have a laptop in a conference room connected to a large TV monitor. Because you forgot the power connector for the mobile computer, you want the battery to last as long as possible. What should you do to conserve the most power during the presentation?

   ❍ **A.** Reduce the brightness settings in the Windows Mobility Center to the lowest setting.

   ❍ **B.** Select External display only in the New Display Detected dialog box.

   ❍ **C.** Select Extended in the New Display Detected dialog box.

   ❍ **D.** Turn on Presentation mode in the Windows Mobility Center.

3. You work as the desktop support specialist at Acme.com. You have a Bluetooth-enabled handheld device added to a user's personal area networks (PAN). What do you need to do so that the device can be discovered?

   ❍ **A.** Configure the passkey and ensure that the device is discoverable.

   ❍ **B.** Configure the appropriate wireless security method and ensure that the device is discoverable.

   ❍ **C.** Turn on the Network Discovery and configure the passkey.

   ❍ **D.** Configure the passkey and ensure that the mobile device is WiFi enabled.

4. You work as the desktop support technician at Acme.com. You plan to give a presentation on a Tablet PC workstation. During the presentation, you need to temporarily block notifications and disable your screen saver during the presentation. What should you do?

   ❍ **A.** Set the screen saver to None in the Display Settings.

   ❍ **B.** Select Extended in the New Display Detected dialog box.

   ❍ **C.** Turn on and configure Presentation mode in the Windows Mobility Center.

   ❍ **D.** Click Connect External Display in the Windows Mobility Center.

5. You work as the desktop support technician at Acme.com. You are in the office and get an emergency call to visit a client. You want to stop your work as quick as possible and resume as quickly as possible when you get to the client site. You also want to be protected from data loss if there is a power problem. What do you suggest?

   ❍ **A.** Ensure that the laptop workstations have the power saving logo. You should configure Hybrid Sleep on the laptop workstations.

   ❍ **B.** Ensure that the users are administrators. You should configure Hybrid Sleep on the laptop workstations.

   ❍ **C.** Ensure that there is available disk space equivalent to the amount of RAM. Configure Sleep on the laptop workstations.

   ❍ **D.** Ensure that there is available disk space equivalent to the amount of RAM. You should configure Hybrid Sleep on the laptop workstations.

   ❍ **E.** Ensure that there is available disk space equivalent to the amount of RAM. Configure Hibernation on the laptop workstations.

6. You work as the desktop support technician at Acme.com. You have a user who shuts down by clicking the power button icon on the Start menu. Yet, when the user starts the computer back up, the same programs that were opened during the shutdown are opened when the computer is started. What do you need to do so that the machine does a complete shutdown?

   ❍ **A.** Open Power Options and click the Choose What Power Buttons Do link and choose the option to shut down the computer when the power button is pressed.

   ❍ **B.** Open Power Options and click the Change When Computer Sleeps link and choose the option to never put the computer to sleep when it is running on battery.

   ❍ **C.** Open Advanced Settings for the current power plan in Power Options. Change the Start menu power button setting to Shut Down.

   ❍ **D.** Change the On Battery setting in the Sleep After category to Never.

7. You work as the desktop support technician at Acme.com. When you close the lid on your Windows Vista computer, you want to start working as soon as you start the computer back up. You also don't want to use any battery power while the computer is shut down. What should you do?

   ❍ **A.** Configure the computer to hibernate when lid is closed.

   ❍ **B.** Configure the computer to sleep when lid is closed.

   ❍ **C.** Configure the computer to shut down when lid is closed.

   ❍ **D.** Configure the computer to go into standby when lid is closed.

8. You work as the desktop support technician at Acme.com. You are using Windows Vista Ultimate edition, which is configured to synchronize calendar information on your work PC. Although the cell phone can play music through the computer's Media Player, you discover that you improve the phone's battery life if you turn off the ability to play music through the computer's Media Player. What should you do?

   ❍ **A.** Open the Windows SideShow and then turn off the Windows Media Player gadget.

   ❍ **B.** Open the Sync Center and disable sync with the Windows Media Player.

   ❍ **C.** Open the Windows Sidebar and turn off the Windows Media Player gadget.

   ❍ **D.** Open the Windows Media Player, and then remove the appropriate plug-in.

9. You work as the desktop support technician at Acme.com. You have a user who uses a Tablet PC. She wants to perform more quickly certain tasks that she uses a lot, such as copy and paste. What should you do?

   ❍ **A.** Configure pen options in Pen and Input Devices on the Tablet PC.

   ❍ **B.** Configure flicks in Pen and Input Devices on the Tablet PC.

   ❍ **C.** Enable Automatic Learning on the Tablet PC.

   ❍ **D.** Configure gestures in the Input Panel Options on the Tablet PC.

Answers to Exam Prep Questions

1. **Answer A is correct.** If you want to use the project as the main monitor, open the display settings in the Control Panel. Then, select the icon that represents the projector and make it the main monitor. Answer B is incorrect because if you extend the desktop onto this monitor, the monitor and the project will act together as if they were sitting side by side. Answers C and D are incorrect because the taskbar has nothing to do with the monitor configuration.

2. **Answer B is correct.** The LCD panel is one of the components on a laptop computer that uses the most power. Therefore, by disabling the LCD panel, you conserve power. Therefore, you should select External Display Only. Answer A is incorrect because although reducing the brightness settings reduces power consumption, it does not save as much power as shutting off the LCD panel. Answers C and D are incorrect because selecting Extended in the New Display Detected dialog box and turning on Presentation mode does not reduce power consumption.

3. **Answer A is correct.** When you configure a Bluetooth-enabled handheld device, you need to enable Bluetooth and assign a passkey. Answers B, C, and D are incorrect because they are used to configure a wireless network connection.

4. **Answer C is correct.** When you turn on Presentation mode, your mobile PC stays awake and system notifications are turned off. You can also choose to turn off the screen saver, adjust the speaker volume, and change your desktop background image. Answer A is not the best answer because this affects only the screen saver. It will not turn off system notifications, or adjust speaker volume. Answers B and D affect only display settings.

5. **Answer D is correct.** When you perform Hybrid Sleep, it will keep the memory alive so that you can do a quick restart to where you left off. It also writes to the hard drive in case power is interrupted. Answer A is incorrect because you don't have to have the power-saving logo to use Sleep or Hybrid Sleep mode. Answer B is incorrect because you don't have to be an administrator to go into Hybrid Sleep mode. Answer C does not protect against power interruption. Answer E is incorrect because Hibernate mode is slower than Sleep and Hybrid Sleep to restart.

6. **Answer C is correct.** When the shutdown button is clicked, the system goes into either Sleep mode or Hibernate mode. Therefore, you need to configure the power button to perform a shutdown instead of Sleep or Hibernate mode. Answer A is incorrect because you have to go into the Advanced Options to change the power plans. Answer B is incorrect because you have to go into the Advanced Options to change the power plans and there is not an option to never put to sleep mode. Answer D is incorrect because there is no such option.

7. **Answer A is correct.** You should configure the computer to hibernate when the lid is closed. Answer B is incorrect because Hibernate mode is faster. Answer C is incorrect because Shutdown is the slowest option to bring back on. Answer D is incorrect because there is no Standby mode in Windows Vista.

8. **Answer A is correct.** Media Player can be accessed through SideShow. Therefore, you need to disable using the Control Panel. Answer B is incorrect because Sync is for data files, not Windows Media Player. Answer C is incorrect because the Windows Media Player gadget is handled in the SideShow, not Sidebar. Answer D is not correct because to access the Windows Media Player on the remote computer you use the SideShow, not a Windows Media Player plug-in.

9. **Answer B is correct.** To program the pen actions, you need to configure flicks. Answers A and C are incorrect because they have nothing to do with pen actions. Answer D is incorrect because there is no such thing as gestures.

Recommended Readings and Resources

Stanek, William R., *Introducing Microsoft Windows Vista* (Redmond, Washington: Microsoft Press, 2006).

Tulloch, Mitch, Tony Northrup, Jerry Honeycutt, Ed Wilson, Ralph Ramos, and the Windows Vista Team, *Windows Vista Resource Kit (Pro. Resource Kit)* (Redmond, Washington: Microsoft Press, 2007).

13

CHAPTER THIRTEEN

Practice Exam 1

Now it's time to put to the test the knowledge that you've learned from reading this book! Write down your answers to the following questions on a separate sheet of paper. You will be able to take this sample test multiple times that way. After you answer all the questions, compare your answers with the correct answers in Chapter 14, "Answers to Practice Exam 1." The answer keys for both exams immediately follow each Practice Exam chapter. When you can correctly answer at least 45 of the 50 practice questions (90 percent) in each Practice Exam, you are ready to start using the PrepLogic Practice Exams CD-ROM at the back of this *Exam Cram 2*. Using the Practice Exams for this *Exam Cram 2*, along with the PrepLogic Practice Exams, you can prepare yourself for the actual 70-620 Microsoft certification exam. Good luck!

Exam Questions

1. You work as a desktop support technician at Acme.com. You need to install Windows Vista Business edition to your marketing department computers. The marketing computers have the following specifications:

   - Pentium M 1.6-GHz processor
   - 512 MB of RAM
   - 20-GB hard drive
   - SVGA video card
   - Integrated sound card
   - 10/100 integrated network adapter

   What do you need to do for these machines to meet the minimum hardware to install Windows Vista Business?

   ❍ **A.** You should upgrade the processor.

   ❍ **B.** You should upgrade the RAM.

   ❍ **C.** You should upgrade the video card.

   ❍ **D.** You should upgrade the hard drive.

   ❍ **E.** You should upgrade the network adapter.

   ❍ **F.** No components need to be upgraded. All components meet the minimum requirements to install Windows Vista Business.

2. You work as a desktop support technician at Acme.com. You insert the Windows Vista DVD into the DVD drive, but the computer does not boot from the DVD. Instead, it tries to boot from the hard drive. What should you do or check first?

   ❍ **A.** Replace the Windows Vista DVD.

   ❍ **B.** Replace the DVD drive.

   ❍ **C.** Enter the BIOS setup program and configure the system to boot from the CD/DVD drive first.

   ❍ **D.** See whether the system has a SCSI drive. If it does, it needs to have an IDE drive instead.

3. Which versions of Windows Vista can you upgrade a Windows XP Table PC to without doing a clean install?

   ❍ **A.** Windows Vista Home Basic Edition

   ❍ **B.** Windows Vista Home Premium Edition

   ❍ **C.** Windows Vista Business Edition

   ❍ **D.** Windows Vista Ultimate Edition

4. Which of the following can upgrade to Windows Vista Business edition?

   ❍ **A.** Starter

   ❍ **B.** Home Basic

   ❍ **C.** Home Premium

   ❍ **D.** Enterprise

   ❍ **E.** Ultimate

5. You have purchased some devices that have been sitting on the shelf at a store for several months and are about ready to be discontinued. You installed the drivers for those devices, and now your system has some sporadic errors. What should you do?

   ❍ **A.** Look on the Windows CD for more up-to-date drivers.

   ❍ **B.** Check with the manufacturer's website and the Windows update website for more up-to-date drivers.

   ❍ **C.** Upgrade Windows Vista to the Ultimate edition so that it can make proper use of the drivers.

   ❍ **D.** Disable the prompting of unsigned driver warnings.

6. You have a new computer with Windows Vista on it. When you visit certain websites using Internet Explorer, you click the link and nothing happens. What is the problem?

   ❍ **A.** You have been denied access to the website by the network administrator.

   ❍ **B.** The website has been taken offline.

   ❍ **C.** The link generates a pop-up window, which is blocked by default.

   ❍ **D.** The website is not on your trusted list.

7. You have Windows Vista loaded on a computer with one primary volume that holds Windows, your applications, and your data files. What will happen if the C: drive starts to run out of disk space? (Choose all that apply.)

❍ **A.** Your computer will run slower.

❍ **B.** Your machine will be less reliable.

❍ **C.** If you attempt to move files from one location to another drive such as a USB drive, Windows might say that you are out of disk space.

❍ **D.** Windows will shift into Compression mode to save disk space.

8. You work as a desktop support technician at Acme.com. You have a new computer running Windows Vista Ultimate edition. What features must you enable to use Windows Aero? (Choose all that apply.)

❍ **A.** Set Theme to Windows Vista.

❍ **B.** Set the monitor settings to a refresh rate higher than 10.

❍ **C.** Set the resolution to 1280x1024 or higher.

❍ **D.** Set Color to 32 bit.

❍ **E.** Set Color Scheme to Windows Aero.

9. How much graphics memory do you need to support Windows Aero?

❍ **A.** 32 MB

❍ **B.** 64 MB

❍ **C.** 128 MB

❍ **D.** 256 MB

10. You are a parent who wants your children to run only certain programs that you allow on the computer. What can you do?

❍ **A.** Use parental controls on your computer to allow only certain programs.

❍ **B.** Use Ease of Access on your computer to allow only certain programs.

❍ **C.** Adjust your NTFS permissions so that they cannot install applications on your computer.

❍ **D.** Configure the firewall to block all ports not being used.

11. You have a computer in the bedroom of your children. What can you use to make sure they do not use it in the middle of the night when you are sleeping?

❍ **A.** Use group policies to specify when they use the computer.

❍ **B.** Use parental controls to specify when they can use the computer.

❍ **C.** Set a timer using the scheduler to shut down the PC at a certain time.

❍ **D.** All of the above.

12. You have a user that made some changes to the advanced options in Internet Explorer. Unfortunately, the user cannot access certain websites. What can you do to reset those options?

❍ **A.** Reinstall Internet Explorer 7.0.

❍ **B.** Navigate to the Advanced tab in Internet Options and click Restore Advanced Settings.

❍ **C.** Navigate to the Advanced tab in Internet Options and click Reset.

❍ **D.** Navigate to the Security tab in Internet Options and click Reset All Zones to Default Level.

13. How do you turn off the prompts generated by User Account Control? (Choose two answers.)

❍ **A.** Use local or group policies.

❍ **B.** Click the Turn User Account Control Off link under User Accounts.

❍ **C.** Use the Computer Management console.

❍ **D.** Open the System properties of the computer and click the Turn Off button under the UAC.

14. When you have a domain account, where is the domain account stored?

❍ **A.** It is stored with the Windows Vista registry.

❍ **B.** It is stored in Active Directory, which is stored on domain controllers.

❍ **C.** It is stored in a users.dat file on the Windows Vista machine.

❍ **D.** It is stored with Active Directory on the Windows Vista machine.

15. What happens if a local user account does not have a password?

- ❍ **A.** The user will not be able to log in to the computer.
- ❍ **B.** The user will not be able to log in as an administrator.
- ❍ **C.** The user will not be able to remotely access the computer.
- ❍ **D.** The user will not be able to run the Computer Management and related consoles.

16. Which two utilities can you use to disable start programs that may cause problems during startup? (Choose two answers.)

- ❍ **A.** Software Explorer, which can be found in Windows Defender
- ❍ **B.** The Add/Remove Programs, found in the Control Panel
- ❍ **C.** The Computer Management console
- ❍ **D.** The msconfig program

17. How do you disable ActiveX in Internet Explorer?

- ❍ **A.** Open Internet Options and click the Security tab.
- ❍ **B.** Open Internet Options and click the Advanced tab.
- ❍ **C.** Open Internet Options and click the Privacy tab.
- ❍ **D.** Use Add/Remove Programs in the Control Panel.

18. You have over 50 laptop computers that run Windows Vista Business that you need to connect to your corporate wireless network. What is the easiest way to do that?

- ❍ **A.** Log in to each computer and manually configure the wireless settings.
- ❍ **B.** Copy the wireless settings to a shared folder and then copy the wireless settings to each computer.
- ❍ **C.** Save the wireless network settings to a USB flash drive and use that flash drive on each computer to copy the configuration.
- ❍ **D.** Use the Autodetect feature of Windows Vista to detect the wireless settings.
- ❍ **E.** Use group policies to automatically configure the wireless settings.

19. You are a desktop technician for Acme.com. You are in Sacramento, California, and Joe is in Cleveland, Ohio. You got a call from Joe, who is saying he getting a strange error when he runs a program. You would like to see these errors as they happen. What can you do?

❍ **A.** You can use Remote Assistant to view Joe's desktop so that you can see the errors as they happen.

❍ **B.** You can use Remote Desktop to view Joe's desktop so that you can see the errors as they happen.

❍ **C.** You can run telnet so that you can take over Joe's command prompt so that you can see the errors as they happen.

❍ **D.** Have Joe use Remote Desktop on a server so that you can see the errors as they happen.

20. You are at work and you want to use Remote Desktop to connect to your computer at home, which is running Windows Vista Home Basic edition. However, your home computer is not responding. What is the problem?

❍ **A.** Remote Desktop connection is not available in Windows Vista Home Basic edition.

❍ **B.** You do not have a user account with a password.

❍ **C.** You did not enable Remote Desktop on your Home edition.

❍ **D.** Your account does not have permission to use Remote Desktop on your home computer.

21. What is the paging file use for?

❍ **A.** It is used as a database that keeps track of your files on your drive.

❍ **B.** It is used to simulate RAM by using disk space.

❍ **C.** It is used to provide backward compatibility with older versions of Windows.

❍ **D.** It is used to increase your performance of your system.

22. You think some of your boot files have gotten corrupt, which is causing Windows Vista not to load properly. What can you do to fix the problem?

    ❍ **A.** Start Safe mode and run further diagnostics to figure out which file is causing the problem.

    ❍ **B.** Insert the Windows Vista installation disc, and use the Startup Repair tool to fix the problem.

    ❍ **C.** Insert the Windows Vista installation disc and start Windows in Safe mode.

    ❍ **D.** Insert the Windows Vista installation disc and start Windows from the CD. Then, run further diagnostics to figure out which file is causing the problem.

23. A user from your office has reported some strange errors. Where can you look at the logs to see whether they report some of the errors?

    ❍ **A.** Use Log Trace in Administrative Tools.

    ❍ **B.** Use the Event Viewer in the Computer Management console.

    ❍ **C.** Use Logging in the Control Panel.

    ❍ **D.** Use Debugging Logs in Administrative Tools.

24. A Windows Vista computer is accessed by several users through shared folders. How do you make sure that only users with local user accounts and passwords can access the shared folders?

    ❍ **A.** Set the Network Location type to Domain Share.

    ❍ **B.** Turn on Public Folder Sharing.

    ❍ **C.** Turn off Network Discovery in the Network and Sharing Center.

    ❍ **D.** Turn on the Password Protected Sharing option in the Network and Sharing Center.

25. Which of the following is not a TCP/IP private address?

    ❍ **A.** 10.1.2.50

    ❍ **B.** 172.16.23.42

    ❍ **C.** 172.32.34.202

    ❍ **D.** 192.168.4.5

26. What is the difference between IPv4 and IPv6?

❍ **A.** IPv4 is based on 32-bit addresses, whereas IPv6 is based on 128-bit addresses.

❍ **B.** IPv6 includes enhanced security including built-in IPSec support.

❍ **C.** IPv4 is faster than IPv6 because of the bigger addresses.

❍ **D.** IPv6 has built-in name resolution.

27. You are configuring the Windows Fax and Scan on a Windows Vista computer. You scanned some images using the HP scanner. Now you need them to automatically go to the marketing team lead so that they can be used in some marketing material.

❍ **A.** Open the Tools menu and select the Scan Settings to Be Forwarded to an E-mail Address.

❍ **B.** Select all the scanned images and click the Forward button.

❍ **C.** Open the Tools menu and select the Scan Routing option to Configure the New Faxes to Be Forwarded to an E-mail Address option.

❍ **D.** Have the computer logged in as the marketing team lead so that they will automatically be sent to her e-mail address.

28. You are configuring Windows Calendar on a Windows Vista computer. The user that will be using this computer needs to keep track of staff meetings, client meetings, and personal appointments. He would like to see all the appointments together and separately. What should you do?

❍ **A.** Create one calendar and three groups (staff meeting, client meeting, and personal appointments).

❍ **B.** Create three calendars (staff meeting, client meeting, and personal appointments). Then, create one calendar group.

❍ **C.** Create three calendars and three groups.

❍ **D.** Create three calendars.

29. You have several laptops that you are trying to make as secure as possible in case they are stolen. What should you implement to protect the entire volume?

❍ **A.** NTFS

❍ **B.** Share permissions

❍ **C.** BitLocker

❍ **D.** EFS

30. You suspect that a program that you started is using too much memory. How can you verify this?

- ❍ **A.** Use the Event Viewer.
- ❍ **B.** Use the Task Manager.
- ❍ **C.** Use the Computer Management console.
- ❍ **D.** Use Windows Defender.

31. Which utility would you use to prepare an installed system so that its image can be copied to multiple computers?

- ❍ **A.** ImageX
- ❍ **B.** Setup
- ❍ **C.** Diskpart
- ❍ **D.** Sysprep

32. You are looking at the Device Manager. You see a device that has a down arrow on it. What is the problem?

- ❍ **A.** The device is having a problem.
- ❍ **B.** The device is disabled.
- ❍ **C.** The device is sleeping.
- ❍ **D.** The device is not connected.

33. What command can be used to show network connectivity to a computer?

- ❍ **A.** **ipconfig**
- ❍ **B.** **arp**
- ❍ **C.** **ping**
- ❍ **D.** **nslookup**

34. Which account is disabled by default?

- ❍ **A.** Administrator
- ❍ **B.** Guest
- ❍ **C.** First user created
- ❍ **D.** RemoteUser account

35. What is a unique identifier that is automatically generated when a user account is created that consists of a computer or domain security ID prefix combined with a unique relative ID for the user?

- ❍ **A.** MIB
- ❍ **B.** CID
- ❍ **C.** SID
- ❍ **D.** UserID

36. Which editions of Windows Vista include MPEG-2 decoders that enable you to watch DVDs?

- ❍ **A.** Windows Vista Home Basic
- ❍ **B.** Windows Vista Home Premier
- ❍ **C.** Windows Vista Business
- ❍ **D.** Windows Vista Ultimate

37. You want to set up a Windows Vista workstation that can record two movies and play back a movie at the same time. What do you need?

- ❍ **A.** Microsoft Windows Vista Enterprise and two TV tuners
- ❍ **B.** Microsoft Windows Vista Home Basic and three TV tuners
- ❍ **C.** Microsoft Windows Vista Home Premium and two TV tuners
- ❍ **D.** Microsoft Windows Vista Home Premium and three TV tuners

38. What is used to make sure that DVDs are not played in other countries where the DVD has not yet been released?

- ❍ **A.** NTFS permissions
- ❍ **B.** BitLocker
- ❍ **C.** Regions
- ❍ **D.** Codecs

39. You have to have Bluetooth-enabled speakers added to your PC's personal area networks (PAN). What do you need to do for the device to be recognized?

- ❍ **A.** Turn on the Network Discovery and configure the passkey.
- ❍ **B.** Configure the passkey and ensure that the mobile devices are WiFi enabled.
- ❍ **C.** Configure the passkey and ensure that the device is discoverable.
- ❍ **D.** Configure the appropriate wireless security method and ensure that the device is discoverable.

40. You have a user who uses a Tablet PC. She wants to perform certain tasks that she uses a lot such as copy and paste to be performed quicker. What should you do?

❍ A. You need to enable Automatic Learning on the Tablet PC.

❍ B. You need to configure gestures in the Input Panel Options on the Tablet PC.

❍ C. You need to configure Pen options in Pen and Input Devices on the Tablet PC.

❍ D. You need to configure flicks in Pen and Input Devices on the Tablet PC.

41. Which of the following will you not find in the Windows Mobility Center?

❍ A. Brightness

❍ B. Battery status

❍ C. Pointer devices

❍ D. Presentation settings

42. What do you call when a processor uses a lower voltage and a lesser clock speed so that it consumes less power?

❍ A. Step down

❍ B. Throttling

❍ C. Stepping

❍ D. Nonturbo

43. When you configure your power settings, you can save them so that you can call them up quickly. What do you call this?

❍ A. Profile

❍ B. Power scheme

❍ C. Power plan

❍ D. Power settings

44. What do you call an XML file that scripts the answers for a series of graphical user interface (GUI) dialog boxes and other configuration settings used to install Windows?

❍ A. Answer file

❍ B. Installation script

❍ C. Windows image

❍ D. Catalog

45. What do you call the feature built in to Windows Setup that automatically checks for new drivers, compatibility updates, and security fixes while Windows is being installed.

❍ **A.** Dynamic Update

❍ **B.** Auto Update

❍ **C.** Automatic Updates

❍ **D.** Windate

46. Which utility would you use to migrate the files and settings to removable media or to a network share and later restore the files and settings to the target computer?

❍ **A.** Windows Easy Transfer

❍ **B.** User State Migration Tool

❍ **C.** Windows PE

❍ **D.** Sysprep

47. What do you call the area that includes a clock and small icons that show the status of certain programs and computer settings?

❍ **A.** Notification area

❍ **B.** Start menu

❍ **C.** Status area

❍ **D.** Windows area

48. When using Microsoft Mail, what would you set if you want to receive only messages from people or domain names on your Safe Senders list?

❍ **A.** No Automatic Filtering

❍ **B.** Low

❍ **C.** High

❍ **D.** Safe List Only

49. What is the act of sending an e-mail to a user falsely claiming to be an established legitimate organization in an attempt to scam the user into surrendering private information that will be used for identity theft? The e-mail directs the user to visit a website where that user is asked to update personal information, such as passwords and credit card, social security, and bank account numbers, that the legitimate organization already has.

❍ **A.** Phishing

❍ **B.** IP spoofing

❍ **C.** ARP spoofing

❍ **D.** Poisoning

50. What is the pane that keeps your gadgets organized and always available on your desktop?

❍ **A.** Control Panel

❍ **B.** Administrative Tools

❍ **C.** Windows Sidebar

❍ **D.** Gadget Panel

14

CHAPTER FOURTEEN

Answers to Practice Exam 1

1. F
2. C
3. C, D
4. A, B
5. B
6. C
7. A, B, C
8. A, B, D, E
9. B
10. A
11. B
12. B
13. A, B
14. B
15. C
16. A, D
17. A
18. C
19. A
20. A
21. B
22. B
23. B
24. D
25. C
26. A, B
27. C
28. B
29. C
30. B
31. D
32. B
33. C
34. B
35. C
36. B, D
37. C
38. C
39. C
40. D
41. C
42. B
43. C
44. A
45. A
46. B
47. A
48. D
49. A
50. C

Question 1

Answer F is correct. All components meet the minimum requirements to install Windows Vista Business. The minimum requirements for a Vista Capable computer are an 800-MHz processor, 512 MB RAM, an SVGA monitor, 20-GB hard drive with 15 GB free, and a CD drive. Because the computer meets or exceeds all of these, all the other answers (A, B, C, D, and E) are incorrect.

Question 2

Answer C is correct. The first thing you should check is to see whether your system is configured to boot first from the optical drive rather than the hard drive. Answers A and B are incorrect because although these are possible causes for this problem, it is best to first check the BIOS setup program. Answer D is incorrect because Windows Vista will install to any bootable hard drive, including IDE and SCSI hard drives.

Question 3

Answers C and D are correct because they support in-place upgrades. Answers A and B are incorrect because they require a clean install.

Question 4

Answers A and B are correct because they can be upgraded without doing a clean install. Answers C and D are incorrect because they require clean installs.

Answer 5

Answer B is correct because it is obvious that these drivers are not the newest. Therefore, check the update website and manufacturer websites for newer drivers. Answer A is not the best answer because the Windows installation disc might not have the newest drivers either. Answer C is incorrect because the edition has no effect on how a driver is loaded. Answer D is incorrect because it is always recommended to load only signed drivers whenever possible.

Question 6

Answer C is correct because, by default, Internet Explorer blocks most pop-up windows. To enable these sites to work properly and to display pop-ups from specific sites, you need open the Pop-up Blocker Settings dialog box, and you need to add the URL of the website to the Allowed Sites list. Answer A is incorrect because if the site has been blocked by the network administrator, you will usually get a message saying that is the case. Answer B is incorrect because you will get a message similar to Site Not Found or Site Not Available. Answer D is incorrect because when a site is not on your trusted list, it will typically stop certain programs from running such as ActiveX controls.

Question 7

Answers A, B, and C are correct. As you run out of disk space, your computer cannot swap information using the paging file and cannot create the needed temporary files when you move files from one drive to another. Your machine also becomes less reliable. Answer D is incorrect because although NTFS supports compression, it will not automatically start compressing files because it is low on disk space.

Question 8

Answers A, B, D, and E are correct because to use Windows Aero, you must set the theme to Windows Vista, set the monitor settings to a refresh rate higher than 10, set the color to 32 bit, and set the color scheme to Windows Aero. Answer C is incorrect because the resolution is not a requirement.

Question 9

Answer B is correct because Windows Aero requires that video cards support at least 64 MB of graphics memory. Therefore, answers A, C, and D are incorrect.

Question 10

Answer A is correct because if the computer is not part of the domain, you can use parental controls. Answer B is incorrect because you configure this with parental controls and not Ease of Access. Answer C is incorrect because configuring NTFS is a more complicated method that takes more time to control access to a computer and is not as effective. Answer D is incorrect because blocking ports is only partially effective and would only block programs from communicating over the network.

Question 11

Answer B is correct because you can use parental controls to specify when a computer can be used. Answer A is incorrect because group policies can be used only with computers that are part of the domain, which a home computer typically is not. Answer C is incorrect because a timer is ineffective. Of course, because answers A and C are incorrect, answer D is incorrect.

Question 12

Answer B is correct because you can use the Restore Advanced Settings button on the Advanced tab of the Internet Options dialog box, which will not impact the other security and privacy setting used by Internet Explorer 7. Answer A would not change settings if you reinstall Internet Explorer, and because Internet Explorer is part of the operating system, this is not an option. Answer C is incorrect because there is no need to use the Reset button on the Advanced tab of the Internet Options dialog box because it would result in all the Internet Explorer settings being reset. Answer D is incorrect because there is no need to reset the zone settings on the Security tab; doing so will impact the security level in Internet Explorer, which is not the problem.

Question 13

Answers A and B are correct because you can shut it off for an individual user account or by using group policies. Answers C and D are incorrect because turning off the User Account Control prompts cannot be controlled using the Computer Management console or by using the System Properties.

Question 14

Answer B is correct because domain accounts are stored in Active Directory on a domain controller. Answers A, C, and D are incorrect because domain accounts are not stored locally on the Windows Vista computer.

Question 15

Answer C is correct because they will not be able to log in as a remote user even if they are an administrator. Answers A, B, and D are incorrect because the user without a password will be able to log in or run these utilities, assuming he has the proper permissions.

Question 16

Answers A and D are correct because these programs can be disabled using Software Explorer and msconfig. Answers B and C are incorrect because the Add/Remove Programs or Computer Management console will not show the programs loaded during startup.

Question 17

Answer A is correct because ActiveX is configured in the Security tab under each of the security zones. Answers B, C, and D are incorrect because you cannot use the other option tabs or the Add/Remove programs.

Question 18

Answer C is correct because using a USB flash drive is the easiest to implement. Answer A is a possible answer but takes more work to perform. Therefore, Answer a is not correct. Answer B is incorrect because although you can copy the configuration to the shared folder, the laptop computers are not able to access the shared drive until the wireless network is configured on each laptop. Answer D is incorrect because the network settings of most corporate networks prevent a network from being autodetected, Answer E is incorrect because there is no group policy that will configure wireless settings and the laptop would have to be connected to the network to get those settings.

Question 19

Answer A is correct because Remote Assistant enables you to see the same screen that Joe is looking at. Answer B is incorrect because although you will see the desktop, you disable Joe's view while you do it. Answer C is incorrect because telnet shows the command prompt only and not the GUI interface. Answer D is incorrect because connecting to a server is not helpful. The problem is on Joe's computer, and you typically do not want users to take control of servers.

Question 20

Answer A is correct because the Windows Vista Home Basic edition does not support Remote Desktop. Answers B, C, and D are incorrect because if you have Windows Vista Home Basic edition, it does not support Remote Desktop. Therefore, you would not be able to access the computer remotely.

Question 21

Answer B is correct because the paging file allows you to run more programs and access more memory by using the paging file as memory. Answers A and C are incorrect because paging files do not keep track of your files on your drive, nor do they provide backward compatibility with older versions of Windows. Answer D is incorrect because paging files will actually slow your system when the paging file has to swap between RAM and disk space.

Question 22

Answer B is correct because the Startup Repair tool will allow you to fix boot problems. Answer A will not work because Windows will not start. Answers C and D are incorrect because you cannot start Windows from the installation disc.

Question 23

Answer B is correct because the Event Viewer shows the logs. Answers A, C, and D are incorrect because none of these utilities exist.

Question 24

Answer D is correct because when you have private shares, you need to turn on Password Protected Sharing. Answer A is incorrect because there is no such thing as Domain Share option. Answer B is incorrect because you don't need to use public folders to protect it. Answer C incorrect because network discovery and Windows Firewall is turned on by default. When Network Discovery is enabled, anyone on the network can locate your computer.

Question 25

Answer C is correct because it does not fall in the range of private addresses. Answers A, B, and D are incorrect because they are private addresses. The private addresses are 10.*x*.*x*.*x*, 172.16.*x*.*x* to 172.31.*x*.*x*, and 192.168.0.*x* and 192.168.255.*x* (256 class C address ranges).

Question 26

Answers A and B are correct because IPv6 has large address space (128 bit), efficient routing, straightforward configuration, and enhanced security. Answer C is incorrect because IPv6 performs routing more efficiently, and answer D is incorrect because IPv6 does not include built-in name resolution.

Question 27

Answer C is correct because you need to select Scan Settings to Be Forwarded to an E-mail Address. Answer A is incorrect because the Scan setting is not available to forward images to an e-mail address. Answer B is incorrect because this is a manual process that needs to be done each time. Answer D is incorrect because this is a secure method and it would not send the images automatically.

Question 28

Answer B is correct because the single group will allow you to view all three calendars combined. Answer A is incorrect because you need to divide the meetings and appointments to three separate calendars. Answer C is incorrect because three groups are too many groups. Answer D is incorrect because the three calendars without the group will not allow you to see all the appointments and meetings together.

Question 29

Answer C is correct because BitLocker is the only one that will protect the entire driver. Answers A, B and D are incorrect because NTFS, share permissions, and EFS do not protect everything on the volume.

Question 30

Answer B is correct because Task Manager will show processor and memory utilization of all processes. Answer A is incorrect because the Event Viewer will show you the logs. Answer C is incorrect because the Computer Management console is used to configure the system. Answer D is incorrect because Windows Defender is used to protect against spyware.

Question 31

Answer D is correct because Sysprep will remove the SID from the image and clean up various user and machine settings and log files. Answer A is incorrect because ImageX is a command-line tool that captures, modifies, and applies installation images for deployment in a manufacturing or corporate environment. Answer B is incorrect because Windows Setup (Setup.exe) installs the Windows Vista operating system, and answer C is incorrect because Diskpart is a command-line hard disk configuration utility.

Question 32

Answer B is correct because the down arrow means that the device is disabled. Answer A is incorrect because the exclamation point indicates a device that is having a problem. Answers C and D are not indicated in the Device Manager.

Question 33

Answer C is correct because the **ping** command is used to test network connectivity. Answer A is incorrect because **ipconfig** is used to show IP addresses of a system. Answer B is incorrect because the **arp** command is used to show the ARP cache. Answer D is incorrect because the **nslookup** command is used to look at DNS problems.

Question 34

Answer B is correct because guest is the account that is disabled when you first install Windows. Answer A is incorrect because the administrator is the primary Windows account. Answer C is incorrect because the first account created is active. Answer D is incorrect because no RemoteUser account comes with Windows.

Question 35

Answer C is incorrect because the security identifier (SID) is a unique identifier that is automatically generated when a user account is created and consists of a computer or domain security ID prefix combined with a unique relative ID for the user. Answer A is incorrect because MIB has nothing to do with user accounts. Answer B is incorrect because a CID does not exist in Windows. Answer D is incorrect because the UserID is used with the SID to easily identify a user.

Question 36

Answers B and D are correct because Windows Vista Home Premier and Window Vista Ultimate include the MPEG-2 decoder. Answers A and C are incorrect because Windows Vista Home Basic and Windows Vista Business do not include the MPEG-2 decoder.

Question 37

Answer C is correct because you need Windows Vista Home Premium or Windows Vista Ultimate to record movies, and you will need to have two tuners to record two movies at the same time. Answers A and B are incorrect because Windows Vista Enterprise and Windows Vista Home Basic do not support recording of movies. Answer D is incorrect because you need only two TV tuners to record two movies at the same time, not three.

Question 38

Answer C is correct because DVDs and DVD players are assigned regions so that they know what area in the world they play in. Answer A is incorrect because NTFS permissions are used to secure files. Answer B is incorrect because BitLocker is used to encrypt a drive. Answer D is incorrect because a codec is a translator for audio and video files.

Question 39

Answer C is correct. When you configure a Bluetooth-enabled handheld device, you need to enable Bluetooth and assign a passkey. Answer A is incorrect because Network Discovery is a network setting that affects whether your computer can see (find) other computers and devices on the network and whether other computers on the network can see your computer. Answers B and D are incorrect because WiFi is used to configure a wireless network connection (802.11b and g).

Question 40

Answer D is correct. To program the pen actions, you need to configure flicks. Answers A and C are incorrect because Automatic Learning and Pen options in Pen and input devices have nothing to do with pen actions. Answer B is incorrect because there is no such thing as gestures.

Question 41

Answer C is correct because you will not find pointer devices in the Windows Mobility Center. Answers A, B, and D are incorrect because you find brightness, battery status, and presentation settings in the Windows Mobility Center.

Question 42

Answer B is correct because when a processor runs at a reduced voltage and smaller clock speed, it is known as throttling. Answers A and D are incorrect because they are not real. Answer C is incorrect because steppings are often referred to as versions of a component such as a processor.

Question 43

Answer C is correct because in Windows Vista, the power settings saved together are called power plans. Answer A is incorrect because a profile consists of files and settings for user accounts. Answer B is incorrect because this is what power plans were called in older versions of Windows. Answer D is incorrect because power settings are what you find in the Control Panel.

Question 44

Answer A is correct because an answer file is an XML file that scripts the answers for a series of GUI dialog boxes and other configuration settings used to install Windows. Answer C is incorrect because a Windows image is a copy of a disk volume saved as file. Answer D is incorrect because a catalog is a binary file (CLG) that contains the state of the settings and packages in a Windows image. Answer B is incorrect because it is a made-up answer.

Question 45

Answer A is correct because Dynamic Update is the feature built in to Windows Setup that automatically checks for new drivers, compatibility updates, and security fixes while Windows is being installed. Answers B and D are incorrect because they are not real answers. Answer C is incorrect because Automatic Updates is the feature that keeps Windows updated automatically after it is installed.

Question 46

Answer B is the correct answer because the User State Migration Tool (USMT) is used to migrate the files and settings to a removable media or to a network share and later restore the files and settings to the target computer. Answer A is incorrect because the Windows Easy Transfer (WET) uses removable media, or over the network it uses WET to perform a side-by-side migration to migrate the settings to a new computer that already runs Windows Vista. Answer C is incorrect because Windows PE is a bootable tool that replaces MS-DOS as the preinstallation environment. Answer D is incorrect because Sysprep is a utility that facilitates image creation for deployment to multiple destination computers.

Question 47

Answer A is correct because the notification area includes a clock and small icons that show the status of certain programs and computer settings. Answer B is incorrect because it is on the opposite side of the screen and is used to start most programs. Answers C and D are incorrect because they are not real.

Question 48

Answer D is the correct answer because Safe List Only allows you receive messages only from people or domain names on your Safe Senders list. E-mail messages from people or domain names that are not on your Safe Senders list are treated as junk e-mail messages. Answer A is incorrect because No Automatic Filtering will stop blocking junk e-mail messages. Windows Mail will continue to block messages from domain names and e-mail addresses on your Blocked Senders list. Answer B is incorrect because Low blocks only the most obvious junk e-mail messages. This is the default setting. Answer C is incorrect because High blocks more junk e-mails and should be used if you receive a lot of junk e-mail.

Question 49

Answer A is correct because the act of capturing private information using fake e-mails and websites is called phishing. Answers B and C are incorrect because IP spoofing and ARP spoofing are used to hide the location of sent messages. Answer D is incorrect because poisoning is a form of denial-of-service (DoS) attack.

Question 50

Answer C is correct because the pane that holds the gadget is known as the Windows Sidebar. Answer A is incorrect because the Control Panel is the main configuration tool used in Windows. Answer B is incorrect because Administrative Tools is the place to find advanced configuring and troubleshooting tools. Answer D is incorrect because the Gadget Panel is not real.

15

CHAPTER FIFTEEN

Practice Exam 2

Now it's time to put to the test the knowledge that you've learned from reading this book! Write down your answers to the following questions on a separate sheet of paper. You can take this sample test multiple times this way. After you answer all the questions, compare your answers with the correct answers in Chapter 16, "Answers to Practice Exam 2." The answer keys for both exams immediately follow each Practice Exam chapter. When you can correctly answer at least 45 of the 50 practice questions (90 percent) in each Practice Exam, you are ready to start using the PrepLogic Practice Exams CD-ROM at the back of this Exam Cram 2. Using the Practice Exams for this Exam Cram 2, along with the PrepLogic Practice Exams, you can prepare yourself quite well for the actual 70-620 Microsoft certification exam. Good luck!

Exam Questions

1. You work as a desktop support technician at Acme.com. You need to install Windows Vista Business edition to your finance department computers. The finance department computers have the following specifications:

   ▶ Intel Pentium 4 processor running at 2.0 GHz

   ▶ 256 MB of RAM

   ▶ 30-GB hard drive

   ▶ SVGA video card

   ▶ Integrated sound card

   ▶ 10/100 integrated network adapter

   What do you need to for these machines to meet the minimum hardware to install Windows Vista Business edition?

   ❍ **A.** You should upgrade the processor.

   ❍ **B.** You should upgrade the RAM.

   ❍ **C.** You should upgrade the video card.

   ❍ **D.** You should upgrade the hard drive.

   ❍ **E.** You should upgrade the network adapter.

   ❍ **F.** No components need to be upgraded. All components meet the minimum requirements to install Windows Vista Business.

2. You work as the network administrator at Acme.com. You have three computers to upgrade running Windows 2000 Professional, Windows XP Home, Windows XP Professional (32-bit), and Windows XP Professional (64-bit). Which of the following can you upgrade to Windows Vista Business edition without doing a clean install? (Choose all that apply.)

   ❍ **A.** Windows 2000 Professional

   ❍ **B.** Windows XP Home

   ❍ **C.** Windows Professional (32-bit)

   ❍ **D.** Windows Professional (64-bit)

3. You are a desktop technician for Acme.com. You have 20 different computers used by your company. You want to quickly check whether they will support a Windows Vista installation. What utility can you use to easily determine their capability to run Windows Vista?

❍ **A.** Run the Windows Vista Upgrade Advisor.

❍ **B.** Run the System Checker program.

❍ **C.** Run the System Information program.

❍ **D.** Run the Computer Management Console.

4. You are a desktop technician for Acme.com. Several months ago, you performed a clean install of Windows Vista Business edition on a new computer that had Windows Vista. Lately, the user has been getting a blue screen of death when he boots the computer in Normal mode or Safe mode. What do you need to do to fix this problem?

❍ **A.** You should uninstall Windows Vista and put Windows XP back on the computer.

❍ **B.** You should use the Windows Vista DVD to reboot the computer and run the Startup Repair utility.

❍ **C.** You should run the Software Explorer via Windows Defender to diagnose the problem.

❍ **D.** You should disable all startup items by running msconfig.exe.

5. Why should you not load unsigned drivers?

❍ **A.** Unsigned drivers have not had a security audit performed on them.

❍ **B.** Unsigned drivers have not been paid for and signed showing that they were delivered.

❍ **C.** Unsigned drivers have not been acknowledged by Microsoft.

❍ **D.** Unsigned drivers have not been thoroughly tested not to cause any problems with Windows Vista.

6. If you suspect that certain websites' pop-up windows are being blocked, what can you do to work around this problem?

   ❍ **A.** Open the Manage Add-Ons dialog box and disable the Pop-up Blocker.

   ❍ **B.** Open the Internet Options dialog box and add the URL to the trusted sites list on the Security tab.

   ❍ **C.** Open the Pop-up Blocker Settings dialog box and add the URL to the allowed sites list.

   ❍ **D.** Open the Internet Options dialog box and add the URL to the allowed sites list on the Privacy tab.

7. To support Windows Aero, what does the video card have to have? (Choose two answers.)

   ❍ **A.** DirectX 9, with Pixel Shader 2.0

   ❍ **B.** Resolution of 1920x1200

   ❍ **C.** 64-bit color

   ❍ **D.** Windows Vista Display Driver Model (WDDM)

8. What console do you use to manage accessibility technology?

   ❍ **A.** Ease of Access Center

   ❍ **B.** Accessibility

   ❍ **C.** Disability

   ❍ **D.** Computer Management

9. When you have a person that has poor vision, what can you do to help them out? (Choose all that apply.)

   ❍ **A.** If you use the Ease of Access Center, you can magnify the screen.

   ❍ **B.** If you use the Ease of Access Center, you can adjust the screen colors for better contrast.

   ❍ **C.** If you use the Ease of Access Center, you can turn off the unnecessary animations and background images.

   ❍ **D.** You can increase the resolution of the screen.

10. When can you not use parental controls? (Choose two answers.)

❍ **A.** When you have Windows Vista Ultimate edition.

❍ **B.** When you are a power user.

❍ **C.** When the computer is part of a domain.

❍ **D.** When you are logged in as an administrator.

11. You are a parent with two children. One of your children found this game site. Unfortunately, they are doing nothing but playing the game site and neglecting school and their chores. What can you do?

❍ **A.** You can use the Window Firewall to block access to the website.

❍ **B.** You can use parental controls to enable Windows Vista web filtering and add the URL of the undesired website to the Blocked Web Sites list.

❍ **C.** You can use NTFS permissions to block access to certain websites.

❍ **D.** You can take away the child's administrative permissions.

12. Which utility would you use to manage the volumes on your system?

❍ **A.** Disk Management applet in the Control Panel

❍ **B.** Computer Management Console found in Administrative Tools

❍ **C.** Disk Administrator found on the desktop

❍ **D.** Disk Runner found in My Computer

13. You have a game that was written for Windows 95. When you run the application, it always gets an unexpected error. What should you try next? (Choose two answers.)

❍ **A.** You should run the application under a Windows 95 Compatibility mode by using the Application Compatibility tab.

❍ **B.** You need to change all NTFS permissions to Full Control to Everyone.

❍ **C.** You can try to run the application as an administrator.

❍ **D.** Turn off the read-only attribute for the files that run the game.

14. When you run a new application, you get a warning saying User Account Control stops unauthorized changes to your computer and that your computer needs your permission to continue. What should you do when you get this warning?

❍ **A.** You need to determine whether the application comes from a reliable source. If it does, click the Continue button.

❍ **B.** You need to verify the NTFS permissions for the application.

❍ **C.** You need to run the application as an administrator.

❍ **D.** You need to log off and log back on as an administrator and retry the application again.

15. If you are a standard user, what can you do?

❍ **A.** Install or uninstall software.

❍ **B.** Install hardware.

❍ **C.** Delete files that are required for the computer to work.

❍ **D.** Change settings on the computer that affect other users.

❍ **E.** Run programs that were installed by another user.

16. If you want a program on your Windows Vista computer to communicate over the Internet, what should you do?

❍ **A.** Add the program to the allow list in parental controls.

❍ **B.** Right-click the program file and select Properties. From the Compatibility tab, click Allow Network Connection.

❍ **C.** Open Windows Firewall and add it to the Exceptions list on the Exceptions tab.

❍ **D.** Add to the Exception list in the Ease of Use Center.

17. In addition to allowing and blocking programs from communicating over the Internet and blocking ports to communicate over, what else can you use the Windows Firewall with Advanced Security console for?

❍ **A.** To monitor network traffic

❍ **B.** To configure IPSec

❍ **C.** To view network attacks

❍ **D.** To manage your antivirus program

❍ **E.** To manage your antispyware program

18. What does Protected mode in Internet Explorer do?

❍ **A.** Prevents Component Object Model (COM) objects, such as ActiveX controls, from automatically modifying files and settings

❍ **B.** Helps stop phishing websites

❍ **C.** Helps stop viruses from infecting your computer

❍ **D.** Helps prevent packet sniffing on the network

19. What would you use to check for but not fix errors on the D: drive?

❍ **A.** Run the **chkdsk D:** command at the command prompt.

❍ **B.** Run the **chkdsk D: /F** command at the command prompt.

❍ **C.** Run the **scandisk D:** command at the command prompt.

❍ **D.** Run the **scandisk D: /F** command at the command prompt.

❍ **E.** Right-click the D: drive and select Scan Disk.

20. Why do you need to keep your drives defragged?

❍ **A.** To keep your drive from filling up

❍ **B.** To keep your drive clean from viruses

❍ **C.** To keep your drive optimized for better performance

❍ **D.** To keep your drive free from disk errors

21. ReadyBoost and ReadyDrive increase performance on your machine. What is the difference between the two? (Choose two answers.)

❍ **A.** Windows ReadyBoost uses USB flash devices as additional sources for caching.

❍ **B.** Windows ReadyDrive uses hybrid drives on laptop computers.

❍ **C.** Windows ReadyBoost uses hybrid drives on laptop computers.

❍ **D.** Windows ReadyDrive uses USB flash devices as additional sources for caching.

22. You loaded a new video card driver, which now causes your machine not to boot properly. What can you do to correct this problem?

❍ **A.** Boot to VGA mode (Base Video) and roll back the old driver.

❍ **B.** Boot to the command prompt and roll back the old driver.

❍ **C.** Boot with the Window Vista CD and run the repair.

❍ **D.** Connect to the Windows Update website to get the correct driver.

23. You have a few programs that are causing some strange errors to appear when Windows starts. You want to isolate which program generates the errors. What can you do?

❍ **A.** Use parental controls to disable each program.

❍ **B.** Use Windows Defender to temporarily disable programs.

❍ **C.** Edit the registry to disable each program.

❍ **D.** Use **msconfig** and temporarily disable programs.

24. Which of the following statements are true when discussing wireless technology used with Windows Vista? (Choose two answers.)

❍ **A.** Personal mode provides authentication via a preshared key or password.

❍ **B.** Enterprise mode provides authentication using IEEE 802.1X and EAP.

❍ **C.** Enterprise mode provides authentication via a preshared key or password.

❍ **D.** Personal mode provides authentication using IEEE 802.1X and EAP.

25. You tried to access a website. Unfortunately, your browser could not find the website. You eventually correct an error on the DNS server, which now knows the correct address to the website. What must you do to access the website?

❍ **A.** You need to run the **ipconfig /registerdns** command.

❍ **B.** You need to run the **ipconfig /flushdns** command.

❍ **C.** You need to shut down your machine and restart it.

❍ **D.** You need to change the IP address of your DNS server.

26. You have a Windows Vista computer used in the office through shared folders. You also want users to be able to remote access the computer to run programs from that computer from their own computers by using Remote Desktop. What do you need to do for them to access the computer?

- ❍ **A.** You need to add the users to the Administrators group.
- ❍ **B.** You need to add users to the Power Users group.
- ❍ **C.** You need to add the users to the Remote Desktop Users group.
- ❍ **D.** You need to add users to the Telnet group.

27. You have a Windows Vista computer that users use Remote Desktop to access. The computer has Windows Vista Ultimate edition. The users have passwords, Remote Desktop is enabled, and users have been added to the Remote Desktop Users group. However, the users still cannot access the computer. What is most likely the problem?

- ❍ **A.** You need to add Remote Desktop through the allow list in parental controls.
- ❍ **B.** You need to add the users to the Administrators group.
- ❍ **C.** You need to register Remote Desktop with Microsoft.
- ❍ **D.** You need to allow Remote Desktop through the Windows Firewall.

28. You are a configuring two Windows Vista computers that are used by one user. This user needs to be able to access e-mail from both computers using Windows Mail, and he must be able to permanently delete the messages from either computer. What do you need to do?

- ❍ **A.** Open the Tools menu and select Accounts. Click the Advanced tab and check the Leave a Copy of Messages on the Server option. Check the Remove from Server When Deleted from Deleted Items option.
- ❍ **B.** Open the Tools menu and select Accounts. Check the Remove from Server When Deleted from Deleted Items option.
- ❍ **C.** Open the Tools menu and check the Auto-Update option.
- ❍ **D.** You don't need to do anything after you link Windows Mail to your mail accounts.

29. You are the desktop support technician for Acme.com. You are configuring Windows Meeting Space so that your team can collaborate on a new project. Some of the members are in your local office, whereas others are in other cities. What do you need to do?

❍ **A.** You need to have the members start their Windows Meeting Space and connect to the meeting.

❍ **B.** You need to send out invitations to the members.

❍ **C.** You need to select the Allow People Near Me to See the Meeting option.

❍ **D.** You need to select the Allow All People to See the Meeting option.

30. You have BitLocker Drive Encryption on a computer that runs Microsoft Windows Business edition, which has the Trusted Platform Mobile (TPM) installed. When you set up the computer, you printed out the recovery password you keep in your files. What do you need to recover the system if a TPM error occurs and the user cannot access the data on the computer?

❍ **A.** Start the computer and enter the recovery password.

❍ **B.** Start the computer with the USB flash drive.

❍ **C.** Start the computer and enter the TMP Management Console.

❍ **D.** Boot the computer with the Windows Vista installation disc. Enter the recovery password when you need to log on.

31. You are looking at the Device Manager. You see a device that has an exclamation point on it. What is the problem?

❍ **A.** The device is having a problem.

❍ **B.** The device is disabled.

❍ **C.** The device is sleeping.

❍ **D.** The device is not connected.

32. What is the command to release an IPv4 address handed out by a DHCP address?

❍ **A.** **ipconfig**

❍ **B.** **ipconfig /registerdns**

❍ **C.** **ipconfig /release**

❍ **D.** **ipconfig /renew**

❍ **E.** **ipconfig /renew6**

33. What command would you use to check what IP address is resolved for a host name?

❍ **A. ipconfig /dns**

❍ **B. nslookup**

❍ **C. NBTStat**

❍ **D. resolve**

34. Link Layer Topology Discovery is installed by default. If you want it to function, what do you need to do?

❍ **A.** You have to enable Network Discovery.

❍ **B.** You need to enable file sharing.

❍ **C.** You need to enable public folder sharing.

❍ **D.** You need to enable password-protected sharing.

35. You work as the desktop support technician at Acme.com. Pat is a member of the Manager group. There is a shared folder called MANAGEMENT on an NTFS partition on a remote Windows Vista computer. Pat is given the write NTFS permission, the Manager group is given the read and execute NTFS permissions, and the Everyone group has the read NTFS permission to the DATA folder. In addition, Pat, Manager, and Everyone are assigned the shared Contributor permission to the MANAGEMENT folder. When Pat logs on his client computer and accesses the MANAGEMENT folder, what would be Pat's permissions? (Choose all that apply.)

❍ **A.** Read the files in the folder

❍ **B.** Write to the files in the folder

❍ **C.** Execute the files in the folder

❍ **D.** Delete the files in the folder

❍ **E.** No access to the files in the folder

36. What do you call a bootable tool that replaces MS-DOS as the preinstallation environment?

❍ **A.** Windows PE

❍ **B.** Installation script

❍ **C.** Windows image

❍ **D.** Catalog

37. What is the name of the answer file used on removable media when you install Windows Vista?

- ❍ **A.** Answer.txt
- ❍ **B.** Answer.xml
- ❍ **C.** Autoattend.xml
- ❍ **D.** Install.xml

38. What two network services are used for name resolution when communicating over a TCP/IP network?

- ❍ **A.** DNS
- ❍ **B.** LMHOSTS
- ❍ **C.** DHCP
- ❍ **D.** WINS

39. What command is used to trace the route that a packet takes to a destination and displays the series of IP routers that are used in delivering packets to the destination?

- ❍ **A.** **ipconfig**
- ❍ **B.** **arp**
- ❍ **C.** **tracert**
- ❍ **D.** **ping**

40. When discussing content zones used in Internet Explorer, what defines the local intranet zone?

- ❍ **A.** Anything that is not assigned to any other zone and anything that is not on your computer, or your organization's network
- ❍ **B.** Computers that are part of the organization's network that do not require a proxy server, as defined by the system administrator
- ❍ **C.** Contains trusted sites that you believe you can download or run files from without damaging your computer or data or that you consider are not a security risk
- ❍ **D.** Contains sites that you do not trust from which downloading or running files may damage your computer or data or that are considered a security risk

41. What is the version of Windows that includes everything?

❍ **A.** Premium

❍ **B.** Enterprise

❍ **C.** Ultimate

❍ **D.** Advanced

42. When you visit several websites using Internet Explorer, additional windows will appear. At times, you try to close these windows, but more windows are appearing faster than you can close then. What should you make sure you have enabled?

❍ **A.** Phishing Protection

❍ **B.** Dynamic Protection

❍ **C.** Pop-up Blocker

❍ **D.** Windows Defender

43. What Microsoft technology is used for developing reusable object-oriented software components and contains controls that are popular in Windows Explorer plug-ins?

❍ **A.** ActiveX

❍ **B.** OLE

❍ **C.** Basic language

❍ **D.** C##

44. What is used as an XML format for syndicating web content that can be automatically read by users as soon as it is published?

❍ **A.** ActiveX

❍ **B.** RSS

❍ **C.** TrueType

❍ **D.** Rich Text Format

45. What is a special microchip in some newer computers that supports advanced security features, including BitLocker encryption?

❍ **A.** ActiveX controls

❍ **B.** Trusted Platform Module

❍ **C.** Dynamic Protection

❍ **D.** NTFS

46. What would you use to encrypt individual files on your system?

- ❍ **A.** NTFS
- ❍ **B.** Compression
- ❍ **C.** EFS
- ❍ **D.** BitLocker

47. To use Windows Remote Desktop, a user must be added to one of two groups. What are the two groups?

- ❍ **A.** Administrator
- ❍ **B.** Power Users
- ❍ **C.** Remote Desktop Administrators
- ❍ **D.** Remote Desktop Users

48. When your machine goes into hibernate, what is the name of the file it saves the contents of the system memory to?

- ❍ **A.** Page.sys
- ❍ **B.** Pagefile.sys
- ❍ **C.** Hiberfil.sys
- ❍ **D.** Power.sys

49. You have two computers that you work on, and both contain Windows Vista Ultimate edition. One computer is a desktop computer, the other is a laptop computer. When working on each computer, you need to have the same current data files available to both computers. What do you need to do?

- ❍ **A.** You need to use offline folders.
- ❍ **B.** You need to create a login script that will copy the files from a shared folder.
- ❍ **C.** You need to set up DFS.
- ❍ **D.** You need to use a local policy to copy the files from a shared folder.

50. What would you use to disable USB connections and Bluetooth connections in Windows Vista?

- ❍ **A.** Windows Hardware Disable tool
- ❍ **B.** Windows Mobility Center
- ❍ **C.** System Configuration (msconfig.exe)
- ❍ **D.** Registry Editor

CHAPTER SIXTEEN

Answers to Practice Exam 2

1. B
2. B and C
3. A
4. B
5. D
6. C
7. A and D
8. A
9. A, B, and C
10. C and D
11. B
12. B
13. A and C
14. A
15. E
16. C
17. B
18. A
19. A
20. C
21. A and B
22. A
23. D
24. A and B
25. B
26. C
27. D
28. A
29. B
30. A
31. A
32. C
33. B
34. A
35. A, B, and C
36. A
37. C
38. A and D
39. C
40. B
41. C
42. C
43. A
44. B
45. B
46. C
47. A and D
48. C
49. A
50. B

Question 1

Answer B is correct. For a system to be Windows Vista capable, it must have at least 512 MB of RAM. Therefore, more RAM should be added to the system. The minimum requirements for a Vista Capable computer is an 800-MHz processor, 512 MB RAM, an SVGA monitor, 20-GB hard drive with 15 GB free, and a CD drive. Therefore, Answers A, C, D, E, and F are incorrect.

Question 2

Answers B and C are correct because you can use an in-place upgrade for Windows XP Pro, Windows XP Home, Windows XP Media Center, and Windows XP Tablet PC. Note that the Windows XP Pro computer requires Service Pack 2 to be installed for an in-place upgrade. Answers A and D are incorrect because they require a clean install, especially if you are upgrading from a 32-bit system to a 64-bit system.

Question 3

Answer A is correct because the Windows Vista Upgrade Advisor is a utility that allows one to access an easy-to-understand report after scanning your computer. This report will specify whether the currently installed hardware will work with Windows Vista. Answer B is incorrect because there is no Microsoft utility called System Checker for Windows Vista. Answer C is incorrect because the System Information gives you a quick view of what components and software your computer has; it does not specify which components do not meet Windows Vista minimum requirements. Answer D is incorrect because the Computer Management Console is used to manage the computer.

Question 4

Answer B is correct because at this point, you can only use the Startup Repair utility to fix the problem. Answers C and D are incorrect because you cannot load Windows in Normal mode or Safe mode to run the Software Explorer or msconfig.exe. Answer A is incorrect because a clean install was done, and therefore, there is no prior information left on the hard drive to revert back to.

Question 5

Answer D is correct because signed drivers have been tested by Microsoft to ensure that they are stable and will not cause any problems. Answer A is incorrect because signed drivers have nothing to do directly with system security.

Answer B is not correct because Microsoft does not keep track of paid drivers. Answer C is incorrect because Microsoft may or may not have acknowledged the driver.

Question 6

Answer C is correct because you have to specify which sites you do not want to block pop-up blockers. Answer A is incorrect because you would use the Manage Add-On dialog box to shut down add-on programs such as Adobe Shockwave Flash. Answer B is incorrect because adding to a trusted site allows websites more permissions, such as running ActiveX. Answer D is incorrect because you need to open the Pop-Up Blocker Settings dialog box and add the URL to the allowed sites list.

Question 7

Answers A and D are correct because Windows Aero requires that the video card includes DirectX 9, with Pixel Shader 2.0 and Windows Vista Display Driver Model (WDDM). Answer B is incorrect because although Windows Aero can use the higher resolution, it is not required. Answer C is incorrect because there is no 64-bit color on computer systems.

Question 8

Answer A is correct because the Ease of Access Center enables you to control the accessibility options. Answers B and C are incorrect because there are not such consoles with those names. Answer D is incorrect because the Computer Management is a powerful console but does not including accessibility options.

Question 9

Answers A, B, and C are correct because all of these options can be controlled using the Ease of Access Center. Answer D is incorrect because increasing the resolution typically makes things smaller on the screen, making it harder to read.

Question 10

Answers C and D are correct because you cannot use parental controls when the computer is part of a domain and when you are logged on as an administrator. Answer A is incorrect because parental controls are available on all editions of Windows Vista. Answer B is incorrect because the Power Users group is mostly used for backward compatibility with applications that were created for older versions of Windows.

Question 11

Answer B is correct because you can use parental controls to block certain websites. Answer A is incorrect because the firewall is used to block certain ports or applications from communicating over the network, not specific websites. Answer C is incorrect because you cannot use NTFS to block websites. Answer D is incorrect because the child should not have administrative permissions.

Question 12

Answer B is correct because volumes are managed using the Computer Management Console, which is found in Administrative Tools. Answers A, C, and D are incorrect because these do not exist.

Question 13

Answers A and C are correct because you should try to run the application as a Windows 95 environment. If that does not work, try to run the application as an administrator. Answers B and D are incorrect because NTFS permissions and file attributes are not the cause of the problem.

Question 14

Answer A is correct because this warning is generated by User Account Control to protect you from an application that may be performing functions that it should not be performing. Answer B is incorrect because the problem is caused by User Account Control and has nothing to do with NTFS permissions. Answer C is incorrect because although you could try running the application as an administrator, this would open up the security on your system. In addition, applications written for older operating systems may not function properly on Windows Vista because of the enhanced security. Answer D is incorrect because it would give you an error saying a file is read-only or not able to save something.

Question 15

Answer E is correct because you can run programs that were installed by another user. Answers A, B, C, and D are incorrect because you must be an administrator to install or uninstall software, install hardware, delete system files, and change settings that affect other users.

Question 16

Answer C is correct because if the Windows Firewall is active, you can allow communication by adding the name of the program file to the Exceptions list. Answers A, B, and D do not have these capabilities.

Question 17

Answer B is correct because the Windows Firewall with Advanced Security is used to manage your IPSec configuration when the firewall rules and IPSec settings conflict with each other. Answers A, C, D, and E are incorrect because the console does none of these.

Question 18

Answer A is correct because Protected mode prevents Component Object Model (COM) objects, such as ActiveX controls, from automatically modifying files and settings. With Protected mode enabled, only users can initiate these types of requests. Answers B, C, and D are incorrect because Protected mode does not do any of these.

Question 19

Answer A is correct because **chkdsk** is used in Windows Vista. Answer B is incorrect because the **/F** parameter will fix errors (such as lost clusters and cross-lined files) that it finds while checking the disk. Answers C and D are incorrect because **scandisk** was used by the Windows 9x versions of Windows. Answer E is incorrect because it is not **scandisk**.

Question 20

Answer C is the correct because disk defragmentation leads to slow disk performance. Answers A and B are incorrect because when you defrag a hard drive, you are relocating clusters. You are not deleting files or clearing out space, and you are not checking for or removing viruses. Answer D is incorrect because disk errors would be found using **chkdsk**.

Question 21

Answers A and B are correct because Windows ReadyBoost boosts system performance by using USB flash devices as additional sources for caching, and Windows ReadyDrive boosts system performance on mobile computers equipped with hybrid drives. Answer C is incorrect because ReadyBoost boosts system performance by using USB flash devices as additional sources for caching. Answer D is incorrect because ReadyDrive boosts system performance on mobile computers equipped with hybrid drives.

Question 22

Answer A is the correct answer because if you load the basic VGA driver rather than the new driver, you can then roll back to the previous driver. Answer B is incorrect because you cannot roll back the driver using the command prompt. Answer C is not correct because you cannot roll back the driver, and you don't want to reinstall Windows. Answer D is incorrect because you cannot connect to the update site until you can boot to Windows.

Question 23

Answer D is correct because **msconfig** enables you to temporarily disable each program one by one to see which one is causing the problem. Answer A is available only when the computer is not part of the domain and is a clumsy way to perform the same tasks. Answers B and C are incorrect because they are clumsy ways to perform the same tasks.

Question 24

Answers A and B are correct because Personal mode provides authentication via a preshared key or password, and Enterprise mode provides authentication using IEEE 802.1X and EAP. Answers C and D are incorrect because they state the opposite.

Question 25

Answer B is correct because you need to flush the DNS cache so that it can get the new address from the DNS server. Answer A is incorrect because it would only register your computer's IP address with the DNS server. Answer C clears the cache, but it is not the most efficient way because rebooting your computer takes far longer than using the **ipconfig** command. Answer D does not correct the problem, because the address is still cached.

Question 26

Answer C is correct. For a user to access a Windows Vista machine using Remote Desktop, the user must be added to the Remote Desktop Users group. Users must also have passwords. Answer A would work, but would most likely be a security problem because a user who is an administrator will have access to everything on the machine; if a person lets a virus on the system, it will spread through the entire system because of the user's rights and permissions. Answer B is incorrect because the Power Users group is for backward compatibility. Answer D is incorrect because there is no Telnet group that comes with Windows.

Question 27

Answer D is correct because it is most likely blocked by the Windows Firewall. Answer A is incorrect because Remote Desktop cannot be controlled through parental controls. Answer B is incorrect because the users who are trying to use Remote Desktop are already members of the Remote Desktop Users group (which has all the permissions needed to access Remote Desktop). In addition, a user who is an administrator would most likely be a security problem because that user would have access to everything on the machine; if a person lets a virus on the system, it will spread through the entire system because of the user's rights and permissions. Answer C is incorrect because you don't have to register Remote Desktop with Microsoft for it to function.

Question 28

Answer A is correct because you need to leave a copy of messages so that when you go to the other computer, the messages will still be there. You also need to check the Remove from Server When Deleted option so that when you delete from one, the message will be gone from the other. Answer B is incorrect because you did not check the Remove from Server box. Answer C is incorrect because there is no Auto-Update option. Answer D is incorrect because Windows Mail does not do these options by default.

Question 29

Answer B is correct because when you have remote users, you need to send out invitations. Answer A is incorrect because the remote users will not see that the meeting is nearby. Answer C is incorrect because Allow People Near Me will only include local users. Answer D is incorrect because there is no Allow All People option.

Question 30

Answer A is correct because you start the computer and enter the recovery password in the BitLocker Driver Encryption Recovery Console. Answer B is incorrect because you did not save the password to disk. Answer C is incorrect because you cannot enter the TMP Management Console. Answer D is incorrect because you cannot access the BitLocker Driver Encryption Recovery Console using the Windows Vista installation disc.

Question 31

Answer A is the correct answer because the exclamation point indicates a problem. Answer B is incorrect because a device that is disabled would have a down arrow. Answers C and D are incorrect because they are not indicated in the Device Manager.

Question 32

Answer C is correct because **ipconfig /release** releases an IPv4 address. Answer A is incorrect because the **ipconfig** command displays the IP address, subnet mask, and default gateway. Answer B is incorrect because the **/registerdns** option will register the IP address with the DNS server. Answers D and E are incorrect because the **/renew** option is used to renew IPv4 addresses, and the **/renew6** is used to renew IPv6 addresses.

Question 33

Answer B is correct because **nslookup** is used to diagnose your DNS infrastructure. Answer A is incorrect because there is no **/dns** option with the **ipconfig** command. Answer C is incorrect because **NBTState** is used troubleshoot NetBIOS name-resolution problems. Answer D is incorrect because no **resolve** command comes with Windows.

Question 34

Answer A is correct because for Link Layer Topology Discovery to function, you have to enable Network Discovery. Answers B, C, and D are incorrect because none of these options enable Link Layer Topology Discovery.

Question 35

Answers A, B, and C are correct because NTFS permissions include write permission combined with read and execute. The Contributor share permission gives the ability to read, write, execute, and delete. When you combine the two, you take the least, so that would be read, write, and execute. Answer D is incorrect because there was no delete NTFS permission given. Because they have permissions, answer E is incorrect.

Question 36

Answer A is correct because Microsoft Windows Preinstallation Environment (Windows PE) is a bootable tool that replaces MS-DOS as the preinstallation environment. Windows PE is not a general-purpose operating system. Instead, it is used to provide operating system features for installation, troubleshooting, and recovery. Answer C is incorrect because a Windows image is a copy of a disk volume saved as file. Answer D is incorrect because a catalog is a binary file (CLG) that contains the state of the settings and packages in a Windows image. Answer B is incorrect because it is a made-up answer.

Question 37

Answer C is correct because the name of the answer file is autoattend.xml. Answers A, B, and D are incorrect because they are fictional answers.

Question 38

Answers A and D are correct. DNS, short for Domain Name System, translates from host name to IP address. WINS, short for Windows Internet Naming Service, translates from computer name (NetBIOS name) to IP address. Answer B is a file that provides name resolution from computer name to IP address. Answer C is incorrect because DHCP is a method to assign IP addresses to hosts.

Question 39

Answer C is correct because **tracert** traces the route that a packet takes and displays the series of IP routers. Answer A is incorrect because **ipconfig** is used to display the IP configuration. Answer B is incorrect because **arp** is used to show the ARP cache. Answer D is incorrect because the **ping** command is used to test a connection to a host.

Question 40

Answer B is correct because an intranet is defined as part of the organization's network that does not require a proxy server. Answer A is incorrect because anything that is not assigned to any other zone and anything that is not on your computer, or your organization's network defines this as the Internet zone. Answer C is incorrect because trusted sites are those that you believe you can download or run files from without damaging your computer or data or that you consider not a security risk. Answer D is incorrect because restricted zone sites are those that you do not trust to download or run files from because they might damage your computer or data, or those that are considered a security risk.

Question 41

Answer C is correct because the Windows Vista Ultimate edition includes everything that all the others offer. Answers A and B include more features than most of the other versions, but Ultimate has additional features. Answer D is incorrect because there is no Advanced edition.

Question 42

Answer C is correct because you need to have a pop-up blocker to stop the windows from opening. Answers A and B are incorrect because they will not stop the pop-up windows. Answer D is incorrect because Windows Defender will protect against spyware. However, Windows Defender will help little against some pop-ups that are generated by spyware programs.

Question 43

Answer A is correct because ActiveX is the popular control used in Internet Explorer. Answer B is incorrect because OLE allows you to cut, copy, and paste objects from one document to another document, even between different applications. Answers C and D are incorrect because these are programming languages.

Question 44

Answer B is correct because RSS, short for Rich Site Summary, is used to get feeds from websites when new content is published. Answer A is incorrect because ActiveX includes special controls used in Internet Explorer plug-ins. Answer C is incorrect because this is a type of font created by Adobe. Rich Text Format is a file format that supports fonts, font styles (such as bold, underline, and italics), and varying font sizes.

Question 45

Answer B is correct because the Trusted Platform Module (TPM) is a special microchip that supports advanced security features. Answer A is incorrect because ActiveX includes special controls used in Internet Explorer plug-ins. Answer C is incorrect because Dynamic Protection is used to make sure web applications cannot access files on the computer. Answer D is incorrect because NTFS is a file system.

Question 46

Answer C is correct because EFS, which is short for Encrypted File System, is used to encrypt individual files. Answer A is incorrect because NTFS is the secure file system used in Windows Vista that supports both compression and EFS. Answer B is incorrect because compression is used to compress files, not encrypt them. Answer D is incorrect because BitLocker is used to encrypt entire disk volumes.

Question 47

Answers A and D are correct. All administrators are automatically given the necessary permission to use Windows Remote Desktop. For other users, you must add them to the Remote Desktop Users group. Answer B is incorrect because the Power Users group is mostly used for backward compatibility. Answer C is incorrect because there is no Remote Desktop Administrators group.

Question 48

Answer C is correct because the file in which the memory content is saved during hibernation is hiberfil.sys. Answer A is a made-up file. Answer B is the name of the paging file used in Windows XP and Vista. Answer D is incorrect because Power.sys is a system file used in Windows to help manage power settings.

Question 49

Answer A is correct. Windows Vista supports offline folders to help keep file synchronized. Answer B is a possible solution, but using a login script requires some skill and can be a lengthy process because it copies files from one drive to another. It might also overwrite newer files. Answer C is incorrect because Distributed File System (DFS) is only available on Windows servers. Answer D is not a viable option.

Question 50

Answer B is correct because the Windows Mobility Center can be used to disable both USB and Bluetooth connections. Answer A is incorrect because the Windows Hardware Disable tool does not exist at the time of this writing. Answer C is incorrect because the System Configuration utility (msconfig.exe) is a troubleshooting tool that can be used to disable startup programs and services. Answer D is incorrect because the Registry Editor is used to edit the registry, which holds most of the configuration information for hardware and software programs.

APPENDIX

What's on the CD-ROM?

The CD-ROM features an innovative practice test engine powered by MeasureUp™, giving you yet another effective tool to assess your readiness for the exam.

Multiple Test Modes

MeasureUp practice tests can be used in Study, Certification, or Custom Mode.

Study Mode

Tests administered in Study Mode allow you to request the correct answer(s) and explanation to each question during the test. These tests are not timed. You can modify the testing environment during the test by selecting the Options button. You can also specify the objectives or missed questions you want to include in your test, the timer length, and other test properties.

In Study Mode, you receive automatic feedback on all correct and incorrect answers. The detailed answer explanations are a superb learning tool in their own right.

Certification Mode

Tests administered in Certification Mode closely simulate the actual testing environment you will encounter when taking a licensure exam and are timed. These tests do not allow you to request the answer or explanation to each question until after the exam.

Custom Mode

Custom Mode allows you to specify your preferred testing environment. Use this mode to specify the categories you want to include in your test, timer length, number of questions, and other test properties. You can modify the testing environment during the test by selecting the Options button.

Attention to Exam Objectives

MeasureUp practice tests are designed to appropriately balance the questions over each technical area covered by a specific exam. All concepts from the actual exam are covered thoroughly to ensure that you're prepared for the exam.

Installing the CD

System Requirements:

- Windows 95, 98, Me, NT 4, 2000, XP, or Vista
- 7MB disk space for testing engine
- An average of 1MB disk space for each individual test
- Control Panel Regional Settings must be set to English (United States)
- PC only

To install the CD-ROM, follow these instructions:

1. Close all applications before beginning this installation.
2. Insert the CD into your CD-ROM drive. If the setup starts automatically, go to step 6. If the setup does not start automatically, continue with step 3.
3. From the Start menu, select **Run**.

4. Click **Browse** to locate the MeasureUp CD. In the Browse dialog box, from the Look In drop-down list, select the CD-ROM drive.
5. In the Browse dialog box, double-click **Setup.exe**. In the Run dialog box, click **OK** to begin the installation.
6. On the Welcome screen, click **MeasureUp Practice Questions** to begin installation.
7. Follow the Certification Prep Wizard by clicking **Next**.
8. To agree to the Software License Agreement, click **Yes**.
9. On the Choose Destination Location screen, click **Next** to install the software to C:\Program Files\Certification Preparation. If you cannot locate MeasureUp Practice Tests on the Start menu, see the section titled "Creating a Shortcut to the MeasureUp Practice Tests," later in this appendix.
10. On the Setup Type screen, select **Typical Setup**. Click **Next** to continue.
11. In the Select Program Folder screen, you can name the program folder where your tests will be located. To select the default, simply click **Next** and the installation continues.
12. After the installation is complete, verify that **Yes, I Want to Restart My Computer Now** is selected. If you select **No, I Will Restart My Computer Later**, you cannot use the program until you restart your computer.
13. Click **Finish**.
14. After restarting your computer, choose **Start > Programs > Certification Preparation > Certification Preparation > MeasureUp Practice Tests**.
15. On the MeasureUp Welcome Screen, click **Create User Profile**.
16. In the User Profile dialog box, complete the mandatory fields and click **Create Profile**.
17. Select the practice test you want to access and click **Start Test**.

Creating a Shortcut to the MeasureUp Practice Tests

To create a shortcut to the MeasureUp Practice Tests, follow these steps.

1. Right-click on your desktop.
2. From the shortcut menu, select **New > Shortcut**.
3. Browse to C:\Program Files\MeasureUp Practice Tests and select the **MeasureUpCertification.exe** or **Localware.exe** file.
4. Click **OK**.
5. Click **Next**.
6. Rename the shortcut MeasureUp.
7. Click **Finish**.

After you complete step 7, use the MeasureUp shortcut on your desktop to access the MeasureUp products you ordered.

Technical Support

If you encounter problems with the MeasureUp test engine on the CD-ROM, please contact MeasureUp at (800) 649-1687 or email support@measureup.com. Support hours of operation are 7:30 a.m. to 4:30 p.m. EST. In addition, you can find Frequently Asked Questions (FAQ) in the Support area at www.measureup.com. If you would like to purchase additional MeasureUp products, call (678) 356-5050 or (800) 649-1687, or visit www.measureup.com.

Glossary

Numbers

802.11 standard An Institute of Electrical and Electronic Engineers (IEEE) set of wireless LAN standards.

A

access control list (ACL) A list of each user account and group that can access a resource and the permissions for that resource.

Active Directory The directory service that is included with Windows Server 2003. Active Directory is based on the X.500 standards and those of its predecessor, Lightweight Directory Access Protocol (LDAP). It stores information about objects on a network and makes this information available to applications, users, and network administrators. Active Directory is also used for authentication to network resources, using a single logon process. It provides network administrators a hierarchical view of the network and a single point of administration for all network objects.

ActiveX controls A loosely defined set of technologies used by browsers to share information among different applications.

Ad Hoc mode A wireless mode that allows a wireless adapter to connect directly to other computers with wireless adapters without using a wireless access point.

add-on (Internet Explorer) A software module used by browsers to display or play different types of audio or video messages.

Add-on Manager Enables you to disable or allow web browser add-ons and delete unwanted ActiveX controls.

Administrative Tools A folder in the Control Panel that contains tools for system administrators and advanced users to manage the computer.

administrator account A predefined account that provides complete access to files, directories, services, and other facilities on the computer.

answer file An Extensible Markup Language (XML) file that scripts the answers for a series of graphical user interface (GUI) dialog boxes and other configuration settings, typically to be used to install Windows or other applications.

Automatic Private IP An address generated by a host when it cannot connect to a DHCP server to get a DHCP address. The Automatic Private IP address will be in the form of 169.254.*xxx.xxx* and the subnet mask of 255.255.0.0.

B

Backup and Restore Center A backup/restore application that can be easily configured to periodically back up files on users' computers.

battery meter A tool that enables the user to monitor the state of the battery on mobile computers.

BitLocker Drive Encryption A technology used to encrypt an entire volume on a Windows Vista computer.

Bluetooth Short-range radio technology aimed at simplifying communications among Internet devices and between devices and the Internet. It also aims to simplify data synchronization between Internet devices and other computers.

broadband connection A connection based on data transmission in which a single medium or wire that can carry several channels simultaneously. Digital Subscriber Line (DSL) and cable modems are often associated with broadband connections.

Business Desktop Deployment Solution Accelerator 2007 (BDD 2007) Software that is part of the Windows Deployment Services that provides end-to-end guidance for planning, building, testing, and deploying Windows Vista.

C

catalog A binary file (CLG) that contains the state of the settings and packages in a Windows image.

Check Disk tool (chkdsk) A tool used to check the integrity of disks and correct many types of common errors found on the disk.

codecs Short for compressor/decompressor, software or hardware used to compress and decompress digital media such as a song or video.

color depth The number of bits that determine the number of possible colors on the screen.

compression Technology used to store or transmit the same amount of data using fewer bits.

Control Panel A graphical tool used to configure the Windows environment and hardware devices.

cookie A message given to a web browser by a web server, which is typically stored in a text file on the PC's hard drive. The message is then sent back to the server each time the browser requests a page from the server. The main purpose of cookies is to identify users and possibly prepare customized web pages for them.

D

data collector set (DCS) Defined elements that can be reused over and over.

default gateway The address that points to the newest router so that it communicates with other networks or subnetworks.

defragmentation The occurrence that slows down hard drive performance because files get stored in separated pieces on the hard drive.

desktop Main screen/graphical space that you see after you turn on your computer and log on to Windows. Like the top of the actual office desk, it serves as a surface for your work.

device drivers A program that controls a device by acting like a translator between the device and programs that use the device.

Device Manager A software component that lists all hardware devices on your computer and allows you to change the properties for any device.

dial-up connection Technology that enables a connection to a network over a public telephone network using an analog or digital modem.

Direct3D An application programming interface (API) developed by Microsoft for manipulating and displaying three-dimensional objects.

Diskpart A command-line hard disk configuration utility.

domain A logical unit of computers that defines a security boundary. A domain uses one database known as Active Directory, which is stored on one or more domain controllers.

Domain Name System (DNS) A directory service used on TCP/IP networks that translates from host names to IP addresses.

domain user accounts User accounts defined in the Active Directory. Through single sign-on, these accounts can access resources throughout a domain/forest.

dual boot Also called a multiboot, an operating system configuration that enables the user to boot the computer system from one of multiple operating systems that are installed on the same hard drive. The operating system that is loaded is given control, typically through a boot management program that will override the original Master Boot Record (MBR) and load instead of an operating system.

dynamic security Options in Internet Explorer that offer multiple security features to defend your computer against malware and data theft.

E

Ease of Access Center A central location that you can use to set up the accessibility settings and programs available in Windows.

e-mail A powerful, sophisticated tool that allows users to send text messages and file attachments (documents, pictures, sound, and movies) to anyone with an e-mail address.

Encrypting File System (EFS) A technology used to encrypt folders and files on an NT file system (NTFS) volume.

encryption The process of disguising a message or data in what appears to be meaningless data (cipher text) to hide and protect the sensitive data from unauthorized access.

end user license agreement (EULA) Type of license used for most software and represents a legal contract between the manufacturer/author and the end user of an application. The EULA details how the software can and cannot be used and any restrictions that the manufacturer imposes.

explicit permissions Permissions that are granted directly to the folder or file. Some of these permissions are granted automatically, such as when a file or folder is created, whereas others have to be assigned manually.

F

FAT32 A file system introduced in the second major release of Windows 95 that is an enhancement to the File Allocation Table (FAT) file system. It uses 32-bit FAT entries, which supports hard drives up to 2 TB and supports long filenames.

File Allocation Table (FAT) An older file system used by DOS. FAT is a simple file system that uses minimum memory. Originally, FAT supported filenames of 11 characters, which include the 8 characters for the filename and 3 characters for the file extension, but it has been expanded to support long filenames.

file system The overall structure in which files are named, stored, and organized. Files systems used in Windows Vista include FAT, FAT32, and NTFS.

flicks Simple pen gestures used to execute commands or actions.

fonts A collection of characters (letters, numerals, symbols, and punctuation marks) that have common characteristics.

fully qualified domain name (FQDNs) Sometimes referred to as just domain names, FQDNs are used to identify computers on a TCP/IP network.

G

gadgets Easy-to-use mini programs (tools) that give you information at a glance for frequently performed tasks such as checking the weather, checking the time (via a digital clock), and checking e-mail (without opening other programs).

guest account A predefined account that is designed for users who need one-time or occasional access.

H

Hibernate mode A method to shut down your computer that saves the contents of the system memory to a file (Hiberfil.sys) on the hard disk. Because it is saved to the hard disk, no power is required to maintain this state. When you boot your computer, you can then continue where you left off within a short time.

HOSTS file A file used to translate the host name to IP address.

Hybrid Sleep mode A combination of Sleep and Hibernate that saves your work to your hard disk and puts your mobile PC into a power-saving state. If you suffer a power failure on a computer when it is in a Hybrid Sleep state, your data will not be lost.

I

ImageX A command-line tool that captures, modifies, and applies installation images for deployment in a manufacturing or corporate environment.

Infrastructure mode Adapter connects to a wireless access point.

inherited permissions Permissions that flow down from the folder into the subfolders and files, indirectly giving them permissions to a user or group.

Internet Explorer (IE) Software found on Windows that enables the user to view web pages.

Internet Protocol Security (IPSec) A set of protocols developed used to support secure exchange of packets at the IP layer.

Internet service provider (ISP) A company that provides access to the Internet.

IP address A unique address that certain electronic devices used to identify and communicate with each other on a computer network utilizing the Internet Protocol (IP) standard.

ipconfig command A command used on Windows computers that shows the TCP/IP configuration of a host.

IPv4 The version of the Internet Protocol that supports 32-bit addresses, which allows up to 4,294,967,296 possible unique addresses.

IPv6 The newest version of the Internet Protocol that supports 128-bit addresses that allows up to 3.403×10^{38} unique host interface addresses.

J–L

junk e-mail Unsolicited e-mail or advertisements, flyers, and catalogs that may or may not contain fraudulent schemes and pornography. Junk e-mail often includes viruses and other forms of malware.

Link Layer Topology Discovery (LLDT) A technology that queries each device to determine its capabilities and to determine the topology of the network.

LMHOSTS file A file used to translate the NetBIOS computer name to an IP address.

local user accounts User accounts defined on a local computer, which have access to the local computer only.

M

malware Software designed specifically to damage or disrupt a system, such as a virus or Trojan horse.

Memory Diagnostic tool A utility used to test memory for a wide assortment of problems.

Microsoft Management Console (MMC) An application that provides a common interface to administer Windows-based environments using snap-ins.

MPEG standard Standards developed by the Moving Pictures Experts Group that define video format.

MPEG-2 A common format used on most video DVDs.

N

Network Diagnostic tool A tool that helps resolve network-related issues.

Notepad A text editor included in Windows.

notification area A software component on the taskbar that includes a clock and small icons that show the status of certain programs and computer settings.

nslookup command A command that displays information that you can use to diagnose your DNS infrastructure.

NTFS (NT File System) The preferred file system used in Windows XP and Windows Vista that supports large hard drives, is more reliable then previous file systems, and offers security through NTFS permissions and encryption. It also offers compression.

O–P

offline folder Technology that saves a copy of files that are accessed over a network so that it can be accessed when you are not connected to the network. When you do connect to the network, the files will be synchronized.

packet filter A filter used in firewalls that protect the computer by using an access control list (ACL), which specifies which packets are allowed through the firewall based on IP address and protocol (specifically the port number).

paging file (pagefile.sys) A file on the disk that is used as memory.

parental controls A software component, mostly designed to protect children while they are online, that allows you to restrict websites and programs and to set time limits.

performance The overall effectiveness of how data moves through the system.

permissions Defines the type of access that is granted to an object or object attribute.

phishing The act of sending an e-mail to a user falsely claiming to be an organization in an attempt to trick the user into giving private information that will be used for identity theft. The e-mail directs users to visit a website where they are asked to update personal information, such as passwords and credit card, social security, and bank account numbers.

ping command A command that uses Internet Control Message Protocol (ICMP) packets to test connectivity to a host on a TCP/IP network.

pixel Short for picture element, a single point or dot in a graphic image.

plug-and-play Technology that gives the ability of a computer system to automatically configure expansion boards and other devices.

pop-up blocker Technology used in browsers to help block most pop-up windows.

port An endpoint to a logical connection that is identified by a port number. For example, port 80 is used for HTTP traffic.

power plans Formerly known as power schemes in earlier versions of Windows, a collection of hardware and system settings that manages how your computer uses and conserves power.

Presentation mode A mode used when displaying presentations that disables screen saves, adjusts the speaker volume, and changes the desktop background image.

Previous Versions Technology that automatically creates daily backup copies of files and folders. If you enable this feature by creating a System Protection Point, you can restore previous versions of the document.

Problem Reports and Solutions A new control panel that enables users to see previously sent problems and any solutions or additional information that is available.

Protected mode A mode used in Internet Explorer used to prevent websites from saving or installing programs on a computer.

public folder A shared folder that is designed to enable users to share files and folders from a single location quickly and easily.

Q–R

Quick Launch toolbar Lets you start programs with one click.

RDF Site Summary (RSS) Also known as Rich Site Summary, an XML format for syndicating web content.

ReadyBoost Technology that boosts system performance by using USB flash devices as additional sources for caching.

ReadyDrive Technology that boosts system performance on mobile computers equipped with hybrid drives.

refresh rate A term that describes the number of times it is refreshed or redrawn per second (hertz).

region A code used by optical drives and disks used to prevent CDs and DVDs from being played in countries in which the CD or DVD was not made for.

reliability A measure of how often a system deviates from configured, expected behavior. Reliability problems occur as the result of application crashes, service freezes and restarts, driver initialization failures, and operating system failures.

Remote Access Server (RAS) A server that allows remote users who are not connected to a network using dial-up or virtual private networking (VPN) technology to gain access to files and print services on the LAN from a remote location.

Remote Assistance Technology that enables you to piggy-back on a user's session, usually used to troubleshoot problems.

Remote Desktop Technology that enables you to remotely control a PC.

Rich Text Format A format used by word processing documents that define fonts, colors, and pictures.

right Authorizes a user to perform certain actions on a computer, such as logging on to a system interactively or back up files and directories.

S

safe list A list found in e-mail programs that specifies those users who are trusted to receive e-mail from.

Safe mode Starting Windows in a mode with a basic GUI interface that runs only essential system services, typically used to troubleshoot startup problems.

screen resolution The screen resolution describes the sharpness and clarity of an image by signifying the number of dots (pixels) on the entire screen, usually described as the number of pixels going across and the number of pixels going down.

search box A software component found with the Start menu that allows you to find things quickly by searching programs, all the folders in your personal folder (which includes Documents, Pictures, Music, Desktop, and other common locations), your e-mail messages, saved instant messages, appointments, contacts, your Internet favorites, and Internet history.

Server Message Block (SMB) A protocol that defines a series of commands used to pass information between networked computers using NetBIOS.

service pack An update to a software version that fixes an existing problem, such as a bug, or provides enhancements to the product that will appear in the next version of the product. Usually multiple updates and fixes are packaged together into a single service pack.

service set identifier (SSID) A 32-character unique identifier attached to the header of packets sent over a wireless LAN (WLAN) that acts as a password when a mobile device tries to connect to an access point.

shared folder A folder that is shared or made available to users on the network.

Sidebar A pane on the side of the Microsoft Windows Vista desktop where you can keep your gadgets organized and always available.

signed driver A device driver that includes a digital signature, which is an electronic security mark that can indicate the publisher of the software and information that can show whether a driver has been altered.

Sleep mode A power-saving state that saves work and opens programs to memory. To maintain the contents of memory while the computer is in Sleep mode, the system still consumes a small amount of power. The advantage of Sleep mode is that you can continue where you left off, typically within a few seconds.

speech recognition Technology that allows the user to activate the computer by voice.

spyware Any software that gathers user information through the user's Internet connection without his or her knowledge, usually for advertising purposes or to steal private information. Spyware applications are typically bundled as a hidden component of freeware or shareware programs that can be downloaded from the Internet.

standard account The account to use for everyday computing that lets a person use most of the capabilities of the computer.

standard file sharing A type of shared folder that offers more security than a public shared folder.

Start menu A software component that enables you to start programs, access folders, make changes to Windows Vista, access help, log off the computer, switch to a different user account, or turn off the computer.

Startup Repair Tool (STR) A tool used to automatically fix many common problems, including incompatible drivers, missing or corrupted startup configuration settings, and corrupted startup files.

stateful firewall A technology used in firewalls that monitors the state of active connections and uses the information gained to determine which network packets are allowed through the firewall. Typically, if the user starts communicating with an outside computer, it will remember the conversation and allow the appropriate packets back in. If an outside computer tries to start communicating with a computer protected by a stateful firewall, those packets will automatically be dropped unless it was granted by the access control list (ACL).

subnet mask Numbers/bits that resemble an IP address used to define which bits describe the network number and which bits describe the host address.

Sync Center Software that enables you to keep data synchronized with another computer.

Sysprep The utility that facilitates image creation for deployment to multiple destination computers. Sysprep prepares an installed system ready to be duplicated as an image by removing the original security identifiers (SIDs) from the image, and cleaning up various user and machine settings and log files.

System Configuration tool (msconfig) An advanced tool used to identify problems that might prevent Windows from starting correctly.

System Performance Assessment A benchmark used by Windows Vista and certain applications such as games to monitor and adjust the system for optimum performance.

system requirements Minimum hardware or software to run, install, or use a hardware or software component.

System Restore A tool used to restore a computer's system files to an earlier point in time.

T

Tablet PC A fully functioning compact PC.

taskbar The long, horizontal bar at the bottom of your screen. By default, the taskbar is always on top, making it always visible even after you open several windows or programs. The taskbar contains the Start button, Quick Launch toolbar, and the notification area.

TCP/IP This Internet protocol suite is the set of communications protocols that implements the protocol stack on which the Internet and many commercial networks run. TCP/IP is named after two of the most important protocols in the protocol suite: the Transmission Control Protocol (TCP) and the Internet Protocol (IP).

text file A basic file that contains only alphanumeric characters and does not include formatting codes such as margins, fonts, colors, or pictures.

theme A collection of visual elements and sounds for your computer desktop. A theme determines the look of the various visual elements of your desktop, such as windows, icons, fonts, and colors, and it can include sounds.

tracert command A command, based on Internet Control Message Protocol (ICMP) packets, that traces the route that a packet takes to a destination and displays the series of IP routers that are used in delivering packets to the destination.

Trusted Platform Module (TPM) A microchip that is built in to a computer and used to store cryptographic information, such as encryption keys. It is used by BitLocker Drive Encryption.

U

Unified Memory Architecture (UMA) A computer that has graphics chips built in to the motherboard that use part of the computer's main memory for video memory.

Universal Naming Convention (UNC) A common syntax to describe the location of a network resource, such as a shared file, directory, or printer. The UNC syntax for Windows systems is *computername**sharedfolder**resource*.

user account Enables a user to log on to a computer or domain with an identity that can be authenticated and authorized for access to the resources of the computer or domain. Because the user account is meant to be assigned to one and only one user, it allows you to assign rights and permissions to a single user and gives the ability to track what users are doing (accountability).

User Account Control (UAC) A feature in Windows that can help prevent unauthorized changes to your computer.

User State Migration Tool (USMT) Software that migrates the files and settings to a removable media or to a network share and later restores the files and settings to the target computer.

V

virtual memory Technology that uses disk space for memory (RAM).

virtual private network (VPN) A network connection generated by creating secured, point-to-point connections across a private network or a public network such as the Internet. A virtual private networking client uses special TCP/IP-based protocols, called tunneling protocols, to make a virtual call to a virtual port on a virtual private networking service, and it is secured by using encryption technology to secure the communication channel.

virus A program or piece of code that is loaded onto your computer without your knowledge and runs against your wishes, often causing a wide range of problems. Viruses can also replicate themselves.

virus scanner A software that detects and removes viruses and other forms of malware.

W

Welcome Center Used to simplify the process of setting up a new computer, a software component that shows tasks you'll most likely want to complete when you set up your computer into a single location.

Wi-Fi Protected Access (WPA) A wireless encryption scheme that provides strong data encryption via Temporal Key Integrity Protocol (TKIP).

Windows activation A process that authorizes Microsoft Windows to fully function.

Windows Aero An interface used in Windows Vista that features a transparent glass design with subtle window animations, new window colors, Windows Flip 3D, and taskbar previews for your open windows.

Windows Calendar A new calendar and task application found in Windows Vista.

Windows Defender Software included with Windows Vista that detects and removes known spyware and other potentially unwanted software.

Windows Deployment Service An updated and redesigned version of Remote Installation Services (RIS) that is installed on Windows Server 2003 to be used to rapidly and remotely deploy Windows operating systems.

Windows Display Driver Model (WDM) A driver technology developed by Microsoft that channels some of the work of the device driver into portions of the code that are integrated into the operating system. These portions of code handle all of the low-level buffer management, including DMA and plug-and-play device enumeration. The WDM device driver becomes more streamlined with less code and works at greater efficiency.

Windows DVD Maker A program that provides the capability to create video DVDs based on a user's content.

Windows Easy Transfer (WET) Software that performs a side-by-side migration to migrate the settings to a new computer that is already running Windows Vista using removable media or over a network.

Windows Fax and Scan A tool found in Windows Vista that enables you to fax and scan documents.

Windows Firewall Software included with Windows Vista to protect a computer connected through a network.

Windows image A single compressed file that contains a collection of files and folders that duplicate a Windows installation on a disk volume.

Windows Internet Naming Service (WINS) A directory service used on TCP/IP networks that translates computer NetBIOS names into IP addresses.

Windows Mail A replacement for Outlook Express used to send, receive, and organize e-mail. Different from Outlook Express, Windows Mail includes a completely replaced mail store (data base/file that stores all of the individual e-mail messages) that improves stability and enables real-time search. It also includes enhanced security that includes a Phishing Filter and a Junk Mail Filter, both of which are regularly updated through Windows Update.

Windows Media Center Provides an application to view TV programs and to record and play back TV programs, DVD, video, and music and photos. As part of the Media Center controls, it includes a large-font interface that can be seen up to 10-feet away.

Windows Media Player Software that enables you to play most media files with an easy-to-use, intuitive interface.

Windows Meeting Space A program that replaces Microsoft NetMeeting that allows you share applications (or your entire desktop) with other users on the local network, or over the Internet using peer-to-peer technology.

Windows Mobility Center A new control panel that allows you to view and control the settings for mobile computers, including brightness, sound, battery level, power scheme selection, wireless network, and presentation settings.

Windows Mobility Device Center A tool used to disable USB connections and Bluetooth connections.

Windows Photo Gallery A photo and movie library management application that allows the user to import JPG files from digital cameras, tag and rate individual items, adjust colors and exposure, create and display slideshows (with pan and fade effects), and burn slideshows to DVD.

Windows Preinstallation Environment (Windows PE) A bootable tool that replaces MS-DOS as the preinstallation environment used to install, troubleshoot, and recover Windows.

Windows PXE Short for Pre-Boot Execution Environment, this technology allows a computer to boot from a server on a network instead of booting from the operating system on the local hard drive.

Windows Reliability and Performance Monitor A Microsoft Management Console (MMC) snap-in that provides tools for analyzing system performance.

Windows Setup (Setup.exe) The program that installs the Windows Vista operating system.

Windows SideShow New technology in Windows Vista that supports a secondary screen on your mobile PC. With this additional display, you can view important information whether your laptop is on, off, or in Sleep mode. For instance, you can run Windows Media Player or check e-mail.

Windows System Image Manager (Windows SIM) A tool that enables you to create answer files and network shares or to modify the files contained in a configuration set.

Windows Vista The latest workstation release of Microsoft Windows operating system that is designed for both home and business users.

Windows Vista Hardware Assessment tool An inventory, assessment, and reporting tool that finds computers on a network and determines whether they are ready to run the Windows Vista operating system. The Windows Vista Hardware Assessment solution accelerator performs three key functions: hardware inventory, compatibility analysis, and readiness reporting.

Windows Vista Startup Repair A Windows recovery tool that can fix certain problems, such as missing or damaged system files that might prevent Windows from starting correctly.

Windows Vista Upgrade Advisor Software that analyzes a computer to determine whether it will support Windows Vista.

Wireless Equivalency Protection (WEP) A basic wireless encryption scheme used to encrypt all data sent over a wireless network. It should be noted that it is easy for someone with a little knowledge or experience to break the shared key because it doesn't change automatically over time. Therefore, it is recommended you use a higher form of wireless encryption then WEP.

wireless network A network that communicates with radio or infrared signals rather than electrical or light signals sent over copper wire or fiber.

WordPad A basic word processor included in Windows.

WPA2 A wireless encryption scheme that provides strong data encryption via Advanced Encryption Standard (AES).

Index

Numbers

128-bit secure (SSL) connections, 239

A

access. *See also* security
  configuring, 110-111
  files, 165-166
  firewalls
    configuring, 215-218
    connection security rules, 221-223
    Windows Firewall with Advanced Security, 219-221
  local, domain user accounts, 189-190
  NTFS permissions, 153-156, 162
  remote, 139
    broadband connections, 141
    dial-up connections, 139-141
    virtual private networking, 141-142
  Users and Groups, 192
  Windows Updates, 71
access control entries (ACEs), 153
access control lists (ACLs), 153, 216
access points (APs), 133
accounts
  administrator, 185
  deleting, 191
  domain user, local user, 189-190
  e-mail, adding, 295
  fax, creating, 303
  groups, configuring, 184-185
  guest, 185
  modifying, 190-191

NTFS permissions, 153-156, 162
passwords, creating, 191
selecting, 189
user
configuring, 184-185
defaults, 185
local, 186-188
managing local logon, 188-193
UAC, 193-200

ACEs (access control entries), 153

ACLs (access control lists), 153, 216

activating Windows Vista, 80

Active Data Object (ADO), 241

ActiveX controls, deleting, 238

ad hoc wireless technology, 133

adapters, wireless, 133

Add User Account Wizard, 295

Add-on Manager, 239

add-ons, Internet Explorer 7.0, 236-238

adding
applications, Quick Launch toolbar, 96
desktop icons, 89
devices, Device Manager, 100-101
e-mail accounts, 295
shortcuts to desktops, 89
wireless connections, 137

addresses
NAT, 126
TCP/IP, 124. *See also* TCP/IP

Administrative Tools, 114-115

administrator accounts, 185

ADO (Active Data Object), 241

Advanced Encryption Standard. *See* AES

advanced startup options, 267-268

Advanced Television Systems Committee (ATSC), 287

adware, 208. *See also* spyware

Aero (Windows), 106-110

AES (Advanced Encryption Standard), 56, 134

aligning desktop icons, 90

answers
exam layout and design, 29-42
files, 66
Practice Exam 1, 353-363
Practice Exam 2, 379-390

antiphishing filters, 56

antispyware, Windows Defender, 56

antivirus programs
spyware, 208-209
Windows Defender, 209-215

anxiety, dealing with test, 27-28

applications
accessibility, configuring, 110-111
exceptions, configuring as, 218
notification area, 96
parental control, configuring, 112-113
productivity, 294
Notepad, configuring, 294
Sidebar, 309-310
Windows Calendar, 300-303
Windows Fax and Scan, 303-307
Windows Mail, 294-300
Windows Meeting Space, 307-309
Windows WordPad, configuring, 294
Search box, 93-94
Windows Media Center, 286-288
Windows Media Player, 282
codecs, 284
regions, 285-286
security, 282-283
Windows Vista, 51-53

applying Windows Mail, 295-296
appointments (calendars), creating, 302-303
APs (access point), 133
architecture, UMA, 108
ASCII characters, 56
assigning user accounts, 184
atomic transaction operations, 53
ATSC (Advanced Television Systems Committee), 287
attaching files to e-mail, 296
audio
- codecs, 284
- controls, 50
- descriptions, starting, 106
- Windows Media Center, 286-288

authentication
- exemptions, 222
- user account passwords, 188

auto-tuning network stack, 55
AutoComplete settings, 235
automatic scanning, Windows Defender, 211-212

B

Backup and Restore Center, 50
balanced power plans, 321
batteries
- meters, 323-324
- status, mobile computers, 318

BDD 2007 (Business Desktop Deployment Solution Accelerator 2007), 65-67
behavior, modifying UAC messages, 199
BitLocker Drive Encryption, 56, 166, 170-174
Blocked Senders list, 299
blocking privileges, Windows Defender, 213
Bluetooth connections, 328-329
booting
- advanced startup options, 267-268
- dual, 79
- multiboot configurations, 152
- Startup Repair tool, 269
- Windows Defender, 212

brightness, configuring mobile computers, 318
broadband connections, 141
browsing history, configuring, 234
Business Desktop Deployment Solution Accelerator 2007. *See* BDD 2007

C

cable connections, 141
caching, 54, 328
calendars, 52
candidate background and experience, 16-17
catalogs, 67
Category view, 97
CD-ROM
- installing, 392-393
- test modes
  - certification mode, 391
  - custom mode, 392
  - study mode, 391

cell phones, 318
certificates, 169. *See also* EFS
certification
- mode (CD-ROM), 391
- self-assessment, 15, 17
  - candidate background and experience, 16-17
  - dealing with test anxiety, 27-28

educational background, 17-18
exam preparation, 21-22, 25-27
hands-on experience, 18-20
Microsoft certification in real world situations, 15
studying for exams, 22-23
testing for exam readiness, 24-25

characters, ASCII, 56
Check Disk, running, 258-259
Chess Titans, 52
Classic view, 98
clean installation, 65-70
co-owner permissions, 162
codecs, Windows Media Player, 284
colors, modifying, 105
commands
ipconfig, 131-132
nslookup, 131-132
ping, 131
tracert, 131-132

communities, Microsoft SpyNet, 210
compatibility, 197
components, Windows Vista, 48
application enhancements, 51-53
core technologies, 53-55
end-user features, 48-51
security enhancements, 55-56

compression
codecs, 284
NTFS, 174-175

Computer folder, 95
Computer Management Console, 192
Computer Management tool, 114
configuring
accessibility, 110-111
advanced startup options, 267-268
display settings, 102-106
Event Viewer, 269
firewalls, 215-218
connection security rules, 221-223
Windows Firewall with Advanced Security, 219-221
groups, 184-185
Internet Explorer 7.0, 233-236
content zones, 240-241
cookies/privacy, 239-240
Dynamic Security, 242-246
resetting default settings, 247
RSS feeds, 246-247
IP, 128-130
mobile computers
battery meter, 323-324
Control Panel, Windows Mobility Center, 318-320
file and data synchronization, 325-329
power management, 320-322
presentations, 329-331
shutdown options, 323-324
Tablet PCs, 332-333
Windows SlideShow, 331-332
multiboot configurations, 152
NTFS permissions, 155
parental control, 112-113
passwords, 191
permissions, 163
Problems Reports and Solutions tool, 270
productivity applications, 294
Notepad, 294
Windows Calendar, 300-303
Windows Fax and Scan, 303-307
Windows Mail, 294-300
Windows Meeting Space, 307-309

Windows Sidebar, 309-310
Windows WordPad, 294
refresh rates, 104
Startup Repair tool, 269
System Configuration tool, 266-267
System Restore, 271
Themes, Windows Aero, 108
user accounts, 184-185
defaults, 185
local, 186-188
managing local login accounts, 188-193
UAC, 193-200
virtual memory, 262
Windows Defender, 211
Windows Media Center, 286-288
Windows Media Player, 282
codecs, 284
regions, 285-286
security, 282-283
wireless connections, 135-138

Connect To folder, 95

connections
connection-specific rules, 216
mobile devices, 328-329
NTFS, sharing files and folders, 156-157
remote, 273
remote access, 139
broadband connections, 141
dial-up connections, 139-141
virtual private networking, 141-142
TCP/IP, 124
configuring IP, 128-130
IPv4 TCP/IP addressing, 124-126
IPv6 TCP/IP addressing, 126-127
name resolution, 127-128
troubleshooting, 131-132
Windows Firewall, 220-223
wireless, 133
adapters, 133
configuring, 135-138
mobile computers, 318
security, 134-135

Connectix Corporation, 20

content zones, Internet Explorer 7.0, 240-241

contrast, modifying, 105

contributor permissions, 162

Control Panel, 95-97
Administrative Tools, 114-115
BitLocker, 174
Personalize Appearance and Sounds, 103
Windows Firewall, enabling/disabling, 217
Windows Mobility Center, 318-320

controlling UAC, 197-200

controls, audio, 50

cookies
deleting, 232
Internet Explorer 7.0, 239-240

core technologies, Windows Vista, 53-55

credentials, UAC, 200

credit cards, spyware, 208

cryptographic extensions, 56

CTEC (Microsoft Certified Training and Education Center), 20

custom mode (CD-ROM), 392

Custom Scan (Windows Defender), 211

customizing
authentication, 223
e-mail, filtering, 298

offline files, 327
presentation settings, 330
shutdown, 323-324
Windows Mobility Center, 318-320

D

Data Collector Set (DCS), 254
Data Sources (ODBC) tool, 114
data synchronization, 325-326
connections, 328-329
offline folders, 326-327
DCS (Data Collector Set), 254
dealing with test anxiety, 27-28
decoders (codecs), 284
decompression, codecs, 284
Default Programs folder, 95
default settings, resetting Internet Explorer 7.0, 247
default user accounts, 185
Defender (Windows), 209-215
deleting
accounts, 191
ActiveX controls, 238
desktop icons, 89-90
permissions, 154
Deny permission, 155
deploying
Windows Deployment Services, 54
Windows Vista, WDS, 65-67
desktops, 88
display settings, 102-106
icons, managing, 89-91
Remote Desktop, 271-273
taskbars, 91
Windows Aero, 106-110
Windows Sidebar, 91
detecting
phishing websites, 299
spyware, 208-209
Windows Defender, 209-215
Device Manager, 100-101
devices
drivers
Device Manager, 100-101
managing, 99
plug-and-play, 100
signed, 100
mobile computers. *See* mobile computers
USB, 133
DHCP (Dynamic Host Configuration Protocol), 125
diagnostic tools, 264
advanced startup options, 267-268
Event Viewer, 269
Memory Diagnostic, 264-265
Network Diagnostic, 265
Problems Reports and Solutions tool, 270
Startup Repair tool, 269
System Configuration, 266-267
System Restore, 271
dial-up connections, 139-141
dialog boxes
Display Settings, 104
New Scan, 304
Properties, 155
User Accounts, 190
Wireless Network Connection Status, 135
Digital Cable Tuner, 288
digital signatures, 239
Digital Subscriber Line (DSL) connections, 141

Digital Video Broadcasting Terrestrial television (DVB-T), 287

directories, NTFS permissions, 153-162

disabling
- add-ons, 237-238
- BitLocker Drive Encryption, 173-174
- devices, 101
- UAC, 197-200, 213
- Windows Defender, 214
- Windows Firewall, 216

Disk Defragmenter, 259-260

Diskpart, 67

disks
- optimizing, 258
  - defragging hard drives, 259-260
  - running Check Disk, 258-259
- ReadyBoost/ReadyDrive, 262-264

display settings, 102-103
- screen resolution, modifying, 103-106

Display Settings dialog box, 104

DNS (Domain Name System), 127

documents
- Notepad, configuring, 294
- scanning, 304. *See also* scanning
- Search box, 93-94
- Windows WordPad, configuring, 294

Documents folder, 94

Domain Name System. *See* DNS

domain user accounts, 185
- local access, 189-190

Driver Rollback, 102

drivers
- devices
  - Device Manager, 100-101
  - managing, 99
  - plug-and-play, 100
  - signed, 100
- troubleshooting, 270

drives, mapping network, 165-166

DSL (Digital Subscriber Line) connection, 141

dual booting, 79

DVB-T (Digital Video Broadcasting Terrestrial television), 287

DVDs
- player regions, 285-286. *See also* Windows Media Player
- Windows DVD Maker, 52

DVR-MS files (Microsoft Digital Video Recording), 285

Dynamic Host Configuration Protocol. *See* DHCP

E

e-mail
- documents, sending scanned, 305
- forwarding, 304
- spyware, 208
- Windows Mail, 52
  - applying, 295-296
  - configuring, 294-297
  - filtering, 297-298
  - Phishing Filter, 299
  - security, 300

EAP (Extensible Authentication Protocol), 135

Ease of Access Center, 110

ECC (Elliptic Curve Cryptography), 56

editing appointments, 302

educational background, self-assessment, 17-18

EFS (Encrypting File System), 166-170

Elliptic Curve Cryptography. *See* ECC

enabling
BitLocker Drive Encryption, 173-174
devices, 101
standard file sharing, 161-163
UAC, 197-200
Windows Defender, 214
Windows Firewall, 216
encoders (codecs), 284
Encrypting File System. *See* EFS
encryption, 134, 166. *See also* security
AES, 134
BitLocker Drive Encryption, 56, 170-174
EFS, 167-170
IPSec, 141
MPPE, 141
end user license agreement. *See* EULA
end-user features, Windows Vista, 48-51
energy. *See* power management
error-reporting, 54
EULA (end user license agreement), 208
Event Viewer, 114, 269
exams
dealing with test anxiety, 27-28
layout and design, 29-42
MeasureUp, 392-394
Practice Exam 1, 339
answers, 353-363
questions, 340-352
Practice Exam 2
answers, 379-390
questions, 365-378
preparing for, 21-27
resources, 45-46
strategies, 42-44
studying for, 22-23
test-taking strategies, 44-45
testing for readiness, 24-25
exceptions, configuring firewalls, 218
explicit permissions, 155
Export Wizard, 169
Extensible Authentication Protocol. *See* EAP
Extensible Markup Language. *See* XML
external display settings, mobile computers, 319

F

FAT (File Allocation Table), 152
Favorites Center, 232
Fax Setup Wizard, 303
faxing, 303-307
feeds
RSS, 246-247
subscribing, 232
File Allocation Table (FAT), 152
File Sharing Wizard, 163
file systems, NTFS, 152-153
accessing folders, 165-166
BitLocker Drive Encryption, 170-174
compression, 174-175
EFS, 167-170
encryption, 166
navigating, 157-159
permissions, 153-162
Public folders, 160-161
sharing files and folders, 156-157
standard file sharing, 161-163
files
answer, 66
e-mail, attaching, 296
paging, 260-262
Search box, 93-94

synchronization, 325-326
connections, 328-329
offline folders, 326-327
WIM, 54, 67

filters
antiphishing, 56
e-mail, 297-298
Phishing Filter, 299

firewalls. *See also* security
configuring, 215-218
connection security rules, 221-223
Windows Firewall, 56
Windows Firewall with Advanced Security, 115, 219-221

flash memory, 54

flicks, 332

folders
Administrative Tools, 114-115
compression, 174-175
Computer, 95
Connect To, 95
Control Panel, 95
Default Programs, 95
Documents, 94
encryption, 166
BitLocker Drive Encryption, 170-174
EFS, 167-170
Games, 94
Help and Support, 95
Music, 94
Network, 95
NTFS permissions, 154
offline file and data synchronization, 326-327
personal, 94
Picture, 94
Public, 160-161
Recent Items, 95
search, 95
sharing, 156-157, 165-166

fonts, new features, 50

formatting
calendars, 301-303
passwords, 191

forms, deleting, 232

forwarding e-mail, 304

FQDNs (fully qualified domain names), 127

fragmentation, running Disk Defragmenter, 259-260

Full Scan (Windows Defender), 211

fully qualified domain names. *See* FQDNs

G

gadgets, 49

games, 52

Games folder, 94

Group Policy settings, 54

groups
calendars, creating, 301-303
configuring, 184-185
NTFS permissions, 153-162

guest accounts, 185

H

hands-on experience, self-assessment, 18-20

Handwriting Recognition Personalization Tool, 332

hardware
Device Manager, 100-101
Windows Vista installation requirements, 64

help, 394

Help and Support folder, 95

Hibernation mode, 323
hiding desktop icons, 90
high performance power plans, 321
history, configuring, 234
hosts, 124
Hybrid Sleep, 323

I

ICS (iCalendar format), 303
IEEE (Institute of Electrical and Electronics Engineers), 133
images
- scanning, 304
- Search box, 93-94
- Windows Photo Gallery, 52

ImageX, 67
in-place upgrade installations, 65
inbound rules, 216
- Windows Firewall with Advanced Security, 219

information bar messages, 244
infrastructure, wireless adapters, 133
inherited permissions, 155
installing
- CD-ROM, 392-393
- devices, 100-101
- user accounts, 185
- Windows Vista
  - clean installation, 68-70
  - methods, 65
  - migrating user settings to, 76
  - restoring previous versions, 78-79
  - system requirements, 64-65
  - troubleshooting, 79-80
  - upgrading between Windows Vista editions, 77-78
  - upgrading from previous versions, 72-77
  - Windows Updates, 71-72

Instant Search box, 232
Institute of Electrical and Electronics Engineers (IEEE), 133
interfaces
- desktops, 88
  - managing icons, 89-91
  - taskbars, 91
  - Windows Sidebar, 91
- display settings, 102-106
- Internet Explorer 7.0
  - add-ons, 236-238
  - configuring, 233-236
  - content zones, 240-241
  - cookies, 239-240
  - Dynamic Security, 242-246
  - new features, 232-233
  - plug-ins, 236-238
  - reconfiguring, 247
  - RSS feeds, 246-247
  - scripting languages, 236-238
  - security, 238-239
- MUI, 54
- Sync Center, 325-326
  - mobile device connections, 328-329
  - offline folders, 326-327
- Windows Aero, 106-110
- Windows Vista, 48

Internet Explorer 7.0
- add-ons, 236-238
- configuring, 233-236
- new features, 232-233
- plug-ins, 236-238
- reconfiguring, 247
- RSS feeds, 246-247

scripting languages, 236-238
security, 238-239
content zones, 240-241
cookies, 239-240
Dynamic Security, 242-246
Internet, publishing calendars, 303
Internet service provider (ISP), 139
Internet zone, 240
IP (Internet Protocol), configuring, 128-130
IP security (IPSec), 141
ipconfig command, 131-132
IPSec (IP security), 141
IPv4 (Internet Protocol version 4), TCP/IP addressing, 124-126
IPv6 (Internet Protocol version 6), 53, 126-127
iSCSI Initiator, 114
isolation, 222
ISP (Internet service provider), 139

J-K-L

junk e-mail, filtering, 297-298

Kernel Transaction Manager, 53

L2TP (Layer 2 Tunneling Protocol), 141
laptops, 318. *See also* mobile computers
Layer 2 Tunneling Protocol (L2TP), 141
levels, modifying security, 241
licenses, EULA, 208
Link Layer Topology Discovery. *See* LLDT
links, right pane, 94-95
lists
Blocked Senders, 299
Safe Senders, 299
LLDT (Link Layer Topology Discovery), 157-159
local intranet zone, 240
local logon accounts, 188-193
Local Security Policy, 114
local user accounts, 184-188
deleting, 191
Local Users and Groups console, 185
logons
configuring user account security, 184
managing, 188-193

M

Magnifier, starting, 106
Mahjong Titans, 52
Mail. *See* Windows Mail
malware, 56. *See also* security
managing
desktop icons, 89-91
device drivers, 99
Device Manager, 100-101
plug-and-play, 100
signed, 100
Favorites Center, 232
local logon accounts, 188-193
memory, 260-262
network services, 157-159
NTFS permissions, 156
power
battery meter, 323-324
mobile computers, 320-322
shutdown options, 323-324
user accounts, 185
Windows Calendar, 300-303
Windows Sidebar, 309-310
mapping network drives, 165-166

MeasureUp practice tests, 392
shortcuts, creating, 394
media applications
Windows Media Center, 286-288
Windows Media Player, 282
codecs, 284
regions, 285-286
security, 282-283
Meeting Space, 307-309
meetings, Windows Meeting Space, 52
memory, 54
managing, 260-262
UMA, 108
virtual, configuring, 262
Memory Diagnostics Tool, 114, 264-265
menus, Start, 91-93
right pane, 94-95
Search box, 93-94
Windows Vista, 49
messages
e-mail. *See also* e-mail
creating, 296
moving, 299
information bar, 244
UAC, modifying, 199
methods, Windows Vista installation, 65
clean, 68-70
migrating user settings to, 76
restoring previous versions, 78-79
troubleshooting, 79-80
upgrading
from previous versions, 72-77
between Windows Vista editions, 77-78
Windows Updates, 71-72
Microsoft certifications, 15. *See also* certification
Microsoft Certified Training and Education Center (CTEC), 20
Microsoft Digital Video Recording (DVR-MS) files, 285
Microsoft Management Console. *See* MMC
Microsoft Point-to-Point Encryption (MPPE), 141
Microsoft Speech Recognition, 52
Microsoft SpyNet community, 210
Microsoft testing formats, 40-42
Microsoft Windows Preinstallation Environment. *See* Windows PE
migration
troubleshooting, 77
Windows Vista
from previous versions, 72-74
user settings to, 76
Windows Vista installations, 65
MMC (Microsoft Management Console), 114
mobile computers
Control Panel, Windows Mobility Center, 318-320
file and data synchronization, 325-326
connections, 328-329
offline folders, 326-327
power management, 320
battery meter, 323-324
power plans, 320-322
shutdown options, 323-324
presentations, 329-331
Tablet PCs, 332-333
types of, 318
Windows SlideShow, 331-332
mobile phones, 318
modifying
accounts, 190-191
passwords, 191

permissions, 154
screen resolution, 103-106
security levels, 241
UAC messages, 199

monitoring
battery meters, 323-324
firewalls
configuring, 215-218
connection security rules, 221-223
Windows Firewall with Advanced Security, 219-221
Windows Defender, 210-215
Windows Reliability and Performance Monitor, 254-258

movies, Windows Media Center, 286-288

moving
desktop icons, 90
e-mail messages, 299

MPEG (Moving Pictures Experts Group), 285

MPEG-2 (Moving Picture Experts Group-2), 287

MPPE (Microsoft Point-to-Point Encryption), 141

MUI (Multilingual User Interface), 54

multiboot configurations, 152

Multilingual User Interface (MUI), 54

multiple TV tuner hardware devices, 288

Music folder, 94

N

names
FQDNs, 127
NetBIOS, 128
resolution, 127-128
UNC, 157
WINS, 128

Narrator, starting, 106

NAT (Network Address Translation), 126

National Television Standards Committee (NTSC), 287

navigating
Control Panel, 97
desktops, 88
managing icons, 89-91
taskbars, 91
Windows Sidebar, 91
Internet Explorer 7.0
add-ons, 236-238
configuring, 233-236
content zones, 240-241
cookies, 239-240
Dynamic Security, 242-246
new features, 232-233
plug-ins, 236-238
reconfiguring, 247
RSS feeds, 246-247
scripting languages, 236-238
security, 238-239
NTFS, 157-159
Start menu, 91-93
right pane, 94-95
Search box, 93-94
taskbars, 95
notification area, 96
Quick Launch toolbar, 96
Welcome Center, 98-99

NetBIOS (network basic input/output system), 128, 156

.NET Framework 3.0, 55

NetMeeting. *See* Meeting Space

Network Address Translation. *See* NAT

Network and Sharing Center, 157-159

network basic input/output system. *See* NetBIOS

Network Diagnostic tool, 265

Network folder, 95
network interface cards. *See* NICs
networks
NTFS, 152
accessing folders, 165-166
BitLocker Drive Encryption, 170-174
compression, 174-175
EFS, 167-170
encryption, 166
file systems, 152-153
navigating, 157-159
permissions, 153-162
Public folders, 160-161
sharing files and folders, 156-157
standard file sharing, 161-163
remote access, 139
broadband connections, 141
dial-up connections, 139-141
virtual private networking, 141-142
security
connection security rules, 221-223
firewall settings, 215-218
spyware, 208-215
Windows Firewall with Advanced Security, 219-221
TCP/IP, 124
configuring IP, 128-130
IPv4 TCP/IP addressing, 124-126
IPv6 TCP/IP addressing, 126-127
name resolution, 127-128
troubleshooting, 131-132
wireless connections, 133
adapters, 133
configuring, 135-138
security, 134-135
New Authentication Rule Wizard, 222
New Connection Security Rule Wizard, 222
new features
Internet Explorer 7.0, 232-233
Windows Vista, 48
application enhancements, 51-53
core technologies, 53-55
end-user features, 48-51
security enhancements, 55-56
New Scan dialog box, 304
NICs (network interface cards), 67
notebook computers, 318. *See also* mobile computers
Notepad, configuring, 294
Notification, 239
notification area, 96
nslookup command, 131-132
NTFS (NT File System), 152
files, 152-153
accessing, 165-166
BitLocker Drive Encryption, 170-174
compression, 174-175
EFS, 167-170
encryption, 166
sharing, 156-157
navigating, 157-159
permissions, 153-162
Public folders, 160-161
standard file sharing, 161-163
NTSC (National Television Standards Committee), 287

O

ODBC (Open Database Connectivity), 114
offline folders, 326-327

Open Database Connectivity. *See* ODBC
opening
Favorites Center, 232
ports in Windows Firewall, 218
Windows Mobility Center, 320
operating systems
dual booting, 79
Windows Vista
application enhancements, 51-53
core technologies, 53-55
end-user features, 48-51
features of, 48
security enhancements, 55-56
Windows Vista, 57-58, 65. *See also* Windows Vista
optimizing
applications, new features, 51-53
disks, 258
defragging hard drives, 259-260
running Check Disk, 258-259
performance, ReadyBoost/ReadyDrive, 262-264
security, 55-56
Windows Reliability and Performance Monitor, 254-258
options, Internet Explorer 7.0, 234
outbound rules, 216, 219
owner permissions, 162

P

packets, 124
paging files, 260-262
PAL (Phase Alternating Line), 287
parental controls, 50
configuring, 112-113
partnerships, creating sync, 329
passwords. *See also* security
creating, 191
deleting, 232
spyware, 208
user accounts, 188
PCI (Peripheral Component Interconnect) cards, 133
PDAs (personal digital assistants), 318
PDF (Portable Document Format), 236
performance
ReadyBoost/ReadyDrive, 262-264
System Performance Assessment, 51
Windows Reliability and Performance Monitor, 254-258
Peripheral Component Interconnect. *See* PCI
permissions
configuring, 163
NTFS, 153-162
UAC, 194
user accounts, 188
personal digital assistants. *See* PDAs
personal folders, 94
Personalize Appearance and Sounds (Control Panel), 103
Phase Alternating Line (PAL), 287
phishing, 56
Phishing Filter, 238, 299
phones, mobile, 318
physical memory, 260
Memory Diagnostic tool, 264-265
Pictures folder, 94
pictures, Windows Media Center, 286-288
ping command, 131
plans, power, 320-322
plug-and-play devices, managing, 100
plug-ins, Internet Explorer 7.0, 236-238
Point-to-Point Tunneling Protocol (PPTP), 141
policies, UAC, 198-199

Pop-up Blocker, 238

Portable Document Format. *See* PDF

portable media players, 318

ports, opening in Windows Firewall, 218

power management, mobile computers, 320

- battery meters, 323-324
- power plans, 320-322
- shutdown options, 323-324

power save power plans, 321

PPTP (Point-to-Point Tunneling Protocol), 141

Practice Exam 1, 339

- answers, 353-363
- questions, 340-352

Practice Exam 2

- answers, 379-390
- questions, 365-378

practice exams, MeasureUp, 392-394

Pre-boot Execution Environment (PXE), 67

preinstallation, Windows PE, 67

preparing for exams, 21-27

presentation settings, mobile computers, 319

presentations on mobile computers, 329-331

previous versions, 50

- migrating user settings to, 76
- Windows Vista
  - restoring, 78-79
  - upgrading, 72-77

Print Management tool, 114

printing

- calendars, 303
- web pages, 232

privacy, Internet Explorer 7.0, 239-240

privileges

- UAC, 55
- Windows Defender, 213

problem reports and solutions, 50

Problems Reports and Solutions tool, 270

processes, rogue, 55

productivity applications, 294

- Notepad, configuring, 294
- Windows Calendar, 300-303
- Windows Fax and Scan, 303-307
- Windows Mail
  - applying, 295-296
  - configuring, 294-297
  - filtering, 297-298
  - Phishing Filter, 299
  - security, 300
- Windows Meeting Space, 307-309
- Windows Sidebar, 309-310
- Windows WordPad, configuring, 294

program compatibility, 197

Program Compatibility Wizard, 197

projectors, 54

Properties dialog box, 155

Protected mode, 238

protected mode, Internet Explorer 7.0, 242-246

protocols

- DHCP, 125
- EAP, 135
- L2TP, 141
- PPTP, 141
- TCP/IP, 124
  - configuring IP, 128-130
  - IPv4 TCP/IP addressing, 124-126
  - IPv6 TCP/IP addressing, 126-127

name resolution, 127-128
troubleshooting, 131-132
TKIP, 134
tunneling, 141
Public folders, 160-161
publishing calendars, 303
Purble Place, 52
PXE (Pre-boot Execution Environment), 67

Q-R

QoS (quality of service), 157
qualifications, candidate background and experience, 16-17
quality of service. *See* QoS
questions
exam layout and design, 29-42
Practice Exam 1, 340-352
Practice Exam 2, 365-378
Quick Launch toolbar, 96
Quick Scan (Windows Defender), 211

RAM (random access memory), 260
RDF Site Summary (RSS), 51, 246-247
RDS (Remote Data Services), 241
reader permissions, 162
readiness, testing for exam, 24-25
ReadyBoost, 54, 262-264
ReadyDrive, 54, 262-264
real-time protection
enabling, 214
Windows Defender, 209
receiving faxes, 306
Recent Items folder, 95
reenabling add-ons, 238
refresh rates, configuring, 104
regions, Windows Media Player, 285-286
Reliability and Performance Monitor, 114
remote access, 139, 273
broadband connections, 141
dial-up connections, 139-141
virtual private networking, 141-142
Remote Assistance, 271, 273
Remote Data Services (RDS), 241
Remote Desktop, 271, 273
reports, problem reports and solutions, 50
requirements, BitLocker Drive Encryption, 172-173
resolution
modifying screen, 103-106
names, 127-128
Resource Kits, 20
resources, exams, 45-46
restoring
Backup and Restore Center, 50
drivers to previous versions, 270
previous versions of Windows, 78-79
System Restore, 271
restricted sites zone, 240
right pane, 94-95
rights, user accounts, 188
rogue processes, 55
rolling back drivers, 102
RSS (RDF Site Summary), 51, 246-247
rules
connection security, 221-223
firewalls, 216

S

Safe Senders list, 299
saved passwords, deleting, 232
saving faxes, 306

scanning, 303-307
Windows Defender, 210-212
schedules, Windows Calendar, 300-303
screens. *See also* interfaces
resolution, modifying, 103-106
rotation setting, mobile computers, 319
scripting languages, Internet Explorer 7.0, 236-238
Search box, 93-94
Search folder, 95
searching
appoints, 303
Windows Search, 49
SECAM (Sequential Color with Memory), 287
Secure Sockets Layer. *See* SSL
security
encryption, 166
BitLocker Drive Encryption, 170-174
EFS, 167-170
firewalls
configuring, 215-218
connection security rules, 221-223
Windows Firewall with Advanced Security, 219-221
groups/user accounts
configuring, 184-185
defaults, 185
local, 186-188
managing local logon accounts, 188-193
UAC, 193-200
Internet Explorer 7.0, 238-239
content zones, 240-241
cookies, 239-240
Dynamic Security, 242-246
passwords, creating, 191
spyware, 208-215
Windows Firewall with Advanced Security, 115
Windows Mail, 300
Windows Media Player, 282-283
Windows Vista enhancements, 55-56
wireless, 134-135
security identifiers. *See* SIDs
selecting accounts, 189
self-assessment, 15,
candidate background and experience, 16-17
educational background, 17-18
exam preparation, 21-27
dealing with test anxiety, 27-28
studying for, 22-23
testing readiness, 24-25
hands-on experience, 18-20
Microsoft certification in real world situations, 15
Sequential Color with Memory (SECAM), 287
server message block (SMB), 156
servers
DHCP, 125
DNS, 127
server to server authentication, 222
service set identifier (SSID), 136
services, managing networks, 157-159
Services tool, 114
Setup.exe, 67
shader support, 53
sharing
files, 156-157
accessing, 165-166
BitLocker Drive Encryption, 170-174
EFS, 167-170
encryption, 166
Network and Sharing Center, 157-159

Public folders, 160-161
standard file, 161-163
shortcuts
desktops, adding, 89
MeasureUp practice tests, creating, 394
shutdown options, 323-324
Sidebar (Windows), 91, 309-310
SIDs (security identifiers), 67, 188
signed devices, managing, 100
Sleep mode, 323
preventing from going to, 331
SlideShow, 331-332
SMB (server message block), 156
Software Explorer, Windows Defender, 212
Speech Recognition, 52
SpyNet community (Microsoft), 210
spyware, 208
Windows Defender, 209-215
SRT (Startup Repair Tool), 54, 79, 269
SSID (service set identifier), 136
SSL (Secure Sockets Layer), 56
standard file sharing, 161-163
standards, wireless, 133
Start menu, 91-93
right pane, 94-95
Search box, 93-94
Windows Vista, 49
starting
advanced startup options, 267-268
Narrator, 106
Quick Launch toolbar, 96
Remote Assistance, 273
Remote Desktop, 273
Startup Repair tool, 269
Windows Defender, 212
Windows Reliability and Performance Monitor, 255
Windows Vista, 80
Startup Repair Tool (SRT), 54, 79, 269
status
notification area, 96
Wireless Network Connection Status dialog box, 135
strategies
exam, 42-44
test-taking, 44-45
study mode (CD-ROM), 391
studying for exams, 22-23
subnet masks, 125
SuperFetch, 54
Sync Center
configuring, 325-326
mobile computers, 319
mobile device connections, 328-329
offline folders, 326-327
synchronization, 325
connections, 328-329
offline folders, 326-327
Sysprep, 67
System Configuration tool, 114, 266-267
System Performance Assessment, 51
System Recovery, 79-80
system requirements
BitLocker Drive Encryption, 172-173
CD-ROM installations, 392
Windows Vista installation, 64-65
System Restore, 271

T

Tablet PCs, 332-333. *See also* mobile computers
task panes, Windows Vista, 49
Task Scheduler, 115
taskbars, 91
- navigating, 95
- notification area, 96
- Quick Launch toolbar, 96

TCP/IP (Transmission Control Protocol/Internet Protocol), 124
- IP, configuring, 128-130
- IPv4 TCP/IP addressing, 124-126
- IPv6 TCP/IP addressing, 126-127
- name resolution, 127-128
- troubleshooting, 131-132

technical support, 394
television, Windows Media Center, 52
Temporal Key Integrity Protocol (TKIP), 134
temporary files, deleting, 232
test modes (CD-ROM)
- certification mode, 391
- custom mode, 392
- study mode, 391

tests. *See* exams
text
- Narrator, starting, 106
- Notepad, configuring, 294
- Windows WordPad, configuring, 294

themes
- modifying, 105
- Windows Aero, 108

TKIP (Temporal Key Integrity Protocol), 134
TLS (Transport Layer Security), 56
toolbars, Quick Launch, 96
tools
- Administrative Tools, 114-115
- BDD 2007, 66
- Check Disk, running, 258-259
- Computer Management, 114
- Data Sources (ODBC), 114
- diagnostic, 264
  - advanced startup options, 267-268
  - Event Viewer, 269
  - Memory Diagnostic, 264-265
  - Network Diagnostic, 265
  - Problems Reports and Solutions tool, 270
  - Startup Repair tool, 269
  - System Configuration, 266-267
  - System Restore, 271
- Disk Defragmenter, running, 259-260
- Event Viewer, 114
- Handwriting Recognition Personalization Tool, 332
- iSCSI Initiator, 114
- Local Security Policy, 114
- Memory Diagnostics Tool, 114
- Print Management, 114
- Reliability and Performance Monitor, 114
- Remote Assistance, 271-273
- Remote Desktop, 271-273
- Services, 114
- SRT, 54
- System Configuration, 114
- Task Scheduler, 115
- TCP/IP, 131-132
- Windows Defender, 209-215
- Windows Firewall with Advanced Security, 115
- Windows Reliability and Performance Monitor, 254-258

TPM (Trusted Platform Module), 170-172

tracert command, 131-132

transactions, 53

Transmission Control Protocol/Internet Protocol. *See* TCP/IP

Transport Layer Security. *See* TLS

troubleshooting

Backup and Restore Center, 50
Check Disk, running, 258-259
clean installations, 70
devices, 102
diagnostic tools, 264
advanced startup options, 267-268
Event Viewer, 269
Memory Diagnostic, 264-265
Network Diagnostic, 265
Problems Reports and Solutions tool, 270
Startup Repair tool, 269
System Configuration, 266-267
System Restore, 271
drivers, 270
installations, 77-80
memory, 260-262
Memory Diagnostics Tool, 114
Remote Assistance, 271-274
Remote Desktop, 271-273
spyware, 208-215
SRT, 54
System Performance Assessment, 51
TCP/IP, 131-132
Windows Reliability and Performance Monitor, 254-258
Windows Updates, 71-72

Trusted Platform Module. *See* TPM

trusted sites zone, 240

tunneling

authentication, 222
protocols, 141

types

of memory, 260
of mobile computers, 318
of user accounts, 184-185

U

UAC (User Account Control), 55, 193-196, 213

controlling, 197-200
program compatibility, 197

Ultra-Mobile computers, 318. *See also* mobile computers

UMA (Unified Memory Architecture), 108

UNC (Uniform Naming Convention), 157

uncompressing files and folders, 175

Unified Memory Architecture (UMA), 108

Uniform Naming Convention (UNC), 157

uninstalling devices, 101

universal serial bus. *See* USB

updating

devices, 102
Windows Updates, 71-72

Upgrade Advisor (Windows Vista), 73-74

upgrading

in-place upgrade installations, 65
troubleshooting, 77

USB (universal serial bus), 133, 286

connections, 328-329

User Account Control. *See* UAC

user accounts

configuring, 184-185
defaults, configuring, 185

deleting, 191
local, configuring, 186-188
local logon accounts, managing, 188-193
passwords, creating, 191
UAC, 193-196
controlling, 197-200
program compatibility, 197
user settings, migrating, 76
User State Migration Tool V3.0 (USMT), 76
Users Account dialog box, 190
Users and Groups, accessing, 192
USMT (User State Migration Tool V3.0), 76

V

versions
drives, restoring to previous, 270
Previous Versions, 50
Windows Vista, 57-58
application enhancements, 51-53
core technologies, 53-55
end-user features, 48-51
features of, 48
migrating user settings to, 76
restoring previous versions, 78-79
security enhancements, 55-56
upgrading between Windows Vista editions, 77-78
upgrading from previous, 72-77
video
codecs, 284
Windows Media Center, 286-288
viewing
add-ons, 237
calendars, 301-303
desktop icons, 90
Event viewer, 114, 269
permissions, 154
views
Category, 97
Classic, 98
virtual memory, 260-262
Virtual PC, 20
virtual private networking, remote access, 141-142
Vista. *See* Windows Vista
VMware, 20
volume, mobile computers, 318

W

WDDM (Windows Vista Display Driver Model), 53
WDS (Windows Deployment Services), 65-67
web pages
history, deleting, 232
printing, 232
RSS feeds, 246-247
Zoom feature, 233
websites, detecting phishing, 299
Welcome Center, 98-99
WEP (Wireless Equivalency Protection), 134
WET (Windows Easy Transfer), 76
Wi-Fi Protected Access (WPA), 134
WiFi connections, 328-329
WIM (Windows IMage) files, 54, 67
window frame transparency, turning on, 105
Window Mobility Center, 318-320
Windows Aero, 106-110
Windows Calendar, 52, 300-303
Windows Defender, 209-215. *See also* security

Windows Deployment Services. *See* WDS

Windows DVD Maker, 52

Windows Easy Transfer (WET), 76

Windows Explorer, configuring permissions, 163

Windows Fax and Scan, 303-307

Windows Firewall, 56

Windows Firewall with Advanced Security, 115, 219-221

Windows IMage. *See* WIM files

Windows Internet Name Service. *See* WINS

Windows Mail, 52

- applying, 295-296
- configuring, 294-297
- filtering, 297-298
- Phishing Filter, 299
- security, 300

Windows Media Center, 52, 286-288

Windows Media Player, 282

- codecs, 284
- regions, 285-286
- security, 282-284

Windows Meeting Space, 52, 307-309

Windows Mobile devices, 318

Windows Mobility Center, 50

Windows PE (Microsoft Windows Preinstallation Environment), 67

Windows Photo Gallery, 52

Windows Reliability and Performance Monitor, 254-258

Windows Search, 49

Windows Setup (Setup.exe), 67

Windows Sidebar, 49, 91, 309-310

Windows SlideShow, 331-332

Windows System Image Manager (Windows SIM), 66

Windows Touch Technology, 332

Windows Update, 50, 71-72

Windows Vista, 48

- activating, 80
- deployment, WDS, 65-67
- dual booting, 79
- features of, 48
  - application enhancements, 51-53
  - core technologies, 53-55
  - end-user features, 48-51
  - security enhancements, 55-56
- installation
  - clean, 68-70
  - methods, 65
  - migrating user settings to, 76
  - restoring previous versions, 78-79
  - system requirements, 64-65
  - troubleshooting, 79-80
  - upgrading between Windows Vista editions, 77-78
  - upgrading from previous versions, 72-77
  - Windows Updates, 71-72
- IP, configuring, 128-130
- search box, 93-94
- Upgrade Advisor, 73-74
- versions, 57-58

Windows Vista Business, 57

Windows Vista Display Driver Model (WDDM), 53

Windows Vista Enterprise, 57

Windows Vista Home Basic, 57

Windows Vista Home Premium, 57

Windows Vista Ultimate, 58

Windows WordPad, configuring, 294

Windows XP, dual booting, 79

WINS (Windows Internet Name Service), 128

wireless connections, 133

adapters, 133

configuring, 135-138

mobile computers, 318

security, 134-135

Wireless Equivalency Protection (WEP), 134

Wireless Network Connection Status dialog box, 135

wizards

Add User Account Wizard, 295

Export, 169

Fax Setup Wizard, 303

File Sharing, 163

New Authentication Rule, 222

New Connection Security Rule, 222

Program Compatibility Wizard, 197

WPA (Wi-Fi Protected Access), 134

X-Z

XML (Extensible Markup Language), 51

zones, Internet Explorer 7.0, 240-241

Zoom feature, 233

THIS BOOK IS SAFARI ENABLED

INCLUDES FREE 45-DAY ACCESS TO THE ONLINE EDITION

The Safari® Enabled icon on the cover of your favorite technology book means the book is available through Safari Bookshelf. When you buy this book, you get free access to the online edition for 45 days.

Safari Bookshelf is an electronic reference library that lets you easily search thousands of technical books, find code samples, download chapters, and access technical information whenever and wherever you need it.

TO GAIN 45-DAY SAFARI ENABLED ACCESS TO THIS BOOK:

- Go to **www.examcram.com/safarienabled**
- Complete the brief registration form
- Enter the coupon code found in the front of this book on the "Copyright" page

If you have difficulty registering on Safari Bookshelf or accessing the online edition, please e-mail customer-service@safaribooksonline.com.